250

EGYPTIAN MYTHS
AND LEGENDS

EGYPTIAN MYTHS AND LEGENDS

Originally titled *Egyptian Myth and Legend*

DONALD A. MACKENZIE

ILLUSTRATED

GRAMERCY BOOKS
NEW YORK • AVENEL

Originally published under the title
Egyptian Myth and Legend.

Foreword copyright © 1978 by Crown Publishers, Inc.

This 1994 edition is published by Gramercy Books,
distributed by Random House Value Publishing, Inc.
40 Engelhard Avenue,
Avenel, New Jersey 07001

Printed and bound in the United States of America

Library of Congress Cataloging-in-Publication Data

MacKenzie, Donald Alexander, 1873-1936.
Egyptian myths and legends / Donald A. MacKenzie.
p. cm.
Includes index.
ISBN 0-517-11915-3
1. Mythology, Egyptian. 2. Legends—Egypt. 3. Egypt—History.
I. Title.
BL2441.2.M33 1994
299'.31—dc20
94-14845
CIP

8 7 6 5 4 3 2 1

A NOTE ON THE TEXT

This book was first published in the early years of the twentieth century and it must be recognized that it represents the ideas of that time.

This edition has not been altered or revised in any way and there are no additions or inclusions that relate to modern scholarship or to more current attitudes.

CONTENTS

v

CONTENTS

LIST OF COLOR ILLUSTRATIONS

_____

FOREWORD

The ancient Egyptians were among the most civilized peoples of their time. They left a large and varied literature that has been deciphered to a great extent during the last hundred years. Egyptian religion, myth, and legend, however, cannot be easily comprehended. Compared with the structured world of Greek mythology, they offer instead a vast and exuberant collection of separate beliefs which are often obscure and contradictory. Only a few scholars have attempted to deal with the seeming chaos of belief, most preferring to stay in the more coherent realm of its art. The ancient Egyptians were aware of the diversity of their legends and gods, but they thought that this diversity reflected the complicated sequence of natural phenomena in the world, and thought that thus they did justice to the world's complexity.

Even among the multitude of local and regional gods one can discern certain principal elements of Egyptian religion. The sun is foremost, as it dominates the Egyptian landscape and provides warmth and sustenance for the crops. The all-engulfing power of the sun led to its personification as "Ra," the supreme god and later creator god. Another natural phenomenon—the annual life-giving flooding of the Nile—tremendously influenced the Egyptian world view. They saw it as a sacred event that would remain unchanged unless countered by man through successive rituals. There were thus annual festivals connected with the rising of the Nile and the end of the inundation, as well as with the resurrection of Osiris, who symbolized the fertility of the earth. His life replicated the life of the river. Certain animals that were essential to the livelihood of the Egyptian farmers were also made major deities—Amun is represented as a ram-headed god, and the popular Hathor is portrayed as a woman with

ix

FOREWORD

the head of a cow.

Many peoples have used solar, as well as plant and animal, symbols to express their relationship with the surrounding world in mythical terms. Peculiarly Egyptian is the simultaneous use of these three sets of images with their connotations—the power of the sun associated with creation, that of the earth with resurrection, and that of the cattle with procreation. The prevalence of these concepts through the course of Egyptian history transcends the chaos of the many local cults.

In this book, Donald Mackenzie has recorded the fascinating plethora of Egyptian myths and legends. Clearly, his work has been the result of painstaking and accurate transcription from ancient hieroglyphs, documented also by references to further authoritative sources, and he has put the myths in historical perspective. Perhaps best of all, he has illustrated his accounts with diverse anecdotes and stories, giving the reader a vivid sense of the world and world view of the ancient Egyptian.

FATMA TURKKAN

PREFACE TO THE FIRST EDITION

In this volume the myths and legends of ancient Egypt are embraced in a historical narrative which begins with the rise of the great Nilotic civilization and ends with the Græco-Roman Age. The principal deities are dealt with chiefly at the various periods in which they came into prominence, while the legends are so arranged as to throw light on the beliefs and manners and customs of the ancient people. Metrical renderings are given of such of the representative folk songs and poems as can be appreciated at the present day.

Egyptian mythology is of highly complex character, and cannot be considered apart from its racial and historical aspects. The Egyptians were, as a Hebrew prophet has declared, a "mingled people", and this view has been confirmed by recent ethnological research: "the process of racial fusion begun in the Delta at the dawn of history", says Professor Elliot Smith, "spread through the whole land of Egypt". In localities the early Nilotic inhabitants accepted the religious beliefs of settlers, and fused these with their own. They also clung tenaciously to the crude and primitive tribal beliefs of their remote ancestors, and never abandoned an archaic conception even when they acquired new and more enlightened ideas; they accepted myths literally, and regarded with great sanctity ancient ceremonies and usages. They even showed a tendency to multiply rather than to reduce the number of their gods and goddesses, by symbolizing their attributes. As a result, we find it necessary to deal with a bewildering number of deities and a confused mass of beliefs, many of which are obscure and contradictory. But the average Egyptian was never dismayed by inconsistencies in religious matters: he seemed rather to be fascinated by them. There was, strictly speaking, no orthodox creed in Egypt; each provincial centre had its own distinctive theological system, and the religion of an individual appears to have depended mainly on his habits of life. "The Egyptian", as Professor Wiedemann has said, "never attempted to systematize his conceptions of the different divinities into a homogeneous religion. It is open to us to speak of the religious ideas of the Egyptians, but not of an Egyptian religion."

In our introduction we deal with the divergent character of some of the ancient myths so as to simplify the study of a difficult but extremely fascinating subject. It is shown that one section of the people recognized a Creator like Ptah, who begot himself and "shaped his limbs" ere he fashioned the Universe, while another section perpetuated the idea of a Creatrix who gave birth to all things. At the dawn of history these rival conceptions existed side by side, and they were perpetuated until the end. It is evident, too, that the theologies which were based on these fundamental ideas had undergone, ere the fusion of peoples occurred, a sufficiently prolonged process of separate development to give them a racial, or, at any rate, a geographical significance. As much is suggested by the divergent ideas which obtained regarding the world. One section, for instance, had conceived of land surrounded by sky-supporting mountains, peopled by gods and giants, round which the sun ass galloped to escape the night serpent; another section believed that the world was embraced by the "Great Circle"—Ocean—and that the Nile flowed from sea to sea; a third conception was of a heavenly and an underground Nile. There were also two Paradises—the Osirian and the Ra (sun god's). Osiris judged men according to their deeds. He was an agricultural deity, and the early system of Egyptian ethics seems to have had its origin in the experiences enshrined in the text: "Whatsoever a man soweth that shall he also reap". Admission to the Paradise of the sun cult was secured, on the other hand, by the repetition of magical formulæ. Different beliefs obtained also regarding the mummy. In the *Book of the Dead* it would appear that the preservation of the body was necessary for the continued existence of the soul. Herodotus, however, was informed that after a period of 3000 years the soul returned to animate the dead frame, and this belief in transmigration of souls is illustrated in the Anpu-Bata story, and is connected with a somewhat similar conception that the soul of a father passed to a son, who thus became "the image of his sire", as Horus was of Osiris, and "husband of his mother".

Of special interest in this connection are the various forms of the archaic chaos-egg myth associated with the gods Ptah, Khnûmû, Seb, Osiris, and Ra. As the European giant hides his soul in the egg, which is within the duck, which is within the fish, which is within the deer and so on, and Bata hides his soul in the blossom, the bull, and the tree ere he becomes "husband of his mother", so does Osiris "hide his essence in the shrine of Amon", while his manifestations include a tree, the Apis bull, the boar, the goose, and the Oxyrhynchus fish. Similarly when Set was slain he became a "roaring serpent", a hippopotamus, a crocodile, or a boar. The souls of Ra,

Ptah, and Khnûmû are in the chaos egg like two of the prominent Hindu and Chinese gods. Other Egyptian deities who are "hidden" include Amon, Sokar, and Neith. This persistent myth, which appears to have been associated with belief in transmigration of souls, may be traced even in Akhenaton's religion. We have "Shu (atmosphere god) in his Aton (sun disk)", and a reference in the famous hymn to the "air of life" in the "egg". There can be little doubt that the Transmigration theory prevailed at certain periods and in certain localities in ancient Egypt, and that the statement made by Herodotus was well founded, despite attempts to discredit it.

It is shown that the conception of a Creator was associated with that form of earth, air, and water worship which was perpetuated at Memphis, where the presiding Deity was the hammer god Ptah, who resembles the Chinese Pan-ku, Indra of the Aryans, Tarku and Sutekh of Asia Minor, Hercules, Thor, &c. The Creatrix, on the other hand, was more closely associated with lunar, earth, and water worship, and appears to have been the principal Deity of the Mediterranean race which spread into Asia Minor and Europe. In Scotland, for instance, as we show, she is called Cailleach Bheur, and, like other archaic tribal deities and ghosts, she was the enemy of mankind. Similarly the Egyptian goddesses Sekhet and Hathor were destroyers, and Tefnut was goddess of plagues. Even the sun god Ra "produced calamity after thy (Osiris's) heart", as one of the late temple chants puts it.

In the chapter dealing with animal worship the racial aspect of early beliefs, which were connected with fixed and definite ceremonies, is illustrated in the Horus-Set myth. The "black pig" was Set (the devil) in Egypt, pork was "taboo", and the swineherd was regarded as "an abomination", and not allowed to enter temples. The Gauls and Achæans, on the other hand, honoured the swineherd and ate pork freely, while in the Teutonic Valhal and the Celtic (Irish) Paradise, swine's flesh was the reward of heroes. In Scotland, however, the ancient prejudice against pork exists in localities even at the present day, and the devil is the "black pig". Professor Sir John Rhys, in his *Celtic Folklore*, records that in Wales the black sow of All-Hallows was similarly regarded as the devil. Even in parts of Ireland the hatred of pork still prevails, especially among certain families. This evidence, considered with that afforded by the study of skull forms, suggests that Mediterranean racial ideas may not yet be wholly extinct in our own country. "Strange to say," writes Mr. R. N. Bradley, in his recent work on *Malta and the Mediterranean Race*, "it is in these lands remote from the origin that some of the best indications of the (Mediterranean) race are to be found." The Gaulish treatment of the boar appears to be Asiatic. Brahma, in one of the Hindu creation myths, assumes the form of a boar, the "lord of creatures", and tosses up the earth with his tusks from the primordial deep.

Another myth which seems to have acquired a remote racial colouring is the particular form of the dragon story which probably radiated from Asia Minor. The hero is represented in Egypt by Horus, with his finger on his lips, in his character as Harpocrates, as the Greeks named this mysterious form of the god. The god Sutekh of Rameses II, as we show, was also a dragon slayer. So was Hercules, who fought with the Hydra, and Thor, who at Ragnarok overcame the Midgard Serpent. Sigurd, Siegfried, the Teutonic heroes, and the Celtic Finn-mac-Coul suck a finger or thumb after slaying the dragon, or one of its forms, and cooking part of it, to obtain "knowledge" or understand "the language of birds". In an Egyptian folk tale Ahura, after killing the "Deathless Snake", similarly understands "the language of birds, fishes", &c. Harpocrates appears to be the god Horus as the dragon-slaying Sutekh, the imported legend being preserved in the Ahura tale of the Empire period, when Egypt received so many Asiatic immigrants that the facial type changed as the statuary shows. Professor Elliot Smith considers that while the early Egyptian was "the representative of his kinsman the Neolithic European . . . the immigrant population into both Europe and Egypt" represented "two streams of the same Asiatic folk". Racial myths appear to have followed in the tracks of the racial drift.

In our historical narrative the reader is kept in touch with the great civilizations of the Cretans, Hittites, Babylonians, Assyrians, &c., which influenced and were influenced by Egypt. Special attention is also devoted to Palestine and the great figures in Biblical narrative—Joseph, Moses, Isaiah, Jeremiah, Nahum, and the notable kings of Israel and Judah. There are numerous quotations from the Old Testament, and especially from the prophets who dealt with the political as well as the religious problems of their times. To students of the Bible this part of the volume should make special appeal. It is impossible to appreciate to the full the power and sagacity of Isaiah's sublime utterances without some knowledge of the history of ancient Egypt.

DONALD A. MACKENZIE

INTRODUCTION

"Cleopatra's Needle", on the Thames Embankment, affords us an introduction to ancient Egypt, "the land of marvels" and of strange and numerous deities. This obelisk was shaped from a single block of red granite quarried at Assouan by order of one of the old Pharaohs; it is 68 feet 5½ inches high, and weighs 186 tons. Like one of our own megalithic monuments, it is an interesting relic of stone worship. Primitive man believed that stones were inhabited by spirits which had to be propitiated with sacrifices and offerings, and, long after higher conceptions obtained, their crude beliefs survived among their descendants. This particular monument was erected as a habitation for one of the spirits of the sun god; in ancient Egypt the gods were believed to have had many spirits.

The "Needle" was presented to the British Government in 1820, and in 1877–8 was transported hither by Sir Erasmus Wilson at a cost of £10,000. For about eighteen centuries it had been a familiar object at Alexandria. Its connection with the famous Queen Cleopatra is uncertain; she may have ordered it to be removed from its original site on account of its archæological interest, for it was already old in her day. It was first erected at Heliopolis thirty-two centuries ago. But even then Egypt was a land of ancient memories; the great Pyramids, near Cairo, were aged about 500 years, and the Calendar had been in existence for over fourteen centuries.

Heliopolis, "the city of the sun", is called On in the Bible. It was there that Moses was educated, and became "mighty in word and in deed". Joseph had previously married, at On, Asenath, the daughter of Potiphera, a priest of the sun temple, the site of which, at modern Matarieh, is marked by an erect obelisk of greater antiquity even than the "Needle". Near by are a holy well and a holy tree, long invested with great sanctity by local tradition. Coptic Christians and native Mohammedans still relate that when Joseph and Mary fled with the infant Christ into Egypt, to escape the fierce King Herod, they rested under the tree, and that Mary washed in the well the swaddling clothes of the holy child.

When "Cleopatra's Needle" was erected at On, which is also called Beth-shemesh[1], "the house of the sun god", in the Hebrew Scriptures, the priests taught classes of students in the temple colleges. For about thirty centuries the city was the Oxford of Egypt. Eudoxus and Plato, in the course of their travels, visited the priestly professors and heard them lecture. As ancient tradition has credited Egypt with the origin of geometry, Euclid, the distinguished mathematician, who belonged to the brilliant Alexandria school, no doubt also paid a pilgrimage to the ancient seat of learning. When he was a student he must have been familiar with our "Needle"; perhaps he puzzled over it as much as some of us have puzzled over his problems.

At On the Egyptian students were instructed, among other things, to read and fashion those strange pictorial

---

[1] The Babylonian form is "shamash".

signs which appear on the four sides of the "Needle". These are called hieroglyphics, a term derived from the Greek words *hieros*, "sacred", and *glypho*, "I engrave", and first applied by the Greeks because they believed that picture writing was used only by Egyptian priests for religious purposes. Much of what we know regarding the myths, legends, and history of the land of the Pharaohs has been accumulated since modern linguists acquired the art of reading those pictorial inscriptions. The ancient system had passed out of human use and knowledge for many long centuries when the fortunate discovery was made of a slab of black basalt on which had been inscribed a decree in Greek and Egyptian. It is called the "Rosetta Stone", because it was dug up at Rosetta by a French officer of engineers in 1799, when Napoleon, who had invaded Egypt, ordered a fort to be rebuilt. It was afterwards seized by the British, along with other antiquities collected by the French, and was presented by George III to the British Museum in 1802.

Copies of the Rosetta Stone inscriptions were distributed by Napoleon, and subsequently by British scholars, to various centres of learning throughout Europe. It was found that the Greek section recorded a decree, issued by the native priests to celebrate the first anniversary of Pharaoh Ptolemy V in 195 B.C. The mysterious Egyptian section was rendered in hieroglyphics and also in Demotic, a late form of the cursive system of writing called Hieratic. In 1814 two distinguished linguists—Dr. Thomas Young in Britain, and Professor Champollion in France—engaged in studying the quaint pictorial signs. The credit of having first discovered the method of reading them is claimed for both these scholars, and a heated controversy waged for long years over the matter. Modern opinion inclines to the view that Young and Champollion solved the secret simultaneously and independently of each other. The translation of other Egyptian texts followed in course; and of late years so great has been the skill attained by scholars that they are able to detect blunders made by ancient scribes. Much uncertainty exists, however, and must ever exist, regarding the proper pronunciation of the language.

Another source of knowledge regarding the civilization of Egypt is the history of Manetho, a native priest, who lived at the beginning of the third century before Christ. His books perished when Alexander the Great conquered Egypt, but epitomes survive in the writings of Julius Africanus, Eusebius, and George the Syncellus, while fragments are quoted by Josephus. Manetho divided the history of his country into thirty dynasties, and his system constitutes the framework upon which our knowledge of the great Egyptian past has accumulated.

Divergent views exist regarding the value of Manetho's history, and these are invariably expressed with point and vigour. Professor Breasted, the distinguished American Egyptologist, for instance, characterizes the chronology of the priestly historian as "a late, careless, and uncritical compilation", and he holds that it "can be proven wrong from the contemporary monuments in the vast majority of cases". "Manetho's dynastic totals", he says, "are so absurdly high throughout that they are not worthy of a moment's credence, being often nearly or quite double the maximum drawn from contemporary monuments. Their accuracy is now maintained only by a small and constantly decreasing number of modern scholars." Breasted goes even further than that by adding: "The compilation of puerile folk tales by Manetho is hardly worthy of the name history".

Professor Flinders Petrie, whose work as an excavator

has been epochmaking, is inclined, on the other hand, to attach much weight to the history of the native priest. " Unfortunately," he says, " much confusion has been caused by scholars not being content to accept Manetho as being substantially correct in the main, though with many small corruptions and errors. Nearly every historian has made large and arbitrary assumptions and changes, with a view to reducing the length of time stated. But recent discoveries seem to prove that we must accept the lists of kings as having been correct, however they may have suffered in detail. . . . Every accurate test that we can apply shows the general trustworthiness of Manetho apart from minor corruptions."

Breasted, supported by other leading Egyptologists, accepts what is known as the " Berlin system of Egyptian chronology ". The following tables illustrate how greatly he differs from Petrie:—

	Breasted.	Petrie.
Mena's Conquest	3400 B.C.	5550 B.C.
Twelfth Dynasty	2000 B.C.	3400 B.C.
Eighteenth Dynasty ...	1580 B.C.	1580 B.C.

The Hyksos invasion took place, according to Manetho, at the beginning of the Fifteenth Dynasty, and he calculated that the Asiatic rulers were in Egypt for 511 years. Breasted's minimum is 100 years. King and Hall, like Newberry and Garstang, allow the Hyksos a little more than 200 years, while Hawes, the Cretan explorer, whose dating comes very close to that of Dr. Evans, says that " there is a growing conviction that Cretan evidence, especially in the eastern part of the island, favours the minimum (Berlin) system of Egyptian chronology ". Breasted, it will be seen, allows 420 years for the period between the Twelfth and Eighteenth Dynasties, while Petrie gives 1820—a difference of 1400 years.

From 1580 B.C., onward, the authorities are in practical agreement; prior to that date the chronology is uncertain.

This confusion has been partly caused by the Egyptians having ignored the leap year addition of one day. Their calendar of 365 days lost about a quarter of a day each twelvemonth and about a whole day every four years. New Year's Day began with the rising of the star Sirius (Sothos) on 17 June, and it coincided with the beginning of the Nile inundation. But in a cycle of 1461 years Sirius rose in every alternate month of the Egyptian year. When, therefore, we find in the Egyptian records a reference, at a particular period, to their first month (the month of Thoth), we are left to discover whether it was our April or October; and in dating back we must allow for the "wanderings of Sirius". Much controversial literature has accumulated regarding what is known as the Egyptian "Sothic Cycle".

Throughout this volume the dates are given in accordance with the minimum system, on account of the important evidence afforded by the Cretan discoveries. But we may agree to differ from Professor Petrie on chronological matters and yet continue to admire his genius and acknowledge the incalculable debt we owe him as one who has reconstructed some of the most obscure periods of Egyptian history. The light he has thrown upon early Dynastic and pre-Dynastic times, especially, has assured him an undying reputation, and he has set an example to all who have followed by the thoroughness and painstaking character of his work of research.

It is chiefly by modern-day excavators in Egypt, and in those countries which traded with the Nilotic kingdom in ancient times, that the past has been conjured up before us. We know more about ancient Egypt now than did the Greeks or the Romans, and more about pre-Dynastic times and the early Dynasties than even those Egyptian scholars who took degrees in the Heliopolitan colleges when "Cleopatra's Needle" was first erected. But our knowledge is withal fragmentary. We can but trace the outlines of Egyptian history; we cannot command that unfailing supply of documentary material which is available, for instance, in dealing with the history of a European nation. Fragments of pottery, a few weapons, strings of beads, some rude drawings, and tomb remains are all we have at our disposal in dealing with some periods; others are made articulate by inscriptions, but even after civilization had attained a high level we occasionally find it impossible to deal with those great movements which were shaping the destinies of the ancient people. Obscure periods recur all through Egyptian history, and some, indeed, are almost quite blank.

When "Cleopatra's Needle" was erected by Thothmes III, the Conqueror, and the forerunner of Alexander the Great and Napoleon, Egyptian civilization had attained its highest level. Although occasionally interrupted by internal revolt or invasions from north and south, it had gradually increased in splendour until Thothmes III extended the empire to the borders of Asia Minor. The Mediterranean Sea then became an "Egyptian lake". Peace offerings were sent to Thothmes from Crete and Cyprus, the Phœnicians owed him allegiance, and his favours were courted by the Babylonians and Assyrians: the "Needle" records the gifts which were made by the humbled King of the Hittites.

After the passing of Thothmes, who flourished in the Eighteenth Dynasty, decline set in, and, although lost ground was recovered after a time, the power of Egypt gradually grew less and less. "Cleopatra's Needle" may be regarded as marking the "halfway house" of Egyptian civilization. It was erected at the beginning of the Age of Empire. The chief periods before that are known as the Pre-Dynastic, the Archaic Age, the Old Kingdom, the Middle Kingdom, and the Hyksos Age; after the fall of empire, in the Twentieth Dynasty, we have the periods of Libyan, Ethiopian, and Assyrian supremacy. Then came "The Restoration", or Saite period, which ended with the Persian Conquest. Subsequently the Greeks possessed the kingdom, which was afterwards seized by the Romans. Arabs and Turks followed, and to-day we witness a second Restoration under British rule. But not since the day when Ezekiel declared, in the Saite period: "There shall be no more a prince of the land of Egypt" (*Ezek.*, xxx, 13) has a ruler of the old Egyptian race sat upon the throne of the Pharaohs.

The mythology of Egypt was formulated prior to the erection of the "Needle". Indeed, in tracing its beginnings we must go back to the pre-Dynastic times, when the beliefs of the various peoples who mingled in the ancient land were fused and developed under Egyptian influences.

We are confronted by a vast multitude of gods and goddesses. Attempts to enumerate them result, as a rule, in compilations resembling census returns. One of the Pharaohs, who lived about 4000 years ago, undertook the formidable task of accommodating them all under one roof, and caused to be erected for that purpose a great building which Greek writers called "The Labyrinth"; he had separate apartments dedicated to the various deities, and of these it was found necessary to construct no fewer than 3000. The ancient Egyptians lived in a world which swarmed with spirits, "numerous as gnats upon the evening beam". They symbolized everything; they gave concrete form to every abstract idea; they had deities which represented every phase and function of life, every act and incident of import, and every hour and every month; they had nature gods, animal gods and human gods, and gods of the living and gods of the dead. And, as if they had not a sufficient number of their own, they imported gods and goddesses from other countries.

In the midst of this mythological multitude, which a witty French Egyptologist calls "the rabble of deities", a few, comparatively speaking, loom vast and great. But some of these are but differentiated forms of a single god or goddess, whose various attributes were symbolized, so that deities budded from deities; others underwent separate development in different localities and assumed various names. If we gather those linking deities together in groups, the task of grappling with Egyptian mythology will be greatly simplified.

An interesting example of the separating process is afforded by Thoth of Hermopolis. That god of quaint and arresting aspect is most usually depicted with a man's body and the head of an ibis, surmounted by a lunar disk and crescent. As the divine lawyer and recorder, he checked the balance in the Judgment Hall of the Dead when the human heart was weighed before Osiris; as a Fate, he measured out at birth the span of human life on a rod with serrated edge; he was also a patron of architects, a god of religious literature who was invoked by scribes, and a god of medicine. Originally he was a lunar deity, and was therefore of great antiquity, for, as Mr. Payne has emphasized in his *History of the New World*, a connection is traced between the lunar phenomena and the food supply in an earlier stage of civilization than that in which a connection is traced between the food supply and the solar phenomena.

The worship of the moon preceded in Egypt, as in many other countries, the worship of the sun. It still survives in Central Africa, and among primitive peoples elsewhere throughout the world. Even in highly civilized Europe we can still trace lingering evidences of belief in the benevolence of the lunar spirit, the ancient guide and protector of mankind.

The moon was believed to exercise a direct influence upon Nature as a generative agency; agriculturists were of opinion that seeds sown during its period of increase had more prolific growth than those sown when it was on the wane. Pliny said that "the blood of men grows and diminishes with the light of the moon, while leaves and herbage also feel the same influence". Crops were supposed to receive greater benefit in moonlight than in sunshine. In one of the Egyptian temple chants, the corn god is entreated to "give fecundity in the nighttime". The "harvest moon" was "the ripening moon", and many poets have in all ages sung its praises. It was followed in Scotland, where archaic Mediterranean beliefs appear to have tardy survival, by "the badger's moon", which marked the period for laying in winter stores, and then by "the hunter's moon", an indication that lunar worship prevailed in the archæological "hunting period". Indeed the moon bulks as largely in European as in ancient Egyptian folklore: it is still believed in certain localities to cure diseases and to inspire love; until a comparatively recent date quaint ceremonies were performed in Scotland during its first phase by women who visited sculptured stones to pray for offspring.

Although the strictly lunar character of the Egyptian god Thoth is not apparent at first sight, it can be traced through his association with kindred deities. At Hermopolis and Edfu he was fused with Khonsu (or Khensu), who had developed from Ah, the lunar representative of the male principle, which was also "the fighting principle". Khonsu was depicted as a handsome youth, and he symbolized, in the Theban group of gods, certain specialized influences of the moon. He was the love god, the Egyptian Cupid, and the divine physician; he was also an explorer (the root *khens* signifies "to traverse") and the messenger and hunter of the gods. Special offerings were made to him at the Ploughing Festival, just before the seed was sown, and at the Harvest Festival, after the grain was reaped; and he was worshipped as the increaser of flocks and herds and human families. Like Thoth, he was a "measurer", and inspirer of architects, because the moon measures time. But in this direction Thoth had fuller development; he was a "lawyer" because the orderly changes of the moon suggested the observance of well-defined laws, and a "checker" and "scribe" because human transactions were checked and recorded in association with lunar movements. Time was first measured by the lunar month.

Moon gods were also corn gods, but Thoth had no pronounced association with agricultural rites. That phase of his character may have been suppressed as a result of the specializing process; it is also possible that he was differentiated in the pastoral and hunting period when the lunar spirit was especially credited with causing the growth of trees. In the Nineteenth Dynasty Thoth was shown recording the name of a Pharaoh on the sacred sycamore. He must have been, therefore, at one time a tree spirit, like Osiris. Tree spirits, as well as corn spirits, were manifestations of the moon god.

Thoth also links with Osiris, and this association is

of special interest. Osiris was originally an ancient king of Egypt who taught the Egyptians how to rear crops and cultivate fruit trees. He was regarded as a human incarnation of the moon spirit. As a living ruler he displayed his lunar qualities by establishing laws for the regulation of human affairs and by promoting agriculture and gardening; when he died, like the moon, he similarly regulated the affairs of departed souls in the agricultural Paradise of the Egyptians; he was the great Judge of the Dead, and in the Hall of Judgment Thoth was his recorder.

Like Thoth, Osiris was identified with the tree spirit. His dead body was enclosed in a tree which grew round the coffin, and Isis voyaged alone over the sea to recover it. Isis was also the herald of the Nile inundation; she was, indeed, the flood. The myth, as will be seen, is reminiscent of archaic tree and well worship, which survives at Heliopolis, where the sacred well and tree are still venerated in association with the Christian legend. In Ireland the tree and corn god Dagda has similarly for wife a water goddess; she is called Boann, and personifies Boyne River.

Osiris had many manifestations, or, rather, he was the manifestation of many gods. But he never lost his early association with the moon. In one of the Isis temple chants, which details his various attributes and evolutionary phases, he is hailed as the god—

> Who cometh to us as a babe each month.

He is thus the moon child, a manifestation of the ever-young, and ever-renewing moon god. The babe Osiris is cared for by Thoth—

> He lays thy soul in the Maadit boat
> By the magic of thy name of Ah (moon god).

Thoth utters the magic "password" to obtain for Osiris his seat in the boat which will carry him over the heavens. This reference explains the line in the complex hymn to Osiris-Sokar:—

Hail, living soul of Osiris, crowning him with the moon.[1]

We have now reached a point where Thoth, Osiris, Khonsu, and Ah are one; they are but various forms of the archaic moon spirit which was worshipped by primitive hunters and agriculturists as the begetter and guardian of life.

According to Dr. Budge, whose works on Egyptian mythology are as full of carefully compiled facts as were Joseph's great storehouses of grain, the ancient Egyptians, despite their crowded labyrinth, "believed in the existence of one great God, self-produced, self-existent, almighty, and eternal, who created the 'gods', the heavens, and the sun, moon and stars in them, and the earth and everything on it, including man and beast, bird, fish, and reptile. . . . Of this god", Dr. Budge believes, "they never attempted to make any figure, form, likeness, or similitude, for they thought that no man could depict or describe Him, and that all His attributes were quite beyond man's comprehension. On the rare occasions in which He is mentioned in their writings, He is always called 'Neter', i.e. God, and besides this He has no name. The exact meaning of the word 'Neter' is unknown."[2]

Dr. Budge explains the multiplication of Nilotic deities by saying that the behests of "God Almighty . . . were performed by a number of gods, or, as we might say, emanations or angels", which were "of African rather

---

[1] *The Burden of Isis*, Dennis, p. 54.
[2] Osiris-Sokar is also "the mysterious one, he who is unknown to mankind", and the "hidden god" (*The Burden of Isis*, Dennis, pp. 53, 54).

than Asiatic origin". He prefers to elucidate Egyptian mythology by studying surviving African beliefs "in the great forests and on the Nile, Congo, Niger, and other great rivers", and shows that in these districts the moon god is still regarded as the creator.

A distinction is drawn by Dr. Budge between the Libyan deities and those of Upper Egypt, and his theory of one God has forcible application when confined to the archaic lunar deity. He refers to the period prior to the minglings of peoples and the introduction of Asiatic beliefs. But in dealing with historic Egyptian mythology we must distinguish between the African moon spirit, which is still identified by savage peoples with the creator god, and the representative Egyptian lunar deity, which symbolized the male principle, and was not the "first cause", but the son of a self-produced creating goddess. The difference between the two conceptions is of fundamental character.

It is apparent that some of the great Egyptian deities, and especially those of Delta origin, or Delta characterization, evolved from primitive groups of Nature spirits. At Heliopolis, where archaic Nilotic and other beliefs were preserved like flies in amber, because the Asiatic sun worshippers sought to include all existing forms of tribal religion in their own, a creation myth makes reference to the one God of the primordial deep. But associated with him, it is significant to note, were "the Fathers and the Mothers".

The "Mothers" appear to be represented by the seven Egyptian Fates who presided at birth. These were called "the seven Hathors", but their association with the Asiatic Hathor, who was Ishtar, was evidently arbitrary. The Mediterranean people, who formed the basis of the Egyptian race, were evidently worshippers of the "Mothers". In southern and western Europe, which they peopled in early times, various groups of "Mothers" were venerated. These included "Proximæ (the kinswomen), Dervonnæ (the oak spirits), Niskai (the water spirits), Mairæ, Matronæ, Matres or Matræ (the mothers), Quadriviæ (the goddesses of crossroads). The Matres, Matræ, and Matronæ are often qualified by some local name. Deities of this type appear to have been popular in Britain, in the neighbourhood of Cologne, and in Provence. In some cases it is uncertain", comments Professor Anwyl, from whose *Celtic Religion in Pre-Christian Times* we quote, "whether some of these grouped goddesses are Celtic or Teutonic." They were probably pre-Celtic and pre-Teutonic. "It is an interesting parallel", he adds, "to the existence of these grouped goddesses, when we find that in some parts of Wales 'Y Mamau' (the mothers) is the name for the fairies. These grouped goddesses take us back to one of the most interesting stages in the early Celtic religion, when the earth spirits or the corn spirits had not yet been completely individualized."[1]

Representatives of the groups of Egyptian spirits called "the Fathers" are found at Memphis, where Ptah, assisted by eight earth gnomes called Khnumu, was believed to have made the universe with his hammer by beating out the copper sky and shaping the hills and valleys. This group of dwarfs resemble closely the European elves, or male earth spirits, who dwelt inside mountains as the Khnumu dwelt underground.

In the process of time the various groups of male and female spirits were individualized. Some disappeared, leaving the chief spirit alone and supreme. When Ptah

---

[1] Herodotus says: "The Pelasgians did not distinguish the gods by name or surname. . . . They called them gods, which by its etymology means 'disposers'" (fates).

became a great god, the other earth gnomes vanished from the Memphis creation myth. Other members of groups remained and were developed separately. This evolutionary process can be traced, we think, in the suggestive association of the two sister goddesses Isis and Nepthys. In one of the temple chants both are declared to be the mothers of Osiris, who is called—

> The bull, begotten of the two cows, Isis and Nepthys . . .
> He, the progeny of the two cows, Isis and Nepthys,
> The child surpassingly beautiful![1]

At the same time he is son of "his mother Nut". Osiris has thus three mothers. The conception may be difficult to grasp, but we must remember that we are dealing with vague beliefs regarding ancient mythological beings. Heimdal, the Norse god, had nine mothers, "the daughters of sea-dwelling Ran".[2] The Norse god, Tyr's grandmother,[3] was a giantess with nine hundred heads. If we reduce that number to nine, it might be suggested that she represented nine primitive earth spirits, which were multiplied and individualized by the tellers of wonder tales of mythological origin. The Egyptian Great Mother deities had sons, and practically all of these were identified with Osiris. It is not improbable, therefore, that the Mediterranean moon spirit, whom Osiris represented, had originally as many mothers as he had attributes. The "mothers" afterwards became "sisters" of the young god. Nepthys sings to Osiris:

> All thy sister goddesses are at thy side
> And behind thy couch.

---

[1] *The Burden of Isis* (Wisdom of the East), James Teackle Dennis.
[2] See *Teutonic Myth and Legend*.
[3] There is no trace in Egypt of a "grandmother" or of a "great grandmother" like "Edda" of Iceland. With "the mother", however, these may represent a triad of nature spirits. A basis of Mediterranean beliefs is traceable in Norse mythology.

The Heliopolitan reference to "the Fathers" and the "Mothers" indicates that fundamental beliefs of divergent origin were fused by the unscientific but diplomatic priestly theorists of the sun cult. It is evident that the people who believed in "Father spirits" were not identical with the people who believed in "Mother spirits".

We may divide into two classes the primitive symbolists who attempted to solve the riddle of the universe:

1. Those who conceived that life and natural phenomena had a female origin;
2. Those who conceived that life and natural phenomena had a male origin.

Both "schools of thought" were represented in Egypt from the earliest times of which we have any definite knowledge; but it may be inferred that the two rival conceptions were influenced by primitive tribal customs and habits of life.

It is possible that the theory of the female origin of life evolved in settled communities among large tribal units. These communities could not have come into existence, or continued to grow, without laws. As much may be taken for granted. Now, the earliest laws were evidently those which removed the prime cause of rivalries and outbreaks in tribal communities by affording protection to women. As primitive laws and primitive religions were inseparable, women must have been honoured on religious grounds. In such communities the growth of religious ideas would tend in the direction of exalting goddesses or mother spirits, rather than gods or father spirits. The men of the tribe would be regarded as the sons of an ancestress, and the gods as the sons of a goddess. The Irish tribe known as "Tuatha de Danann", for instance, were "the children of Danu", the mother of the Danann gods.

The theory of the male origin of life, on the other hand, may have grown up among smaller tribal units of wandering or mountain peoples, whose existence depended more on the prowess and activities of the males than on the influence exercised by their females, whom they usually captured or lured away. Such nomads, with their family groups over which the fathers exercised supreme authority, would naturally exalt the male and worship tribal ancestors and regard gods as greater than goddesses.

In Egypt the "mother-worshipping" peoples and the "father-worshipping" peoples were mingled, as we have indicated, long before the dawn of history. Nomadic peoples from desert lands and mountainous districts entered the Delta region of the Mediterranean race many centuries ere yet the Dynastic Egyptians made appearance in Upper Egypt. The illuminating researches of Professor Flinders Petrie prove conclusively that three or four distinct racial types were fused in pre-Dynastic times in Lower Egypt.

The evidence obtained from the comparative study of European mythologies tends to suggest that the "mother" spirits and the Great Mother deities were worshipped by the Mediterranean peoples, who multiplied rapidly in their North African area of characterization, and spread into Asia Minor and Europe and up the Nile valley as far as Nubia, where Thoth, the lunar god, was the son of Tefnut, one of the Great Mothers. But that matriarchal conception did not extend, as we have seen, into Central Africa. The evidence accumulated by explorers shows that the nomadic natives believe, as they have believed from time immemorial, in a Creator (god) rather than a Creatrix (goddess). Mungo Park found that the "one god" was worshipped only "at the appearance of the new moon".[1] In Arabia, the "mothers" were also prominent, and certain ethnologists have detected the Mediterranean type in that country. But, of course, all peoples who worshipped "mother spirits" were not of Mediterranean origin. In this respect, however, the Mediterraneans, like other races which multiplied into large settled communities, attained early a comparatively high degree of civilization on account of their reverence for motherhood and all it entailed.

The Great Mother deity was believed to be self-created and self-sustaining. In the Isis chants addressed to Osiris we read—

> Thy mother Nut cometh to thee in peace;
> She hath built up life from her own body.

> There cometh unto thee Isis, lady of the horizon,
> Who hath begotten herself alone.[2]

According to the Greeks, the Great Mother Neith declared to her worshippers—

> I am what has been,
> What is,
> And what shall be.

A hymn to Neith, of which Dr. Budge gives a scholarly and literal translation, contains the following lines :—

> Hail! Great Mother, not hath been uncovered thy birth;
> Hail! Great Goddess, within the underworld doubly hidden;
> Thou unknown one—
> Hail! thou divine one,
> Not hath been unloosed thy garment.

[1] The Accadians also believed that the moon had prior existence to the sun.
[2] *The Burden of Isis*, Dennis.

The typical Great Mother was a virgin goddess who represented the female principle, and she had a fatherless son who represented the male principle. Like the Celtic Danu, she was the mother of the gods, from whom mankind were descended. But the characteristics of the several mother deities varied in different localities, as a result of the separating and specializing process which we have illustrated in dealing with some of the lunar gods. One Great Mother was an earth spirit, another was a water spirit, and a third was an atmosphere or sky spirit.

The popular Isis ultimately combined the attributes of all the Great Mothers, who were regarded as different manifestations of her, but it is evident that each underwent, for prolonged periods, separate development, and that their particular attributes were emphasized by local and tribal beliefs. An agricultural people, for instance, could not fail, in Egypt, to associate their Great Mother with the Nile flood; a pastoral people, like the Libyans, on the other hand, might be expected to depict her as an earth spirit who caused the growth of grass.

As a goddess of maternity the Great Mother was given different forms. Isis was a woman, the Egyptianized Hathor was a cow, Apet of Thebes was a hippopotamus, Bast was a cat, Tefnut was a lioness, Uazit was a serpent, Hekt was a frog, and so on. All the sacred animals and reptiles were in time associated with Isis.

In Asia Minor the Great Mother was associated with the lioness, in Cyprus she was "My Lady of Trees and Doves", in Crete she was the serpent goddess; in Rome, Bona Dea was an earth goddess, and the Norse Freyja was, like the Egyptian Bast, a feline goddess—her car was drawn by cats.

One of the least known, but not the least important,

of Great Mothers of Europe is found in the Highlands of Scotland, where, according to the ethnologists, the Mediterranean element bulks considerably among the racial types. She is called Cailleach Bheur, and is evidently a representative survival of great antiquity. In Ireland she degenerated, as did other old gigantic deities, into a historical personage. An interesting Highland folk tale states that she existed "from the long eternity of the world". She is described as "a great big old wife". Her face was "blue black",[1] and she had a single watery eye on her forehead, but "the sight of it" was "as swift as the mackerel of the ocean".

Like the Egyptian Ptah, this Scottish hag engaged herself in making the world. She carried upon her back a great creel filled with rocks and earth. In various parts of northern Scotland small hills are said to have been formed by the spillings of her creel. She let loose the rivers and formed lochs. At night she rested on a mountain top beside a spring of fresh water. Like the Libyan Neith she was evidently the deity of a pastoral and hunting people, for she had herds of deer, goats, and sheep, over which she kept watch.

In the springtime the Cailleach, or hag, was associated with the tempests. When she sneezed, she was heard for many miles. But her stormy wrath, during the period in spring called in Gaelic "Cailleach", was especially roused because her son fled away on a white horse with a beautiful bride. The hag pursued him on a steed which leapt ravines as nimbly as the giant Arthur's[2] horse leapt over the Bristol Channel. But the

---

[1] The Egyptians would have said "true lapis lazuli". The face of the Libyan goddess Neith was green. Isis was "the green one whose greenness is like the greenness of earth" (Brugsch).

[2] Arthur of "the round table" was originally a giant, and, like other giants, became associated with the fairies. "Arthur's Seat", Edinburgh, is reminiscent of his

son would not give up the bride, who had, it seems, great dread of the terrible old woman. The hag, however, managed to keep the couple apart by raising storm after storm. Her desire was to prevent the coming of summer. She carried in her hand a magic wand, or, as some stories have it, a hammer, which she waved over the earth to prevent the grass growing. But she could not baffle Nature. She, however, made a final attempt to keep apart her son and the young bride, who was evidently the spirit of summer, by raising her last great storm, which brought snow and floods, and was intended to destroy all life. Then her son fought against her and put her to flight. So "the old winter went past", as a Gaelic tale has it.

One of the many versions of the Scottish Hag story makes her the chief of eight "big old women" or witches. This group of nine suggests Ptah and his eight earth gnomes, the nine mothers of Heimdal the Norse god, and the Ennead of Heliopolis.

An Egyptian Great Mother, who was as much dreaded as the Scottish Hag, was Sekhet, the lioness-headed deity, who was the wife of Ptah. In a Twelfth-Dynasty story she is referred to as the terrible goddess of plagues. All the feline goddesses "represented", says Wiedemann, "the variable power of the sun, from genial warmth to scorching heat. Thus a Philæ text states in reference to Isis-Hathor, who there personified all goddesses in one: 'Kindly is she as Bast, terrible is she as Sekhet'. As the conqueror of the enemies of the Egyptian gods, Sekhet carried a knife in her hand, for she it was who, under the name of the 'Eye of Ra', entered upon the

giant form. If there was once a king named Arthur, who was a popular hero, his name may have been given to a giant god originally nameless. The Eildon Hills giant was called Wallace.

task of destroying mankind. Other texts represent her as ancestress of part of the human race."[1]

The oldest deities were evidently those of most savage character.[2] Sekhet must, therefore, have been a primitive conception of the Great Mother who rejoiced in slaughter and had to be propitiated. The kindly Bast and the lovable Isis, on the other hand, seem to be representative of a people who, having grown more humane, invested their deities with their own qualities. But the worship of mother goddesses was ever attended by rites which to us are revolting. Herodotus indicates the obscene character of those which prevailed in the Delta region. Female worshippers were unmoral (rather than immoral). In Asia Minor the festivals of the Great Mother and her son, who symbolized the generative agency in nature, were the scenes of terrible practices. Men mutilated their bodies and women became the "sacred wives" of the god. There are also indications that children were sacrificed. In Palestine large numbers of infants' skeletons have been found among prehistoric remains, and although doubt has been thrown on the belief that babies were sacrificed, we cannot overlook in this connection the evidence of Isaiah, who was an eye-witness of many terrible rites of Semitic and pre-Semitic origin.

"Against whom", cried the Hebrew prophet, "do ye sport yourselves? against whom make ye a wide mouth and draw out the tongue? are ye not children of transgression, a seed of falsehood, enflaming your-

---

[1] *Religion of the Ancient Egyptians*, A. Wiedemann. In old Arabia the sun deity was female, and there are traces of a sun goddess among the earlier Hittites (H. Winckler, *Mitteilungen der Deutschen Orient-Gesellschaft*; Berlin, 1907).

[2] Ra, in one of the Isis temple chants, "hath produced calamity after the desire of thy (Osiris's) heart," and Osiris-Sokar is "the lord of fear who causeth himself to come into being". Sokar, who fused with Ra and Osiris, is one of the oldest Egyptian deities.

selves with idols under every green tree, slaying the children in the valleys under the clifts of the rocks" (*Isaiah*, lvii, 4 and 5).

In Ireland similar rites obtained "before the coming of Patrick of Macha", when the corn god, the son of the Great Mother, was dreaded and propitiated. He was called Cromm Cruaich, and was probably the archaic Dagda, son of Danu.

> To him without glory
> They would kill their piteous, wretched offspring
> With much wailing and peril,
> To pour their blood around Cromm Cruaich.
>
> Milk and corn
> They would ask from him speedily
> In return for one-third of their healthy issue:
> Great was the horror and the scare of him.
> —*Celtic Myth and Legend.*

Neith, the Libyan Great Mother, was an earth goddess. Nut, on the other hand, was a sky goddess, and associated with her was an earth god called Seb. Sometimes she is depicted with Seb alone, and somtimes a third deity, the atmosphere god, Shu, is added. Shu separates the heavens from the earth, and is shown as "the uplifter", supporting Nut, as Atlas supports the world. Nut is also pictured with another goddess drawn inside her entire form; within the second goddess a god is similarly depicted. This triad suggests Osiris and his two mothers. A mummy drawing of Nut, with symbols figured upon her body, indicates that she was the Great Mother of the sun disk and lunar disk and crescent. In one of the myths of the sun cult, Ra, the solar god, is said to be "born of Nut" each morning.

The most representative Egyptian Great Father was

Ptah in his giant form and in his union with Tanen, the earth god. He was self-created; "no father begot thee", sang a priestly poet, "and no mother gave thee birth"; he built up his own body and shaped his limbs. Then he found "his seat" like a typical mountain giant; his head supported the sky and his feet rested upon the earth. Osiris, who also developed into a Great Father deity, was fused with Ptah at Memphis, and, according to the Pyramid texts, his name signifies "the seat maker". The sun and the moon were the eyes of the Great Father, the air issued from his nostrils and the Nile from his mouth. Other deities who link with Ptah include Khnumu, Hershef, and the great god of Mendes. These are dealt with in detail in Chapter XIV.

It is possible that Ptah was imported into Egypt by an invading tribe in pre-Dynastic times. He was an artisan god and his seat of worship was at Memphis, the home of the architects and the builders of the Pyramids and limestone mastabas. According to tradition, Egypt's first temple was erected to Ptah by King Mena.

The skilled working of limestone, with which Memphis was closely associated, made such spontaneous appearance in Egypt as to suggest that the art was developed elsewhere. It is of interest to find, therefore, that in Palestine a tall, pre-Semitic blonde race constructed wonderful artificial caves. These were "hewn out of the soft limestone", says Professor Macalister, "with great care and exactness. . . . They vary greatly in size and complexity; one cave was found by the writer that contained no less than sixty chambers. This was quite exceptional; but caves with five, ten, or even twenty chambers large and small are not uncommon. The passages sometimes are so narrow as to make their exploration difficult; and the chambers are sometimes so large that it requires a bright light such as that of magnesium wire to illuminate them sufficiently for examination. One chamber, now fallen in, was found to have been 400 feet long and 80 feet high. To have excavated these gigantic catacombs required the steady work of a long-settled population." They are "immense engineering works". The hewers of the artificial caves "possessed the use of metal tools, as the pick marks testify".

These caves, with their chambers and narrow passages, suggest the interiors of the Pyramids. A people who had attained such great skill in limestone working were equal to the task of erecting mountains of masonry in the Nile valley if, as seems possible, they effected settlement there in very early times. As they were of mountain characterization, these ancient artisans may have been Ptah worshippers.

The Pyramids evolved from mastabas.[1] Now in Palestine there are, to the north of Jerusalem, "remarkable prehistoric monuments". These, Professor Macalister says, "consist of long, broad walls in one of which a chamber and shaft have been made, happily compared by Père Vincent to an Egyptian mastaba".[2]

Legends regarding this tall people make reference to giants, and it is possible that with other mountain folk their hilltop deities, with whom they would be identified, were reputed to be of gigantic stature and bulk. They are also referred to in the Bible. When certain of the spies returned to Moses from southern Canaan "they brought up an evil report of the land which they had searched". They said: "It is a land that eateth up the inhabitants thereof; and all the people that we saw in it

---

[1] Oblong platform tombs which were constructed of limestone. The body was concealed in a secret chamber. See Chapter VIII.
[2] *A History of Civilization in Palestine*, R. A. S. Macalister.

are men of great stature. And there we saw the giants, the sons of Anak, which come of the giants" (*Numbers*, xiii, 32–33). In other words, they were "sons of their gods".

It is evident that this tall, cave-hewing people had attained a high degree of civilization, with a well-organized system of government, ere they undertook engineering works on such a vast scale. Although they had established themselves in such close proximity to the Delta region, no reference is made to them in any surviving Egyptian records, so that they must have flourished at a remote period. They preceded the Semites in southern Palestine, and the Semites appeared in Egypt in pre-Dynastic times. Professor Macalister considers that they may be "roughly assigned to 3000 B.C.". A long period must be allowed for the growth of their art of skilled stone working.

When the mysterious cave-dwellers were at the height of their power, they must have multiplied rapidly, and it is not improbable that some of their surplus stock poured into the Delta region. Their mode of life must have peculiarly fitted them for residence in towns, and it may be that the distinctive character of the mythology of Memphis was due to their presence in no inconsiderable numbers in that cosmopolitan city.

There is no indication that the Dynastic Egyptians, who first made their appearance in the upper part of the Nile valley, utilized the quarries prior to their conquest of Lower Egypt. They were a brick-making people, and their early tombs at Abydos were constructed of brick and wood. But after King Mena had united the two kingdoms by force of arms, stone working was introduced into Upper Egypt. A granite floor was laid in the tomb of King Usephais of the First Dynasty. This sudden transition from brick making to granite working is very remarkable. It is interesting to note, however, that the father of Usephais is recorded to have erected a stone temple at Hierakonpolis. Probably it was constructed of limestone. As much is suggested by the finish displayed in the limestone chamber of the brick tomb of King Khasekhemui of the Second Dynasty. Brick, however, continued in use until King Zoser of the Third Dynasty, which began about 2980 B.C., had constructed of stone, for his tomb, the earliest Egyptian pyramid near Memphis.

It is highly probable that it was the experienced limestone workers of the north, and not the brickmakers of Upper Egypt, who first utilized granite. The Pharaohs of the First Dynasty may have drafted southward large numbers of the skilled workers who were settled at Memphis, or in its vicinity. We seem to trace the presence of a northern colony in Upper Egypt by the mythological beliefs which obtained in the vicinity of the granite quarries at Assouan. The chief god of the First Cataract was Khnumu, who bears a close resemblance to Ptah, the artisan god of Memphis. (See Chapter XIV.)

We have now dealt with two distinct kinds of supreme deities—the Great Father, and the Great Mother with her son. It is apparent that they were conceived of and developed by peoples of divergent origin and different habits of life, who mingled in Egypt under the influence of a centralized government. The ultimate result was a fusion of religious beliefs and the formulation of a highly complex mythology which was never thoroughly systematized at any period. The Great Father then became the husband of the Great Mother, or the son god was exalted as "husband of his mother". Thus Ptah was given for wife Sekhet, the fierce lioness-headed mother, who re-

sembles Tefnut and other feline goddesses. Osiris, the
son of Isis and Nepthys, on the other hand, became " husband of his mother ", or mothers ; he was recognized as
the father of Horus, son of Isis, and of Anubis, son of
Nepthys. Another myth makes him displace the old
earth god Seb, son of Nut. Osiris was also a son of
Nut, an earlier form of Isis. So was Seb, who became
" husband of his mother ". That Seb and Osiris were
fused is evident in one of the temple chants, in which
Isis, addressing Osiris, says : " Thy soul possesseth the
earth ".

In Asia Minor, where the broad-headed patriarchal
Alpine hill people blended with the long-headed matriarchal Mediterranean people, the Pappas[1] god (Attis,
Adon) became likewise the husband of the Ma goddess
(Nana). A mythological scene sculptured upon a cliff
at Ibreez in Cappadocia is supposed to represent the
marriage of the two Great Father and Mother deities,
and it is significant to find that the son accompanies the
self-created bride. As in Egypt, the father and the son
were fused and at times are indistinguishable in the
legends.

It now remains with us to deal with the worship of
the solar disk. This religion was unknown to the early
Mediterranean people who spread through Europe and
reached the British Isles and Ireland. Nor did it rise
into prominence in the land of the Pharaohs until after
the erection of the Great Pyramids near Cairo. The
kings did not become " sons of the sun " until the Fifth
Dynasty.

There is general agreement among Egyptologists that

---

[1] The Phrygian name of the father deity, also called "Bagaios" (Slav, *bogu*, god).
The roots "pa", "ap", "da", "ad", "ta", and "at" signify "father", while "ma",
"am", "na", and "an" signify "mother".

sun worship was imported from Asia and probably from Babylonia. It achieved fullest development on Egyptian lines at Heliopolis, "the city of the sun". There Ra, the solar deity, was first exalted as the Great Father who created the universe and all the gods and goddesses, from whom men and animals and fish and reptiles were descended. But the religion of the sun cult never achieved the popularity of the older faiths. It was embraced chiefly by the Pharaohs, the upper classes, and the foreign sections of the trading communities. The great masses of the people continued to worship the gods of the moon, earth, atmosphere, and water until Egyptian civilization perished of old age. Osiris was ever the deity of the agriculturists, and associated with him, of course, were Isis and Nepthys. Set, the red-haired god of prehistoric invaders, who slew Osiris, became the Egyptian Satan, and he was depicted as a black serpent, a black pig, a red mythical monster, or simply as a red-haired man; he was also given half-animal and half-human form.

As we have indicated, the policy adopted by the priests of the sun was to absorb every existing religious cult in Egypt. They permitted the worship of any deity, or group of deities, so long as Ra was regarded as the Great Father. No belief was too contradictory in tendency, and no myth was of too trivial a character, to be embraced in their complex theological system. As a result we find embedded, like fossils, in the religious literature of Heliopolis, many old myths which would have perished but for the acquisitiveness of the diplomatic priests of the sun.

The oldest sun god was Tum, and he absorbed a primitive myth about Khepera, the beetle god. After Ra was introduced into Egypt the solar deity was called Ra-Tum. A triad was also formed by making Ra the noonday sun, Tum the evening sun, and Khepera the sun at dawn.

Khepera is depicted in beetle form, holding the sun disk between his two fore legs. To the primitive Egyptians the winged beetle was a sacred insect. Its association with the resurrected sun is explained by Wiedemann as follows: "The female (*Ateuchus sacer*) lays her eggs in a cake of dung, rolls this in the dust and makes it smooth and round so that it will keep moist and serve as food for her young; and finally she deposits it in a hole which she has scooped out in the ground; and covers it with earth. This habit had not escaped the observation of the Egyptians, although they failed to understand it, for scientific knowledge of natural history was very slight among all peoples of antiquity. The Egyptians supposed the Scarabæus to be male, and that it was itself born anew from the egg which it alone had made, and thus lived an eternal life. . . ."

The Scarabæus became a symbol of the resurrection and the rising sun. The dawn god raised up the solar disk as the beetle raised up the ball containing its eggs ere it set it a-rolling. Similarly souls were raised from death to life eternal.

Another myth represented the new-born sun as the child Horus rising from a lotus bloom which expanded its leaves on the breast of the primordial deep. Less poetic, but more popular, apparently, was the comedy about the chaos goose which was called "Great Cackler", because at the beginning she cackled loudly to the chaos gander and laid an egg, which was the sun. Ra was identified with the historical egg[1], but at Heliopolis the priests claimed that it was shaped by Ptah on his potter's wheel; Khnûmû, the other artisan god, was similarly

[1] The "soul and egg" myth is dealt with in Chapter V.

credited with the work. The gander was identified with Seb, the earth god, and in the end Amon-Ra, the combined deity of Thebes, was represented as the great chaos goose and gander in one. The "beautiful goose" was also sacred to Isis.

Of foreign origin, probably, was the myth that the sun was a wild ass, which was ever chased by the Night serpent, Haiu, as it ran round the slopes of the mountains supporting the sky. These are probably the world-encircling mountains, which, according to the modern Egyptians, are peopled by giants (genii). Belief in mountain giants survive among the hillmen of Arabia, Syria, Asia Minor, and Europe. The most popular old Egyptian idea was that the earth was surrounded by the ocean; the same opinion obtained in Greece. The wild ass, as we have seen, was also Set, the Nilotic Satan.

A similar myth represents the sun as a great cat, which was originally a female, but was identified with Ra as a male. It fought with the Night serpent, Apep, below the sacred tree at Heliopolis, and killed it at dawn. In this myth Set is identified with the serpent.

The cat and the wild ass enjoyed considerable popularity at Heliopolis. In the *Book of the Dead* it is declared: "I have heard the word of power (the magic word) which the ass spake to the cat in the house of Hapt-ra", but the "password" which was used by the souls of the dead is not given.

Another belief regarding the sun had its origin apparently among the moon worshippers. It can be traced in one of the Nut pictures. Shu, the atmosphere god, stands beneath the curving body of the Great Mother and receives in one of his hands a white pool of milk, which is the sun. In the mummy picture, already referred to, the sun disk is drawn between the breasts of the sky goddess.

Nut is sometimes called the "mother of Ra", but in a creation myth she is his wife, and her secret lover is Seb, the earth god.

It was emphasized at Heliopolis that Ra, as the Great Father, called Nut, Seb, and Shu into being. Those deities which he did not create were either his children or their descendants.

The creation story in which the priests of Heliopolis fused the old myths will be found in Chapter I. It familiarizes the reader with Egyptian beliefs in their earliest and latest aspects.

The second chapter is devoted to the Osiris and Isis legends, which shows that these deities have both a tribal and seasonal significance. In the chapters which follow, special attention is devoted to the periods in which the religious myths were formulated and the greater gods came into prominence[1], while light is thrown on the beliefs and customs of the ancient people of Egypt by popular renderings of representative folk tales and metrical versions of selected songs and poems.

[1] Aten worship is dealt with fully in its relation to primitive Egyptian myths in Chapter XXVI.

EGYPTIAN MYTHS
AND LEGENDS

CHAPTER I

Creation Legend of Sun Worshippers

The Primordial Deep—Ra's "Soul Egg" arises—The Elder Gods—Isis and the Serpent—Plot to rival Ra—How his Magic Name was obtained—Ra seeks to destroy Mankind—An Avenging Goddess—The Deluge—Worshippers are spared—Origin of Sacrifice—Ra ascends to Heaven—Earth God's Reptile Brood—Thoth the Deputy—The Sun God's Night Journey—Perils of the Underworld—Rebirth of Sun at Dawn.

AT the beginning the world was a waste of water called Nu, and it was the abode of the Great Father. He was Nu, for he was the deep, and he gave being unto the sun god who hath said: "Lo! I am Khepera at dawn, Ra at high noon, and Tum at eventide". The god of brightness first appeared as a shining egg which floated upon the water's breast, and the spirits of the deep, who were the Fathers and the Mothers, were with him there, as he was with Nu, for they were the companions of Nu.

Now Ra was greater than Nu from whom he arose. He was the divine father and strong ruler of gods, and those whom he first created, according to his desire, were Shu, the wind god, and his consort Tefnut, who had the

1

head of a lioness and was called "The Spitter" because she sent the rain. In aftertime these two deities shone as stars amidst the constellations of heaven, and they were called "The Twins".

Then came into being Seb, the earth god, and Nut, the goddess of the firmament, who became the parents of Osiris and his consort Isis and also of Set and his consort Nepthys.

Ra spake at the beginning of Creation, and bade the earth and the heavens to rise out of the waste of water. In the brightness of his majesty they appeared, and Shu, the uplifter, raised Nut upon high. She formed the vault, which is arched over Seb, the god of earth, who lies prostrate beneath her from where, at the eastern horizon, she is poised upon her toes to where, at the western horizon, bending down with outstretched arms, she rests upon her finger tips. In the darkness are beheld the stars which sparkle upon her body and over her great unwearied limbs.

When Ra, according to his desire, uttered the deep thoughts of his mind, that which he named had being. When he gazed into space, that which he desired to see appeared before him. He created all things that move in the waters and upon the dry land. Now, mankind were born from his eye, and Ra, the Creator, who was ruler of the gods, became the first king upon earth. He went about among men; he took form like unto theirs, and to him the centuries were as years.

Ra had many names that were not known unto gods or men, and he had one secret name which gave to him his divine power. The goddess Isis, who dwelt in the world as a woman, grew weary of the ways of mankind; she sought rather to be amidst the mighty gods. She was an enchantress, and she desired greatly to have power equal with Ra in the heavens and upon the earth. In her heart, therefore, she yearned to know the secret name[1] of the ruling god, which was hidden in his bosom and was never revealed in speech.

Each day Ra walked forth, and the gods who were of his train followed him, and he sat upon his throne and uttered decrees. He had grown old, and as he spake moisture dripped from his mouth and fell upon the ground. Isis followed after him, and when she found his saliva she baked it with the earth on which it lay. In the form of a spear she shaped the substance, and it became a venomous serpent. She lifted it up; she cast it from her, and it lay on the path which Ra was wont to traverse when he went up and down his kingdom, surveying that which he had made. Now the sacred serpent which Isis created was invisible to gods and men.

Soon there came a day when Ra, the aged god, walked along the path followed by his companions. He came nigh to the serpent, which awaited him, and the serpent stung him. The burning venom entered his body, and Ra was stricken with great pain. A loud and mighty cry broke from his lips, and it was heard in highest heaven.

Then spake the gods who were with him, saying: "What hath befallen thee?" and "What thing is there?"

Ra answered not; he shook; all his body trembled and his teeth clattered, for the venom overflowed in his flesh as does the Nile when it floods the land of Egypt. But at length he possessed himself and subdued his heart and the fears of his heart. He spake, and his words were:

"Gather about me, ye who are my children, so that I may make known the grievous thing which hath be-

[1] The secret name was called Ran; it was one of the god's spirits. See Chapter VII.

fallen me even now. I am stricken with great pain by something I know not of . . . by something which I cannot behold. Of that I have knowledge in my heart, for I have not done myself an injury with mine own hand. Lo! I am without power to make known who hath stricken me thus. Never before hath such sorrow and pain been mine."

He spake further, saying: "I am a god and the son of a god; I am the Mighty One, son of the Mighty One. Nu, my father, conceived my secret name which giveth me power, and he concealed it in my heart so that no magician might ever know it, and, knowing it, be given power to work evil against me.

"As I went forth, even now, beholding the world which I have created, a malignant thing did bite me. It is not fire, yet it burns in my flesh; it is not water, yet cold is my body and my limbs tremble. Hear me now! My command is that all my children be brought nigh to me so that they may pronounce words of power which shall be felt upon earth and in the heavens."

All the children of Ra were brought unto him as was his desire. Isis, the enchantress, came in their midst, and all sorrowed greatly, save her alone. She spoke forth mighty words, for she could utter incantations to subdue pain and to give life unto that from which life had departed. Unto Ra spake Isis, saying: "What aileth thee, holy father? . . . Thou hast been bitten by a serpent, one of the creatures which thou didst create. I shall weave spells; I shall thwart thine enemy with magic. Lo! I shall overwhelm the serpent utterly in the brightness of thy glory."

He answered her, saying: "A malignant thing did bite me. It is not fire, yet it burns my flesh. It is not water, yet cold is my body, and my limbs tremble.

Mine eyes also have grown dim. Drops of sweat fall from my face."

Isis spake unto the divine father and said: "Thou must, even now, reveal thy secret name unto me, for, verily, thou canst be delivered from thy pain and distress by the power of thy name."

Ra heard her in sorrow. Then he said: "I have created the heavens and the earth. Lo! I have even framed the earth, and the mountains are the work of my hands; I made the sea, and I cause the Nile to flood the land of Egypt. I am the Great Father of the gods and the goddesses. I gave life unto them. I created every living thing that moves upon the dry land and in the sea depths. When I open my eyes there is light: when I close them there is thick darkness. My secret name is known not unto the gods. I am Khepera at dawn, Ra at high noon, and Tum at eventide."

So spake the divine father; but mighty and magical as were his words they brought him no relief. The poison still burned in his flesh and his body trembled. He seemed ready to die.

Isis, the enchantress, heard him, but there was no sorrow in her heart. She desired, above all other things, to share the power of Ra, and she must needs have revealed unto her his sacred name which Nu conceived and uttered at the beginning. So she spake to Ra, saying:

"Divine father, thou hast not yet spoken thy name of power. If thou shalt reveal it unto me I will have strength to give thee healing."

Hotter than fire burned the venom in the heart of Ra. Like raging flames it consumed his flesh, and he suffered fierce agony. Isis waited, and at length the Great Father spake in majesty and said:

"It is my will that Isis be given my secret name, and that it leave my heart and enter hers."

When he had spoken thus, Ra vanished from before the eyes of the gods. The sun boat was empty, and there was thick darkness. Isis waited, and when the secret name of the divine father was about to leave his heart and pass into her own, she spake unto Horus her son and said:

"Now, compel the ruling god, by a mighty spell, to yield up also his eyes, which are the sun and the moon."[1]

Isis then received in her heart the secret name of Ra, and the mighty enchantress said:

"Depart, O venom, from Ra; come forth from his heart and from his flesh; flow out, shining from his mouth. . . . I have worked the spell. . . . Lo! I have overcome the serpent and caused the venom to be spilled upon the ground, because that the secret name of the divine father hath been given unto me. . . . Now let Ra live, for the venom hath perished."

So was the god made whole. The venom departed from his body and there was no longer pain in his heart or any sorrow.

As Ra grew old ruling over men, there were those among his subjects who spake disdainfully regarding him, saying: "Aged, indeed, is King Ra, for now his bones are silvern and his flesh is turned to gold, although his hair is still true lapis lazuli (dark)."

Unto Ra came knowledge of the evil words which were spoken against him, and there was anger in his heart, because that there were rebellious sayings on the lips of men and because they sought also to slay him. He spake unto his divine followers and said:

"Bring before me the god Shu and the goddess

[1] Hence the reference to "Horus the Ra".

Tefnut, the god Seb and his consort Nut, and the fathers and mothers who were with me at the beginning when I was in Nu. Bring Nu before me also. Let them all come hither in secret, so that men may not behold them, and, fearing, take sudden flight. Let all the gods assemble in my great temple at Heliopolis."

The gods assembled as Ra desired, and they made obeisance before him. They then said: "Speak what thou desirest to say and we will hear."

He addressed the gods, saying: "O Nu, thou the eldest god, from whom I had my being, and ye ancestral gods, hear and know now, that rebellious words are spoken against me by mankind, whom I did create. Lo! they seek even to slay me. It is my desire that ye should instruct me what ye would do in this matter. Consider well among yourselves and guide me with wisdom. I have hesitated to punish mankind until I have heard from your lips what should now be done regarding them.

"For lo! I desire in my heart to destroy utterly that which I did create. All the world will become a waste of water through a great flood as it was at the beginning, and I alone shall be left remaining, with no one else beside me save Osiris and his son Horus. I shall become a small serpent invisible to the gods. To Osiris will be given power to reign over the dead, and Horus will be exalted on the throne which is set upon the island of fiery flames."

Then spake forth Nu, god of primeval waters, and he said: "Hear me now, O my son, thou who art mightier far than me, although I gave thee life. Steadfast is thy throne; great is the fear of thee among men. Let thine eye go forth against those who are rebels in the kingdom."

Ra said: "Now do men seek escape among the hills; they tremble because of the words they have uttered."

The gods spake together, saying: "Let thine eye go forth against those who are rebels in the kingdom and it shall destroy them utterly. When it cometh down from heaven as Hathor, no human eye can be raised against it."

Ra heard, and, as was his will, his eye went forth as Hathor against mankind among the mountains, and they were speedily slain. The goddess rejoiced in her work and drave over the land, so that for many nights she waded in blood.

Then Ra repented. His fierce anger passed away, and he sought to save the remnant of mankind. He sent messengers, who ran swifter than the storm wind, unto Elephantine, so that they might obtain speedily many plants of virtue. These they brought back, and they were well ground and steeped with barley in vessels filled with the blood of mankind. So was beer made and seven thousand jars were filled with it.

Day dawned and Hathor[1] went upstream slaughtering mankind. Ra surveyed the jars and said: "Now shall I give men protection. It is my will that Hathor may slay them no longer."

Then the god gave command that the jars should be carried to the place where the vengeful goddess rested for the night after that day of slaughter. The jars were emptied out as was his desire, and the land was covered with the flood.

When Hathor awoke her heart was made glad. She

---

[1] The feline goddess Sekhet is also given as the slaughterer. In one of the temple chants we read: "Hathor overcometh the enemy of her sire by this her name of Sekhet".

stooped down and she saw her beauteous face mirrored in the flood. Then began she to drink eagerly, and she was made drunken so that she went to and fro over the land, nor took any heed of mankind.

Ra spake unto her, saying: "Beautiful goddess, return to me in peace."

Hathor returned, and the divine father said: "Henceforward shall comely handmaidens, thy priestesses, prepare for thee in jars, according to their number, draughts of sweetness, and these shall be given as offerings unto thee at the first festival of every New Year.[1]

So it came that from that day, when the Nile rose in red flood, covering the land of Egypt, offerings of beer were made unto Hathor. Men and women partook of the draughts of sweetness at the festival and were made drunken like the goddess.

Now when Hathor had returned to Ra he spake unto her with weariness, saying:

"A fiery pain torments me, nor can I tell whence it comes. I am still alive, but I am weary of heart and desire no longer to dwell among men. Lo! I have not destroyed them as I have power to do."

The gods who followed Ra said: "Be no longer weary. Power is thine according to thy desire."

Ra answered them, saying: "Weary indeed are my limbs and they fail me. I shall go forth no longer alone, nor shall I wait until I am stricken again with pain. Help shall be given unto me according to my desire."

Then the ruler of the gods called unto Nu, from whom he had being, and Nu bade Shu, the atmosphere god, and Nut, goddess of the heavens, to give aid unto Ra in his distress.

[1] 20 July, when the star Sirius (Sothis) appears as the morning star. The Nile is then in full flood.

Nut took the form of the Celestial Cow, and Shu lifted Ra upon her back. Then darkness came on. Men issued forth from their hiding places in great fear, and when they beheld Ra departing from them they sorrowed because of the rebellious words which had been spoken against his majesty. Indeed they cried unto Ra, beseeching him to slay those of his enemies who remained. But Ra was borne through the darkness, and men followed him until he appeared again and shed light upon the earth. Then did his faithful subjects arm themselves with weapons, and they sallied forth against the enemies of the sun god and slaughtered them in battle.

Ra beheld that which his followers among men had done, and he was well pleased. He spake unto them saying: "Now is your sin forgiven. Slaughter atones for slaughter. Such is sacrifice and the purport thereof."

When Ra had thus accepted in atonement for the sin of men the sacrifice of his enemies who desired to slay him, he spake unto the heavenly goddess Nut, saying:

"Henceforth my dwelling place must be in the heavens. No longer will I reign upon the earth."

So it happened, according to his divine will. The great god went on his way through the realms which are above, and these he divided and set in order. He spake creating words, and called into existence the field of Aalu, and there he caused to assemble a multitude of beings which are beheld in heaven, even the stars, and these were born of Nut. In millions they came to praise and glorify Ra. Unto Shu, the god of atmosphere, whose consort is Nut, was given the keeping of the multitude of beings that shine in thick darkness. Shu raised his arms, uplifting over his head the Celestial Cow[1] and the millions and millions of stars.

[1] Hathor, the sky goddess, in her cow form, displaces Nut.

Then Ra spake unto the earth god, who is called Seb, and said:

"Many fearsome reptiles dwell in thee. It is my will now that they may have dread of me as great as is my dread of them. Thou shalt discover why they are moved with enmity against me. When thou hast done that, thou shalt go unto Nu, my father, and bid him to have knowledge of all the reptiles in the deep and upon the dry land. Let it be made known unto each one that my rays shall fall upon them. By words of magic alone can they be overcome. I shall reveal the charms by which the children of men can thwart all reptiles, and Osiris, thy son, shall favour the magicians who protect mankind against them."

He spake again and called forth the god Thoth who came into being by his word.

"For thee, O Thoth," he said, "I shall make a resplendent abode in the great deep and the underworld which is Duat. Thou shalt record the sins of men, and the names of those who are mine enemies; in Duat thou shalt bind them. Thou shalt be temporary dweller in my place; thou art my deputy. Lo! I now give messengers unto thee."

So came into being by his power the ibis, the crane, and the dog ape,[1] the messengers of Thoth.

Ra spake again, saying: "Thy beauty shall be shed through the darkness; thou shalt join night with day."

So came into being the moon (Ah) of Thoth, and Ra said: "All living creatures shall glorify and praise thee as a wise god."

When all the land is black, the sun bark of Ra passes through the twelve hour-divisions of night in Duat. At

---

[1] Here the old lunar deity Thoth is associated with the dawn. The chattering of apes at sunrise gave origin to the idea that they worshipped the rising sun.

eventide, when the god is Tum, he is old and very frail.
Five-and-seventy invocations are chanted to give him
power to overcome the demons of darkness who are his
enemies.   He then enters the western gate, through
which dead men's souls pass to be judged before Osiris.
In front of him goes the jackal god, Anubis, for he is
"Opener of the Ways".   Ra has a sceptre in one hand:
in the other he carries the Ankh, which is the symbol of
life.

When the sun bark enters the river Ûrnes of the
underworld the companions of Ra are with him.   Watch-
man is there, and Striker, and Steersman is at the helm,
and in the bark are also those divinities who are given
power, by uttering magical incantations, to overcome the
demons of evil.

The gloomy darkness of the first hour-division is
scattered by the brightness of Ra.   Beside the bark
gather the pale shades of the newly dead, but none of
them can enter it without knowledge of the magical
formulæ which it is given unto few to possess.

At the end of the first hour-division is a high and
strong wall, and a gate is opened by incantations so that
the bark of Ra may pass through.   So from division
to division, all through the perilous night, the sun
god proceeds, and the number of demons that must be
thwarted by magic and fierce fighting increases as he goes.
Apep, the great Night serpent, ever seeks to overcome
Ra and devour him.

The fifth hour-division is the domain of dreaded
Sokar, the underworld god, with three human heads, a
serpent's body, and mighty wings between which appears
his hawk form.   His abode is in a dark and secret place
which is guarded by fierce sphinxes.   Nigh to him is the
Drowning Pool, watched over by five gods with bodies

like to men and animals' heads. Strange and mysterious
forms hover nigh, and in the pool are genii in torture,
their heads aflame with everlasting fire.

In the seventh hour-division sits Osiris, divine judge
of the dead. Fiery serpents, which are many-headed,
obey his will. Feet have they to walk upon and hands,
and some carry sharp knives with which to cut to pieces
the souls of the wicked. Whom Osiris deems to be
worthy, he favours; such shall live in the Nether
World: whom he finds to be full of sin, he rejects;
and these do the serpents fall upon, dragging them away,
while they utter loud and piercing cries of grief and
agony, to be tortured and devoured; lo! the wicked
perish utterly. In this division of peril the darksome
Night serpent Apep attacks the sun bark, curling its
great body round the compartment of Ra with ferocious
intent to devour him. But the allies of the god contend
against the serpent; they stab it with knives until it is
overcome. Isis utters mighty incantations which cause
the sun bark to sail onward unscathed nor stayed.

In the eighth division are serpents which spit forth
fire to illumine the darkness, and in the tenth are fierce
water reptiles and ravenous fishes. The god Horus
burns great beacons in the eleventh hour-division; ruddy
flames and flames of gold blaze aloft in beauty: the
enemies of Ra are consumed in the fires of Horus.

The sun god is reborn in the twelfth hour-division.
He enters the tail of the mighty serpent, which is named
"Divine Life", and issues from its mouth in the form
of Khepera, which is a beetle. Those who are with the
god are reborn also. The last door of all is guarded by
Isis, wife of Osiris, and Nepthys, wife of Set, in the form
of serpents. They enter the sun bark with Ra.

Now Ûrnes, the river of Duat, flows into the primeval

ocean in which Nu has his abode.   And as Ra was lifted out of the deep at the beginning, so he is lifted by Nu at dawn.   He is then received by Nut, goddess of the heavens; he is born of Nut and grows in majesty, ascending to high noon.

The souls of the dead utter loud lamentations when the sun god departs out of the darkness of Duat.[1]

---

[1] The myths from which this chapter has been constructed date from the Empire period, and especially the Nineteenth and Twentieth Dynasties. Ra is first a human god (the Pharaoh), then a world god like Ptah in his giant form, and lastly a cosmic deity. The priests were evidently engaged in systematizing the theology of the sun cult. Ra, the sun, is shown to be greater than his father Nu, and a concession is made to the worshippers of Isis in the legend which credits Ra with imparting to her the powers she possessed. Horus is given recognition; he possesses himself of the "eyes" of Ra (the sun and moon). Thoth also, as Ah, has control of the moon. The result of the compromising process was to leave everything vague and even confused, but the greatness of Ra was made manifest.

CHAPTER II
The Tragedy of Osiris

Osiris the Wise King—Introduction of Agriculture—Isis the Strong
Queen—Conspiracy of Set—The Tragic Feast—Osiris is slain—The Quest
of Isis—Set the Oppressor—"The Opener of the Ways"—Birth of Horus—
Thoth the Healer—Tree encloses Osiris's Body—Isis as a Foster-mother—
Her Swallow Guise—Flames of Immortality—Osiris brought back to Egypt
—Torn in Pieces by Set, the Boar Hunter—Isis recovers Fragments—Ghost
of Murdered King—Horus as Hamlet—Succession of Uncle and Son—Agri-
cultural Rites—The Inundation—Lamentations at Sowing Time and Harvest
—Osiris and Isis as Corn Spirits—Hapi, the Nile Deity—Isis as a Male.

WHEN Osiris was born, a voice from out of the heavens
proclaimed: "Now hath come the lord of all things."
The wise man Pamyles had knowledge of the tidings in
a holy place at Thebes, and he uttered a cry of gladness,
and told the people that a good and wise king had appeared among men.

When Ra grew old and ascended unto heaven, Osiris
sat in his throne and ruled over the land of Egypt.
Men were but savages when he first came amongst them.
They hunted wild animals, they wandered in broken
tribes hither and thither, up and down the valley and
among the mountains, and the tribes contended fiercely
in battle. Evil were their ways and their desires were
sinful.

Osiris ushered in a new age. He made good and
binding laws, he uttered just decrees, and he judged with
wisdom between men. He caused peace to prevail at
length over all the land of Egypt.

Isis was the queen consort of Osiris, and she was a

woman of exceeding great wisdom.   Perceiving the need of mankind, she gathered the ears of barley and wheat which she found growing wild, and these she gave unto the king.   Then Osiris taught men to break up the land which had been under flood, to sow the seed, and, in due season, to reap the harvest.   He instructed them also how to grind corn and knead flour and meal so that they might have food in plenty.   By the wise ruler was the vine trained upon poles, and he cultivated fruit trees and caused the fruit to be gathered.   A father was he unto his people, and he taught them to worship the gods, to erect temples, and to live holy lives.   The hand of man was no longer lifted against his brother.   There was prosperity in the land of Egypt in the days of Osiris the Good.

When the king perceived the excellent works which he had accomplished in Egypt, he went forth to traverse the whole world with purpose to teach wisdom unto all men, and prevail upon them to abandon their evil ways. Not by battle conquest did he achieve his triumphs, but by reason of gentle and persuasive speech and by music and song.   Peace followed in his footsteps, and men learned wisdom from his lips.

Isis reigned over the land of Egypt until his return. She was stronger than Set, who regarded with jealous eyes the good works of his brother, for his heart was full of evil and he loved warfare better than peace.   He desired to stir up rebellion in the kingdom.   The queen frustrated his wicked designs.   He sought in vain to prevail in battle against her, so he plotted to overcome Osiris by guile.   His followers were seventy and two men who were subjects of the dusky queen of Ethiopia.[1]

---

[1] After the period of Ethiopian supremacy (Twenty-fifth Dynasty) Set was identified with the Ethiopians.

When Osiris returned from his mission, there was great rejoicing in the land. A royal feast was held, and Set came to make merry, and with him were his fellow conspirators. He brought a shapely and decorated chest, which he had caused to be made according to the measurements of the king's body. All men praised it at the feast, admiring its beauty, and many desired greatly to possess it. When hearts were made glad with beer-drinking, Set proclaimed that he would gift the chest unto him whose body fitted its proportions with exactness. There was no suspicion of evil design among the faithful subjects of Osiris. The guests spoke lightly, uttering jests one against another, and all were eager to make trial as Set had desired. So it happened that one after another entered the chest on that fateful night, until it seemed that no man could be found to win it for himself. Then Osiris came forward. He lay down within the chest, and he filled it in every part. But dearly was his triumph won in that dark hour which was his hour of doom. Ere he could raise his body, the evil followers of Set sprang suddenly forward and shut down the lid, which they nailed fast and soldered with lead. So the richly decorated chest became the coffin of the good king Osiris, from whom departed the breath of life.

The feast was broken up in confusion. Merry-making ended in sorrow, and blood flowed after that instead of beer. Set commanded his followers to carry away the chest and dispose of it secretly. As he bade them, so did they do. They hastened through the night and flung it into the Nile. The current bore it away in the darkness, and when morning came it reached the great ocean and was driven hither and thither, tossing among the waves. So ended the days of Osiris and the years of his wise and prosperous reign in the land of Egypt.

When the grievous tidings were borne unto Isis, she was stricken with great sorrow and refused to be comforted. She wept bitter tears and cried aloud. Then she uttered a binding vow, cut off a lock of her shining hair, and put on the garments of mourning. Thereafter the widowed queen wandered up and down the land, seeking for the body of Osiris.

Nor would she rest nor stay until she found what she sought. She questioned each one she encountered, and one after another they answered her without knowledge. Long she made search in vain, but at length she was told by shoreland children that they had beheld the chest floating down the Nile and entering the sea by the Delta mouth which takes its name from the city of Tanis.[1]

Meanwhile Set, the usurper, ascended the throne of Osiris and reigned over the land of Egypt. Men were wronged and despoiled of their possessions. Tyranny prevailed and great disorder, and the followers of Osiris suffered persecution. The good queen Isis became a fugitive in the kingdom, and she sought concealment from her enemies in the swamps and deep jungle of the Delta. Seven scorpions followed her, and these were her protectors. Ra, looking down from heaven, was moved to pity because of her sore distress, and he sent to her aid Anubis, "the opener of the ways", who was the son of Osiris and Nepthys, and he became her guide.

One day Isis sought shelter at the house of a poor woman, who was stricken with such great fear when she beheld the fearsome scorpions that she closed the door against the wandering queen. But a scorpion gained entrance, and bit her child so that he died. Then loud and long were the lamentations of the stricken mother.

---

[1] Tanis was during the later Dynasties associated with the worship of Set as Sutekh

The heart of Isis was touched with pity, and she uttered magical words which caused the child to come to life again, and the woman ministered unto the queen with gratitude while she remained in the house.

Then Isis gave birth unto her son Horus; but Set came to know where the mother and babe were concealed, and he made them prisoners in the house.[1]

It was his desire to put Horus to death, lest he should become his enemy and the claimant of the throne of Osiris. But wise Thoth came out of heaven and gave warning unto Isis, and she fled with her child into the night. She took refuge in Buto, where she gave Horus into the keeping of Uazit, the virgin goddess of the city, who was a serpent,[2] so that he might have protection against the jealous wrath of Set, his wicked uncle, while she went forth to search for the body of Osiris. But one day, when she came to gaze upon the child, she found him lying dead. A scorpion had bitten him, nor was it in her power to restore him to life again. In her bitter grief she called upon the great god Ra. Her voice ascended to high heaven, and the sun boat was stayed in its course. Then wise Thoth came down to give aid. He worked a mighty spell; he spoke magical words over the child Horus, who was immediately restored to life again.[3] It was the will of the gods that he should grow into strong manhood and then smite his father's slayer.

The coffin of Osiris was driven by the waves to Byblos, in Syria, and it was cast upon the shore. A sacred tree sprang up and grew round it, and the body of the dead ruler was enclosed in its great trunk. The king of that

---

[1] Another version of the myth places the birth of Horus after the body of Osiris was found.

[2] She took the form of a shrew mouse to escape Set when he searched for Horus.

[3] Thoth in his lunar character as divine physician.

alien land marvelled greatly at the wonderful tree, because that it had such rapid growth, and he gave command that it should be cut down. As he desired, so it was done. Then was the trunk erected in his house as a sacred pillar, but to no man was given knowledge of the secret which it contained.

A revelation came unto Isis, and she set out towards Byblos in a ship. When she reached the Syrian coast she went ashore clad in common raiment, and she sat beside a well, weeping bitterly. Women came to draw water, and they spoke to her with pity, but Isis answered not, nor ceased to grieve, until the handmaidens of the queen drew nigh. Unto them she gave kindly greetings. When they had spoken gently unto her she braided their hair, and into each lock she breathed sweet and alluring perfume. So it chanced that when the maidens returned unto the king's house the queen smelt the perfume, and commanded that the strange woman should be brought before her. Then it was that Isis found favour in the eyes of the queen, who chose her to be the foster-mother of the royal babe.

But Isis refused to suckle the child, and to silence his cries for milk she put her finger into his mouth. When night came she caused fire to burn away his flesh, and she took the form of a swallow and flew, uttering broken cries of sorrow, round about the sacred pillar which contained the body of Osiris. It chanced that the queen came nigh and beheld her babe in the flames. She immediately plucked him forth; but although she rescued his body she caused him to be denied immortality.[1]

Isis again assumed her wonted form, and she confessed

---

[1] We have here a suggestion of belief in cremation, which was practised by the cave-dwellers of southern Palestine. The ghost of Patroklos says: "Never again will I return from Hades when I receive from you my meed of fire".—*Iliad*, xxiii, 75.

unto the queen who she was.   Then she asked the king
that the sacred pillar be given unto her.   The boon was
granted, and she cut deep into the trunk and took forth
the chest which was concealed therein.   Embracing it
tenderly, she uttered cries of lamentation that were so
bitter and keen that the royal babe died with terror.
Then she consecrated the sacred pillar, which she wrapped
in linen and anointed with myrrh, and it was afterwards
placed in a temple which the king caused to be erected
to Isis, and for long centuries it was worshipped by the
people of Byblos.

The coffin of Osiris was borne to the ship in which
the queen goddess had sailed unto Syria.   Then she
went aboard, and took with her Maneros, the king's
first-born, and put forth to sea.   The ship sped on, and
the land faded from sight.   Isis yearned to behold once
again the face of her dead husband, and she opened the
chest and kissed passionately his cold lips, while tears
streamed from her eyes.   Maneros, son of the King of
Byblos, came stealthily behind her, wondering what secret
the chest contained.   Isis looked round with anger, her
bright eyes blinded him, and he fell back dead into the
sea.

When Isis reached the land of Egypt she concealed
the body of the dead king in a secret place, and hastened
towards the city of Buto to embrace her son Horus; but
shortlived was her triumph.   It chanced that Set came
hunting the boar[1] at full moon in the Delta jungle, and
he found the chest which Isis had taken back from Syria.
He caused it to be opened, and the body of Osiris was
taken forth and rent into fourteen pieces, which he cast
into the Nile, so that the crocodiles might devour them.
But these reptiles had fear of Isis and touched them not,

[1] The Osiris boar.   See Chapter V.

and they were scattered along the river banks.[1] A fish (Oxyrhynchus) swallowed the phallus.

The heart of Isis was filled with grief when she came to know what Set had done. She had made for herself a papyrus boat and sailed up and down the Delta waters, searching for the fragments of her husband's body, and at length she recovered them all, save the part which had been swallowed by the fish. She buried the fragments where they were found, and for each she made a tomb. In after days temples were erected over the tombs, and in these Osiris was worshipped by the people for long centuries.

Set continued to rule over Egypt, and he persecuted the followers of Osiris and Isis in the Delta swamps and along the seacoast to the north. But Horus, who was rightful king, grew into strong manhood. He prepared for the coming conflict, and became a strong and brave warrior. Among his followers were cunning workers in metal who were called Mesniu (smiths), and bright and keen were their weapons of war. The sun hawk was blazoned on their battle banners.

One night there appeared to Horus in a dream a vision of his father Osiris.[2] The ghost urged him to overthrow Set, by whom he had been so treacherously put to death, and Horus vowed to drive his wicked uncle and all his followers out of the land of Egypt. So he gathered his army together and went forth to battle. Set came against him at Edfu and slew many of his followers. But Horus secured the aid of the tribes that remained faithful to Osiris and Isis, and Set was again attacked and driven towards the eastern frontier. The usurper uttered a

---

[1] The crocodile worshippers held that their sacred reptile recovered the body of Osiris for Isis.

[2] This is the earliest known form of the Hamlet myth.

great cry of grief when he was forced to take flight.
He rested at Zaru, and there was the last battle fought.
It was waged for many days, and Horus lost an eye.
But Set was still more grievously wounded,[1] and he was
at length driven with his army out of the kingdom.

It is told that the god Thoth descended out of heaven
and healed the wounds of Horus and Set. Then the
slayer of Osiris appeared before the divine council and
claimed the throne. But the gods gave judgment that
Horus was the rightful king, and he established his power
in the land of Egypt, and became a wise and strong ruler
like to his father Osiris.

Another version of the legend relates that when the
fragments of the body of Osiris were recovered from the
Nile, Isis and Nepthys lamented over them, weeping
bitterly. In one of the temple chants Isis exclaims:

Gods, and men before the face of the gods, are weeping for thee
    at the same time when they behold me!
Lo! I invoke thee with wailing that reacheth high as heaven—
Yet thou hearest not my voice. Lo! I, thy sister, I love thee more
    than all the earth—
And thou lovest not another as thou dost thy sister!

Nepthys cries,

Subdue every sorrow which is in the hearts of us thy sisters . . .
Live before us, desiring to behold thee.[2]

The lamentations of the goddesses were heard by Ra,
and he sent down from heaven the god Anubis, who,
with the assistance of Thoth and Horus, united the
severed portions of the body of Osiris, which they
wrapped in linen bandages. Thus had origin the mummy
form of the god. Then the winged Isis hovered over

---

[1] He was mutilated by Horus as he himself had mutilated Osiris.
[2] *The Burden of Isis*, translated by J. T. Dennis (Wisdom of the East Series).

the body, and the air from her wings entered the nostrils of Osiris so that he was imbued with life once again. He afterwards became the Judge and King of the Dead.

Egyptian burial rites were based upon this legend. At the ceremony enacted in the tomb chapel two female relatives of the deceased took the parts of Isis and Nepthys, and recited magical formulæ so that the dead might be imbued with vitality and enabled to pass to the Judgment Hall and Paradise.

Osiris and Isis, the traditional king and queen of ancient Egyptian tribes, were identified with the deities who symbolized the forces of Nature, and were accordingly associated with agricultural rites.

The fertility of the narrow strip of country in the Nile valley depends upon the River Nile, which overflows its banks every year and brings down fresh soil from the hills. The river is at its lowest between April and June, the period of winter. Fed by the melting snows on the Abyssinian hills, and by the equatorial lakes, which are flooded during the rainy season, the gradual rise of the river becomes perceptible about the middle of June. The waters first assume a reddish tint on account of the clay which they carry. For a short period they then become greenish and unwholesome. Ere that change took place the Ancient Egyptians were wont to store up water for domestic use in large jars. By the beginning of August the Nile runs high. It was then that the canals were opened in ancient days, so that the waters might fertilize the fields.

"As the Nile rose," writes Wilkinson,[1] "the peasants were careful to remove the flocks and herds from the lowlands; and when a sudden irruption of the water, owing to the bursting of a dike, or an unexpected and

[1] *The Ancient Egyptians*, Sir J. Gardner Wilkinson.

unusual increase of the river, overflowed the fields and pastures, they were seen hurrying to the spot, on foot or in boats, to rescue the animals and to remove them to the high grounds above the reach of the inundation. . . . And though some suppose the inundation does not now attain the same height as of old, those who have lived in the country have frequently seen the villages of the Delta standing, as Herodotus describes them, like islands in the Ægean Sea, with the same scenes of rescuing the cattle from the water." According to Pliny, "a proper inundation is of 16 cubits . . . in 12 cubits the country suffers from famine, and feels a deficiency even in 13; 14 causes joy, 15 scarcity, 16 delight; the greatest rise of the river to this period was of 18 cubits".

When the river rose very high in the days of the Pharaohs, "the lives and property of the inhabitants", says Wilkinson, "were endangered"; in some villages the houses collapsed. Hence the legend that Ra sought to destroy his enemies among mankind.

The inundation is at its height by the end of September, and continues stationary for about a month. Not until the end of September does the river resume normal proportions. November is the month for sowing; the harvest is reaped in Upper Egypt by March and in Lower Egypt by April.

It was believed by the ancient agriculturists that the tears of Isis caused the river to increase in volume. When Sirius rose before dawn about the middle of July it was identified with the goddess. In the sun-cult legend this star is Hathor, "the eye of Ra", who comes to slaughter mankind. There are evidences that human sacrifices were offered to the sun god at this period.

E. W. Lane, in his *Manners and Customs of the Modern Egyptians*, tells that the night of 17 June is called "Leylet-

en-Nuktah", or "the Night of the Drop", because "it
is believed that a miraculous drop then falls into the Nile
and causes it to rise". An interesting ceremony used to
be performed at "the cutting of the dam" in old Cairo.
A round pillar of earth was formed, and it was called the
"bride", and seeds were sown on the top of it. Lane
says that an ancient Arabian historian "was told that the
Egyptians were accustomed, at the period when the Nile
began to rise, to deck a young virgin in gay apparel, and
throw her into the river, as a sacrifice to obtain a plentiful
inundation ".

When the ancient Egyptians had ploughed their fields
they held a great festival at which the moon god, who,
in his animal form, symbolized the generative principle,
was invoked and worshipped. Then the sowing took
place, amidst lamentations and mourning for the death
of Osiris. The divine being was buried in the earth;
the seeds were the fragments of his body. Reference
is made to this old custom in Psalm cxxvi: "They that
sow in tears shall reap in joy. He that goeth forth and
weepeth, bearing precious seed, shall doubtless come
again with rejoicing, bringing his sheaves with him".

When harvest operations began, the Egyptians
mourned because they were slaying the corn spirit.
Diodorus Siculus tells that when the first handful of
grain was cut, the Egyptian reapers beat their breasts
and lamented, calling upon Isis. When, however, all
the sheaves were brought in from the fields, they rejoiced
greatly and held their "harvest home".

Both Osiris and Isis were originally identified with
the spirits of the corn. The former represented the
earth god and the latter the earth goddess. But after
the union of the tribes which worshipped the human
incarnations of ancient deities, the rival conceptions were

fused.   As a result we find that the inundation is symbolized now as the male principle and now as the female
principle; the Nile god, Hapi, is depicted as a man with
female breasts.   In an Abydos temple chant Isis makes
reference to herself as " the woman who was made a male
by her father, Osiris ".[1]

The Scottish Osiris

(JOHN BARLEYCORN)

THERE were three kings into the east,
   Three kings both great and high,
And they hae sworn a solemn oath
   John Barleycorn should die.

They took a plough and plough'd him down,
   Put clods upon his head,
And they hae sworn a solemn oath
   John Barleycorn was dead.

But the cheerful spring came kindly on,
   And show'rs began to fall;
John Barleycorn got up again,
   And sore warpris'd them all.

But the cheerful spring came kindly on,
   And show'rs began to fall;
John Barleycorn got up again,
   And sore surpris'd them all.

The sultry suns of summer came,
   And he grew thick and strong,
His head weel arm'd wi' pointed spears,
   That no one should him wrong.

The sober autumn enter'd mild,
   When he grew wan and pale;
His bending joints and drooping head
   Show'd he began to fail.

[1] *The Burden of Isis*, Dennis, p. 49.

His colour sicken'd more and more,
  He faded into age;
And then his enemies began
  To show their deadly rage.

They've ta'en a weapon long and sharp,
  And cut him by the knee;
Then ty'd him fast upon a cart,
  Like a rogue for forgerie.

They laid him down upon his back,
  And cudgell'd him full sore;
They hung him up before the storm,
  And turn'd him o'er and o'er.

They fillèd up a darksome pit
  With water to the brim,
They heavèd in John Barleycorn—
  There let him sink or swim.

They laid him out upon the floor,
  To work him farther woe;
And still, as signs of life appear'd,
  They tossed him to and fro.

They wasted, o'er a scorching flame,
  The marrow of his bones;
But the miller us'd him worst of all,
  For he crush'd him between two stones.

And they hae ta'en his very heart's blood,
  And drank it round and round;
And still the more and more they drank,
  Their joy did more abound.

John Barleycorn was a hero bold
  Of noble enterprise;
For if you do but taste his blood,
  'Twill make your courage rise.

'Twill make a man forget his woe;
  'Twill heighten all his joy;
'Twill make the widow's heart to sing,
  Tho' the tear were in her eye.

Then let us toast John Barleycorn,
  Each man a glass in hand;
And may his great posterity
  Ne'er fail in old Scotland.
                  Burns.

CHAPTER III

Dawn of Civilization

Early Peoples—The Mediterranean Race—Blonde Peoples of Morocco and Southern Palestine—Fair Types in Egypt—Migrations of Mediterraneans—They reach Britain—Early Nilotic Civilizations—Burial Customs—Osiris Invasion—The Set Conquest—Sun Worshippers from Babylonia—Settlement in North—Coming of Dynastic Egyptians—The Two Kingdoms—United by Mena—The Mathematicians of the Delta—Introduction of Calendar—Progressive Pharaohs—Early Irrigation Schemes.

In the remote ages, ere the ice cap had melted in northern Europe, the Nile valley was a swamp, with growth of jungle like the Delta. Rain fell in season, so that streams flowed from the hills, and slopes which are now barren wastes were green and pleasant grassland. Tribes of Early Stone Age savages hunted and herded there, and the flints they chipped and splintered so rudely are still found in mountain caves, on the surface of the desert, and embedded in mud washed down from the hills.

Other peoples of higher development appeared in time,[1] and after many centuries elapsed they divided the valley between them, increasing in numbers and breaking off in tribes. Several small independent kingdoms were thus formed. When government was ultimately centralized after conquest, these kingdoms became provinces,

---

[1] The early Palæolithic men were probably of Bushman type and the later of Mediterranean. Evidences of development from the Palæolithic to the Neolithic Age have been forthcoming

called nomes,[1] and each had its capital, with its ruling god and local theological system. The fusion of peoples which resulted caused a fusion of religious beliefs, and one god acquired the attributes of another without complete loss of identity.

The early settlers came from North Africa, which was possessed by tribes of the Mediterranean race. They were light-skinned "long heads" of short stature, with slender bodies, aquiline noses, and black hair and eyes. In the eastern Delta they were the Archaic Egyptians; in the western Delta and along the coast, which suffered from great subsidences in later times, they were known as the Libyans. Tribes of the latter appear to have mingled with a blonde and taller stock.[2] On the northern slopes of the Atlas Mountains this type has still survival; a similar people occupied southern Palestine in pre-Semitic times. Blue-eyed and light-haired individuals thus made appearance in the Nile valley at an early period. They were depicted in tomb paintings, and, although never numerous, were occasionally influential. There are fair types among modern-day Berbers. The idea that these are descendants of Celts or Goths no longer obtains.

As they multiplied and prospered, the Mediterranean peoples spread far from their North African area of characterization. Their migration southward was arrested in Nubia, where the exploring tribes met in conflict hordes of dusky Bushmen, with whom they ultimately blended. Fusion with taller negroes followed in later times. Thus had origin the virile Nubian people, who were ever a menace to the Dynastic Pharaohs.

---

[1] The Greek name; the old Egyptian name was "hesp".

[2] There were Libyans in the western Delta; on its borders were the "Tehenu", and beyond these the "Lebu", and still farther west were the "Meshwesh", the Maxyes of the Greeks. All were referred to as Libyans.

But the drift of surplus Mediterranean stock appears to have been greater towards the north than the south. Branching eastward, they poured into Palestine and Asia Minor. They were the primitive Phœnicians who ultimately fused with Semites, and they were the Hittites who blended with Mongols and Alpine (or Armenoid) "broad heads". Possessing themselves of large tracts of Italy and Greece, they became known to history as the Italici, Ligurians, Pelasgians, &c., and they founded a great civilization in Crete, where evidences have been forthcoming of their settlement as early as 10,000 B.C.

The western migration towards Morocco probably resulted in periodic fusions with blonde mountain tribes, so that the stock which entered Spain across the Straits of Gibraltar may have been more akin in physical type to the Libyans than to the Archaic Egyptians. The early settlers spread through western Europe, and are known to history as the Iberians. They also met and mingled with the tribes branching along the seacoast from Greece. Moving northward through the river valleys of France, the Iberians crossed over to Britain, absorbing everywhere, it would appear, the earlier inhabitants who survived the clash of conflict. These were the men of the Late Stone Age, which continued through vast intervals of time.

A glimpse of the early Mediterranean civilization is obtained in the Delta region. The dwellings of the Archaic Egyptians were of mud-plastered wickerwork, and were grouped in villages, round which they constructed strong stockades to ward off the attacks of desert lions and leopards, and afford protection for their herds of antelopes, goats, and ostriches. The cat and the dog were already domesticated. Men tattooed their bodies and painted their faces; they wore slight garments of goatskin, and adorned their heads with ostrich feathers. The women, who affected similar habits, but had fuller attire, set decorated combs in their hair, and they wore armlets and necklets of shells, painted pebbles, and animals' teeth which were probably charms against witchcraft.

These early settlers were herdsmen and hunters and fishermen, and among them were artisans of great skill, who chipped from splintered flint sharp lances and knives and keen arrowheads, while they also fashioned artistic pottery and hollowed out shapely stone jars. In their small boats they sailed and rowed upon the Nile; they caught fish with bone hooks, and snared birds in the Delta swamps. Their traders bartered goods constantly among the tribes who dwelt on the river banks. They were withal fierce and brave warriors, as fearless in the chase as in battle, for they not only slew the wild ox, but made attack with lance and bow upon the crocodile and hippopotamus, and hunted the wild boar and desert lion in moonlight.

As day followed night, so they believed that life came after death. They buried their dead in shallow graves, clad in goatskin, crouched up as if taking rest before setting forth on a journey, while beside them were placed their little palettes of slate for grinding face paint, their staffs and flint weapons and vessels of pottery filled with food for sustenance and drink for refreshment.

Long centuries went past, and a new civilization appeared in Lower Egypt. Tribes from the east settled there and effected conquests, introducing new arts and manners of life and new beliefs. The people began to till the soil after the Nile flood subsided, and they raised harvests of barley and wheat. It was the age of Osiris and Isis.

Each king was an Osiris, and his symbols of power were the shepherd's staff and the flail. The people worshipped their king as a god, and, after thirty years' reign, devoured him at their Sed festival[1] with cannibalistic ceremonial, so that his spirit might enter his successor and the land and the people have prosperity. The gnawed bones of monarchs have been found in tombs.[1]

Laws, which were stern and inexorable as those of Nature, disciplined the people and promoted their welfare. Social life was organized under a strict system of government. Industries were fostered and commerce flourished. Traders went farther afield as the needs of the age increased, and procured ivory from Nubia, silver from Asia, and from Araby its sweet perfumes and precious stones, and for these they bartered corn and linen and oil; there was also constant exchange of pottery and weapons and ornaments. Centuries went past, and this civilization at length suffered gradual decline, owing, probably, to the weakening of the central power.

Then followed a period of anarchy, when the kingdom, attracting plunderers, sustained the shock of invasion. Hordes of Semites, mingled probably with northern mountaineers, poured in from Syria and the Arabian steppes, and overthrew the power of the Osirian ruler. They were worshippers of Set (Sutekh), and they plundered and oppressed the people. Their sway, however, was but slight in the region of the western Delta, where frequent risings occurred and rebellion was ever fostered. Warfare disorganized commerce and impoverished the land. Art declined and an obscure period ensued.

But the needs of a country prevail in the end, and

[1] Petrie's view. See *Researches in Sinai*, p. 185.
[2] Maspero. This opinion, however, has been sharply challenged.

the north flourished once again with growing commerce and revived industries. On their pottery the skilled artisans painted scenes of daily life. Men and women were, it appears, clad in garments of white linen, and the rich had belts and pouches of decorated leather and ornaments of silver and gold set with precious stones. Tools and weapons of copper had come into use, but flint was also worked with consummate skill unsurpassed by any other people.

The land was a veritable hive of industry. Food was plentiful, for the harvests yielded corn, and huntsmen found wild animals more numerous as beasts of prey were driven from their lairs and lessened in number. Great galleys were built to trade in the Mediterranean, and each was propelled by sixty oarsmen. The ships of other peoples also visited the ports of Egypt, probably from Crete and the Syrian coast, and caravans crossed the frontier going eastward and north, while alien traders entered the land and abode in it. Battle conflicts with men of various races were also depicted on the pottery, for there was much warfare from time to time.

Growing communities with Babylonian beliefs effected settlements in the north. These were the sun worshippers whose religion ultimately gained ascendancy all over Egypt. From primitive Pithom (house of Tum) they may have passed to On (Heliopolis), which became sacred to Ra-Tum and was the capital of a province and probably, for a period, of the kingdom of Lower Egypt.

A masterful people also appeared in Upper Egypt. They came from or through Arabia, and had absorbed a culture from a remote civilization, which cannot be located, in common with the early Babylonians. Crossing the lower end of the Red Sea, they entered the verdurous valley of the Nile over a direct desert route, or through the highlands of Abyssinia. They were armed with weapons of copper, and effected their earliest settlement, it would appear, at Edfu. Then by gradual conquest they welded together the various tribes, extending their sway over an ever-increasing area. New and improved methods of agriculture were introduced. Canals were constructed for purposes of irrigation. The people increased in number and prosperity, and law and order was firmly established in the land.

These invaders were sun worshippers of the Horus-hawk cult, but they also embraced the religious beliefs of the people with whom they mingled, including the worship of the corn god Osiris. From Edfu and Hierakonpolis they pressed northward to sacred Abydos, the burial place of kings, and to Thinis, the capital of four united provinces. Several monarchs, who wore with dignity the white crown of Upper Egypt, reigned and "abode their destined hour". Then arose a great conqueror who was named Zaru, "The Scorpion". He led his victorious army down the Nile valley, extending his kingdom as he went, until he reached the frontier of the Fayum province, which was then a great swamp. There his progress was arrested. But a new era had dawned in Egypt, for there then remained but two kingdoms—the Upper and the Lower.

King Zaru was not slain at the Sed festival in accordance with the suggested ancient custom. He impersonated Osiris, throned in solitary dignity and wearing his crown, within a small curtained enclosure which opened at the front, and he held the crook in one hand and the flail in the other. The people made obeisance before him. It is not possible to follow the details of the ceremony, but from pictorial records it appears that large numbers of captives and oxen and cattle were offered up in sacrifice, so that slaughter might be averted by slaughter. The monarch was believed to have died a ceremonial death and to have come to life again with renewed energy which prolonged his years. An Abydos inscription declares of an Osiris ruler in this connection: "Thou dost begin thy days anew; like the holy moon child thou art permitted to prosper . . . thou hast grown young and thou art born to life again."[1] An important event at the festival was the appearance before the Pharaoh of his chosen successor, who performed a religious dance; and he was afterwards given for wife a princess of the royal line, so that his right to the throne might be secured.

The closing years of Zaru's reign were apparently occupied in organizing and improving the conquered territory. As befitted an Osirian king, he devoted much attention to agriculture, and land was reclaimed by irrigation. An artist depicted him in the act of digging on the river bank with a hoe, as if performing the ceremony of "cutting the first sod" of a new canal. The people are shown to have had circular dwellings, with fruit trees protected by enclosures. Their square fields were surrounded by irrigating ditches.

When the king died he was buried at Abydos, like other rulers of his line, in one of the brick tombs of the time. The investigation of these by Flinders Petrie has made possible the reconstruction in outline of the history of Egypt immediately prior to the founding of the First Dynasty. It is significant to note that the dead were buried at full length instead of in contracted posture as in Lower Egypt.

---

[1] The Horus worshippers had evidently absorbed the beliefs of the Nilotic moon cult. Some authorities credit the Dynastic Egyptians with the introduction of Osiris worship. The close resemblance of Osiris to similar deities in Asia Minor and Europe favours the view that Osiris first entered Lower Egypt. See *Golden Bough*—Adonis, Attis, Osiris volume. The Osirian heaven was of Delta character.

The next great monarch was Narmer, who is believed by certain authorities to have been Mena. Petrie, however, holds that they were separate personalities. Another view is that the deeds of two or three monarchs were attributed to Mena, as in the case of the Sesostris of the Greeks. Evidently many myths attached to the memory of the heroic figure who accomplished the conquest of the northern kingdom and founded the First Dynasty of united Egypt. Mena was represented, for instance, as the monarch who taught the people how to gorge luxuriously while he lay upon a couch and slaves massaged his stomach, and tradition asserted that he met his death, apparently while intoxicated, by falling into the Nile, in which he was devoured by a hippopotamus. But these folk tales hardly accord with the character of a conqueror of tireless energy, who must have been kept fully occupied in organizing his new territory and stamping out the smouldering fires of rebellion.

The initial triumph of the traditional Mena, in his Narmer character, was achieved in the swampy Fayum, the buffer state between Upper and Lower Egypt. It had long resisted invasion, but in the end the southern forces achieved a great victory. The broad Delta region then lay open before them, and their ultimate success was assured. King Narmer is shown on a slate palette clutching with one hand the headlocks of the Fayum chief—who kneels in helpless posture—while with the other he swings high a mace to smite the final blow. A composed body servant waits upon the conquering monarch, carrying the royal sandals and a water jar. The hawk symbol is also depicted to signify that victory was attributed to Horus, the tribal god. Two enemies take flight beneath, and above the combatants are two cow heads of the pastoral and sky goddess Hathor.

This great scene was imitated, in the true conservative spirit of the ancient Egyptians, on the occasion of similar acts of conquest in after time. Indeed, for a period of 3000 years each succeeding Pharaoh who achieved victory in battle was depicted, like Narmer, smiting his humbled foeman, and his importance was ever emphasized by his gigantic stature. It was an artistic convention in those ancient days to represent an Egyptian monarch among his enemies or subjects like a Gulliver surrounded by Lilliputians.

After the conquest of the Fayum, the Libyans appear to have been the dominating people in Lower Egypt. Their capital was at Sais, the seat of their goddess Neith. The attributes of this deity reflect the character of the civilization of her worshippers. Her symbol was a shield and two arrows. She was depicted with green hands and face, for she was an earth spirit who provided verdure for the flocks of a pastoral people. A weaver's shuttle was tattooed upon her body, to indicate apparently that she imparted to women their skill at the loom.

Mena conquered the Libyans in battle, and many thousands were slain, and he extended his kingdom to the shores of the Mediterranean. Then he assumed, in presence of his assembled army, the red crown of Lower Egypt. He appears also to have legitimatized the succession by taking for wife Neithhotep, "Neith rests", a princess of the royal house of Sais.

So was the Horus tribe united with the Libyans who worshipped a goddess. In aftertime the triad of Sais was composed of Osiris, Neith, and Horus. Neith was identified with Isis.

The race memory of the conquest of Lower Egypt is believed to be reflected in the mythical tale of Horus overcoming Set. The turning-point in the campaign was the Fayum conflict where the animal gods of Set were slain. Petrie urges with much circumstantial detail the striking view that the expulsion of Set from Egypt signifies the defeat of the military aristocracy of "Semites"[1] by the Horus people, who, having espoused the religion of Osiris, also espoused the cause of the tribe which introduced his worship into the land. It is evident, from an inscription on a temple of southern Edfu, that many conquests were effected in the Delta region ere the union was accomplished. One version of the great folk tale states that when Horus overcame Set he handed him over to Isis bound in chains. She failed, however, to avenge her husband's death, and set her oppressor at liberty again. In his great wrath Horus then tore the crown from her head. This may refer particularly to the circumstances which led to the Libyan conquest. "We can hardly avoid", says Petrie, "reading the history of the animosities of the gods as being the struggles of their worshippers."

The Libyans were ever a troublesome people to the Pharaohs, whose hold on the western district of the Delta was never certain. Mena apparently endeavoured to break their power by taking captive no fewer than 120,000 prisoners. His spoils included also 400,000 oxen and 1,420,000 goats.

This displacement of so large a proportion of the inhabitants of the north was not without its effect in the physical character of the Nile-valley peoples. The differences of blend between north and south were well marked prior to the conquest. After the union of the two kingdoms the ruling classes of Upper Egypt approximated closely to the Delta type. It is evident that the great

---

[1] It is possible that Set (Sutekh) was the god of a pre-Semitic people whose beliefs were embraced by certain Semitic tribes.

The girl wife and the Bata bull
Page 54

The farmer plunders the peasant
Page 126

Senuhet slays the warrior of Tonu
Page 212

Queen Ahmes (wife of Thothmes I), mother of the
famous Queen Hatshepsut
Page 286

Luring the doom serpent
Page 299

Pastime in ancient Egypt three thousand years ago
Page 304

Farm scene: the counting and inspection of geese
In the upper register the seated scribe is preparing to make
a list of the geese, which are being marshalled before him.
Below we see a group of gooseherds with their flock, who
are making obeisance before him, whilst one of their
number places the birds in baskets. The scribe has risen
and is engaged in unrolling a new papyrus, whereon to
inscribe his list. The horizontal line of hieroglyphics above
the geese contains an exhortation of one gooseherd to
another to "make haste", so that he may bring his flock
before the scribe. In front of the scribe is a red leather
sack, or bag, in which he kept his clothes, &c., and round
it is rolled the mat on which he sat.

Fowling scene

The deceased, accompanied by his wife and daughter, stands in a reed canoe in a marsh filled with large papyrus reeds, and is occupied in knocking down birds with a stick, which is made in the form of a snake. In front of him is his hunting cat, which has seized three birds, one with its hind claws, one with its fore claws, and one by the wings with its mouth. Numerous butterflies are represented, and the lake is well stocked with fish. The line of hieroglyphics at the back of the deceased indicates that the scene is supposed to represent the state of felicity that he will enjoy in the next world.

native civilization which flourished in the Nile valley for over forty centuries owed much to the virility and genius of the Mediterranean race, which promoted culture wherever its people effected settlements. One is struck, indeed, to note in this connection that the facial characteristics of not a few Pharaohs resemble those of certain great leaders of men who have achieved distinction among the nations of Europe.

The culture of the Horite conquerors was evidently well adapted for the Nile valley. It developed there rapidly during the three centuries which elapsed before the Delta was invaded, and assumed a purely Egyptian character. Hieroglyphics were in use from the beginning, copper was worked by "the smiths", and superior wheel-turned pottery made its appearance. But the greatest service rendered to ancient Egypt by the Horites was the ultimate establishment of settled conditions over the entire land in the interests of individual welfare and national progress.

The contribution of the north to Dynastic culture was not inconsiderable. In fact, it cannot really be over-estimated. The Delta civilization was already well developed prior to the conquest. There was in use among the people a linear script which resembled closely the systems of Crete and the Ægean and those also that appeared later in Karia and Spain. Its early beginnings may be traced, perhaps, in those rude signs which the pioneers of the Late Stone Age in western Europe scratched upon the French dolmens. Archaic Phœnician letters show that the great sea traders in after time simplified the system and diffused it far and wide.[1] Our alphabet is thus remotely North African in origin.

[1] Professor Macalister is inclined to credit the Philistines instead of the Phœnicians with the work of systematizing the script.

It was in the Delta also that the Calendar was invented by great mathematicians of the Late Stone Age, over sixty centuries ago, who recognized that an artificial division of time was necessary for purposes of accurate record and calculation. They began their year with the rising of the star Sirius (Sothos) at the height of the Nile inundation, and it was divided into twelve months of thirty days each, five extra days being added for religious festivals associated with agricultural rites. This Calendar was ultimately imported and adjusted by the Romans, and it continues in use, with subsequent refinements, all over the world until the present day. Under Mena's rule there are evidences of the progress which is ever fostered when ideas are freely exchanged and a stimulating rivalry is promoted among the people. The inventive mind was busily at work. Pottery improved in texture and construction, and was glazed in colours. Jewellery of great beauty was also produced, and weapons and tools were fashioned with artistic design. Draughtboards and sets of "ninepins" were evidently in demand among all classes for recreation in moments of leisure.

Meanwhile the administration of the united kingdom was thoroughly organized. Officials were numerous and their duties were strictly defined. Various strategic centres were garrisoned so as to prevent outbreaks and to secure protection for every industrious and law-abiding citizen. Memphis became an important city. According to tradition it was built by Mena, but the local theological system suggests that it existed prior to his day. It is probable that he erected buildings there, including a fortification, and made it a centre of administration for the northern part of his kingdom.

When Mena died he was buried at Abydos, and he was succeeded by his son Aha, "the fighter". Under the new monarch a vigorous military campaign was conducted in the south, and another province was placed under the sway of the central government. The peaceful condition of the north is emphasized by his recorded visit to Sais, where he made offerings at the shrine of Neith, the goddess of his mother's people.

Meanwhile the natural resources of the Nile valley were systematically developed. Irrigation works were undertaken everywhere, jungle was cleared away, and large tracts of land were reclaimed by industrious toilers. These activities were promoted and controlled by royal officials. King Den, a wise and progressive monarch, inaugurated the great scheme of clearing and draining the Fayum, which was to become in after time a fertile and populous province. The surveyors set to work and planned the construction of a canal, and the scheme was developed and continued by the monarchs who followed. It was as shrewdly recognized in the time of the First Dynasty as it is in our own day, that the progress and welfare of the Nile-valley people must ever depend upon the development of the agricultural resources of the country. The wealth of Egypt is drawn from the soil. All the glory and achievements of the Dynasties were made possible by the systems of government which afforded facilities and protection for the men who "cast their bread upon the waters" so that abundant return might be secured "after many days". When we are afforded, therefore, a glimpse of daily life on the land, as is given in the ancient and treasured folk tale which follows,[1] we are brought into closer touch with the people who toiled in contentment many thousands of years ago in the land of Egypt than is possible when we contem-

---

[1] It assumed its final form in the Empire period, and is evidently of remote antiquity.

plate with wonder their exquisite works of art or great architectural triumphs. The spirit which pervaded the ancient peasantry of the Nile valley is reflected in the faithful and gentle service and the winning qualities of poor Bata, the younger brother. It gives us pause to reflect that the story of his injured honour and tragic fate moved to tears those high-born dames whose swaddled mummies now lie in our museums to be stared at by holidaymakers who wonder how they lived and what scenes surrounded their daily lives.

CHAPTER IV

The Peasant who became King

The Two Brothers—Peasant Life—The Temptress—Wrath of Anpu—Attempt to slay his Brother—Flight of Bata—Elder Brother undeceived—Kills his Wife—Bata hides his Soul—His Wife—Sought by the King—Bata's Soul Blossom destroyed—Wife becomes a Queen—Recovery of Lost Soul—Bata as a Bull—Slaughtered for the Queen—Bata a Tree—Bata reborn as Son of his Wife—The King who slew his Wife-mother—Belief in Transmigration of Souls.

THERE were once two brothers, and they were sons of the same father and of the same mother. Anpu was the name of the elder, and the younger was called Bata. Now Anpu had a house of his own, and he had a wife. His brother lived with him as if he were his son, and made garments for him. It was Bata who drove the oxen to the field, it was he who ploughed the land, and it was he who harvested the grain. He laboured continually upon his brother's farm, and his equal was not to be found in the land of Egypt; he was imbued with the spirit of a god.

In this manner the brothers lived together, and many days went past. Each morning the younger brother went forth with the oxen, and when evening came on he drove them again to the byre, carrying upon his back a heavy burden of fodder which he gave to the animals to eat, and he brought with him also milk and herbs for Anpu and his wife. While these two ate and drank together in the house, Bata rested in the byre with the cattle and he slept beside them.

When day dawned, and the land grew bright again, the younger brother was first to rise up, and he baked bread for Anpu and carried his own portion to the field and ate it there. As he followed the oxen he heard and he understood their speech. They would say: "Yonder is sweet herbage", and he would drive them to the place of their choice, whereat they were well pleased. They were indeed noble animals, and they increased greatly.

The time of ploughing came on, and Anpu spake unto Bata, saying: "Now get ready the team of oxen, for the Nile flood is past and the land may be broken up. We shall begin to plough on the morrow; so carry seed to the field that we may sow it."

As Anpu desired, so did Bata do. When the next day dawned, and the land grew bright, the two brothers laboured in the field together, and they were well pleased with the work which they accomplished. Several days went past in this manner, and it chanced that on an afternoon the seed was finished ere they had completed their day's task.

Anpu thereupon spake to his younger brother saying: "Hasten to the granary and procure more seed."

Bata ran towards the house, and entered it. He beheld his brother's wife sitting upon a mat, languidly pleating her hair.

"Arise," he said, "and procure corn for me, so that I may hasten back to the field with it. Delay me not."

The woman sat still and said: "Go thou thyself and open the storeroom. Take whatsoever thou dost desire. If I were to rise for thee, my hair would fall in disorder."

Bata opened the storeroom and went within. He took a large basket and poured into it a great quantity of seed. Then he came forth carrying the basket through the house.

The woman looked up and said: " What is the weight of that great burden of thine?"

Bata answered: "There are two measures of barley and three of wheat. I carry in all upon my shoulders five measures of seed."

"Great indeed is thy strength," sighed the woman. "Ah, thee do I contemplate and admire each day!"

Her heart was moved towards him, and she stood up saying: "Tarry here with me. I will clothe thee in fine raiment."

The lad was made angry as the panther, and said: "I regard thee as a mother, and my brother is like a father unto me. Thou hast spoken evil words and I desire not to hear them again, nor will I repeat unto any man what thou hast just spoken."

He departed abruptly with his burden and hastened to the field, where he resumed his labour.

At eventide Anpu returned home and Bata prepared to follow after him. The elder brother entered his house and found his wife lying there, and it seemed as if she had suffered violence from an evildoer. She did not give him water to wash his hands, as was her custom. Nor did she light the lamp. The house was in darkness. She moaned where she lay, as if she were in sickness, and her garment was beside her.

"Who hath been here?" asked Anpu, her husband.

The woman answered him: "No one came nigh me save thy younger brother. He spoke evil words unto me, and I said: 'Am I not as a mother, and is not thine elder brother as a father unto thee?' Then was he angry, and he struck me until I promised that I would not inform thee. . . . Oh! if thou wilt allow him to live now, I shall surely die."

The elder brother became like an angry panther. He

sharpened his dagger and went out and stood behind the door of the byre with purpose to slay young Bata when he came nigh.

The sun had gone down when the lad drove the oxen into the byre, carrying on his back fodder and herbs, and in one hand a vessel of milk, as was his custom each evening.

The first ox entered the byre, and then it spoke to Bata, saying: "Beware! for thine elder brother is standing behind the door. In his hand is a dagger, and he desires to slay thee. Draw not nigh unto him."

The lad heard with understanding what the animal had said. Then the second ox entered and went to its stall, and spake likewise words of warning, saying: "Take speedy flight."

Bata peered below the byre door, and he saw the legs of his brother, who stood there with a dagger in his hand. He at once threw down his burden and made hurried escape. Anpu rushed after him furiously with the sharp dagger.

In his sore distress the younger brother cried unto the sun god Ra-Harmachis, saying: "O blessed lord! thou art he who distinguisheth between falsehood and truth."

The god heard his cry with compassion, and turned round.[1] He caused a wide stream to flow between the two brothers, and, behold! it was full of crocodiles. Then it came that Anpu and Bata stood confronting one another, one upon the right bank and the other upon the left. The elder brother twice smote his hands with anguish because that he could not slay the youth.

Bata called out to Anpu, saying: "Tarry where thou art until the earth is made bright once again. Lo! when

---

[1] Ra is here in his human form, walking through Egypt.

Ra, the sun god, riseth up, I shall reveal in his presence
all that I know, and he shall judge between us, discerning
what is false and what is true. . . . Know thou that I
may not dwell with thee any longer, for I must depart
unto the fair region of the flowering acacia."

When day dawned, and the sun god Ra appeared
in his glory, the two brothers stood gazing one upon the
other across the stream of crocodiles. Then the lad
spake to his elder brother, saying: "Why didst thou
come against me, desiring to slay me with treachery ere
yet I had spoken for myself? Am I not thy younger
brother, and hast thou not been as a father and thy wife
as a mother unto me? Hear and know now that when
I hastened to procure seed thy wife spoke, saying:
'Tarry thou with me.' But this happening hath been
related unto thee in another manner."

So spake Bata, and he told his brother what was true
regarding the woman. Then he called to witness the
sun god, and said: "Great was thy wickedness in desiring to murder me by treachery." As he spoke he cut off
a piece of his flesh and flung it into the stream, where it
was devoured by a fish.[1] He sank fainting upon the
bank.

Anpu was stricken with anguish; tears ran from his
eyes. He desired greatly to be beside his brother on
the opposite bank of the stream of crocodiles.

Bata spake again, saying: "Verily, thou didst desire
an evil thing, but if thy desire now is to do good, I shall
instruct thee what thou shouldst do. Return unto thy
home and tend thine oxen, for know now that I may not
dwell with thee any longer, but must depart unto the fair
region of the flowering acacia. What thou shalt do is to
come to seek for me when I need thine aid, for my soul

---

[1] He was thus mutilated like Osiris, Attis, Adonis, and other gods.

shall leave my body and have its dwelling in the highest blossom of the acacia. When the tree is cut down, my soul will fall upon the ground. There thou mayest seek it, even if thy quest be for seven years, for, verily, thou shalt find it if such is thy desire. Thou must then place it in a vessel of water, and I shall come to life again and reveal all that hath befallen and what shall happen thereafter. When the hour cometh to set forth on the quest, behold! the beer given to thee will bubble, and the wine will have a foul smell. These shall be as signs unto thee."

Then Bata took his departure, and he went into the valley of the flowering acacia, which was across the ocean.[1] His elder brother returned home. He lamented, throwing dust upon his head. He slew his wife and cast her to the dogs, and abandoned himself to mourning for his younger brother.

Many days went past, and Bata reached at length the valley of the flowering acacia. He dwelt there alone and hunted wild beasts. At eventide he lay down to rest below the acacia, in whose highest blossom his soul was concealed. In time he built a dwelling place and he filled it with everything that he desired.

Now it chanced that on a day when he went forth he met the nine gods, who were surveying the whole land. They spoke one to another and then asked of Bata why he had forsaken his home because of his brother's wife, for she had since been slain. "Return again," they said, "for thou didst reveal unto thine elder brother the truth of what happened unto thee."

They took pity on the youth, and Ra spoke, saying: "Fashion now a bride for Bata, so that he may not be alone."

[1] Probably in Syria.

Then the god Khnumu[1] fashioned a wife whose body was more beautiful than any other woman's in the land, because that she was imbued with divinity.

Then came the seven Hathors[2] and gazed upon her. In one voice they spoke, saying: "She shall surely die a speedy death."

Bata loved her dearly. Each day she remained in his house while he hunted wild beasts, and he carried them home and laid them at her feet. He warned her each day, saying: "Walk not outside, lest the sea may come up and carry thee away. I could not rescue thee from the sea spirit,[3] against whom I am as weak as thou art, because my soul is concealed in the highest blossom of the flowering acacia. If another should find my soul I must needs fight for it."

Thus he opened unto her his whole heart and revealed its secrets.

Many days went past. Then on a morning when Bata had gone forth to hunt, as was his custom, his girl wife went out to walk below the acacia, which was nigh to the house.

Lo! the sea spirit beheld her in all her beauty and caused his billows to pursue her. Hastily she fled away and returned to the house, whereat the sea spirit sang to the acacia: "Oh, would she were mine!"

The acacia heard and cast to the sea spirit a lock of the girl wife's hair. The sea bore it away towards the land of Egypt and unto the place where the washers of the king cleansed the royal garments.

Sweet was the fragrance of the lock of hair, and it perfumed the linen of the king. There were disputes among the washers because that the royal garments smelt

---

[1] A creative god who resembles Ptah.   [2] The seven Fates.
[3] A non-Egyptian conception apparently.

of ointment, nor could anyone discover the secret thereof. The king rebuked them.

Then was the heart of the chief washer in sore distress, because of the words which were spoken daily to him regarding this matter. He went down to the seashore; he stood at the place which was opposite the floating lock of hair, and he beheld it at length and caused it to be carried unto him. Sweet was its fragrance, and he hastened with it to the king.

Then the king summoned before him his scribes, and they spake, saying: "Lo! this is a lock from the hair of the divine daughter of Ra, and it is gifted unto thee from a distant land. Command now that messengers be sent abroad to seek for her. Let many men go with the one who is sent to the valley of the flowering acacia so that they may bring the woman unto thee.[1]

The king answered and said: "Wise are your words, and they are pleasant unto me."

So messengers were sent abroad unto all lands. But those who journeyed to the valley of the flowering acacia returned not, because that Bata slew them all; the king had no knowledge of what befel them.

Then the king sent forth more messengers and many soldiers also, so that the girl might be brought unto him. He sent also a woman, and she was laden with rare ornaments . . . and the wife of Bata came back with her.

Then was there great rejoicing in the land of Egypt. Dearly did the king love the divine girl, and he exalted her because of her beauty. He prevailed upon her to reveal the secrets of her husband, and the king then said: "Let the acacia be cut down and splintered in pieces."

---

[1] An early version of the Cinderella story.

Workmen and warriors were sent abroad, and they reached the acacia. They severed from it the highest blossom, in which the soul of Bata was concealed. The petals were scattered, and Bata dropped down dead.[1]

A new day dawned, and the land grew bright. The acacia was then cut down.

Meanwhile Anpu, the elder brother of Bata, went into his house, and he sat down and washed his hands.[2] He was given beer to drink, and it bubbled, and the wine had a foul smell.

He seized his staff, put on his shoes and his garment, and armed himself for his journey, and departed unto the valley of the flowering acacia.

When he reached the house of Bata he found the young man lying dead upon a mat. Bitterly he wept because of that. But he went out to search for the soul of his brother at the place where, below the flowering acacia, Bata was wont to lie down to rest at eventide. For three years he continued his search, and when the fourth year came his heart yearned greatly to return to the land of Egypt. At length he said: "I shall depart at dawn to-morrow."

A new day came, and the land grew bright. He looked over the ground again at the place of the acacia for his brother's soul. The time was spent thus. In the evening he continued his quest also, and he found a seed, which he carried to the house, and, lo! the soul of his brother was in it. He dropped the seed into a vessel filled with cold water, and sat down as was his custom at evening.

Night came on, and then the soul absorbed the water.

---

[1] Like the typical giant of European folklore, who conceals his soul and is betrayed by his wife.

[2] The Egyptians always washed their hands before and after meals.

The limbs of Bata quivered and his eyes opened and
gazed upon his elder brother, but his heart was without
feeling.   Then Anpu raised the vessel which contained
the soul to the lips of Bata, and he drank the water.
Thus did his soul return to its place, and Bata was as he
had been before.

The brothers embraced and spoke one to the other.
Bata said: "Now I must become a mighty bull with
every sacred mark.   None will know my secret.   Ride
thou upon my back, and when the day breaks I shall be
at the place where my wife is.   Unto her must I speak.
Lead me before the king, and thou shalt find favour in
his eyes.   The people will wonder when they behold me,
and shout welcome.   But thou must return unto thine
own home."

A new day dawned, and the land grew bright.   Bata
was a bull, and Anpu sat upon his back and they drew
nigh to the royal dwelling.   The king was made glad,
and he said: "This is indeed a miracle."   There was
much rejoicing throughout the land.   Silver and gold
were given to the elder brother, and he went away to
his own home and waited there.

In time the sacred bull stood in a holy place, and the
beautiful girl wife was there.   Bata spoke unto her,
saying: "Look thou upon me where I stand, for, lo!
I am still alive."

Then said the woman: "And who art thou?"

The bull made answer: "Verily, I am Bata.   It was
thou who didst cause the acacia to be cut down; it was
thou who didst reveal unto Pharaoh that my soul had
dwelling in the highest blossom, so that it might be
destroyed and I might cease to be.   But, lo! I live on,
and I am become a sacred bull."

The woman trembled; fear possessed her heart when

Bata spoke unto her in this manner. She at once went out of the holy place.

It chanced that the king sat by her side at the feast, and made merry, for he loved her dearly. She spoke, saying: "Promise before the god that thou wilt do what I ask of thee."

His Majesty took a vow to grant her the wish of her heart, and she said: "It is my desire to eat of the liver of the sacred bull, for he is naught to thee."[1]

Sorrowful was the king then, and his heart was troubled, because of the words which she spake. . . .

A new day dawned, and the land grew bright. Then the king commanded that the bull should be offered in sacrifice.

One of the king's chief servants went out, and when the bull was held high upon the shoulders of the people he smote its neck and it cast two drops of blood[2] towards the gate of the palace, and one drop fell upon the right side and one upon the left. There grew up in the night two stately Persea trees[3] from where the drops of blood fell down.

This great miracle was told unto the king, and the people rejoiced and made offerings of water and fruit to the sacred trees.

A day came when his majesty rode forth in his golden chariot. He wore his collar of lapis lazuli, and round his neck was a garland of flowers. The girl wife was with him, and he caused her to stand below one of the trees, and it whispered unto her:

"Thou false woman, I am still alive. Lo! I am even Bata, whom thou didst wrong. It was thou who didst cause the acacia to be cut down. It was thou who

---

[1] It was believed that the soul was in the liver.
[2] The belief that the soul was in the blood.
[3] One tree for the spirit and one for the soul.

didst cause the sacred bull to be slain, so that I might cease to be."

Many days went past, and the woman sat with the king at the feast, and he loved her dearly. She spake, saying: "Promise now before the god that thou wilt do what I ask of thee."

His Majesty made a vow of promise, and she said: "It is my desire that the Persea trees be cut down so that two fair seats may be made of them."

As she desired, so was it done. The king commanded that the trees should be cut down by skilled workmen, and the fair woman went out to watch them. As she stood there, a small chip of wood entered her mouth, and she swallowed it.

After many days a son was born to her, and he was brought before the king, and one said: "Unto thee a son is given."

A nurse and servants were appointed to watch over the babe.

There was great rejoicing throughout the land when the time came to name the girl wife's son. The king made merry, and from that hour he loved the child, and he appointed him Prince of Ethiopia.

Many days went past, and then the king chose him to be heir to the kingdom.

In time His Majesty fulfilled his years, and he died, and his soul flew to the heavens.

The new king (Bata) then said: "Summon before me the great men of my Court, so that I may now reveal unto them all that hath befallen me and the truth concerning the queen."

His wife[1] was then brought before him. He re-

---

[1] Who was also his mother. Bata was reborn as the son of his wife. The tale is based upon belief in the transmigration of souls.

vealed himself unto her, and she was judged before the great men, and they confirmed the sentence.[1]

Then Anpu was summoned before His Majesty, and he was chosen to be the royal heir.

When Bata had reigned for thirty years,[2] he came to his death, and on the day of his burial his elder brother stood in his place.

Egyptian Love Songs

(Collected by Scribes over 3000 years ago, and laid in tombs so that they might be sung by departed souls in Paradise.)

THE WINE OF LOVE

Oh! when my lady cometh,
    And I with love behold her,
I take her to my beating heart
    And in mine arms enfold her;
My heart is filled with joy divine
For I am hers and she is mine.

Oh! when her soft embraces
    Do give my love completeness,
The perfumes of Arabia
    Anoint me with their sweetness;
And when her lips are pressed to mine
I am made drunk and need not wine.

[1] The sentence is not given, but is indicated by the prophecy of the seven Hathors, who said she would die "a speedy death" (a death by violence).

[2] This suggests that he was sacrificed at the Sed festival.

THE SNARE OF LOVE

(Sung by a girl snarer to one she loves.)

With snare in hand I hide me,
    I wait and will not stir;
The beauteous birds of Araby
    Are perfumed all with myrrh—
Oh, all the birds of Araby,
    That down to Egypt come,
Have wings that waft the fragrance
    Of sweetly smelling gum!

I would that, when I snare them,
    Together we could be,
I would that when I hear them
    Alone I were with thee.
If thou wilt come, my dear one,
    When birds are snared above,
I'll take thee and I'll keep thee
    Within the snare of love.

THE SYCAMORE SONG

A sycamore sang to a lady fair,
    And its words were dropping like honey dew.
"Now ruby red is the fruit I bear
    All in my bower for you.

"Papyri green are my leaves arrayed,
    And branch and stem like to opal gleam;
Now come and rest in my cooling shade
    The dream of your heart to dream.

"A letter of love will my lady fair
    Send to the one who will happy be,
Saying: 'Oh, come to my garden rare
    And sit in the shade with me!

"'Fruit I will gather for your delight,
　Bread I will break and pour out wine,
I'll bring you the perfumed flow'rs and bright
　On this festal day divine.'

"My lady alone with her lover will be,
　His voice is sweet and his words are dear—
Oh, I am silent of all I see,
　Nor tell of the things I hear!"

THE DOVE SONG

I hear thy voice, O turtle dove—
　The dawn is all aglow—
Weary am I with love, with love,
　Oh, whither shall I go?

Not so, O beauteous bird above,
　Is joy to me denied. . . .
For I have found my dear, my love,
　And I am by his side.

We wander forth, and hand in hand
　Through flow'ry ways we go—
I am the fairest in the land,
　For he hath called me so.

JEALOUSY

My face towards the door I'll keep
　Till I my love behold,
With watching eyes and list'ning ears
　I wait . . . and I turn cold,
　　　I sigh and sigh;
　　　He comes not nigh.

My sole possession is his love
　All sweet and dear to me;

And ever may my lips confess
  My heart, nor silent be.
      I sigh and sigh;
      He comes not nigh.

But now . . . a messenger in haste
  My watching eyes behold . . .
He went as swiftly as he came.
  "I am delayed", he told.
      I sigh and sigh;
      He comes not nigh.

Alas! confess that thou hast found
  One fairer far than me.
O thou so false, why break my heart
  With infidelity?
      I sigh and sigh;
      He 'll ne'er come nigh.

THE GARDEN OF LOVE

Oh! fair are the flowers, my beloved,
  And fairest of any I wait.
A garden art thou, all fragrant and dear,
  Thy heart, O mine own, is the gate.

The canal of my love I have fashioned,
  And through thee, my garden, it flows—
Dip in its waters refreshing and sweet,
  When cool from the north the wind blows.

In our beauteous haunt we will linger,
  Thy strong hand reposing in mine—
Then deep be my thoughts and deeper my joy,
  Because, O my love, I am thine.

Oh! thy voice is bewitching, beloved,
  This wound of my heart it makes whole—
Ah! when thou art coming, and thee I behold,
  Thou 'rt bread and thou 'rt wine to my soul.

LOVE'S PRETENCE

With sickness faint and weary
  All day in bed I 'll lie;
My friends will gather near me
  And she 'll with them come nigh.
She 'll put to shame the doctors
  Who 'll ponder over me,
For she alone, my loved one,
  Knows well my malady.

CHAPTER V

Racial Myths in Egypt and Europe

Worship of Animals—Possessed by Spirits of Good and Evil—Reptiles as Destroyers and Protectors—Pigs of Set and Osiris—The Moon Eater—Horus Solar and Storm Myth—The Devil Pig in Egypt and Scotland—Contrast with Gaulish, Irish, and Norse Beliefs—Animal Conflicts for Mastery of Herd—Love God a Pig—Why Eels were not eaten—The Sacred Bull—Irish and Egyptian Myths—Corn Spirits—The Goose Festival in Europe—The Chaos Egg—Giant's Soul Myth—Nilotic and other Versions—Wild Ass as Symbol of Good and Evil.

ONE of the most interesting phases of Nilotic religion was the worship of animals. Juvenal ridiculed the Egyptians for this particular practice in one of his satires, and the early fathers of the Church regarded it as proof of the folly of pagan religious ideas. Some modern-day apologists, on the other hand, have leapt to the other extreme by suggesting that the ancient philosophers were imbued with a religious respect for life in every form, and professed a pantheistic creed. Our task here, however, is to investigate rather than to justify or condemn ancient Egyptian beliefs. We desire to get, if possible, at the Egyptian point of view. That being so, we must recognize at the outset that we are dealing with a confused mass of religious practices and conceptions of Egyptian and non-Egyptian origin, which accumulated during a vast period of time and were perpetuated as much by custom as by conviction. The average Egyptian of the later Dynasties might have been as little able to account for his superstitious regard for the crocodile or the serpent as is the society lady of to-day to explain her dread of being one of a dinner party of thirteen, or of spilling salt at table; he worshipped animals because they had always been worshipped, and, although originally only certain representatives of a species were held to be sacred, he was not unwilling to show reverence for the species as a whole.

We obtain a clue which helps to explain the origin of animal worship in Egypt in an interesting Nineteenth-Dynasty papyrus preserved in the British Museum. This document contains a calendar in which lucky and unlucky days are detailed in accordance with the ideas of ancient seers. Good luck, we gather, comes from the beneficent deities, and bad luck is caused by the operations of evil spirits. On a particular date demons are let loose, and the peasant is warned not to lead an ox with a rope at any time during the day, lest one of them should enter the animal and cause it to gore him. An animal, therefore, was not feared or worshipped for its own sake, but because it was liable to be possessed by a good or evil spirit.

The difference between good and evil spirits was that the former could be propitiated or bargained with, so that benefits might be obtained, while the latter ever remained insatiable and unwilling to be reconciled. This primitive conception is clearly set forth by Isocrates, the Greek orator, who said: "Those of the gods who are the sources to us of good things have the title of Olympians; those whose department is that of calamities and punishments have harsher titles. To the first class both private persons and states erect altars and temples; the second is not worshipped either with prayers or burnt sacrifices, but in their case we perform ceremonies of riddance".

"Ceremonies" of riddance are, of course, magical

ceremonies. It was by magic that the Egyptians warded off the attacks of evil spirits. Ra's journey in the sun bark through the perilous hour-divisions of night was accomplished by the aid of spells which thwarted the demons of evil and darkness in animal or reptile form.

In Egypt both gods and demons might possess the same species of animals or reptiles. The ox might be an incarnation of the friendly Isis, or of the demon which gored the peasant. Serpents and crocodiles were at once the protectors and the enemies of mankind. The dreaded Apep serpent symbolized everything that was evil and antagonistic to human welfare; but the beneficent mother goddess Uazit of Buto, who shielded Horus, was also a serpent, and serpents were worshipped as defenders of households; images of them were hung up for "luck" or protection, as horseshoes are in our own country even at the present day; the serpent amulet was likewise a protective agency, like the serpent stone of the Gauls and the familiar "lucky pig" which is still worn as a charm.

In certain parts of Egypt the crocodile was also worshipped, and was immune from attack;[1] in others it was ruthlessly hunted down. As late as Roman times the people of one nome waged war against those of another because their sacred animals were being slain by the rival religious organization.

Here we touch upon the tribal aspect of animal worship. Certain animals or reptiles were regarded as the protectors of certain districts. A particular animal might be looked upon by one tribe as an incarnation of their deity, and by another as the incarnation of their Satan. The black pig, for instance, was associated by the Egyptians with Set, who was the god of a people who conquered

---

[1] Snake worshippers in India are careful not to injure or offend a serpent, and believe that "the faithful" are never stung.

and oppressed them in pre-Dynastic times. Horus is depicted standing on the back of the pig and piercing its head with a lance; its legs and jaws are fettered with chains. But the pig was also a form of Osiris, "the good god".

Set was identified with the Apep serpent of night and storm, and in certain myths the pig takes the place of the serpent. It was the Set pig, for instance, that fed upon the waning moon, which was the left eye of Horus. How his right eye, the sun, was once blinded is related in a Heliopolitan myth. Horus sought, it appears, to equal Ra, and desired to see all things that had been created. Ra delivered him a salutory lesson by saying: "Behold the black pig". Horus looked, and immediately one of his eyes (the sun) was destroyed by a whirlwind of fire. Ra said to the other gods: "The pig will be abominable to Horus". For that reason pigs were never sacrificed to him.[1] Ra restored the injured eye, and created for Horus two horizon brethren who would guard him against thunderstorms and rain.

The Egyptians regarded the pig as an unclean animal. Herodotus relates that if they touched it casually, they at once plunged into water to purify themselves.[2] Swineherds lost caste, and were not admitted to the temples. Pork was never included among the meat offerings to the dead. In Syria the pig was also "taboo". In the Highlands, even in our own day, there survives a strong prejudice against pork, and the black pig is identified with the devil.

On the other hand, the Gauls, who regarded the pig

---

[1] Evidently because the sun cult was opposed to lunar rites which included the sacrifice of pigs.

[2] Before the Greeks sacrificed a young pig, in connection with the mysteries of Demeter and Dionysos, they washed it and themselves in the sea. Plutarch: *Vit. Phoc* xxviii.

as sacred, did not abstain from pork. Like their kinsmen, the Achæans, too, they regarded swineherds as important personages; these could even become kings. The Scandinavian heroes in Valhal feast upon swine's flesh, and the boar was identified with Frey, the corn god. In the Celtic (Irish) Elysium presided over by Dagda, the corn god, as the Egyptian Paradise was presided over by Osiris, there was always "one pig alive and another ready roasted".[1] Dagda's son, Angus, the love god, the Celtic Khonsu, had a herd of swine, and their chief was the inevitable black pig.

In *The Golden Bough*, Professor Frazer shows that the pig was tabooed because it was at one time a sacred animal identified with Osiris. Once a year, according to Herodotus, pigs were sacrificed in Egypt to the moon and to Osiris. The moon pig was eaten, but the pigs offered to Osiris were slain in front of house doors and given back to the swineherds from whom they were purchased.

Like the serpent and the crocodile, the pig might be either the friend or the enemy of the corn god. At sowing time it rendered service by clearing the soil of obnoxious roots and weeds which retard the growth of crops. When, however, the agriculturists found the—

Snouted wild boar routing tender corn,

they apparently identified it with the enemy of Osiris— it slew the corn god. The boar hunt then ensued as a matter of course. We can understand, therefore, why the Egyptians sacrificed swine to Osiris because, as Plutarch says, "not that which is dear to the gods but that which

---

[1] *Celtic Myth and Legend*, p. 136. This is a tribal phase of pig worship, apparently, of different character to that which obtained in Egypt. It may be that the reverence for the good pig was greater than the hatred of the black and evil pig.

is contrary is fit to be sacrificed". The solution of the problem may be that at sowing time the spirit of Osiris entered the boar, and that at harvest the animal was possessed by the spirit of Set.

This conclusion leads us back to the primitive conception of the Great Mother Deity. In the archaic Scottish folk tale, which is summarized in our Introduction, she is the enemy of mankind.[1] But her son, the lover of the spirit of summer—he is evidently the prototype of the later love god—is a beneficent giant; he fights against his mother, who separated him from his bride and sought to destroy all life. Ra similarly desired to slay "his enemies", because he created evil as well as good. Seb, the Egyptian earth god, was the father of Osiris, "the good god", and of Set, the devil; they were "brothers". Osiris was a boar, and Set was a boar. The original "battle of the gods" may, therefore, have been the conflict between the two boars for the mastery of the herd—a conflict which also symbolized the warfare between evil and good, winter and summer. Were not the rival forces of Nature created together at the beginning? The progeny of the Great Father, or the Great Mother, included evil demons as well as good gods.

The Greek Adonis was slain by a boar; Osiris was slain by Set, the black boar; the Celtic Diarmid was slain by a boar which was protected by a Hag who appears to be identical with the vengeful and stormy Scottish Earth Mother. The boar was "taboo" to the worshippers of Adonis and Osiris; in Celtic folklore "bonds" are put upon Diarmid not to hunt the boar. Evidently Adonis, Osiris, and Diarmid represented the "good" boars.

---

[1] Ghosts also were enemies. A dead wife might cause her husband to be stricken with disease. Budge's *Osiris and the Egyptian Resurrection*, vol. ii, p. 211.

These three deities were love gods; the love god was identified with the moon, and the primitive moon spirit was the son of the Great Mother; the Theban Khonsu was the son of Mut; the Nubian Thoth was the son of Tefnut. Now Set, the black boar of evil, devoured the waning moon, and in doing so he devoured his brother Osiris. When the Eyptians, therefore, sacrificed a pig to the moon, and feasted upon it like Set, they ate the god. They did not eat the pig sacrificed to Osiris, because apparently it represented the enemy of the god; they simply slew it, and thus slew Set.

It would appear that there were originally two moon pigs—the "lucky pig" of the waxing moon and the black pig of the waning moon. These were the animal forms of the moon god and of the demon who devoured the moon—the animal form of the love god and the thwarted rebel god; they also symbolized growth and decay—Osiris was growth, and Set symbolized the slaughter of growth: he killed the corn god.

The primitive lunar myth is symbolized in the legend which tells that Set hunted the boar in the Delta marshes. He set out at full moon, just when the conflict between the demon and the lunar deity might be expected to begin, and he found the body of Osiris, which he broke up into fourteen parts—a suggestion of the fourteen phases of lunar decline. We know that Set was the moon-eating pig. The black boar of night therefore hunts, slays, and devours the white boar of the moon. But the generative organ of Osiris is thrown into the river, and is swallowed by a fish: similarly Set flings the wrenched-out "eye" of Horus into the Nile.

Now the fish was sacred in Egypt. It had a symbolic significance; it was a phallic symbol. The Great Mother of Mendes, another form of Isis, is depicted with a fish upon her head. Priests were not permitted to eat fish, and the food which was "taboo" to the priests was originally "taboo" to all the Egyptians. In fact, certain fish were not eaten during the Eighteenth Dynasty and later, and fish were embalmed. Those fish which were included among articles of dietary were brought to the table with fins and tails removed. The pig which was eaten sacrificially once a year had similarly its tail cut off. Once a year, on the ninth day of the month of Thoth, the Egyptians ate fried fish at their house doors: the priests offered up their share by burning them. Certain fish were not eaten by the ancient Britons. The eel is still abhorred in Scotland: it was sacred and tabooed in Egypt also.[1]

Osiris was worshipped at Memphis in the form of the bull Apis, Egyptian *Hapi*, which was known to the Greeks as "Serapis", their rendering of *Asar-Hapi* (Osiris-Apis). This sacred animal was reputed to be of miraculous birth, like the son of the Great Mother deity. "It was begotten", Plutarch was informed, "by a ray of generative light flowing from the moon." "Apis", said Herodotus, "was a young black bull whose mother can have no other offspring." It was known by its marks; it had "on its forehead a white triangular spot, on its back an eagle, a beetle lump under its tongue, while the hair of its tail was double". Plutarch said that "on account of the great resemblance which the Egyptians imagine between Osiris and the moon, its more bright and shining parts being shadowed and obscured by those that are of darker hue, they call the Apis the living image of Osiris". The bull, Herodotus says, was "a fair and beautiful image of the soul of Osiris". Diodorus similarly states that Osiris mani-

[1] The Egyptian sacred fish were the Oxyrhinchus, Lepidotus, Latus, and Phagrus.

fested himself to men through successive ages as Apis. "The soul of Osiris migrated into this animal", he explains.

That this bull represented the animal which obtained mastery of the herd is suggested by the popularity of bull fights at the ancient sports; there are several representations on the ancient tombs of Egyptian peasants, carrying staves, urging bulls to battle one against another. Worshippers appear to have perpetuated the observance of the conflict between the male animals in the mock fights at temples. Herodotus relates that when the votaries of the deity presented themselves at the temple entrance they were armed with staves. Men with staves endeavoured to prevent their admission, and a combat ensued between the two parties, "in which many heads were broken, and, I should suppose," adds Herodotus, "many lives lost, although this the Egyptians positively deny". Apparently Set was the thwarted male animal—that is, the demon with whom the Egyptianized Set (Sutekh) was identified.

The sacred Apis bull might either be allowed to die a natural death, or it was drowned when its age was twenty-eight years—a suggestion of the twenty-eight phases of the moon and the violent death of Osiris. The whole nation mourned for the sacred animal; its body was mummified and laid in a tomb with much ceremony. Mariette, the French archæologist, discovered the Eighteenth-Dynasty tombs of the Memphite bulls in 1851. The sarcophagi which enclosed the bodies weighed about 58 tons each. One tomb which he opened had been undisturbed since the time of the burial, and the footprints of the mourners were discoverable after a lapse of 3000 years.[1]

---

[1] Apis worship was of great antiquity. Reference is made to the Apis priests in the Fourth Dynasty.

After the burial the priests set out to search for the successor of the old bull, and there was great rejoicing when one was found; its owner was compensated with generous gifts of gold. In the Anpu-Bata story, which is evidently a version of the Osiris myth, the elder brother is honoured and becomes rich after he delivers the Bata bull to the Pharaoh. It will be noted that the Osiris soul was believed to be in the animal's liver, which was eaten—here we have again the ceremony of eating the god. Before the bull was transferred to its temple it was isolated for forty days, and was seen during that period by women only.

At Heliopolis the soul of Osiris entered the Mnevis bull. This sacred animal was evidently a rival to Apis. Ammianus Marcellinus says that Apis was dedicated to the moon and Mnevis to the sun.

In Upper Egypt the sacred bull was Bakh (Bacis) a form of Mentu; it was ultimately identified with Ra.

The worship of Apis ultimately triumphed, and in Roman times became general all over Egypt.

Like the Osiris boar, the Osiris bull was identified with the corn spirit. But its significance in this regard is not emphasized in the Egyptian texts. That may have been because different tribes regarded different animals as harvest deities. The association of Apis with Ptah is therefore of interest. We have suggested that Ptah was originally worshipped by a people of mountain origin. In the great caves of southern Palestine there survive rude scratchings of cows and bulls, suggesting that this pastoral people venerated their domesticated animals. In Europe the corn spirit was identified with the bull and cow principally by the Hungarians, the Swiss, and the Prussians, and by some of the French, for the "corn bull" was slain at Bordeaux. On the other hand, it may be that in the Irish legend regarding the conflict between the Brown Bull of Ulster and the White-horned Bull of Connaught we have a version of a very ancient myth which was connected with Osiris in Egypt. Both Irish animals were of miraculous birth; their mothers were fairy cows.

Like the Egyptian Anpu-Bata story, the Irish legend is characterized by belief in the transmigration of souls. It relates that the rival bulls were originally swineherds. One served Bodb, the fairy king of Munster, who was a son of Dagda, the Danann corn god; the other served Ochall Ochne, the fairy king of Connaught, the province occupied by the enemies of the beneficent Danann deities. The two herds fought one against another. " Then, the better to carry on their quarrel, they changed themselves into two ravens and fought for a year; next they turned into water monsters, which tore one another for a year in the Suir and a year in the Shannon; then they became human again, and fought as champions; and ended by changing into eels. One of these eels went into the River Cruind in Cualgne in Ulster, where it was swallowed by a cow belonging to Daire of Cualgne; and the other into the spring of Uaran Garad, in Connaught, where it passed into the belly of a cow of Queen Medb's. Thus were born those two famous beasts, the Brown Bull of Ulster and the White-horned Bull of Connaught."[1] The brown bull was victorious in the final conflict; it afterwards went mad, burst its heart with bellowing, and fell dead. In this myth we have the conflict between rival males, suggested in the Osiris-Set boar legend and the mock fights at the Egyptian bull temple.

The sacred cow was identified with Isis, Nepthys, Hathor, and Nut. Isis was also fused with Taurt, the

[1] *Celtic Myth and Legend*, pp. 164-5.

female hippopotamus, who was goddess of maternity and was reputed to be the mother of Osiris. Even the crocodile was associated with the worship of the corn god; in one of the myths this reptile recovers the body of Osiris from the Nile.

Bast, another Great Mother who was regarded as a form of Isis, was identified with the cat, an animal which was extremely popular as a household pet in Egypt. Herodotus relates that when a house went on fire the Egyptians appeared to be occupied with no thought but that of preserving their cats. These animals were prone to leap into the flames, and when a family lost a cat in such circumstances there was universal sorrow. A Roman soldier was once mobbed and slain because he killed a household cat.[1] The cat was identified in France with the corn spirit: the last portion of grain which was reaped was called "the cat's tail".[2]

We have referred in the Introduction to the goose which laid the sun egg. Apparently this bird was at one time sacred. Although it was a popular article of diet in ancient Egypt, and was favoured especially by the priests, it was probably eaten chiefly in the winter season. The goose and the duck were sacred in Abyssinia, where the Mediterranean type has been identified in fusion with Semitic, Negroid, and other types. In the Highlands of Scotland the goose was eaten, until recently, on Christmas Day only. Throughout England it was associated with Michaelmas. "If you eat goose at Michaelmas", runs an old saying, "you will never want money all the year round." The bird was evidently identified with the corn spirit. In Shropshire the shearing of the last portion of

---

[1] Similarly British soldiers got into trouble recently for shooting sacred pigeons.

[2] In Ireland the cat deity was the god Cairbre *cinn cait*, "of the cat's head". He was a god of the Fir Bolg, the enemies of the Gaulish Danann people.

grain was referred to as "cutting the gander's neck". When all the corn was gathered into a stackyard in Yorkshire an entertainment was given which was called "The Inning Goose". During the reign of Henry IV the French subjects of the English king called the harvest festival the "Harvest Gosling". The Danes had also a goose for supper after harvest.

The sun god Ra, of Egypt, was supposed to have been hatched from the egg which rose from the primordial deep. This belief is reminiscent of the folk tale of the European giant who hid his soul in an egg, as Anpu hid his soul in the blossom of the acacia.

In one Scottish version of the ancient mythical story the giant's soul is in a stump of a tree, a hare, a salmon, a duck, and an egg; in another it is in a bull, a ram, a goose, and an egg. Ptah was credited with making the sun egg which concealed his own soul, or the soul of Ra. So was Khnûmû. These artisan gods appear to be of common origin (see Chapter XIV); they became giants in their fusion with the primitive earth god, who was symbolized as a gander, while they were also identified with the ram and the bull. Khnûmû received offerings of fish, so that a sacred fish may be added. Anpu's soul passed from the blossom to a bull, and then to a tree. It may be that in these folk tales we have renderings of the primitive myth of a pastoral people which gave origin to the Egyptian belief in the egg associated with Ra, Ptah, and Khnûmû. In the *Book of the Dead* reference is made to the enemies of Ra, "who have cursed that which is in the egg". The pious were wont to declare: "I keep watch over the egg of the Great Cackler" (the chaos goose), or, according to another reading: "I am the egg which is in the Great Cackler" (Budge). Set, the earth deity, was believed to have flown through the air at the beginning in the form of the chaos goose.   The Celtic deities likewise appeared to mankind as birds.

The hare was identified with a god of the underworld. Doves and pigeons were sacred; the ibis was an incarnation of Thoth, the hawk of Horus, and the swallow of Isis.   The mythical phœnix, with wings partly of gold and partly of crimson, was supposed to fly from Arabia to Heliopolis once every five hundred years.   It was reputed to spring from the ashes of the parent bird, which thus renewed its youth.

The frog was sacred, and the frog goddess Hekt was a goddess of maternity.   Among the gods identified with the ram were Amon and Min and the group of deities resembling Ptah.   Anubis was the jackal.   Mut, the Theban Great Mother, and the primitive goddess Nekhebat were represented by the vulture.   The shrew mouse was sacred to Uazit, who escaped from Set in this form when she was the protector of Horus, son of Isis.   The dog-faced ape was a form of Thoth; the lion was a form of Aker, an old, or imported, earth god.

There were two wild asses in Egyptian mythology, and they represented the good and evil principles.   One was Set, and the other the sun ass, which was chased by the night serpent.   Although the souls of the departed, according to the *Book of the Dead*, boasted that they drove back the "Eater of the Ass" (the serpent which devoured the sun); they also prayed that they would "smite the ass" (the devil ass) "and crush the serpent".   When Set was driven out of Egypt he took flight on the back of the night ass, which was another form of the night serpent.   Set was also the Apep serpent and the "roaring serpent", which symbolized the tempest.

Herodotus has recorded that although the number of beasts in ancient Egypt was comparatively small, both those which were wild and those which were tame were regarded as sacred.   They were fed upon fish, and ministered to by hereditary lay priests and priestesses.   "In the presence of the animals", the Greek historian wrote, "the inhabitants of the cities perform their vows.   They address themselves as suppliants to the deity who is believed to be manifested by the animal in whose presence they are. . . . . It is a capital offence to kill one of these animals."

CHAPTER VI

The City of the Elf God

Now, when there was corn in Egypt "as the sand of the sea", traders from foreign countries crossed the parched deserts and the perilous deep, instructed, like the sons of Jacob, to "get you down thither and buy for us from thence". So wealth and commerce increased in the Nile valley. A high civilization was fostered, and the growing needs of the age caused many industries to flourish.

The business of the country was controlled by the cities which were nursed into prosperity by the wise policy of the Pharaohs. Among these Memphis looms prominently in the history of the early Dynasties. Its ruling deity was, appropriately enough, the artificer god Ptah, for it was not only a commercial but also an important industrial centre; indeed it was the home of the great architects and stone builders whose activities culminated in the erection of the Pyramids, the most sublime achievements in masonry ever accomplished by man.

To-day the ruins of Old Memphis lie buried deep in the sand. The fellah tills the soil and reaps the harvest in season above its once busy streets and stately temples, its clinking workshops and noisy markets. "I have heard the words of its teachers whose sayings are on the lips of men. But where are their dwelling places? Their walls have been cast down and their homes are not, even as though they had never been." Yet the area of this ancient city was equal to that of modern London from Bow to Chelsea and the Thames to Hampstead, and it had a teeming population.

> O mighty Memphis, city of "White Walls",
> The habitation of eternal Ptah,
> Cradle of kings . . . on thee the awful hand
> Of Vengeance hath descended. . . . Nevermore
> Can bard acclaim thy glory; nevermore
> Shall harp, nor flute, nor timbrel, nor the song
> Of maids resound within thy ruined halls,
> Nor shouts of merriment in thee be heard,
> Nor hum of traffic, nor the eager cries
> Of merchants in thy markets murmurous;
> The silence of the tomb hath fallen on thee,
> And thou art faded like a lovely queen,
> Whom loveless death hath stricken in the night,
> Whose robe is rent, whose beauty is decayed—
> And nevermore shall princes from afar
> Pay homage to thy greatness, and proclaim
> Thy wonders, nor in reverence behold
> Thy sanctuary glories . . .
>   Are thy halls
> All empty, and thy streets laid bare
> And silent as the soundless wilderness?
> O Memphis, mighty Memphis, hath the morn
> Broken to find thee not?

Memphis was named after King Pepi,[1] and is called Noph in the Old Testament. Its early Dynastic name

---

[1] The Greek rendering of "Men-nofer", the name of Pepi's pyramid. Another Egyptian name was Hiku-ptah, or, according to Budge, "Het-Ka-Ptah, 'House of the Double of Ptah', from which the Greek name of Egypt is derived".

was "White Walls", the reference being probably to the fortress erected there soon after the Conquest. Of its royal builder we know little, but his mother, Queen Shesh, enjoyed considerable repute for many centuries afterwards as the inventor of a popular hair wash which is referred to in a surviving medical papyrus.

After Egypt was united under the double crown of the Upper and the Lower Kingdoms, and the Pharaoh became "Lord of the Two Lands", the seat of government remained for a long period at Thinis, in the south. The various nomes, like the present-day states of North America, had each their centres of local administration. Pharaoh's deputies were nobles who owed him allegiance, collected the Imperial taxes, supplied workmen or warriors as desired, and carried out the orders of the Court officials regarding the construction and control of canals. The temple of the nome god adorned the provincial capital.

Ptah, the deity of Memphis, is presented in sharp contrast to the sun god Ra, who was of Asiatic origin, and the deified King Osiris, whose worship was associated with agricultural rites. He was an earth spirit, resembling closely the European elf. The conception was evidently not indigenous, because the god had also a giant form, like the hilltop deities of the mountain peoples (see Chapter XII). He was probably imported by the invaders who constituted the military aristocracy at Memphis in pre-Dynastic times. These may have been the cave-dwellers of Southern Palestine, or tall and muscular "broad heads" of Alpine or Armenoid type who prior to the Conquest appear to have pressed southward from Asia Minor through the highlands of Palestine, and, after settlement, altered somewhat the physical character of the "long heads" of the eastern Delta.

Allowance has to be made for such an infusion in accounting for the new Dynastic type as well as for the influence exercised by the displacement of a great proportion of the mingled tribes of Libyans. The Palestine cave-dwellers may have been partly of Alpine origin.

A people seldom remember their early history, but they rarely forget their tribal beliefs. That being so, the god Ptah is of special interest in dealing with the tribal aspect of mythology. Among all the gods of Egypt his individuality is perhaps the most pronounced. Others became shadowy and vague, as beliefs were fused and new and greater conceptions evolved in the process of time. But Ptah never lost his elfin character, even after he was merged with deities of divergent origin. He was the chief of nine earth spirits (that is, eight and himself added) called Khnûmû, the modellers. Statuettes of these represent them as dwarfs, with muscular bodies, bent legs, long arms, big broad heads, and faces of intelligent and even benign expression. Some wear long moustaches,[1] so unlike the shaven or glabrous Egyptians.

At the beginning, according to Memphite belief, Ptah shaped the world and the heavens, assisted by his eight workmen, the dwarfish Khnûmû. He was also the creator of mankind, and in Egyptian tombs are found numerous earthenware models of these "elves", who were believed to have had power to reconstruct the decaying bodies of the dead. As their dwellings were underground, they may have also been "artisans of vegetation", like the spirits associated with Tvashtar, the "master workman" of the Rig-Veda hymns and the

---

[1] The suggestion that these represented serpents is not supported by anything we know about Ptah worship. There was a winged serpent goddess in the Delta named Uazit. The Greeks called her Buto, and identified her with their Leto.

"black dwarfs" of Teutonic mythology. A particular statuette of Ptah, wearing a tight-fitting cap, suggests the familiar "wonder smith"[1] of the Alpine "broad heads" who were distributed along Asiatic and European mountain ranges from Hindu Kush to Brittany and the British Isles and mingled with the archaic Hittites in Asia Minor. The Phœnician sailors carried figures of dwarfs in their ships, and worshipped them. They were called "pataikoi". In the Far East a creation artificer who resembles Ptah is Pan Ku, the first Chinese deity, who emerged from a cosmic egg.

Like Ra, Ptah was also believed to have first appeared as an egg, which, according to one of the many folk beliefs of Egypt, was laid by the chaos goose which came to be identified with Seb, the earth god, and afterwards with the combined deities Amon-Ra. Ptah, as the primeval "artificer god", was credited with making "the sun egg" and also "the moon egg", and a bas-relief at Philæ shows him actively engaged at the work, using his potter's wheel.

A higher and later conception of Ptah[2] represents him as a sublime creator god who has power to call into existence each thing he names. He is the embodiment of mind from which all things emerge, and his ideas take material shape when he gives them expression. In a philosophic poem a Memphite priest eulogizes the great deity as "the mind[3] and tongue of the gods", and even as the creator of other gods as well as of "all people, cattle, and reptiles", the sun, and the habitable world.

---

[1] Ptah has been compared to the Greek Hephæstos (Vulcan). He was not a fire god. His consort Sekhet symbolized fire and sun heat, but his association with her was arbitrary.

[2] Eighteenth Dynasty

[3] The poet says "heart", which was believed by the Egyptians to be the seat of intelligence. At the judgment of the dead the heart is weighed in the balance.

Thoth is also credited with similar power, and it is possible that in this connection both these deities were imparted with the attributes of Ra, the sun god.

According to the tradition perpetuated by Manetho, the first temple in Egypt was erected at Memphis, that city of great builders, to the god Ptah at the command of King Mena. It is thus suggested that the town and the god of the ruling caste existed when the Horite sun worshippers moved northward on their campaign of conquest. As has been shown, Mena also gave diplomatic recognition to Neith, the earth goddess of the Libyans, "the green lady" of Egypt, who resembles somewhat the fairy, and especially the banshee, of the Iberians and their Celtic conquerors.

The Ptah worshippers were probably not the founders of Memphis. An earlier deity associated with the city is the dreaded Sokar (Seker). He was a god of the dead, and in the complex mythology of later times his habitation was located in the fifth hour-division of night.[1] When sun worship became general in the Nile valley Sokar was identified with the small winter sun, as Horus was with the large sun of summer. But the winged and three-headed monster god, with serpent body, suffers complete loss of physical identity when merged with the elfin deity of Memphis. Ptah-Sokar is depicted as a dwarf and one of the Khnûmû. Another form of Sokar is a hawk, of different aspect to the Horus hawk, which appears perched on the Ra boat at night with a sun disk upon its head.[2]

Ptah-Sokar was in time merged with the agricultural

[1] See Chapter I.

[2] Osiris-Sokar is "the brilliant one", "lord of great fear and trembling", "the mysterious one, he who is unknown to mankind", and "enlightener of those who are in the underworld".—*The Burden of Isis*, Dennis, p. 52-54 (Hymn to Osiris-Sokar).

Osiris whose spirit passed from Pharaoh to Pharaoh. Ptah-Osiris was depicted as a human-sized mummy, swathed and mute, holding firmly in his hands before him the Osirian dadu (pillar) symbol. The triad, Ptah-Sokar-Osiris, gives us a combined deity who is a creator, a judge of the dead, and a traditional king of Egypt. The influence of the sun cult prevailed when Sokar and Osiris were associated with the worship of Ra.

Memphis, the city of Ptah, ultimately became the capital of United Egypt. It was then at the height of its glory; a great civilization had evolved. Unfortunately, however, we are unable to trace its progress, because the records are exceedingly scanty. Fine workmanship in stone, exquisite pottery, &c., indicate the advanced character of the times, but it is impossible to construct from these alone an orderly historical narrative. We have also the traditions preserved by Manetho. Much of what he tells us, however, belongs to the domain of folklore. We learn, for instance, that for nearly a fortnight the Nile ran with honey, and that one of the Pharaohs, who was a giant about 9 feet high, was "a most dangerous man". It is impossible to confirm whether a great earthquake occurred in the Delta region, where the ground is said to have yawned and swallowed many of the people, or whether a famine occurred in the reign of one Pharaoh and a great plague in that of another, and if King Aha really engaged his leisure moments compiling works on anatomy. The story of a Libyan revolt at a later period may have had foundation in fact, but the explanation that the rebels broke into flight because the moon suddenly attained enormous dimensions shows how myth and history were inextricably intertwined.

Yet Manetho's history contains important material.

His list of early kings is not imaginative, as was once supposed, although there may be occasional inaccuracies. The Palermo Stone, so called because it was carried to the Sicilian town of that name by some unknown curio collector, has inscribed upon it in hieroglyphics the names of several of the early kings and references to notable events which occurred during their reigns. It is one of the little registers which were kept in temples. Many of these, no doubt, existed, and some may yet be brought to light.

Four centuries elapsed after the Conquest ere Memphis became the royal city. We know little, however, regarding the first three hundred years. Two dynasties of Thinite kings ruled over the land. There was a royal residence at Memphis, which was the commercial capital of the country—the marketplace of the northern and southern peoples. Trade flourished and brought the city into contact with foreign commercial centres. It had a growing and cosmopolitan population, and its arts and industries attained a high level of excellence.

The Third Dynasty opens with King Zoser, who reigned at Memphis. He was the monarch for whom the first pyramid was erected. It is situated at Sakkara, in the vicinity of his capital. The kings who reigned prior to him had been entombed at Abydos, and the new departure indicates that the supremacy of Memphis was made complete. The administrative, industrial, and religious life of the country was for the time centred there.

Zoser's preference for Memphis had, perhaps, a political bearing. His mother, the wife of Khasekhemui,[1] the last of the Thinite kings, was probably a daughter of

---

[1] This king's brick tomb at Abydos contains a limestone chamber, which suggests the employment of the Memphite artisans.

the ruling noble of "White Walls". It was the custom of monarchs to marry the daughters of nome governors, and to give their sons his daughters in marriage also. The aristocracy was thus closely connected with the royal house; indeed the relations between the Pharaoh and his noblemen appear to have been intimate and cordial.

The political marriages, however, were the cause of much jealous rivalry. As the Pharaoh had more than one wife, and princes were numerous, the choice of an heir to the crown was a matter of great political importance. The king named his successor, and in the royal harem there were occasionally plots and counterplots to secure the precedence of one particular prince or another. Sometimes methods of coercion were adopted with the aid of interested noblemen whose prestige would be increased by the selection of a near relative—the son, perhaps, of the princess of their nome. In one interesting papyrus roll which survives there is a record of an abortive plot to secure the succession of a rival to the Pharaoh's favourite son. The ambitious prince was afterwards disposed of. In all probability he was executed along with those concerned in the household rebellion. Addressing his chosen heir, the monarch remarks that "he fought the one he knew, because it was unwise that he should be beside thy majesty".

It may be that these revolts explain the divisions of the lines of early kings into Dynasties. Zoser's personality stands out so strongly that it is evident he was a prince who would brook no rival to the throne. His transference of the seat of power to the city of Ptah suggests, too, that he found his chief support there.

With the political ascendancy of Memphis begins the great Pyramid Age; but ere we make acquaintance with the industrial and commercial life in the city, and survey the great achievements of its architects and builders, we shall deal with the religious conceptions of the people, so that it may be understood why the activities of the age were directed to make such elaborate provision for the protection of the bodies of dead monarchs.

CHAPTER VII

Death and the Judgment

The Human Triad—Ghosts—Spirits of the Living—Why the Dead were given Food—Souls as Birds—The Shadow and the Name—Beliefs of Divergent Origin—Burial Customs—The Crouched Burial—Secondary Interment—Extended Burials—Mummies—Life after Death—Two Conceptions—Souls in the Sun Boat—The Osirian Paradise—Journey to the Other World—Perils on the Way—Conflicts with Demons—The River of Death—The Judgment Hall—Weighing the Heart—The Happy Fields.

IN the maze of Egyptian beliefs there were divergent views regarding the elements which constitute the human personality. One triad was a unity of the Ka, spirit; the Khu, soul; and Khat, the body. Another grouped Khaybet, the shadow, with Ba, the soul, and Sahu, the mummy. The physical heart was called Hati; it was supposed to be the seat of the intelligence, and its "spirit" was named Ab, which signified the will and desires. The "vital spark", or controlling force, was symbolized as the Sekhem, and the Ran was the personal name.

The Ka of the first triad is the most concrete conception of all. It was probably, too, the oldest. The early people appear to have believed that the human personality combined simply the body and the spirit. In those tomb scenes which depict the birth of kings the royal babe is represented by two figures—the visible body and the invisible "double". The Ka began to be at birth; it continued to live on after death.

But a human being was not alone in possessing a

Ka. Everything that existed was believed to have its "double". A fish or other animal had a Ka; so also had a tree; and there were spirits in water, in metals, in stone, and even in weapons and other articles manufactured by man. These spirits were invisible to all save the seers, who were able to exercise on occasion the "faculty" which Scottish Highlanders call "second sight".

It was conceived that the Ka could leave the human body during sleep, or while the subject lay in a trance. It then wandered forth and visited people and places, and its experience survived in memory. Dreams were accounted for in this way as actual happenings. When a man dreamt of a deceased friend, he believed that his Ka had met with the Ka of the dead, held converse with it, and engaged in the performance of some Other-World duty. Sometimes the wandering Ka could be observed at a distance from where the sleeper reposed. It had all the appearance of the individual, because it was attired in the "doubles" of his clothing and might carry the "double" of his staff. Ghosts, therefore, included "the spirits of the living", which were not recognized to be spirits until they vanished mysteriously. They might also be simply heard and not seen.

In the story of Anpu and Bata is contained the belief that the Ka could exist apart from the body. Its habitation was a blossom, and when the petals were scattered the younger brother fell dead. He revived, however, when the seed was placed in a vessel of water. This conception was associated with belief in the transmigration of souls. Bata entered a new state of existence after he left his brother.

During normal life the Ka existed in the human body. It was sustained by the "doubles" of everything that was partaken of.   After death it required food and drink, and offerings were made to it at the grave.   The practice of feeding the dead continues in Egypt even in our own day.

In ancient times a cult believed that the Ka could be fed by magic.   Mourners or ancestor worshippers who visited the tomb simply named the articles of food required, and these were immediately given existence for the spirit.   The "good wishes" were thus considered to be potent and practical.

It was essential that the dead should receive the service of the living, and those who performed the necessary ceremonies and made the offerings were called the "servants".   Thus the Egyptian word for "priest" signified a "servant".   But the motive which prompted the mourners to serve the departed was not necessarily sorrow or undying affection, but rather genuine fear. If the Ka or ghost were neglected, and allowed to starve, it could leave the grave and haunt the offenders.   Primitive man had a genuine dread of spirits, and his chief concern was ever to propitiate them, no matter how great might be the personal sacrifice involved.

Sometimes a small "soul house" was provided by the wayside for the wandering Ka, but oftener an image of wood or stone was placed for its use in the grave. The statues of kings which have been found in their tombs were constructed so that their disembodied spirits might be given material bodies, and those which they caused to be erected in various parts of the kingdom were primarily intended for a similar purpose and not merely to perpetuate their fame, although the note of vanity is rarely absent in the inscriptions.

The Khu, or "soul", was a vague conception.   It was really another form of the Ka, but it was the "double" of the intellect, will, and intentions, rather than the "double" of the physical body. The Khu was depicted as a bird,[1] and was called "the bright one" or "the glorious one".

The Ba of the second triad was a conception uniting both the Ka and the Khu. It is represented in bird form with a human head, hovering over the Sahu, or mummy, on which it gazes wistfully, always seeking to re-enter the bandaged form. Like the Ka, it required nourishment, which was provided, however, by the goddess of the consecrated burial ground.

The Khaybet, or shadow, is evidently the survival of an early belief. It is really another manifestation of the Ka. Like all primitive peoples, the archaic Egyptians believed that their shadows were their souls. Higher conceptions evolved in time, but their cultured descendants clung to the old belief, which was perpetuated by folk customs associated with magical practices. Spells were wrought by casting shadows upon a man, and he might be insulted or injured if an offence were committed against his shadow.

The Ran, or name, was also a manifestation of the Ka. Power could be exercised by uttering the name, because there was magical influence in those words which were believed to have spiritual "doubles". A personal name was the spirit identified; its service was secured when the name was uttered. The spirit was the name and the name was the spirit. If a magician desired to work evil against an individual, he made use of the name when uttering potent magical formulæ. The dead were similarly conjured up when their names were spoken

---

[1] According to Celtic folk belief the dead sometimes appear as birds. This idea may be a survival of the transmigration-of-souls conception; the soul passed through many animals before re-entering a human body.

in invocations; evil spirits were cast out by those who knew their names.[1] To guard himself against wizards who uttered "words of power", or verbal spells, the Egyptian therefore considered it necessary to have two names—the big name and the little name, or the true name and the good name. He kept his "big, true name" secret, because it was the Ran; his "good little name" was his nickname, and was not a part of his living being.

The naming ceremony was conducted in secret. The child's fate was bound up in the true name and his character was influenced by it. After it was conferred, a nickname was used, but the true name was the grave name and was uttered when the welfare of the spirit was secured by the utterance of magical spells which "opened the way" in the land of the dead. The gods had Rans also. When Isis obtained the secret name of Ra, she became his equal.

The divergent conceptions regarding the soul in Egyptian religion arose from the mingling of beliefs caused by the mingling of peoples, and also the Egyptian tendency to cling to every belief, or form of belief, which evolved in the course of time in Egypt. A people who believed in the existence of "doubles" and in the transmigration of souls had many vague and complex conceptions. Incoherencies were a feature of their religious beliefs. It must be borne in mind, at the same time, that our review covers a vast period of time, during which various religious cults exercised supreme influence in moulding Egyptian thought. One cult predominated at one period; another cult arose in turn to teach its own peculiar tenets, with the result that all beliefs were ultimately accepted. This process is clearly indicated by the

---

[1] The "ceremony of riddance" referred to by Isocrates.

various burial customs and the complex religious ceremonies which prevailed in different ages.

As we have seen, the early people buried their dead
crouched up in shallow graves with due provision of
nourishment and implements.[1] They appear to have
believed that the Ka remained beside the body until the
flesh decayed.   Then it either ceased to be, or it haunted
the cemetery.   Among primitive peoples at the present
day much concern is evinced regarding the ghosts of the
newly dead.   When a negro, for instance, is questioned
about his remote ancestors, he is unable to express an
opinion as to whether or not their spirits continue to
exercise any influence upon the living, but he trembles
if asked about his dead father.

The Egyptian tree worshippers conceived of a tree
goddess which gave food cakes and poured out drink to
disembodied Kas.   The influence of this ancient cult is
traced in the Osiris and Bata folk tales.   In late Dynastic
times tree worship was revived when the persisting beliefs
of the common people gained ascendancy, and it has not
yet wholly disappeared in the Delta region.   The sacred
tree and the holy well are still regarded with reverence.

The Horites, or Dynastic Egyptians, who pressed
northward on their gradual campaign of conquest, introduced a new burial custom.   Instead of digging shallow
graves they erected brick-lined tombs, in which the dead
were laid upon their backs, fully extended, clad in state,
and adorned with articles of jewellery.   In the inscriptions the Ka and Khu are referred to.   But no attempt
was made, even in the First and Second Dynasties, to
preserve the body from decay, and sumptuous offerings
were placed in the tombs.

---

[1] This burial custom survived at least as late as the Fifth Dynasty, when mum-
mification was well established.

Another burial custom involved secondary interment, as was the case in those European districts where early graves have been found to contain disconnected skeletons. In Egypt attempts were sometimes made to arrange the bones in proper position, but they were often heaped in confusion. It appears that temporary interment was a ceremony of riddance, the object being probably to hasten the departure of the Ka. Dismemberment was also practised, and many graves show that decapitation was effected after death.

In one of the sacred books of ancient Egypt the mutilation of dead bodies is referred to with horror. "I shall not be destroyed," we read, "my head will not be cut off, nor my tongue taken out, nor will the hair of my head or my eyebrows be shaved off. My body will endure for all time."

The revolt against dismemberment took place at the beginning of the Third Dynasty, about 3000 B.C. Massive stone tombs were then constructed and the bodies of the dead were mummified. The idea was either that the Ka would ultimately return and cause the dead to live again, or that the existence of the soul in the Nether World depended upon the existence of the body upon earth. The embalming of the dead ultimately became general throughout Egypt, but the belief in dismemberment survived in the practise of disjointing one of the mummy's feet. During the Middle Kingdom period the dead were laid on their left sides, as if to peer through the Osiris or Horis eyes depicted outside the mummy cases.

Herodotus, who visited Egypt in the fifth century before Christ, found the people "adhering contentedly to the customs of their ancestors, and averse to foreign manners". He related that when an influential man died, the females of the household smeared their hands and faces with dirt, and ran through the streets with their clothes in disorder, beating their bodies and lamenting aloud. The men behaved in similar manner after the corpse was removed from the house.

Embalmers were licensed to practise their profession, and they displayed much ingenuity and surgical skill. When a body was carried to them, they produced models of mummies and arranged a price. The quality of their work depended on the amount of money expended by the dead man's friends.

The costliest method of embalming was as follows. The brain was extracted through the nostrils with the aid of instruments and after the infusion of a chemical preparation. Then a stone knife was used to make an incision on one side of the body. The liver, heart, lungs, and intestines were immediately drawn out, and, after being cleansed, they were steeped in palm wine and sprinkled with rich perfume. The body was dried, and stuffed with powdered myrrh, cassia, &c., and sewn up. It was afterwards covered with nitre for seventy days. Then it was washed all over and carefully wrapped in bandages which had been dipped in a strong gum. As soon as it was carried back to the home it was placed in a large coffin, shaped like a human form, which was inscribed with magical charms and decorated with sacred symbols and figures of gods and goddesses. The face of the dead was carved upon the lid; in the Roman period it was painted.

A cheaper method of embalmment was to inject a chemical preparation before the body was covered with nitre. At the end of seventy days the intestines were drawn out. Nothing then remained except the skin and bones; the flesh had been eaten away by the nitre. Poor people could only afford to have a cheap preservative injected into the veins, after which the body was left in nitre for the usual period.

The intestines were placed in four canopic jars, on the lids of which were often shaped the heads of the four protecting gods, who were the sons of Horus, and represented the north, south, east, and west. These were Amset, with human face, who guarded the stomach and large intestines; Hapi, with dog's head, who guarded the small intestines; Dûamûtef, with jackal's head, who guarded lungs and heart, and Kebeh-senuf, the hawk-headed, who guarded the liver and gall bladder. These jars were placed in a chest and deposited in the tomb. The organs they contained were those which were believed to have caused the various sins to be committed.

The funeral procession was a solemn and touching spectacle. All the family were present, and women mourners wailed aloud on the way to the cemetery on the western bank of the Nile. The mummy was drawn upon a sledge. When the tomb was reached, the coffin was set up on end, facing the south, and an elaborate ceremony was gone through. It was conducted by the chief mourner, who recited the ritual from a papyrus roll, while responses were made by the relatives. Two females represented Isis and Nepthys, for a part of the ceremony was a reproduction of the scene enacted around the body of Osiris when it was restored and prepared for burial. The dead had also to be instructed how to reach the Egyptian heaven. The journey could not be accomplished in safety without the aid of magical formulæ. So these were spoken into the ears of the corpse, as was probably the custom in the days of crouched burials. But the danger was ever present that the dead would fail to remember all the priestly instructions which were repeated over them. The formulæ were therefore in-

scribed on the coffin and on the walls of the tomb, and
as time went on it became customary to prepare rolls of
papyrus, which were ultimately collected into *The Book
of the Dead*. This papyrus might be wrapped under the
mummy bandages, or else laid within the coffin. A bull
was slaughtered to provide food for the sustenance of
the Ka and as a sacrifice to the gods.

The coffin was afterwards lowered down the grave
shaft to the secret chamber in which had been placed
the image of the dead, his weapons and clothing, his
ornaments and perfumes and, perhaps, several articles
of furniture. Then the entrance was closed up with
stonework. A funeral feast in the antechamber concluded a ceremony which grew more and more elaborate
as time went on. Food offerings were afterwards brought
at intervals by faithful mourners.

There were two distinct conceptions of the after-life
and these became confused in the ages that followed.
The sun worshippers believed that the souls of the dead
passed to the first division of night, where those who
were privileged to utter the magical spells, which could
compel the obedience of the gods, were permitted to
enter the bark of Ra. In their tombs were placed
models of the sun boat.

The Other-World conception of the Osirian cult
made more permanent appeal to the Egyptian mind.
Heaven is pictured as the "double" of the Delta region,
where apparently the conception had its origin. But,
before it can be reached, the soul must needs travel a long
and weary way which is beset with many perils. The
Paradise of Aalu is situated in the west. Bleak and water-
less deserts have to be crossed, and these are infested by
fierce reptiles; boiling streams also intercept the pilgrim,
who is ever in danger of being compelled to turn back.

When the soul sets forth, he takes with him his staff and his weapons, and food for nourishment.   He climbs the western mountains and then enters the Kingdom of the Dead.   An immense sycamore tree towers before him with great clusters of fruit amidst its luxuriant foliage. As he approaches it a goddess leans out from the trunk as from a window, displaying the upper part of her body.   In her hands she holds a tray heaped with cakes and fruit; she has also a pot of clear fresh water.   The soul must needs eat of the magic food and drink of the magic water, and thus become a servant of the gods, if he is to proceed farther.   If he rejects the hospitality of the tree goddess, he will have to return again to the dark and narrow tomb whence he came, and lead forever there a solitary and joyless existence.

The soul of him who is faithful eats and drinks as desired, and then proceeds on the journey, facing many perils and enduring great trials.   Evil spirits and fierce demons compass him about, desiring that he should die a second death and cease to be.   A gigantic tortoise rises against him; he must fight against it with his lance; serpents are poised to strike, and they must be overcome. The very insects have venomous stings and must be driven away.   But his most formidable enemy is the fierce god Set, the murderer of Osiris, the terror of the good gods and of men, who appears as an enormous red monster, with a head like a camel and the body of a hound, his long and forked tail erect and venomous. Fain would that wrathful demon devour the pilgrim on his way.

When the evil god is overcome and driven back, the soul goes forward until he reaches the bank of a wide river.   There a magic boat awaits him.   The crew consist of silent divinities who give him no aid.   But ere he can embark he must needs answer each question which the boat addresses to him.   He must know and tell how it is constructed in every part, and if the papyrus roll which was laid beside his mummy contains the secrets of the boat, and the magical formulæ which must also be repeated, he will be ferried over the river and taken to the Osirian kingdom.   The sulky "ferryman" is called "Turnface": his face is always turned away from the dead who call to him.

After entering the boat the soul's journey is not near to an end.   He desires greatly to join those happy beings who have their dwellings in the blessed fields of Aalu, but he must first be tried before Osiris, the King of the Dead and Judge of All.   The only approach to Paradise is through the Hall of Justice, which rises before him stupendous and dark and full of mystery.   The gate is shut fast; no man can draw the bolts or enter without permission of the king.

Alone, and trembling with fear, the pilgrim soul stands before the gate with both hands uplifted in adoration. He is beheld by the shining god who is within.   Then in a clear, full voice the soul cries out in the deep silence:

Hail, unto thee, O thou great god, thou who art lord of truth!
Lo! I draw nigh to thee now, O my lord, and mine eyes behold
    thy beauty.
Thee I know, and I know also the two-and-forty gods assembled
    with thee in the Hall of Justice;
They observe all the deeds of the wicked;
They devour those who seek to do evil;
They drink the blood of those who are condemned before thee, O
    just and good king.
Hail! Lord of Justice; Thee I know,
I come before thee even now to speak what is true;
I will not utter what is false, O Lord of All.

The soul then recites the ritual confession in which he claims to be guiltless of the offences which are punishable.

I have done no evil against any man.
I have never caused my kinsfolk to be put to death,
I have not caused false witnesses to speak in the Hall of Justice.
I have not done that which is hated by the gods.
I am not a worker of wickedness.
I have never oppressed a servant with too much work.
I have not caused men to hunger nor to weep.
I have not been devoid of good works, nor have I acted weakly or with meanness.
I am not a murderer.
I have not conspired to have another put to death.
I have not plotted to make another grieve.
I have not taken away temple offerings.
I have not stinted the food offered to the gods.
I have not despoiled the dead.
I have never committed adultery.
I have not failed to keep myself pure as a priest.
I have not lessened the corn measure.
I have not shortened the hand measure.
I have not tampered with the balance.
I have not deprived children of milk.
I have not stolen cattle from the meadows.
I have not snared the birds consecrated to the gods.
I have not taken fish from holy lakes.
I have not prevented (Nile) water from running (in channels).
I have not turned aside the water.
I have not stolen water from a channel.
I have not put out the fire when it should burn.
I have never kept from the Nine Gods what was their due.
I have not prevented the temple cattle from grazing on my land.
I have not obstructed a god (his image) when he came forth (in a festival procession).

The soul concludes by declaring that he is sinless,

and expresses the hope that no ill will befall him in the Hall of Judgment.

The jackal - headed god Anubis, "Opener of the Ways", then strides from the hall and leads the soul by the hand before Osiris, who had heard the confession in silence. No word is uttered as the dead man enters. The King of the Dead sits in his high throne within a dim pavilion. His crown is upon his head. In one hand he holds the crook and in the other the flail. He is the supreme Judge of the Dead. Before him stands the sure balance on which the heart of the dead man will be weighed. Thoth, the recording god, is beside it, and Horus and Maat, goddess of truth and justice, are there also. The guardian of the balance is a monster which is ready to fall upon sinners who are condemned before the great god. Around the dread hall crouch the two-and-forty animal gods who tear the wicked to pieces.

In the tingling silence which prevails, the pilgrim again recites the confession. Osiris makes no comment. Then, quivering with fear, the soul watches the gods deliberately weighing his heart in the balance, while Maat, the goddess of truth and justice, or her symbol, an ostrich feather, occupies the opposite scale.

The trembling soul cries out to his heart not to witness against him. "O heart that was mine," he says, "do not say 'Behold the things he hath done'. Permit me not to be wronged in presence of the great god."

If the heart is found to be neither too heavy nor too light, the dead man is acquitted. Thoth makes known the result of the weighing to Osiris, who then orders the heart to be restored to the man on trial. "He hath won the victory," the King of the Dead exclaims. "Now let him dwell with the spirits and the gods in the fields of Aalu."

Released and rejoicing, the dead man goes forth to gaze upon the wonders of the Nether World. The divine kingdom is a greater and more glorious Egypt, in which the souls work and hunt and combat against their enemies as in other days. To each man is allotted his task. He must till the soil and reap the grain which grows in abundance and to a great height. The harvest never fails, and famine and sorrow are unknown.

When the soul desires to return to visit familiar scenes upon earth it enters the body of a bird or an animal, or perhaps it blossoms as a flower. It may also visit the tomb as the Ba, and reanimate the mummy and go forth to gaze on scenes which were familiar and dear in other days.

The souls of dead men whom Osiris condemns, because of sins committed upon earth, are subjected to terrible tortures ere they are devoured by the animal gods which crouch, waiting, in the silent and awful Hall of Judgment.

CHAPTER VIII

The Religion of the Stone Workers

Memphite Religion—The Cult of Ptah—Ethical Beliefs—Pharaoh worshipped as a God — "Husband of his Mother"—Magical Incantations — "Mesmerizing the Gods"—The Earliest Mastabas—Endowment of Tomb Chapels—The Servants of the Dead—Scenes of Everyday Life—Zoser's Two Tombs—The First Pyramid—An Architect who became a God—Inspiration of Egyptian Religion—How it promoted Civilization—Mythology of the Stone Builders—Ptah and Khnûmû—The Frog Goddess—A Prototype of Isis—A Negroid Deity—Khnûmû associated with Khufu (Cheops).

WHEN Old Memphis became the leading city of United Egypt the religious beliefs of the mingled peoples were in process of fusion and development. Commerce was flourishing, and ideas were being exchanged as freely as commodities. In the growing towns men of many creeds and different nationalities were brought into close personal contact, and thought was stimulated by the constant clash of opinions. It was an age of change and marked progress. Knowledge was being rapidly accumulated and more widely diffused. Society had become highly organized, and archaic tribal beliefs could no longer be given practical application under the new conditions that obtained throughout the land. A new religion became a necessity—at any rate existing beliefs had to be unified and systematized in the interests of peace and order, especially in a city like Memphis with its large and cosmopolitan population.

The cult which began to mummify the dead had evidently formulated a creed which appealed to the in-

tellectual classes.   Beliefs regarding the after-life took
definite shape.   The "land of shades" was organized
like the land of Egypt.   Ideas of right living and good
government prevailed, and the growth of ethical thought
was reflected in the conception of a Judge of the Dead
who justified or condemned men after consideration of
their actions during life.   The attributes of the principal
gods were defined; their powers and their places were
adjusted; they were grouped in triads and families; and
from the mass of divergent beliefs was evolving a complex mythology which was intended not only to instruct
but to unite the rival beliefs prevailing in a community.

Egyptian religion as a whole, however, was never
completely systematized at this or any subsequent period.
Each locality had its own theological system.   The old
tribal gods remained supreme in their nomes, and when
they were grouped with others; the influence at work
was more political than intellectual in character.   The
growth of culture did not permeate all classes of society,
and the common people, especially in rural districts,
clung to the folk beliefs and practices of their ancestors.
A provincial nobleman, supported by the priests, secured
the loyalty of his followers therefore by upholding the
prestige of their ancient god, who could be linked, if
needs be, with the deity of another tribe with whom a
union had been effected.   If the doctrines of a rival
creed influenced the beliefs of the people of a particular
district the attributes of the rival god were then attached
to their own.   When Ptah, for instance, ceased to make
intellectual appeal as a creation artificer he was exalted
above Ra and the other gods, whom he was supposed to
have called into existence by uttering magical words.

Ptah, as we have seen, was linked with Osiris.   The
combined deity was at once the god of the industrial and

agricultural classes, and the Judge of the Dead.   He was the chief deity of the new religion which controlled the everyday life of the people.   He was the Revealer who made city life possible by promoting law and order as a religious necessity, and by instructing the people how to live honourably and well.   He ordained the fate of all men; he rewarded the virtuous and punished the sinners.   Masters were required to deal humanely with their servants, and servants to perform their duties with diligence and obedience.   Children were counselled to honour their parents lest they might complain to the god and he should hear them.

The supremacy of Ptah was not yet seriously threatened by the sun god Ra, whose cult was gathering strength at Heliopolis.   For a full century the ascendancy of the Memphite cult was complete and unassailable.   The influence of the north was thus predominant. The Horite religion, which was a form of sun worship, had been displaced; it was overshadowed by the Ptah-Osiris creed.   Apparently the people of Lower Egypt had achieved an intellectual conquest of their conquerors. The Osirian Paradise was a duplicate of the Delta region, and the new creed was strongly influenced by Osirian beliefs which had prevailed before Mena's day.

Although great rivalry existed between the various cults throughout the land, the people were united in reverencing the Pharaoh.   He was exalted as a god; indeed he was regarded as an incarnation of the ruling deity.   Until the Fourth Dynasty the monarch was the living Osiris; then he became the earthly manifestation of Ra, the sun god.   The people believed that a deity must needs take human form to associate with mankind. His Ka, therefore, entered the king's body as the king's Ka entered his statue.   In temple scenes we find the people engaged in worshipping Pharaoh; in fact, the Pharaoh might worship himself—he made offerings to his Ka, which was the Ka of a god.

The idea of the divinity of kings was, no doubt, a survival of ancestor worship. Families worshipped the spirit of their dead sire, and tribes that of their departed leader. But the Pharaoh was not like other men, who became divine after death; he was divine from birth. His father had been the ruling god and his mother the god's wife. On the walls of temples elaborate scenes were carved to remind the people of the divine origin of their ruler. At the marriage ceremony the king impersonated the god, and he was accompanied by his divine attendants. As Ptah Tanen he wore "the high feathers" and two ram's horns, and carried the holy symbols; as Osiris he appeared with crook and flail; as Ra he was crowned with the sun disk. The queen was thus married to the god within his temple. In sculptured scenes depicting royal births we see goddesses in attendance as midwives, nurses, and foster mothers. This close association with deities was supposed to continue throughout the Pharaoh's life; he was frequently shown in company of gods and goddesses.

When the king died, the spirit of the god passed to his successor. The son, therefore, according to Egyptian reasoning, became his own father, and, in the theological sense, "husband of his mother". Horus, who was born after Osiris was slain, was "the purified image of his sire". In one of the religious chants the same idea is given expression when it is declared that "the god Seb was before his mother". The new Pharaoh, on ascending the throne, became doubly divine, because both ideas regarding the divinity of kings were perpetuated at the same time.

The worship of a particular Pharaoh did not cease when he died. Like other departed souls he required the service of the living. His priests must assist him to reach the Osirian Paradise of Aalu, or the sun bark of Ra. Even Ra had to be assisted to pass through the perilous hour-divisions of the night. Indeed all the good forces of Nature had to be continually prompted by men who desired to be benefited by them; similarly the evil forces had to be thwarted by the performance of magical ceremonies and the repetition of magical formulæ. Egyptian religion was based upon belief in magic.

Pharaoh's body was therefore mummified, so that his soul might continue to exist and be able to return to reanimate the bandaged form. Food offerings were given regularly for the sustenance of the Ka. Magical ceremonies, which were religious ceremonies, were performed to cause the gods to act and to speak as was desired—to imitate those who impersonated them upon earth. The priests were supposed, as it were, to mesmerize the gods when they went through their elaborate ceremonies of compulsion and their ceremonies of riddance.

It was considered necessary to afford secure protection for the Pharaoh's mummy; his enemies might seek to dismember it with purpose to terminate the life of the soul. Substantial tombs were therefore erected, and the old brick and wood erections which were constructed for the kings at Abydos went out of fashion.

A tomb chamber was hewed out of solid rock, and over it was built an oblong platform structure of limestone called a mastaba. The mummy was lowered down the shaft, which was afterwards filled up with sand and gravel and closed with masonry. This low and flat-roofed building was large enough to accommodate at least a hundred bodies, but it was made solid throughout with the exception of the secret shaft. Robbers would have to wreck it completely before the hiding place of the body could be discovered. On the east side there was a false door through which the Ka could pass when it came from, or departed towards, the western land of shades. In time a little chapel was provided, and the false door was placed at the end of it. This apartment was used for the performance of the ceremonies associated with the worship of the dead; mourners came with offerings, and met in presence of the invisible Ka.

The statue was concealed in an inner chamber, which was built up, but occasionally narrow apertures were constructed through which food and drink were given to the Ka. But only to kings and rich men could this service be rendered for a prolonged period, so the practice ultimately evolved of providing the dead with models of offerings which by a magical process gave sustenance to the hungry spirit.

Mortuary chapels were endowed as early as the First Dynasty. Priests were regularly engaged in worshipping dead kings and princes who had made provision in their wills for the necessary expenses. The son of one monarch in the Fourth Dynasty devoted the revenues of a dozen towns to maintain the priesthood attached to his tomb. This custom created grave financial problems.

In a few generations the whole land might be mortgaged to maintain mortuary chapels, with the result that a revolution involving a change of dynasty became an economic necessity.

> Hearken! ye kings, while horror stalks the land,
> Lo! your poor people fall a ready prey
> Made weak by your oppression, even in death—

Burdened and bruised and terrorized; their lands
Tax ridden for these temples ye endowed,
That fawning priests might meek obeisance make
And render ceaseless homage to your shades.

The walls of the chapel were either sculptured in low relief or painted with scenes of daily life, and from these we gather much of what we know regarding the manners and customs of the ancient people. But such works of art were not intended merely to be decorative or to perpetuate the fame of the dead. It was desired that those scenes should be duplicated in Paradise. The figures of farm servants sowing and reaping corn, of artisans erecting houses, and cooks preparing meals, were expected to render similar services to the departed soul. Magical texts were inscribed with purpose to ensure this happy condition of affairs; others called down curses on the heads of tomb robbers.

Kings and nobles had no pleasure in the prospect that they would have to perform humble tasks in the Nether World. They desired to occupy there the exalted stations which they enjoyed upon earth. It was necessary, therefore, to have numerous employees so that their mansions might be erected, their fields cultivated, and their luxuries provided as of old.

The custom at first obtained of slaying a number of servants to accompany the great dignitary to Paradise. These poor victims were supposed to be grateful, because they were to be rewarded with assured immortality. But the shedding of blood was rendered unnecessary when the doctrine obtained that substitutes could be provided by sculptors and painters.

Another mortuary custom was to provide little figures, called Ushebtiu, "the answerers", inscribed with magical formulæ, which would obey the dead and perform whatever duties he desired of them in Paradise. These were ultimately shaped in mummy form, and in the later Dynasties were made of glazed ware, because wooden figures suffered from the ravages of the white ant.

Many toy-like figures of servants are found in early tombs. Here we discover, perchance, the model of a nobleman's dwelling. An ox is being slain in the back-yard. In the kitchen the staff is engaged cooking an elaborate repast; a little fellow devotes himself entirely to a goose which he turns on a spit before the fire. We have a glimpse of high life in another scene. The nobleman has feasted, and he sits at ease in a large apartment listening to singers and harpers. A dancing girl comes out to whirl before him, while her companions keep time to the music by clapping their hands. Meanwhile artisans are busy in their workshops. We see a potter moulding a vessel of exquisite shape, while near at hand a carpenter saws wood with which he intends to construct an elaborate article of furniture. Boats are rocking at a pier, for the soul may desire to sail down the Nile of the Nether World. Here, in fact, is a boat pursuing its way; a dozen strenuous oarsmen occupy the benches, while the steersman stands erect at the helm with the guiding rope in his hands; armed men are on guard, and the nobleman sits with a friend below an awning on a small deck in the centre of the boat, calmly engaged playing a game of draughts.

King Zoser had two tombs erected for himself. One is a great brick mastaba at Abydos, which may have been a "soul house", in the chapel of which his "double" was worshipped; the other, which is constructed of limestone, is situated on the desert behind Memphis. The latter is of particular interest to students of Egyptian history.

It is a terraced structure nearly 200 feet in height, formed by a series of mastabas of decreasing size superimposed one above another. This wonderful building has been called "the step pyramid of Sakkara"; it is not only the first pyramid which was erected in Egypt, but the earliest great stone structure in the world.

So much attention is paid to the three sublime pyramids at Gizeh that Zoser's limestone tomb is apt to be overlooked. Yet it is of marked importance in the history of the country. It was constructed nearly a hundred years before Khufu (Cheops) ascended the throne, and the experience gained in undertaking a work of such vast dimensions made possible the achievements of later times. The architect was the renowned Imhotep, one of the world's great men. His fame was perpetuated in Egypt until the Saite or Restoration period, when he was worshipped as the god called by the Greeks "Imuthes". He was an inventive and organizing genius, and a statesman who exercised much influence at the Court of King Zoser. Like Solomon, he was reputed to be the wisest man of his Age. He was the author of a medical treatise, and he left behind him a collection of proverbs which endured as long as the old Egyptian language. As a patron of learning his memory was revered by the scribes for over two thousand years, and it was their custom before beginning work to pour out from their jars a libation to his spirit.

The step pyramid was Imhotep's conception. He prepared the plans and overlooked the work of construction. No doubt, too, he was responsible for the organization of the army of labourers and artisans who were employed for a prolonged period in erecting this enduring memorial of a great monarch.

Such a vast undertaking is a sure indication of the

advanced character of the civilization of the times. Much wealth must have accumulated in the royal exchequer. The country was in a settled and prosperous condition, owing to the excellent system of government and the activity of administrators. It was no small task to bring together thousands of workmen, who had to be housed and fed and kept under control. Skilled tradesmen were employed, who had been trained in quarrying and dressing stone. Evidently masonry had flourished in Memphis for a considerable period. There were hundreds of overseers experienced in the organization of labour, and large numbers of educated scribes conversant with the exact keeping of accounts.

Education was no longer confined to the ruling classes. We know that there were schools in Memphis. Boys were instructed in "the three R's", and in a papyrus of maxims it was quaintly remarked that they could "hear with their backs", an indication as to the manner in which corporal punishment was inflicted. The system of writing was the cursive style called "hieratic", which originated in pre-Dynastic times as a rough imitation in outline of hieroglyphics. A knowledge of elementary arithmetic was required in the ordinary transactions of business. Some corrected exercises have survived. Advanced pupils were instructed in geometry—which had its origin in Egypt—in mensuration, and in the simpler problems of algebra.

As the Egyptians were an intensely practical people, school studies were specialized. Boys were trained for the particular profession in which they were to be employed. If they were to become business men they attended commercial classes. The number of "trial pieces" which have been found show that young sculptors attended technical schools, as did also artists and metal workers. In the temple colleges the future officials and lawyers and doctors were made conversant with the accumulated knowledge and wisdom of the age. Education was evidently controlled by the priests.

Memphis was a hive of organized industry. The discipline of business pervaded all classes, and everywhere law and order were promoted. Pharaoh was no idler. His day was fully occupied in the transaction of public business, and to every prince was allotted a responsible post, and his duties had to be efficiently performed. The nation was in its young manhood; the foundations had been securely established of a great civilization, which was to endure for some thirty centuries.

It may be said that the royal house of the Old Kingdom was established upon a rock. When the Pharaoh's builders discarded brick, and began to quarry and hew stones, Egyptian civilization made rapid progress. It had had its beginnings in the struggle with Nature in the Nile valley. An increasing population was maintained under peaceful conditions when the problem of water distribution was solved by the construction of canals. These had to be controlled, and the responsibility of a regulated flow was imposed upon the Pharaoh. Good government, therefore, became a necessity; a failure of water caused famine and insurrection. To those who toiled and those who protected the toiler Nature gave a bountiful reward. More food was produced than was required for home consumption. The surplus yield of corn was, as we have seen, the means of promoting trade, which made Egypt a wealthy country. As capital accumulated, the progress of knowledge was assured, and men entered upon those higher pursuits which promote moral and intellectual advancement.

Egypt might have continued happily on the even

tenor of its way as an agricultural and trading country, but its civilization could never have attained so high a degree of perfection if its arts and industries had not been fostered and developed. We may not think highly of Egyptian religion, of which, after all, we have but imperfect knowledge, but we must recognize that it was the inspiration of the architects and craftsmen whose sublime achievements we regard with wonder and admiration after the lapse of thousands of years. It was undoubtedly a civilizing agency; it promoted culture and refinement, and elevated mankind to love beauty for its own sake. Egyptian art flourished because it was appreciated and was in demand.

The surplus wealth of Egypt was expended largely for religious purposes. Temple building kept those wonderful old architects and sculptors constantly engaged; an ever-increasing class of skilled workers had also to be trained, disciplined, and organized. Men of ability were brought to the front and were judged on their own merits. There is no place for pretenders in the world of Art. When the Pharaohs, therefore, undertook the erection of temples and tombs they not only ensured regularity of labour, but also stimulated intellectual effort, with results that could not have been otherwise than beneficial to society at large.

We may well regard the conquest of stone as one of the greatest conquests which the Egyptians achieved. In our Introduction we have suggested that the new industry may have been introduced by the cave-hewing pre-Semitic inhabitants of southern Palestine. The remarkable skill manifested by the earliest stone workers of Egypt with almost dramatic suddenness was evidently the result of long experience. Deft workmanship was accomplished from the outset; stones were measured and dressed with

wonderful accuracy and skill. The changes which took
place in the burial customs during the early Dynasties
also suggest that influences from without were being felt
in the ancient kingdom.

Whatever the origin of the stone workers may have
been, it is evident that they were closely associated with
Memphis at a very early period. As we have seen, the
art of stone working and stone building on a sublime scale
was first displayed by the worshippers of Ptah, the artificer
god. It is of special interest to find, therefore, that
Manetho has preserved those persistent Egyptian traditions which connect Memphis with the new industry.
He credited Zoser, the builder of the step pyramid at
Sakkara, with the introduction of stonework; he also
recorded that the first temple in Egypt was erected at
Memphis to Ptah by King Mena. The city's name
of "White Walls" suggests that the fortress was constructed of limestone.

We know now that stone was used at Abydos before
Zoser's day—not, however, until after the conquest of
the north—but the traditional association of Memphis
with the new industry is none the less significant. The
probability that a colony of Memphite artisans settled in
the vicinity of the Assouan quarries, and introduced stone
working into Upper Egypt, is emphasized by the worship
of Khnûmû, the god of the First Cataract, who bears so
striking a resembling to Ptah. He was similarly regarded
as the modeller of the world. Like Ptah, he was associated with the chaos egg, and he is depicted shaping the
first man upon his potter's wheel.

Khnûmû was merged at an early date with the ram
god Min, for he is invariably shown with ram's horns or
a ram's head. He was a Great Father, and represented
the male principle. His consort is Hekt, the frog-headed

goddess, who is evidently of great antiquity. The Egyptians believed that frogs were generated spontaneously from Nile-fertilized mud, and they associated Hekt with the origin of life. . This quaint goddess was one of the "mothers" who was supposed to preside at birth, and so persistent was the reverence shown her by the great mass of the people that she was ultimately fused with Hathor. In Coptic times Hekt was a symbol of the resurrection.

Another goddess associated with Khnûmû was named Sati. Her title "Lady of the Heavens" links her with Nut and Hathor. She is usually depicted as a stately woman wearing a cow's horns and the crown of Upper Egypt; she is "the queen of the gods".

An island goddess, called Anukt, belongs to the same group. She has negroid attributes and wears a crown of feathers.

It is apparent that this arbitrary grouping of deities at the First Cataract was the direct result of the mingling of peoples of different origin. Hekt represents a purely Egyptian cult, while Sati is evidently one of the forms of the Great Mother deity of the earliest civilized people in the Nile valley; she resembles closely the historic Isis. Anukt, on the other hand, was probably of Nubian origin, and may have been introduced by those dusky settlers from the south whose aggressive tendencies caused so much concern at the royal Court from time to time. The theory that Khnûmû was the god of the quarries, and builders especially, is supported not only by his resemblance to Ptah, but also by the fact that the Pharaoh who erected the greatest pyramid at Gizeh was called Khnûmû Khufu; this is the monarch whom the Greeks called Cheops.

CHAPTER IX

A Day in Old Memphis

As we gaze upon the scenes depicted in tombs, read the
inscriptions, and piece together fragments of papyri containing old legends, we are afforded vivid glimpses of life
in the Old Kingdom. The great city of Memphis is conjured up before us; its gates lie open, and armed guards
permit us to enter. We walk through the crowded
streets, pausing now and again to gaze upon the people
as they come and go, or, perchance, we loiter in front of
a yard or workshop, watching the busy artisans plying
their trades.

We pass through a main thoroughfare. Most of the
houses are built of brick; the dwellings of the poor are
of wattles daubed with clay. . . . Now we enter a spacious
square, in the centre of which towers a sublime statue of
the Pharaoh. The sun is hot, although it is yet early
forenoon, and we seek the shadow of that vast dominating building round which the city has grown up. It
is the stone temple of the god Ptah, grandly severe in
outline and fronted by two noble pylons of massive pro-

portions. We peer through the gateway as we pass. A procession of priests is crossing an inner court on which lie the broad shadows of great square pillars set widely apart, and supporting immense blocks of limestone. One is impressed by the air of mystery and solemnity which pervades the temple interior.

We can seat ourselves here on the stone bench and watch the crowds pouring from the streets. Memphis is a wonderfully quiet city. You hear a constant hum of voices; it murmurs like a great beehive. But there is no clatter of traffic, for the streets are devoid of vehicles, and horses are as yet unknown in the land of Egypt. Peasants from the country are leading their asses laden with salt, corded bales, rushes for basket makers, bundles of papyrus stalks, and hard stones. Great burdens are carried on the shoulders of labourers; even boys stagger under heavy loads.

Everyone is scantily clad. Men of the lower classes wear only a loincloth, while those of higher social rank have short kilts of linen which are strapped round their waists with leather belts. Women of all ranks are gowned to the ankles, and ladies have skirts so narrow that they walk with short steps, but yet not ungracefully.

Half-naked the men may be, yet it is not difficult to distinguish the various classes. There is no mistaking the labourer, even although his burden has been delivered, or the tradesman, for he carries his tools. Here is a busy merchant knitting his brows, and there a bland-faced scribe with dry, pouting lips and peering eyes set in cobwebs of wrinkles. A few merry students are walking leisurely towards the temple with papyrus rolls under their arms.

A loud clamour of voices in dispute has broken out at a street corner. Two carriers have collided, and the

one who has fallen is an Egyptian; the other is a tall
negro. The smaller man leaps to his feet. Insult has
been added to injury, for the alien is but a slave, and,
fuming with anger, he throws himself on the black man,
who is hampered by his load, and belabours him with
his fists. A crowd collects, and its sympathy is evidently
with the Egyptian. But suddenly a few city guards rush
forward; they smite the combatants with their staves, force
them apart, and cause them to hasten away. The crowd
disperses speedily, and order is again restored.

Note the studied politeness of the greater number of
pedestrians. Age is highly honoured, young men stand
aside to allow their seniors to pass; three lads have risen
from a shaded seat near to us to make room for an old
man who is frail and breathless and desires to rest a little
ere he enters the temple.

Now the moving crowd breaks apart, for somebody
of importance is coming up the street. He is a nobleman and a royal official of high rank. In the Court he
is " Keeper of the Royal Robes " and " Sandal-bearer to
the Pharaoh ". He is also one of those great judges who
sit in the Hall of Justice. In his youth he was a college
friend of the monarch's, and is now privileged at Court
ceremonies to kiss the royal toe instead of the dust on
which it trod. He owns a large estate, and has much
wealth and influence. As he walks past, the pedestrians
salute him respectfully with uplifted arms. He makes
no response; he appears to be oblivious to their presence.
Mark his imperious air and lordly gait. . . . His kilt is
finely embroidered; the upper part of his body is bare;
on his head he wears a great stiff wig which falls down
behind over his shoulders, protecting his neck from the
hot sun. He is square-chested and muscular; he walks
erect, with tilted chin. His face is drawn and severe; he

has firmly set, drooping lips, and his eyes are stern and proud. He is obviously a man accustomed to command and to be obeyed. . . . A servant shuffles after him carrying his sandals and water bottle.

He has just acknowledged with a curt bow the profound obeisance of that rich merchant. But now he meets an equal in the middle of the square—Imhotep, Chief Architect to the King. Ere they speak they both bow gravely, bending their backs, with hands reaching to their knees. Then they converse for a few moments, salute one another again, and turn gravely away.

Some high-born ladies have gathered in the shade. Two carry bunches of lotus flowers, and the others smell them with appreciation. Their faces are refined and vivacious, and one is "black but comely", for she is a Nubian by birth. How they chatter as they flicker their broad fans! Their white gowns are elaborately embroidered in colours, and they all wear sandals, for the builders have left much grit in the streets. Their wigs are drawn low on their foreheads, round which they are clasped by graven bands of silver and gold. Gems sparkle in their necklaces, which are of elaborate design, and one or two wear their wigs set well back to display heavy ear-rings, which are becoming fashionable. A handsome girl is wearing a broad gold armlet which came from Crete. The others examine it with interest, and when they break into laughter, displaying gleaming white teeth, the girl looks sideways in confusion, for they tease her about her far-travelled lover who gifted her that rare ornament. Now they saunter in pairs across the square; they are going down to the quays to sail on the Nile.

There is a variety of racial types about us. The southern Egyptians are almost black, those from the centre of the kingdom are brown, and the Delta people have yellow skins.   That bearded man who has just gone past is a Semite from Arabia; and here comes a soft-featured Syrian, walking with an oblique-eyed Sumerian from Babylonia.   These tall negroes are Nubian mercenaries, who were taken captive in a frontier war.   Of late the stone builders have been purchasing them in large numbers, for they have great muscular strength and make excellent labourers.

There is no mistaking the awkward, wide-eyed peasant who came to the market with salt, and is now surveying the great city of wonderful buildings and endless streets.

That red-haired man who is hurrying past is an Amorite; he came south to barter rugs for corn. He looks behind with an ugly scowl—a carrier has shouted something after him, because an Egyptian peasant dislikes a man who reminds him of red-haired Set, the slayer of Osiris.

Now here comes a handsome stranger who is exciting much interest.   Men and women turn round to look after him.   Children regard him with wonder.   Not only is he taller than the majority of Memphites, but he is distinguished by his lightly coloured hair and his strange blue eyes.   Some would fain know if his cheeks are a natural red or smeared with face paint.   No one doubts whence he came.   He is one of the fair Libyans, and he is evidently a man of some importance, for even royal officials acknowledge his salutations.

Ere we turn away, let us watch that little procession of young peasants walking past.   They are bearers of offerings, and are going to the temple.   One lad has shouldered a live calf, another brings a bundle of papyrus stalks, and a third has a basket of flour upon his head. The girls carry bunches of flowers, doves in pairs, and tame pelicans.   One or two calves are led by boys.   Little notice is taken of the peasants. Processions of similar character are seen daily in Memphis.

We had better cross over quickly, for here comes a great herd of unwilling goats driven by shouting peasants who wield their staves rather freely, nor care whether they miss a goat and strike a pedestrian. The city guards are watching them with interest, for they know their men.

Now turn down this narrow twisting street. Houses are lower here, and some are built with brick, but most of them are constructed of clay-plastered wickerwork. Why not enter this little dwelling? The door lies open, and there is nobody within. Man and wife labour in a potter's yard. The furniture consists of one or two rough stools, a low bed over which hangs a gnat-protecting net, and here and there are a few jars and pots of coarse pottery. Within the window lattice a bunch of lotus leaves is drying in the sun; a cut of salted fish hangs on the wall; a flint knife lies on the floor. The house is used mainly as a sleeping apartment, and if there is a baby it is near the mother in the potter's yard.

Outside, a few children are playing a curious game, which appears to be an imitation of a temple ceremony. Wives of artisans sit gossiping in the shade of a brick building; some are sewing, and others are cutting vegetables which they have brought from the market. Two girls go past with water pots on their heads.

We have glimpses, as they walk on, of long narrow lanes of small and low-roofed houses. There is evidently much congestion in the poorer quarters of the city. Look through that open door and you will see an industrious family. A widow and her three daughters are spinning and weaving fine linen, which might well be mistaken for silk.

Here is a brickyard. Labourers are mixing the clay; others shape the bricks with a binding of straw and lay them out to dry. Carriers come for those which are ready, and take heavy loads in two slings suspended from poles which they lift upon their shoulders. An overseer hastens them on, for the builders cannot be kept waiting.

Farther on is a stoneworker's yard. Under an awning squat several skilled artisans who are engaged making vessels of alabaster and porphyry. The process is slow and arduous. One has shaped and polished a handsome jar with fluted lip and narrow neck, and is hollowing it out with a copper-tipped drill which is fed with ground emery. He pauses for a moment to wipe the perspiration from his forehead, and remarks to a fellow: "This is certainly a handsome vessel." The other looks up and surveys it critically. "It is your masterpiece," he remarks, with a smile, and then goes on drilling a large shallow milk bowl.

Two men are cutting a block of porphyry with a copper saw, while an apprentice supplies the emery, and relieves now one and then the other. See how skilfully those labourers are levering a granite boulder into position; it is mounted on a rounded wooden cradle, and slewed this way and that. A lad is gathering wedges with which to raise it up. One or two naked boys, squatted in a shady corner, are watching the proceedings with interest. They are going to saw stone too, when they grow strong.

We enter another street and our ears are assailed by the clamour of metal workers. It is a noisy quarter. Bang, bang, go the hammers on a large sheet of copper. One would be deafened if he stayed here long. Passersby twitch their eyes and foreheads and hurry on. Look at these naked men kneeling round the blazing furnace, puffing their cheeks and blowing through long pipes. No Egyptian inventor has yet contrived a mechanical bellows. Now the glowing metal is pulled from the furnace, and a dozen exhausted workers rise, with their blowpipes in their hands, coughing and rubbing their eyes, to wait until the hammermen require them again.

Here are goldsmiths at work. A man is weighing precious metal in a balance, and a scribe sits in front of him making careful records on a sheet of papyrus. Near by are men with clever fingers and keen eyes, who engrave and pierce little pieces of gold and silver, shape ear-rings and necklaces, and hammer out sheets of gold which are to be inscribed with hieroglyphics. An overseer moves to and fro from bench to bench and artisan to artisan, surveying everything that is being done with critical eyes.

So we pass from street to street, here watching potters at work, there sculptors and carvers of wood and ivory, and anon the sandal makers and those deft leather cutters who provide gentlemen with slitted network to suspend on the back of their kilts for sitting upon.

Now we reach the principal marketplace. The scene is animated and intensely human. Merchants are squatted beside their stalls, some drowsing in the heat while they await purchasers, and others gesticulating excitedly at bargain making. There is a good deal of wrangling, and voices are often raised in dispute, while friends gather in knots and chatter and laugh or engage in lively argument. Some make purchases with ring money, but the majority engage in barter. Here a merchant has displayed a fine collection of vases and bowls. A lady surveys his wares critically and shakes her head over the prices he demands; but he waits patiently, for he knows she is tempted to purchase and notes that she always returns to a particular porphyry jar of exquisite design.

A woman of the working class leans over a basket of fish, and doubts if they are quite fresh. The vendor lifts one, presses it with his fingers, and smiles to her. "Caught this morning," he says. She decides to have it for her husband's dinner, and gives in exchange a piece of red pottery. Another woman barters a small carved box for ointment and perfume, while a man gives a fan for a bundle of onions.

A steward from a nobleman's house passes from stall to stall, accompanied by two servants, making numerous purchases, because several guests of note are coming to the evening meal. He is welcomed, although a hard bargainer, for he pays with money.

We catch, as we turn away, a soothing glimpse of the broad blue river, and turn towards it, for the streets are dusty and hot, and we know the air is cooler beside the quays. We cross an open space in which are piled up the cargoes of unloaded boats. Here come half a dozen foreign sailors who are going sightseeing. They also intend to make private purchases for their friends at home. You can tell by their pants and characteristic "wasp waists" that they are Cretans. They are short of stature and slim and have sharp features like the Delta coast dwellers, and their movements are active. Their dark hair is pleated in three long coils which fall over their shoulders, and they affect small coloured turbans. They all wear armlets, which are greatly favoured in the distant island kingdom.

A company of Pharaoh's soldiers are marching towards the great limestone fortress. They are naked, save for their loincloths, and about half of them are archers; the others are armed with long spears and

carry wooden shields, square at the bottom and arching
to a point at the top. They go past with a fine swing,
although they have been drilling all forenoon on an open
space two miles southward of the city.

Yonder are boatbuilders at work. The Cretan traders
have brought them a fresh supply of seasoned timber as
well as a raft of drifted logs from Lebanon. Wood is
scarce and dear in Egypt, and watchmen are on duty in
the yard day and night.

Three commodious river boats are being constructed.
The work is well advanced, for the carpenters are fitting
in the benches, which are being pierced and prepared for
jointing on trestles by men who sit astride them. The
artisans are skilled and active, and the overseers who
direct operations are easily recognized; they carry long
staffs in their right hands and constantly urge on the
men.

But what is happening yonder in front of the Government
buildings? A large crowd has assembled, and the
jeers and roars of laughter indicate that something of
amusing character is in progress. We press forward to
find that the city guards have made several arrests, and
are hauling their protesting prisoners through the doorway.
The spectators are delighted to see "the tables
turned", for these are their oppressors—the tax collectors—who
are being taken before the Pharaoh's accountants
so that their accounts may be audited. There
have been several complaints of late of extortionate dealings
and dishonest transactions. In a large hall within
we see the stern auditors kneeling at their low desks, on
which are piled the official records. Scribes record the
proceedings. Each arrested man crouches on his knees,
and is held firmly by a guard while he is sharply questioned
and his accounts are checked. All his private

papers have been seized; he must explain every entry and prove that he is a man above suspicion. It is a rough-and-ready, but effective, manner of doing business. Punishments for dishonesty or oppression are sharp and peremptory.

The Pharaoh is the protector of all his subjects great and small. A poor man may suffer a great wrong and find himself unable to have it righted even in the Hall of Justice; but if the great monarch is appealed to, he will prove to be no respecter of persons, and visit the wrong-doer with punishment of great severity.

A tale has come down the ages which was often related in the dwellings of poor and great alike, to show how Pharaoh might espouse the cause of the humblest man in the kingdom. Scribes recorded it on papyri, and fragments of these still survive.

Once upon a time a peasant had his dwelling in the Fayum, and it was his custom to load his ass with nitre and reeds, salt and stones, and seeds and bundles of wood, and drive it to a town in the south, where in the marketplace he exchanged what he had brought for other things that he and his family required. He began to be prosperous.

One day, when it was nigh to harvesttime, he journeyed townwards and reached the estate of a great royal official named Meritensa. As he passed through it he came to the farm of Hamti, a feudal tenant. The farmer saw him approach, and to himself he said: "May the god permit me to rob the peasant of his ass and its burden. I have need of salt."

The path along the river bank was exceedingly narrow, for Hamti had sowed much land. Between his corn and the water there was scarcely the breadth of a man's body.

Said the farmer to one of his servants: "Bring me a rug from within." The man ran to Hamti's house and came back with a rug, which was spread out upon the path, and it reached from the corn to the river edge.

The peasant drove his ass along the narrow way, past the corn, and when he drew nigh, the farmer called to him, saying: "Observe where you are going; do not soil my rug."

"I will do according to your will," remarked the peasant, "and avoid troubling you."

So he smote his ass and turned it inland to pass round the field. But the farmer would not be satisfied with that even. He shouted with an angry voice, saying: "Would you dare to trample upon my corn? There is no path that way."

"What else can I do?" remonstrated the peasant; "you prevent me from using the path by laying a rug upon it."

As he spoke his ass began to eat the grain, and the farmer seized it and said: "I will take this animal in payment for the damage it has done."

The peasant cried indignantly: "What? first you close the path against me, and now you seize my ass because it has taken a few ears of barley. Dare not to wrong me on this estate; it belongs to the just Meritensa, the great judge, who is a terror to all evildoers in the kingdom. Well you know that I speak truly. Do not imagine that you can oppress me on the land of such a good and high nobleman."

But the farmer laughed. "Heard you not," he asked, "the maxim which says: 'A peasant is esteemed only by himself?' Know now, too, that I am even Meritensa, the judge, of whom you have spoken. I will deal with you here and now."

Having spoken thus, the farmer seized a scourge and lashed the peasant fiercely, seeking to drive him away. But the wronged man refused to depart. His body ached with many wounds. He waited about all day, but neither by threat nor tearful appeal could he prevail upon the farmer to give him back his ass and the burden it carried.

Then the peasant hastened towards the dwelling of Meritensa. He waited the coming forth of that great lord, sitting patiently beside the wall gate. Hours went past, and at length he saw Meritensa walking out to step into a boat at the river side.

"Hail to thee, my lord!" he called. "Bid one of your servants to hear the tale of my wrong."

As the man desired, so did the nobleman do. He bade a scribe to converse with the peasant, who related how he had been wronged by Hamti.

So it happened that, when sitting in the Hall of Justice next morning, Meritensa repeated the accusations which the peasant had made against the farmer. The other judges heard, and then said:

"It is our rule here that these peasants should bring witnesses. We know their ways. If it is proved that the farmer stole some nitre and salt, he can be ordered to make payment, or else he can be scourged. But we must first hear evidence to confirm what is said by this peasant fellow."

Meritensa made no reply. He was indignant at the other judges, and scorned to discuss the matter with them any further. He decided to advise the wronged man what to do.

But the peasant could not find witnesses, and again he waited the coming forth of the good judge. Then he praised him with a loud voice, saying: "Thou art mighty among the mighty ones and the good friend of poor men. May fair winds waft thee on the lake of truth; may no wave smite thee or any terror come nigh. Thou art a father to the fatherless, and a husband to the widow and a brother to the girl in need. I laud thy name, for thou dost give excellent counsel without desire of reward. Thou art the enemy of the wrongdoer and the lover of justice. My cry thou didst hear, and thou hast permitted me to speak. Thou art esteemed by those who are worthy. Now show me mercy and undo my wrong; consider my prayer, enquire regarding me, and thou wilt find that I have been plundered."

Meritensa was on his way to the palace, and he repeated unto Pharaoh what the peasant had said, and related how he had been robbed by the farmer.

His Majesty said: "This man hath great eloquence. See that his wrong is not righted for a little time yet, and arrange that all his fine speeches are recorded by your scribes. I should like to hear them word by word. Meantime see that his wife and his children do not want for food."

The peasant was given a supply of bread each day, and Meritensa arranged that his wife and children should also be supplied with food in abundance.

Daily did the wronged man wait the coming forth of the noble, whom he addressed with great eloquence and poetic fervour. The scribes recorded all the words of his mouth. But Meritensa pretended not to heed him, and he even had him beaten.

Nine times did the peasant make appeal to the judge, and at length two servants went and spoke to the man, who, when he saw them approach, feared that he was about to be scourged once again. But the words which they spake for their lord were:

"You have no cause to be afraid because you addressed the judge these many times. The Pharaoh has read your speeches and has praised them, and you will be rewarded."

Meritensa then caused his scribes to take down the evidence of the peasant regarding the robbery of his ass and its burden of nitre and salt, and he laid the document before His Majesty.

Pharaoh said: "I cannot attend to this matter. Consider it yourself and see that justice is done."

Meritensa then dispatched his officers to the farm, and he caused Hamti's house and all his goods to be confiscated and given unto the peasant.

All that was done was confirmed and approved by the Pharaoh, who commanded that the eloquent peasant should be brought to the palace. His Majesty took delight in his speeches and honoured him greatly, for he caused rich dainties from the royal table to be sent unto the man and his family.

CHAPTER X

The Great Pyramid Kings

Zoser and Sneferu—Their Great Tombs—Sneferu's Battles with Invaders
—Mastabas of Officials—The Grand Vizier—A New Dynasty—Khufu the
Tyrant King—His Great Pyramid—The World's Greatest Stone Structure—
An Army of Workers—How the Pyramids were built—Rocking Machines—
A Religious Revolution—The Gods of the Sun Cult—Ptah excluded—King
Khafra—Menkaura the Just King—The Sacred Heifer—Khufu's Line over-
thrown.

WHEN the great pyramids were being erected Egypt was
already a land of ancient memories. Some of the royal
tombs at Abydos were a thousand years old. Folk tales
had gathered round the memories of notable kings; their
order was confused and not a few were quite forgotten.

Zoser and Sneferu of the Third Dynasty are really
the first Egyptian monarchs of whom we obtain any
accurate idea. They were forceful personalities. We
trace Zoser's activities in Sinai, where he continued to
work the copper mines from which several of his predecessors had obtained supplies of indispensable metal. He
waged war on the southern frontier, which he extended
below the First Cataract, and he imposed his rule firmly
over the north. That peace prevailed all over the kingdom is evident; otherwise he could not have devoted
so much time to the erection of his great tomb, at which
a great army of workmen were kept continuously employed.

Sneferu, whose very name suggests swiftness of

decision and unswerving purpose, impressed himself on
the imagination of the Egyptians for many generations.
When a great national achievement was accomplished it
became customary to remark that no such success had
been attained "since the days of Sneferu". He battled
against Asian hordes who invaded the Delta region, and
erected forts, like a chain of blockhouses, across the
frontier, and these were associated with his name for
over ten centuries. In Sinai there was trouble regarding
the copper mines. Other people had begun to work
them and disputed right of possession with the Egyptians.
Sneferu conducted a vigorous and successful campaign,
and so firmly established his power in that region that
his spirit was worshipped generations afterwards as the
protecting god of the mines. His ambitions were not
confined to land, for he caused great ships to be built
and he traded with Crete and the Syrian coast. The
cedars of Lebanon were then cut and drifted to the Nile
by Egyptian mariners. In the south Nubia was dealt
with firmly. We gather that thousands of prisoners were
captured and taken north as slaves to be employed, apparently, at the building of temples and tombs. Two
pyramids are attributed to Sneferu, the greatest of which
is situated at Medum.

The power and wealth of the officials had increased
greatly. Their mastabas, which surround the royal tombs,
are of greater and more elaborate construction. Pharaoh
was no longer hampered with the details of government.
A Grand Vizier controlled the various departments of
State, and he was the supreme judge to whom final
appeals were made by the Courts. There were also a
"Chancellor of the Exchequer" and officials who controlled the canals and secured an equitable distribution
of water. There were governors of nomes and towns,

and even villages had their "chief men". To secure the effective control of the frontier, always threatened by raids from Nubia, a local vizier was appointed to quell outbreaks, and troops were placed at his disposal. These high offices were usually held by princes and noblemen, but apparently it was possible for men of humble rank to attain distinction and be promoted, like Joseph, to positions of influence and responsibility. In mastaba chapels there are proud records of promotion acquired by capable and successful officials who began life as scribes and were governors ere they died.

The Fourth Dynasty begins with Khufu the Great, the Cheops of the Greeks, who erected the largest pyramid in Egypt. His relationship to Sneferu is uncertain. He was born in the Beni Hassan district, and was probably the son of a nobleman of royal birth. Sneferu may have left no direct heir or one who was a weakling. There is no record or tradition of a revolution, and it may be that Khufu was already a prominent figure at the Court when he seized the crown. In his harem was a lady who enjoyed the confidence of his predecessor, and it is possible that matters were arranged in his interests in that quarter.

No statues of Khufu survive. These were probably destroyed when, a few centuries after his death, his tomb was raided and his mummy torn to pieces, for he was remembered as a great tyrant. So much was he hated that Herodotus was informed by the priests that he "degenerated into the extremest profligacy of conduct". He barred the avenues to every temple and forbade the Egyptians to offer sacrifices. He proceeded next to make them labour as slaves for himself. Some he compelled to hew stones in the quarries of the Arabian mountains and drag them to the banks of the Nile;

others were selected to load vessels. . . . A hundred thousand men were employed." But the memory of ancient wrongs was perpetuated by the priests not merely in sympathy for the workers and those who had to bear the burdens of taxation. A religious revolution was imminent. The sun worshippers at Heliopolis were increasing in numbers and power, and even in Khufu's day their political influence was being felt. In fact, their ultimate ascendancy may have been due to the public revolt against the selfish and tyrannical policy of the pyramid-building kings.

We enjoy a privilege not shared by Greeks or Romans, who heard the Egyptian traditions regarding the masterful monarch. Petrie discovered an ivory statue of Khufu, which is a minute and beautiful piece of work. The features occupy only a quarter of an inch, and are yet animate with life and expression. Khufu's face suggests that of the Duke of Wellington. The nose is large and curved like an eagle's beak; the eyes have a hard and piercing look; the cheek bones are high, the cheeks drawn down to knotted jaws; the chin is firmly cut and the hard mouth has an uncompromising pout; the brows are lowering. The face is that of a thinker and man of action — an idealist and an iron-willed ruler of men—

whose frown
And wrinkled lip and sneer of cold command
Tell that the sculptor well those passions read
Which still survive

stamped on the statuette of the greatest of the pyramid builders. There is withal an air of self-consciousness, and we seem to hear, "My name is Khufu"—

. . . King of Kings;
Look on my works, ye mighty, and despair.

Petrie, the great Egyptian archæologist, calculates that Khufu's vast pyramid is composed of some 2,003,000 blocks of limestone averaging about 2½ tons each. It occupies an area of 13 acres. Each side of the square base originally measured 768 feet, but the removal of the coating which left the sides smooth caused a shrinkage of about 18 feet. The height is now roughly 450 feet, 30 ft. less than when it was completed.

This pyramid is the greatest pile of masonry ever erected by man. Not only is it a monument to a mighty ruler and his great architects and builders, but also to the stone workers of Memphis. Many of the great stones have been cut and dressed with amazing skill and accuracy, and so closely are they placed together that the seams have to be marked with charcoal to be traced in a photograph. Blocks of limestone weighing tons are finished with almost microscopic accuracy, "equal", says Petrie, "to optician's work of the present day".

Volumes have been written to advance theories regarding the purpose of this and other pyramids. The orientation theory has especially been keenly debated. But it no longer obtains among prominent Egyptologists. A pyramid has no astronomical significance whatsoever; the Egyptians were not star worshippers. It is simply a vast burial cairn, and an architectural development of the mastaba, which had been growing higher and higher until Zoser's architect conceived the idea of superimposing one upon the other until an effect was obtained which satisfied his sense of proportion. Geometricians decided its final shape rather than theologians.

There are several chambers in the interior of Khufu's pyramid, whose mummy reposed in a granite sarcophagus in the largest, which is 19 feet high, 34¼ feet in length, and 17 feet in breadth. The entrance is from the north.

Herodotus was informed by the Egyptian priests that 100,000 workers were employed, and were relieved every three months. The limestone was quarried on the eastern side of the Nile, below Cairo, and drifted on rafts across the river. The low ground was flooded, so that the high ground was made an island. We are informed that ten years were spent in constructing a causeway up which the blocks were hauled. A considerable time was also spent in preparing the rocky foundations. The pyramid itself was the work of twenty years.

When the base was completed, the same writer explains, the stones were raised by the aid of "machines" made of "short pieces of wood". Models have been found in tombs of wooden "cradles"—flat on the top and rounded off so that they could be rocked—on which boulders were evidently poised and then slewed into position by haulage and leverage. The "cradles" were raised by wedges. When the block was lifted high enough, it could be tilted and made to slide down skids into position. Herodotus says that according to one account the stones were elevated by the numerous "machines" from step to step, and to another they were lifted into position by one great contrivance. This process was continued until the summit was reached. Then a granite casing was constructed downward to the base, and it was covered over with hieroglyphics which recorded the various sums of money expended for food supplied to the workers. "Cheops (Khufu) exhausted his wealth", adds Herodotus.

The royal exchequer does not appear to have been depleted, because Khufu also erected three smaller pyramids for members of his family, and his successor afterwards undertook the construction of a vast tomb also.

Apart from his pyramid work we know little or

nothing regarding the events of Khufu's reign. Sneferu's military activities had secured peace on the frontiers, and neither dusky Nubian nor bearded Asiatic dared enter the land to plunder or despoil. That the administration was firm and perfectly organized under the iron-willed monarch may be taken for granted.

But a great change was impending which could not be controlled by the will of a single man. Prolonged peace had promoted culture, and the minds of men were centred on the great problems of life and death. Among the educated classes a religious revolution was imminent. Apparently Khufu was raised to power on an early wave of insurrection. It was a period of transition. The downfall of the Ptah cult as a supreme political force was in progress, and the rival cult of Ra, at Heliopolis, was coming into prominence. Already in Sneferu's reign a sun worshipper, one Ra-hotep, occupied the influential position of Superintendent of the South. It remained for the priests of the sun to secure converts among the members of the royal family, so as to obtain political and religious ascendancy, and it can be understood that those who were educated at their temple college were likely to embrace their beliefs. If they failed in that direction, the combined influence of priests and nobles was sufficient to threaten the stability of the throne. A strong ruler might delay, but he could not thwart, the progress of the new movement.

The king's name, as we have stated, was Khnûmû Khufu, which means: "I am guarded by the god Khnûmû". That "modeller" of the universe may have closely re-sembled Ptah, but the doctrines of the two sects developed separately, being subjected to different racial influences. Khnûmû was ultimately merged with the sun god, and his ram became "the living soul of Ra". Khnûmû was regarded at Heliopolis as an incarnation of Osiris, whose close association with agricultural rites perpetuated his worship among the great mass of the people. In the theological system of the sun cult, Osiris became a member of the Ra family, and succeeded to the throne of the "first king" who ruled over Egypt. But Ptah, significantly enough, was never included among the sun god's companions, and the idea that he created Ra was confined to Memphis, and evolved at a later date. The rivalry between the two powerful cults must have been bitter and pronounced.

If Ptolemaic tradition is to be relied upon, Khufu constructed a temple to the goddess Hathor, who, as we have seen, was merged with the frog goddess Hekt, the spouse of Khnûmû. Indeed Hekt came to be regarded as a form of Hathor. Sati, Khnûmû's other spouse, was also a sky and cow goddess, so that she links with Nut, and with Hathor, who displaced Nut.

King Khufu's son and successor must have come under the influence of the Ra cult, for his name, Khaf-ra, signifies "Ra is my glory" or "My brightness is Ra". The sun cult had received their first great concession from the royal house. But not until the following Dynasty did the priests of Heliopolis obtain supreme power, and compel the Pharaoh to call himself "son of the sun", a title which ever afterwards remained in use. Sun worship then became the official religion of Egypt— it gradually coloured every other cult. When the Osirian religion was revived, under the Libyan monarchs, the old deified king, who was an incarnation of the corn god, was also identified with the sun.

King Khafra did not, it would appear, satisfy the ambitions of the Ra worshippers, who desired more than formal recognition. A legend which survives only in fragmentary form relates that "the gods turned away from Khufu and his house". The powerful cult became impatient, and "hope deferred" made them rebels. A political revolution was fostered, and Khufu's Dynasty was doomed.

Khafra, the Chephren of Herodotus, who says Khufu was his brother, erected the second great pyramid, which is only about 30 feet lower than the other. The remains of his temple still survive. It is built of granite, and although the workmanship is less exact, as if the work were more hastily performed than in Khufu's day, the architecture is austerely sublime. Immense square pillars support massive blocks; there are great open spaces, and one is impressed by the simplicity and grandeur of the scheme.

Seven statues of Khafra were discovered by Mariette, so that his "Ka" was well provided for. The great diorite statue preserved in the Cairo museum is one of the enduring triumphs of Egyptian art. The conception is at once grand and imposing. His Majesty is seated on the throne, but he wears the wig of the great ruling judge. At the back of his head is the figure of the protecting Horus hawk. His face is calmer than Khufu's— resolution is combined with dignity and patience. He seems to be imbued with the spirit of Old Kingdom greatness.

Although cut from so hard a material as diorite, there is much muscular detail in the figure, which is that of a strong and vigorous man. His throne is straight-backed, but the stately floral design of the sides, and the lions' heads and fore paws in front are in keeping with the naked majesty of the whole statue, which was originally covered with a soft material.

Again the reign is a blank. The priests informed

Herodotus that Khafra's conduct was similar to that of Khufu. "The Egyptians had to endure every species of oppression and calamity, and so greatly do they hate the memories of the two monarchs that they are unwilling to mention their names. Instead they called their pyramids by the name of the shepherd Philitis, who grazed his cattle near them."

The great Sphinx was long associated with Khafra, whose name was carved upon it during the Eighteenth Dynasty, but it is believed to be of much later date. It is fashioned out of the rock, and is over 60 feet in height. The body is a lion's, and the face was a portrait of a Pharaoh, but it has been so much disfigured by Mohammedans that it cannot be identified with certainty. Nor is there complete agreement as to the significance of the Sphinx. Centuries after its construction the Egyptians regarded it as a figure of the sun god, but more probably it was simply a symbol of royal power and greatness.

There were kindlier memories of Menkaura, the Mycernius of Herodotus, who said that this king was a son of Khufu. He erected the third great pyramid, which is but 218 feet high, and three small ones for his family. He was reputed, however, to have eased the burden of the Egyptians, and especially to have allowed the temples to be reopened, so that the people might offer sacrifices to the gods. As a just monarch he excelled all his predecessors, and his memory was long revered. Not only did he deliver equitable judgments, but was ever ready to hear appeals when complaints were made against officials, and willing to remove and redress wrongs. His statue shows us a less handsome man than either Khufu or Khafra, and the expression of the face accords with his traditional character. Indeed, it is not only unaffected, but melancholy.

A story was told to Herodotus that the king was greatly stricken by the death of his daughter. He had her body enclosed in a heifer made of wood, which was covered over with gold. It was not buried, but placed in a palace hall at Sais. Incense was burned before it daily, and at night it was illuminated. The heifer reclined on its knees. A purple robe covered the body, and between the gilded horns blazed a great golden star. Once a year, in accordance with the request of the dying princess, the image was carried outside so that she might behold the sun. The occasion was an Osirian festival, and the heifer, it is believed, represented Isis.

We know definitely that a daughter of Menkaura was given in marriage to Ptah-shepses, a high official, who became the priest of three obelisks. The appointment is full of significance, because these obelisks were erected to Ra. Sun worship was evidently gaining ground.

The mummy of the king was enclosed in a great sarcophagus of basalt, but was destroyed with the others. Mention is also made of a Fourth-Dynasty monarch named Radadef, but he cannot be placed with certainty. Khufu's line flourished for about a century and a half, and then was overthrown. A new family of kings, who were definitely Ra worshippers, sat on the throne of United Egypt. In the folk tales which follow are interesting glimpses of the life and beliefs of the times.

CHAPTER XI
Folk Tales of Fifty Centuries

A Faithless Lady—The Wax Crocodile—Pharaoh's Decree—Story of the Green Jewel—A Sad-hearted King—Boating on the Lake—How the Waters were divided—Dedi the Magician—His Magical Feats—A Prophecy —Khufu's Line must fall—Birth of the Future Kings—Goddesses as Dancing Girls—Ghostly Music and Song—Tale of a King's Treasure—Fearless Thieves —A Brother's Bravery—Pharaoh's Soldiers are tricked—How a Robber became a Prince—King visits the Underworld.

KING KHUFU sat to hear tales told by his sons regarding the wonders of other days and the doings of magicians. The Prince Khafra stood before him and related the ancient story of the wax crocodile.

Once upon a time a Pharaoh went towards the temple of the god Ptah. His counsellers and servants accompanied him. It chanced that he paid a visit to the villa of the chief scribe, behind which there was a garden with a stately summer house and a broad artificial lake. Among those who followed Pharaoh was a handsome youth, and the scribe's wife beheld him with love. Soon afterwards she sent gifts unto him, and they had secret meetings. They spent a day in the summer house, and feasted there, and in the evening the youth bathed in the lake. The chief butler then went to his master and informed him what had come to pass.

The scribe bade the servant to bring a certain magic box, and when he received it he made a small wax crocodile, over which he muttered a spell. He placed

142

it in the hands of the butler, saying: "Cast this image into the lake behind the youth when next he bathes himself."

On another day, when the scribe dwelt with Pharaoh, the lovers were together in the summer house, and at eventide the youth went into the lake. The butler stole through the garden, and stealthily he cast into the water the wax image, which was immediately given life. It became a great crocodile that seized the youth suddenly and took him away.

Seven days passed, and then the scribe spoke to the Pharaoh regarding the wonder which had been done, and made request that His Majesty should accompany him to his villa. The Pharaoh did so, and when they both stood beside the lake in the garden the scribe spoke magic words, bidding the crocodile to appear. As he commanded, so did it do. The great reptile came out of the water carrying the youth in its jaws.

The scribe said: "Lo! it shall do whatever I command to be done."

Said the Pharaoh: "Bid the crocodile to return at once to the lake."

Ere he did that, the scribe touched it, and immediately it became a small image of wax again. The Pharaoh was filled with wonder, and the scribe related unto him all that had happened, while the youth stood waiting.

Said His Majesty unto the crocodile: "Seize the wrongdoer." The wax image was again given life, and, clutching the youth, leaped into the lake and disappeared Nor was it ever seen after that.

Then Pharaoh gave command that the wife of the scribe should be seized. On the north side of the house she was bound to a stake and burned alive, and what remained of her was thrown into the Nile

Such was the tale told by Khafra. Khufu was well pleased, and caused offerings of food and refreshment to be placed in the tombs of the Pharaoh and his wise servant.

Prince Khafra stood before His Majesty, and said: "I will relate a marvel which happened in the days of King Sneferu, thy father." Then he told the story of the green jewel.

Sneferu was one day disconsolate and weary. He wandered about the palace with desire to be cheered, nor was there aught to take the gloom from his mind. He caused his chief scribe to be brought before him, and said: "I would fain have entertainment, but cannot find any in this place."

The scribe said: "Thy Majesty should go boating on the lake, and let the rowers be the prettiest girls in your harem. It will delight your heart to see them splashing the water where the birds dive and to gaze upon the green shores and the flowers and trees. I myself will go with you."

The king consented, and twenty virgins who were fair to behold went into the boat, and they rowed with oars of ebony which were decorated with gold. His Majesty took pleasure in the outing, and the gloom passed from his heart as the boat went hither and thither, and the girls sang together with sweet voices.

It chanced, as they were turning round, an oar handle brushed against the hair of the girl who was steering, and shook from it a green jewel, which fell into the water. She lifted up her oar and stopped singing, and the others grew silent and ceased rowing.

Said Sneferu: "Do not pause; let us go on still farther."

The girls said: "She who steers has lifted her oar."

Said Sneferu to her: "Why have you lifted your oar?"

"Alas, I have lost my green jewel!" she said; "it has fallen into the lake."

Sneferu said: "I will give you another; let us go on."

The girl pouted and made answer: "I would rather have my own green jewel again than any other."

His Majesty said to the chief scribe: "I am given great enjoyment by this novelty; indeed my mind is much refreshed as the girls row me up and down the lake. Now one of them has lost her green jewel, which has dropped into the water, and she wants it back again and will not have another to replace it."

The chief scribe at once muttered a spell. Then by reason of his magic words the waters of the lake were divided like a lane. He went down and found the green jewel which the girl had lost, and came back with it to her. When he did that, he again uttered words of power, and the waters came together as they were before.

The king was well pleased, and when he had full enjoyment with the rowing upon the lake he returned to the palace. He gave gifts to the chief scribe, and everyone wondered at the marvel which he had accomplished.

Such was Khafra's tale of the green jewel, and King Khufu commanded that offerings should be laid in the tombs of Sneferu and his chief scribe, who was a great magician.

Next Prince Hordadef stood before the king, and he said: "Your Majesty has heard tales regarding the wonders performed by magicians in other days, but I can bring forth a worker of marvels who now lives in the kingdom."

King Khufu said: "And who is he, my son?"

"His name is Dedi," answered Prince Hordadef. "He is a very old man, for his years are a hundred and ten.   Each day he eats a joint of beef and five hundred loaves of bread, and drinks a hundred jugs of beer. He can smite off the head of a living creature and restore it again; he can make a lion follow him; and he knows the secrets of the habitation of the god Thoth, which Your Majesty has desired to know so that you may design the chambers of your pyramid."

King Khufu said: "Go now and find this man for me, Hordadef."

The prince went down to the Nile, boarded a boat, and sailed southward until he reached the town called Dedsnefru, where Dedi had his dwelling.   He went ashore, and was carried in his chair of state towards the magician, who was found lying at his door.   When Dedi was awakened, the king's son saluted him and bade him not to rise up because of his years.   The prince said: "My royal father desires to honour you, and will provide for you a tomb among your people."

Dedi blessed the prince and the king with thankfulness, and he said to Hordadef: "Greatness be thine; may your *Ka* have victory over the powers of evil, and may your *Khu* follow the path which leads to Paradise."

Hordadef assisted Dedi to rise up, and took his arm to help him towards the ship.   He sailed away with the prince, and in another ship were his assistants and his magic books.

"Health and strength and plenty be thine," said Hordadef, when he again stood before his royal father King Khufu.   "I have come down stream with Dedi, the great magician."

His Majesty was well pleased, and said: "Let the man be brought into my presence."

Dedi came and saluted the king, who said: "Why have I not seen you before?"

"He that is called cometh," answered the old man; "you have sent for me and I am here."

"It is told," King Khufu said, "that you can restore the head that is taken from a live creature." [1]

"I can indeed, Your Majesty," answered Dedi.

The king said: "Then let a prisoner be brought forth and decapitated."

"I would rather it were not a man," said Dedi; "I do not deal even with cattle in such a manner."

A duck was brought forth and its head was cut off, and the head was thrown to the right and the body to the left. Dedi spoke magic words. Then the head and the body came together, and the duck rose up and quacked loudly. The same was done with a goose.

King Khufu then caused a cow to be brought in, and its head was cut off. Dedi restored the animal to life again, and caused it to follow him.

His Majesty then spoke to the magician and said: "It is told that you possess the secrets of the dwelling of the god Thoth."

Dedi answered: "I do not possess them, but I know where they are concealed, and that is within a temple chamber at Heliopolis. There the plans are kept in a box, but it is no insignificant person who shall bring them to Your Majesty."

"I would fain know who will deliver them unto me," King Khufu said.

Dedi prophesied that three sons would be born to Rud-dedit, wife of the chief priest of Ra. The eldest would become chief priest at Heliopolis and would

---

[1] This trick is still performed by Egyptian conjurors.

possess the plans.   He and his brothers would one day
sit upon the throne and rule over all the land.

King Khufu's heart was filled with gloom and alarm
when he heard the prophetic words of the great magician.

Dedi then said: "What are your thoughts, O King?
Behold your son will reign after you, and then his son.
But next one of these children will follow."

King Khufu was silent.   Then he spoke and asked:
"When shall these children be born?"

Dedi informed His Majesty, who said: "I will visit
the temple of Ra at that time."

Dedi was honoured by His Majesty, and thereafter-
wards dwelt in the house of the Prince Hordadef.   He
was given daily for his portion an ox, a thousand loaves
of bread, a hundred jugs of beer, and a hundred bunches
of onions.

The day came when the sons of the woman Rud-
dedit were to be born.   Then the high priest of Ra, her
husband, prayed unto the goddess Isis and her sister
Nepthys; to Meskhent, goddess of birth; and to the
frog goddess Hekt; and to the creator god Khnûmû, who
gives the breath of life.   These he entreated to have care
of the three babes who were to become three kings of
Egypt, one after the other.

The deities heard him.   Then came the goddesses
as dancing girls, who went about the land, and the god
Khnûmû followed them as their burden bearer.   When
they reached the door of the high priest's dwelling they
danced before him.   He entreated them to enter, and
they did according to his desire, and shut themselves in
the room with the woman Rud-dedit.

Isis called the first child who was born Userkaf,
and said: "Let no evil be done by him".   The goddess
Meskhent prophesied that he would become King of

Egypt. Khnûmû, the creator god, gave the child strength.

The second babe was named Sahura by the goddess Isis. Meskhent prophesied that he also would become a king. Khnûmû gave him his strength.

The third was called Kaka. Meskhent said: "He shall also be a king", and Khnûmû gave him strength.

Ere the dancing girls took their departure the high priest gave a measure of barley to their burden bearer, and Khnûmû carried it away upon his shoulders.

They all went upon their way, and Isis said: "Now let us work a wonder on behalf of these children, so that their father may know who hath sent us unto his house.

Royal crowns were fashioned and concealed in the measure of barley which had been given them. Then the deities caused a great storm to arise, and in the midst of it they returned to the dwelling of the high priest, and they put the barley in a cellar, and sealed it, saying they would return again and take it away.

It came to pass that after fourteen days Rud-dedit bade her servant to bring barley from the cellar so that beer might be made.

The girl said: "There is none left save the measure which was given unto the dancing girls."

"Bring that then," said Rud-dedit, "and when the dancing girls return I will give them its value."

When the servant entered the cellar she heard the low sounds of sweet music and dancing and song. She went and told her mistress of this wonder, and Rud-dedit entered the cellar, and at first could not discover whence the mysterious sounds issued forth. At length she placed her ear against the sack which contained the barley given to the dancing girls, and found that the music was within it. She at once placed the sack in a chest and locked it, and then told her husband, and they rejoiced together.

Now it happened that one day Rud-dedit was angry with her servant, and smote her heavily. The girl vowed that she would be avenged and said: "Her three children will become kings. . . . I will inform King Khufu of this matter."

So the servant went away and visited her uncle, who was her mother's eldest brother. Unto him she told all that had happened and all she knew regarding the children of her mistress.

He was angry with her and spoke, saying: "Why come to me with this secret? I cannot consent to make it known as you desire."

Then he struck the girl, who went afterwards to draw water from the Nile. On the bank a crocodile seized her, and she was devoured.

The man then went towards the dwelling of Rud-dedit and he found her mourning with her head upon her knees. He spoke, saying: "Why is your heart full of gloom?"

Rud-dedit answered him: "Because my servant girl went away to reveal my secret."

The man bowed and said: "Behold! she came unto me and told me all things. But I struck her, and she went towards the river and was seized by a crocodile."[1]

So was the danger averted. Nor did King Khufu ever discover the babes regarding whom Dedi had prophesied. In time they sat upon the throne of Egypt.

A folk tale regarding the king who reigned in Egypt

---

[1] The manuscript, which is part of the "Westcar Papyrus", ends here. It was purchased in Egypt by a Miss Westcar, and is now preserved in the Berlin museum. The beginning and end had been torn off. The children referred to became the first three kings of the Fifth Dynasty, which marks the political ascendancy of the Ra cult.

before Khufu was related by a priest to Herodotus, the Greek historian.

The monarch was called Rhampsinitus. He built the western portion of the temple of Ptah. He also erected two statues—one to Summer, which faced the north, and was worshipped; and the other to Winter, which faced the south, but was never honoured. The king possessed great wealth, and he caused to be constructed beside the palace a strong stone chamber in which he kept his riches. One of the builders, however, contrived to place a stone in such a manner that it could be removed from the outside.

It chanced that, after the king had deposited his treasure in the chamber, this builder was stricken with illness and knew his end was nigh. He had two sons, and he told them his secret regarding the stone, and gave them the measurements, so that they might locate it.

After the man died the sons went forth in the darkness of night, and when they found the stone they removed it. Then they entered the chamber, and carried away much treasure, and ere they departed they closed up the wall again.

The king marvelled greatly when he discovered that his riches had been plundered, for the seals of the door were unbroken, and he knew not whom to suspect. Again and again the robbers returned, and the treasure diminished greatly. At length the king caused traps to be laid in the chamber, for his guards, who kept watch at the entrances, were unable to prevent the mysterious robberies.

Soon after the brothers returned. They removed the stone, and one of them entered stealthily. He went towards the treasure, as was his custom, but was suddenly caught in a trap. In a moment he realized that escape was impossible, and he reflected that he would be put to death on the morrow, while his brother would be seized and similarly punished. So he said to himself: "I alone will die."

When he had thus resolved to save his brother, he called to him softly in the darkness, bidding him to enter cautiously. He made known his great misfortune, and said: "I cannot escape, nor dare you tarry long lest you be discovered. When they find me here I will be recognized, and they will seize you and put you to death. Cut off my head at once, so that they may not know who I am, and thus save your own life."

With a sad heart the brother did as he was desired, and carried away the head. Ere he escaped in the darkness he replaced the stone, and no man saw him.

When morning came the king was more astounded than ever to find a headless body entrapped in the treasure chamber, for the door had not been opened, and yet two men had entered and one had escaped. He commanded that the corpse should be hung on the palace wall, and stationed guards at the place, bidding them to keep strict watch, so that they might discover if anyone came to sorrow for the dead man. But no one came nigh.

Meanwhile the mother grieved in secret. Her heart was filled with anger because the body was exposed in such a manner, and she threatened to inform the king regarding all that had happened if her other son would not contrive to carry away the corpse. The young man attempted to dissuade her, but she only repeated her threat, and that firmly. He therefore made preparations to obtain possession of the corpse.

He hired several asses, and on their backs he put many skins of wine. In the evening he drove them towards the palace. When he drew near to the guards who kept watch over his brother's body he removed the stoppers of some of the skins. The wine ran forth upon the highway, and he began to lament aloud, and beat his head as if he were in sore distress. The soldiers ran towards the asses and seized them, and caught the wine in vessels, claiming it for themselves. At first the brother pretended to be angry, and abused the men; but when they had pacified him, as they thought, he spoke to them pleasantly and began to make secure the stoppers of all the skins.

In a short time he was chatting with the guards, and pretended to be much amused when they bantered him over the accident. Then he invited them to drink, and they filled their flasks readily. So they began, and the young man poured out wine until they were all made very drunk. When they fell asleep, the cunning fellow took down his brother's body, and laid it upon the back of one of the asses. Ere he went away he shaved the right cheeks of the soldiers. His mother welcomed him on his return in the darkness and was well pleased.

The king was very angry when he discovered how the robber had tricked the guards, but he was still determined to have him taken. He sent forth his daughter in disguise, and she waited for the criminal. She spoke to several men, and at length she found him, because he came to know that he was sought and desired to deal cunningly with her. So he addressed her, and she offered to be his bride if he would tell her the most artful thing and also the most wicked thing he had ever done.

He answered readily: "The most wicked thing I ever did was to cut off my brother's head when he was caught in a trap in the royal treasure chamber, and the most artful was to deceive the king's guards and carry away the body."

The princess tried to seize him, but he thrust forth his brother's arm, which he carried under his robe, and when she clutched it he made speedy escape.

Great was then the astonishment of the king at the cunning and daring of the robber. He caused a proclamation to be made, offering him a free pardon and a generous reward if he would appear at the palace before him. The man went readily, and His Majesty was so delighted with his speeches and great ingenuity that he gave him his daughter in marriage. There is no more artful people than the Egyptians, but this man had not his equal in the land.

It was told that this same king journeyed to the land of Death, where he played dice with the goddess Isis[1] and now won and now lost. She gave to him a napkin embroidered with gold, and on his return a great festival was held, and it was repeated every year thereafter. On such occasions it was customary to blindfold a priest and lead him to the temple of Isis, where he was left alone. It was believed that two wolves met him and conducted him back to the spot where he was found. The Egyptians esteemed Isis and Osiris[2] as the greatest deities of the underworld.

[1] Herodotus gives Demeter (Ceres).
[2] Ceres and Bacchus.

CHAPTER XII

Triumph of the Sun God

Rival Cults—Ptah as a Giant—His Mountain "Seat"—Paradise of Osiris—Paradise of Sun Worshippers—Ideas of Hades—The Devil Serpent—The Great Worm of the Bible—The Nine Gods of Heliopolis—Stone and Sun Worship—The Horus Cult—Various Conceptions of the God—Union with other Deities—Legend of the Winged Disk—Ra's Enemies slain—Set as the "Roaring Serpent"—Sun Worshippers as Kings—Ptah Worshippers as Grand Viziers—Unas the Eater of Gods—The Egyptian Orion.

THE rise of the sun god had both theological and political significance. Ra was elevated as the Great Father of a group of cosmic and human deities, and his high priest, who was evidently of royal descent, sat upon the throne of united Egypt. The folk tale about the prophecy of Dedi and the birth of three children who were to become kings appears to have been invented in later times to give divine origin to the revolution which abruptly terminated the succession of Khufu's descendants.

An interesting contrast is afforded by the two great rival religions of this period of transition. While the theology of Heliopolis was based upon sun worship, that of Memphis was based upon earth worship. Ptah, the creation elf of the latter city, had been united with Tanen (or Tatûnen), the earth giant,[1] who resembles Seb. The dwarfish deity then assumed gigantic proportions, and became a "world god" or Great Father. A hymn addressed to Ptah Tanen declares that his head is in

---

[1] The lion Aker was another earth god.

155

the heavens while his feet are on the earth or in Duat, the underworld. "The wind", declared the priestly poet, "issues from thy nostrils and the waters from thy mouth. Upon thy back grows the grain. The sun and the moon are thine eyes. When thou dost sleep it is dark, and when thou dost open thine eyes it is bright again."

Ptah Tanen was lauded as "a perfect god" who came forth "perfect in all his parts". At the beginning he was all alone. He built up his body and shaped his limbs ere the sky was fashioned and the world was set in order, and ere the waters issued forth. Unlike Ra, he did not rise from the primordial deep. "Thou didst discover thyself", sang the Memphite poet, "in the circumstance of one who made for himself a seat and shaped the Two Lands" (Upper and Lower Egypt). The suggestion is that, therefore, of a mountain giant with his 'seat' or 'chair' upon some lofty peak, an idea which only a hill folk could have imported.

"No father begot thee and no mother gave thee birth," the poet declared; "thou didst fashion thyself without the aid of any other being."

The further union of Ptah with Osiris is reflected in the conception of a material Paradise, where the souls of the dead were employed in much the same manner as the workers in Egypt. Ethical beliefs pervaded this religious system, as we have seen; men were judged after death; their future happiness was the reward of right conduct and good living. Thus we find men declaring in tomb inscriptions:

"I have constructed this tomb by honest means. I have never stolen from another. . . . I have never seized by force what belonged to another. . . . I was never scourged before an official (for law breaking) since I was born. My conduct was admired by all men. . . . I gave food to those who hungered, and those who were destitute I did clothe. . . . No man ever cried out to the god complaining against me as an oppressor."

Men died believing that Osiris would justify their actions. "I shall live like Osiris. He perished not when he died, neither shall I perish when I die."

These professions continued to be recorded after the rise of the sun god. The new religion was embraced mainly by the royal and aristocratic families and the Asiatic element in the population. It was infused by magical rather than ethical beliefs; a man's future happiness depended wholly on his knowledge of magical formula and his devotion to religious rites.

The Paradise of the sun worshippers was of more spiritual character than that believed in by the cult of Ptah-Osiris. Their great hope was to find a place in the sun bark of Ra. The chosen among the dead became shining spirits, who accompanied their god on his safe journey through the perils of darkness, and they partook of his celestial food and shared his celestial drink; they became one with Ra, and yet did not suffer loss of identity.

It was taught by the priests of Heliopolis that after death the souls of mankind travelled towards the west and entered the first hour-division of the dark underworld Duat. There, in Amenti, "the hidden region", they awaited the coming of the bark of Ra. Those who could repeat the necessary magical "passwords" were permitted to enter, and they journeyed onward in the brightness diffused by the god until they reached the eastern horizon at dawn. Then they ascended the heavens and passed through happy fields. They could even visit old friends and old haunts upon earth, but they had to return to the sun bark in the evening, because evil spirits would devour them in the darkness. So they sailed each night through the underworld. They lived in eternal light.

Less fortunate souls resided in the various hour-divisions of Duat. Some were left in the first; others were allowed to enter the sun bark until they reached the particular divisions to which the power of their magical formulæ extended. These remained in darkness, faintly lit up by the fire which serpents spat out and the flames of the torture pools, except for one of the four-and-twenty hours, when the sun bark appeared. Then they enjoyed the blessings of sunlight and the special benefits conferred by Ra. Assembling on the river banks they adored the passing deity, and when he departed their voices were raised in lamentation. They enjoyed the privilege of having food supplied without labour.

The supernatural enemies of Ra were slain nightly by spears, which were sun rays, and knives, which were flames of fire, as well as by powerful magic spells. When the god passed on, all the demons came to life again. Ra's human enemies were those apparently who had not worshipped him upon earth. Such were consigned to torture in lakes of everlasting fire. Later Egyptian beliefs retained the memory of this ancient conception. The Copts peopled hell with demons who had the heads of serpents, crocodiles, lions, and even bears. After death these "avengers" seized the doomed man and wrenched the soul from the body with much violence. Then they stabbed and hacked it with knives, and thrust goads into its sides, and carried it to a river of fire and plunged it in. Afterwards the tortured soul was cast into outer darkness, where it gnashed its teeth in the bitter cold. It might also be consigned to a place of horror which swarmed with poisonous reptiles. But although it could be wounded and hacked to pieces it did not perish. In time the soul passed to the first hour-division of Duat.

Egypt swarmed with serpents in early times, and they were greatly dreaded by the people. Even Ra feared them. He was bitten by the serpent which Isis created, and when he left the earth and ascended to heaven, after reigning over men, he spoke of them as his enemies, and provided magical spells so that they might be overcome. Serpent charmers have not yet disappeared in the land of Egypt. They had great repute in ancient days. Symbolic reference is made to their powers in the Bible. "Their poison", declared the Psalmist, "is like the poison of a serpent; they are like the deaf adder that stopped her ear, which will not hearken to the voice of charmers" (*Psalm* lviii, 4–5). In *Jeremiah*, viii, 17, we read: "I will send serpents, cockatrices, among you which will not be charmed, and they shall bite you"; and in *Ecclesiastes*, x, 11: "Surely the serpent will bite without enchantment". Those who have watched the genuine serpent charmers at work in Egypt have testified to the efficacy of their wonderful powers.[1]

In ancient Egypt serpents were believed, especially by the sun worshippers, to be incarnations of evil spirits.[2] Darkness, the enemy of light, was symbolized as the Apep serpent, which is also referred to as the Great Worm. It rose up each night in the realms of Duat to destroy the sun bark and devour Ra. Occasionally it issued forth in daylight, and appeared in darkening thunder clouds, when a dread battle was waged and lightning spears were hurled against it. At dreaded eclipse it seemed to achieve temporary triumph. In this respect the Apep serpent resembled the Chinese dragon.

[1] See Lane's *Manners and Customs of the Modern Egyptians* (Chapters xi and xx).
[2] See Chapter V.

When Ra was in peril the priests chanted powerful spells to assist him, and the people assembled and shouted together to scare away the monster of darkness and evil. The ordinary ritual of the sun worshippers provided magical formulæ which were recited to render service to the god at regular intervals. Written spells were also considered to be efficacious, and these were inscribed with green ink upon new papyrus, which was burned. Belief in sympathetic magic is reflected in the ceremony of making and destroying a green wax figure of the great serpent. At midnight, when Ra began his return journey, and the power of evil was strongest, the wax figure was placed in a fire and spat upon. As it melted, the pious worshippers of the sun god believed that the Apep serpent suffered loss of power. The ashes of the figure and of the papyrus were afterwards mixed with filth and committed to the flames a second time. It was also customary to make wax models of the serpent fiends which assisted Apep, and they were given the heads of black and white cats, crocodiles, and ducks.[1] Stone knives were stuck in their backs, and they were thrown in the dust and kicked with the left foot.[2]

Symbolic references are also made in the Bible to the great Egyptian serpent. In *Isaiah*, lxvi, 24, we read: "Their worm shall not die, neither shall their fire be quenched, and they shall be an abhorring to all flesh"; and also: "The worm shall eat them like wool" (li, 8). In Coptic literature the Apep serpent is a monster which lies in outer darkness encircling the world and clutching its tail between its jaws, like the Midgard serpent of

[1] The duck-headed serpent recalls the fire drake of the Beowulf poem. Giants with cats' heads and dogs' heads are found in Celtic folklore.

[2] King James in his *Dæmonology* (Book II, Chap. v) says: "The devil teacheth how to make pictures of wax or clay, that by roasting thereof, the persons that they bear the name of may be continually melted or dried away by continual sickness."

Norse mythology. From its mouth issues forth " All ice,[1] dust, cold, disease, and sickness " (*Pistis Sophia*).

The idea that the sun was an incarnation of the Creator was imported from Asia, but the conception of Duat, with its lakes of fire, is of Egyptian origin. In the Babylonian Hades, to which Istar descended, eternal darknesss prevailed, and doomed souls partook of filthy food and drank unclean waters; they were not tortured by flames, but by pestilent odours and by diseases.[2]

Ra theology developed upon Egyptian lines, and was fused with pre-existing local beliefs. The sun bark, which was called " Bark of Millions of Years ", sailed upon an underworld Nile by night and a celestial Nile by day, and the seasonal changes of its course over the heavens were accounted for by the celestial inundation. Ra occupied the Maadit bark in the forenoon, and the Sekti bark in the afternoon. The change was effected at noon, when special magical formulæ were chanted.[3]

As the theology of the sun worshippers developed at Heliopolis, other gods, which were imported or had their origin in Egypt, were included in the divine family. The number three and its multiple had evidently magical significance. Ra, Khepera, and Tum formed the sun triad. The sun god and his children and descendants: Nut, the heavens, Shu, the air, Seb, the earth, with the lioness-headed Tefnut, " the spitter ", Osiris, the deified king and corn spirit, Isis, the Delta " Great Mother ",

---

[1] In the Reign of Rameses II, Khattusil, the Hittite king, visited Egypt. An inscription at Abu Simbel expresses the hope that on his journey homeward he will not be delayed by snow and ice on the mountains. Isaiah makes symbolic reference to the serpent: " In that day the Lord with his sore and great and strong sword shall punish leviathan the piercing (or stiff) serpent, even leviathan that crooked serpent; and he shall slay the dragon that is in the sea" (*Isaiah*, xxvii, 1).

[2] As in the Nifel-hel of Teutonic mythology.

[3] The Mohammedan noonday prayer is probably a survival of the sun worshippers' custom.

and her sister Nepthys, and the Semitic Set, formed the
Ennead of Heliopolis.   The group of Nine Gods varied
at different periods.   In one Horus displaces Set, and
in another Osiris is absent and his place is occupied by
Khepera, the beetle god.   The inclusion of Horus probably marks the union of the Horite creed with that of
Ra.   Attempts were frequently made by kings and priests
to absorb the Osirian cult at Heliopolis, but they were
never successful.   A compromise was evidently effected
in time, for in Duat a "division" was allocated to Osiris,
and there he judged his followers.   Ultimately the two
ideas of Paradise were confused rather than fused, and in
the end the earlier faith achieved the victory after centuries of repression.   We have already noted that Ptah
was rigidly excluded from the Ennead of the sun worshippers.

Archaic religious beliefs also received recognition at
Heliopolis.   The priests of the sun were evidently
prepared to recognize any god so long as Ra was acknowledged as the Great Father.   They not only tolerated but
perpetuated the worship of trees and wells, and of stones
and sacred mounds.   Reverence is still shown for the
well in which Ra was wont to wash his face daily, and
it is called by the Arabs "the spring of the sun".   A
sycamore near it is also regarded with veneration.   Sacrifices were offered up on a holy sand mound, and the
custom prevailed at funeral services in tombs of setting
up the mummy case in erect position on a heap of sand.
One of the spirits[1] of the sun god was believed to in-
habit a great block of stone.   Indeed On, the Egyptian
name of the sacred "city of the sun", signifies "stone
pillar".   In the Fifth Dynasty the Ra kings erected

---

[1] Gods and Pharaohs had several Kas. Ra had fourteen, and he had also seven
Bas (souls).

roofless temples in which there towered great broad obelisks surmounting mastaba-like square platforms. One of these stone idols at Abusir measured 138 feet at the base, and was 111 feet high. Outside the temple was a brick sun bark over 90 feet in length.

This form of temple was discontinued after the Sixth Dynasty, when the political power of the Ra priests was undermined. The tradition of stone worship survived, however, in the custom of erecting in front of temples those shapely obelisks similar to the familiar "Cleopatra's needle" on the Thames Embankment. One still remains erect at Matarieh (Heliopolis) to mark the site of a vanished temple. It bears the name of King Senusert I of the Twelfth Dynasty.

The religion of the Horite sun worshippers, which was introduced by the Dynastic Egyptians who pressed northwards and conquered the whole land, appears to have differed from that of the Ra cult. It is not possible now to distinguish the original form of the tribal god, or to discover what particular religious rites were associated with him. There are several forms of Horus. The most familiar is the hawk, which symbolized the spirit of the sun. It protected the early kings, who were "the priests or descendants of Horus"—a royal title which continued ever afterwards in use. Like the Ra cult, the cult of Horus absorbed Egyptian beliefs, and the conception of the hawk god varied accordingly in different districts.

The two outstanding Horuses are the elder and the younger—the Horus who was the brother of Osiris and the Horus child who was the son of Osiris and Isis.

Horus of Letopolis, near Memphis, was a hawk-headed man and the son of Hathor, the sky goddess. In Upper Egypt he was similarly represented, or simply as a hawk. At Edfu in particular he has the attributes of a sky god, and at Shedenu, a city in Lower Egypt, he was "Horus of the Two Eyes", the sun being one and the moon another, thus resembling the conception of Ptah Tanen. He was also Harmachis, "Horus of the Two Horizons", and in this character became one of the chief forms of Ra. As the "golden Horus" he was a dawn god, and in this character received the dead in the Judgment Hall of Osiris. The planet Saturn was "Horus the Bull", Mars was "Red Horus", and Jupiter "Horus, revealer of secrets". At Letopolis a temple was erected to "Horus of Not Seeing". In this form he is supposed to have represented the sun at solar eclipse, but he may have simply represented the firmament at night. It is possible that Hathor, as the chaos cow, was originally the Great Mother, and that the sky, sun, moon, and stars were the various forms assumed by her son Horus, or her various Horus sons.

When the child Horus became the son of Isis there may have been simply a change of mother. Isis and Hathor are similar conceptions, indeed the deities were ultimately confused. Both also resemble Nut as Great Mothers, but Nut represented Mother Heaven and Isis Mother Earth, while Hathor was the World Cow, representing fertility in that form. Nut was also represented as a cat. In her human form she gave birth to the sun daily, and the moon every month, and in another conception the sun and moon were her eyes. Ere Ra became the "Great Father" he was born of Nut.

The tribal aspect of the Osiris, Isis, and Horus myth is dealt with in a previous chapter. There is abundant evidence in Egyptian mythology that the union of deities signified the union of the tribes which worshipped them. The multiplicity of deities was due to the fact that an original conception remained in its old tribal form, and was perpetuated alongside the new conception. Two gods might be fused into one, but Egypt retained not only the new deity, but the two old deities as well, and thus instead of one god we have three. We need not be surprised, therefore, to find more than one Horus. The name alone may survive in some cases, for the process of blending varied in districts and at various periods. Egyptian religion is made up of many forms of faith.

Horus was united with Ra as Harmachis, and the sun god of Heliopolis became Ra Harmachis. The hawk god was thus symbolized as the winged sun disk. The legend which was invented to account for the change may here be summarized.

When Ra reigned as king over Egypt he sailed up the Nile towards Nubia, because his enemies were plotting against him. At Edfu Horus entered the bark of the great god and hailed him as father. Ra greeted the hawk god and entreated him to slay the rebels of Nubia. Then Horus flew up to the sun as a great winged disk, and he was afterwards called "the great god, the lord of the sky". He perceived the enemies of Ra, and went against them as a winged disk. Their eyes were blinded by his brightness, and their ears were made deaf, and in the confusion they slew one another. Not a single conspirator remained alive.

Horus returned to the bark of Ra, and from that day he became Horus, god of Edfu, in the form of a winged sun disk. Ka embraced him and said: "Thou hast made the water wine-red with blood, and my heart is glad."

Ra afterwards visited the battlefield, and, when he saw the dead bodies of his foes, he said: "Life is pleasant." The name of the place thus became Horbehûdti, which means "Pleasant Life".

The slain men were covered by water (at inundation) and became crocodiles and hippopotami. Then they attacked Horus as he sailed past; but his servants slew them with iron lances. Thoth rejoiced with glad heart when he beheld the enemies of Ra lying dead.

The legend continues in this strain, and relates that Horus pursued the enemies of the god Ra downstream. Apparently Egypt was full of them. We then learn that they were the followers of Set, who was driven towards the frontier. He was afterwards taken prisoner, and with manacled hands and a spear stuck in his neck he was brought before Ra. Then we find that there are two Horuses. The elder Horus is commanded by the sun god to deliver Set to Horus, son of Isis. The younger Horus cuts off the head of Set, and the slayer of Osiris becomes a roaring serpent which seeks refuge in a hole and is commanded to remain there.

Osiris is not mentioned in the legend, and Ra refers to the younger Horus as his own son. Apparently the theorists of Heliopolis desired Ra to supplant Osiris. Place names are played upon so that their origin may be ascribed to something said by the sun god, and grammatical construction is occasionally ignored with this end in view.

Horus worship never became popular in Egypt. It was absorbed by the various cults, so that, as we have indicated, its original form is confused. The religion of the sun cult at Heliopolis, which was imported by the Asiatic settlers, was the religion which received prominence at the beginning of the Fifth Dynasty. A new title was given to the Pharaoh. He became the "Son of the Sun" as well as "Priest of Horus", "Priest of Set", "lord of the north and south", &c.

The rise of the sun god involved far-reaching political

issues.   Although the high priest of Ra sat upon the throne, he did not become a tyrannical dictator like a Fourth-Dynasty king.   A compromise had to be effected with the powerful faction at Memphis, and the high priest of Ptah became the vizier, a post previously held by the Pharaoh's chosen successor.   Nome governors were also given extended powers as administrators, as a reward probably for the share they had taken in the revolution, or at any rate to conciliate them and secure their allegiance.   This decentralizing process weakened the ruling power, but Egypt appears to have prospered as a whole, and the peaceful conditions which prevailed imparted activity to its intellectual life, as we shall see. Small and roughly constructed pyramid tombs were erected by the monarchs, who could no longer command an unlimited supply of labour.

The Fifth Dynasty lasted for about a century and a quarter.   It began with Userkaf, the first babe mentioned in the Dedi folk tale, and he was succeeded in turn by the other two, who were not, however, his brothers.   The ninth and last king of the Dynasty was Unas.   In the so-called "Pyramid Texts", in his own tomb and that of Teta, the first king of the Sixth Dynasty, the monarch was deified as a star god, and has been identified with the constellation of Orion.   The conception is a remarkable one.   It smacks of absolute savagery, and we seem to be confronted with a symbolic revival of pre-Dynastic cannibalistic rites which are suggested, according to Maspero, by the gnawed and disconnected bones found in certain early graves.   At the original Sed festival the tribal king, as Professor Petrie suggests, appears to have been sacrificed and devoured, so that his people might derive from his flesh and blood the power and virtues which made him great.   The

practice was based on belief in contagious magic.   Bulls
and boars were eaten to give men strength and courage,
deer to give fleetness of foot, and serpents to give cunning.   The blood of wounded warriors was drunk so
that their skill and bravery might be imparted to the
drinkers.[1]   King Unas similarly feasts after death on
"the spirits" known at Heliopolis as "the fathers and
the mothers", and on the bodies of men and gods.   He
swallows their spirits, souls, and names, which are contained in their hearts, livers, and entrails, and consequently
becomes great and all-powerful.[2]   The resemblance to
the man-eating giants of Europe is very striking.

The rendering which follows of the remarkable Unas
hymn is fairly close.   It is cast in metrical form with
endeavour to reproduce the spirit of the original.

ORION[3] IN EGYPT

Now heaven rains, and trembles every star
With terror; bowmen scamper to escape;
And quakes old Aker, lion of the earth,
While all his worshippers betake to flight,
For Unas rises and in heaven appears
Like to a god who lived upon his sires
And on his mothers fed.

[1] In the *Nibelungenlied* the Burgundians drink the blood of fallen heroes and are
refreshed and strengthened.   See *Teutonic Myth and Legend.*

[2] Dr. Budge is of opinion that human beings were sacrificed to the sun god.   The
practice was "of vital importance".   Referring to the Ra obelisk in the early sun
temples, he says that "the size and number of conduits to carry away blood bears
evidence of the magnitude of the slaughterings" (*Osiris and the Egyptian Resurrection*
and *Gods of the Egyptians*).

[3] Osiris, in his fusion with Ra, is addressed as "thou first great sun god", and Isis
says: "There proceedeth from thee the strong Orion in heaven at evening, at the resting of every day."—*The Burden of Isis* ("Wisdom of the East" Series), trans. by Dennis,
p. 24.

Unas the lord
Of wisdom is; the secret of his Name
Not e'en his mother knows. . . . His rank is high
In heaven above; his power is like to Tum's,
His sire divine. . . . Greater than Tum is he.

His shadowy doubles follow him behind
As he comes forth.   The uræus on his brow
Uprears; the royal serpent guides him on;
He sees his Ba[1] a flame of living fire.

The strength of Unas shields him. . . He is now
The Bull of Heaven, doing as he wills,
Feeding on what gives life unto the gods—
Their food he eats who would their bellies fill
With words of power from the pools of flame.

Against the spirits shielded by his might,
Unas arises now to take his meal—
Men he devours; he feasts upon the gods
This lord who reckons offerings: he who makes
Each one to bow his forehead, bending low.

Amkenhuu is snarer; Herthertu
Hath bound them well; and Khonsu killer is
Who cuts the throats and tears the entrails out—
'Twas he whom Unas sent to drive them in . . .
Divided by Shesemu, now behold
The portions cooking in the fiery pots.

Unas is feasting on their secret Names;
Unas devours their spirits and their souls—
At morn he eats the largest, and at eve
The ones of middle girth, the small at night:
Old bodies are the faggots for his fire.

Lo! mighty Unas makes the flames to leap
With thighs of agèd ones, and into pots
Are legs of women flung that he may feast.

[1] Soul.

Unas, the Power, is the Power of Powers!
Unas, the mighty god, is god of gods!
Voraciously he feeds on what he finds,
And he is given protection more assured
Than all the mummies 'neath the western sky.

Unas is now the eldest over all—
Thousands he ate and hundreds he did burn;
He rules o'er Paradise. . . . Among the gods
His soul is rising up in highest heaven—
The Crown is he as the horizon lord.

He reckoned livers as he reckoned knots;
The hearts of gods he ate and they are his;
He swallowed up the White Crown and the Red,
And fat of entrails gulped; the secret Names
Are in his belly and he prospers well—
Lo! he devoured the mind of every god,
And so shall live for ever and endure
Eternally, to do as he desires.

The souls of gods are now in his great soul;
Their spirits in his spirit; he obtains
Food in abundance greater than the gods—
His fire has seized their bones, and lo! their souls
Are Unas's; their shades are with their forms.

Unas ascends. . . . Unas ascends with these—
Unas is hidden, is hidden[1]. . . . An One
For him hath ploughed. . . . The seat of every heart
Is Unas's among all living men.

---

[1] " Hail, thou hidden god, Osiris in the underworld."—*The Burden of Isis*, p. 54.

CHAPTER XIII

Fall of the Old Kingdom

Nobles become Little Pharaohs—The Growth of Culture—Temple Building—Maxims of Ptah-hotep—Homely Superstitions—Charms to protect Children—Fear of the Evil Eye—Set and Red-haired Babes—Gruesome Ghosts—Feudal Lords assert Themselves—A Strong Monarch—Military Expeditions—The Promotion of Uni—Coming of the Deng—A Queen's Vengeance—Revolt of Feudal Lords—Pyramids raided.

DURING the Fifth Dynasty the power of the nobles gradually increased until they became little Pharaohs in their own provinces. Even at the Court they could make their influence felt, and when they set out on expeditions their successes received personal acknowledgment and were not recorded to the credit of an overshadowing monarch. They recognized the official religion, but fostered the local religious cult, and in their tombs related the stories of their own lives, boasting of their achievements and asserting the ethical principles which justified them before Osiris. The age thus became articulate. Education was spreading, and the accumulation of wealth promoted culture. The historic spirit had birth, and the scribes began to record the events of the past and compile lists of kings. Among the tomb pictures of everyday life were inscribed fragments of folksong, and it is evident that music was cultivated, for we find groups of harpers and flautists and singers.

The religious energies of the Pharaohs were devoted

more to the building of temples than to the erection of tombs. Ra worship introduced elaborate ceremonials, and large numbers of priests were engaged at Heliopolis. At a later period we learn that over 12,000 persons were directly connected with the temples there. The Pharaohs continued to reside in the vicinity of Memphis, and the Court was maintained with great splendour; their tombs were erected at Abusir, farther south than those of the Khufu line of kings.

No wars of any consequence occurred during the Fifth Dynasty, but exploring expeditions were fitted out, and in the time of Sahura, the second monarch, the coast of Somaliland, which was called Punt, was visited, and there were large imports of gum and resins for incense in the temples, and of wood and precious metals.

The quarries in Sinai continued to be worked, and the name of Isôsi, the eighth monarch, is associated with the working of black granite at Wadi Hammamat. We know little or nothing regarding the personalities of the kings. They appear to have reigned with discretion and ability, for the age was one of political progress and extending culture.

In the reign of King Dedka Ra Isôsi—to give him his full name—that famous collection of maxims, "The Instruction of Ptah-hotep", was compiled. This production survives in the Prisse Papyrus, which was called after the French archæologist who purchased it from a native in 1847. The author was Isôsi's grand vizier, and he was evidently of Memphite birth and a Ptah worshipper, for his name signifies "Ptah is well pleased". He lived over a thousand years before Hammurabi, the wise king of Babylon, and long ages ere Solomon collected his Proverbs at Jerusalem.

The maxims of Ptah-hotep were for centuries copied

by boys in the schools of ancient Egypt. In their papyrus "copybooks" they were wont to inscribe the following phrases:—

> It is excellent for a son to obey his father.
> He that obeys shall become one who is obeyed.
> Carelessness to-day becomes disobedience to-morrow.
> He that is greedy for pleasure will have an empty stomach.
> A loose tongue causes strife.
> He that rouses strife will inherit sorrow.
> Good deeds are remembered after death.

The maxims afford us interesting glimpses of the life and culture of the times. Old Ptah-hotep is full of worldly wisdom, and his motto is: "Do your duty and you will be happy". He advises his son to acquire knowledge and to practise the virtues of right conduct and right living. His precepts are such as we would expect to find among a people who conceived of an Osirian Judgment Hall in the next world.

The "Instruction" is dedicated to King Isôsi. The vizier feels the burden of years, and laments his fate. He opens in this manner:

> O King, my lord, I draw nigh to life's end,
> To me the frailties of life have come
> And second childhood. . . . Ah! the old lie down
> Each day in suffering; the vision fails,
> Ears become deaf and strength declines apace,
> The mind is ill at ease. . . . An old man's tongue
> Has naught to say because his thoughts have fled,
> And he forgets the day that has gone past. . . .
> Meanwhile his body aches in every bone;
> The sweet seems bitter, for all taste is lost—
> Ah! such are the afflictions of old age,
> Which work for evil. . : . Fitful and weak
> His breath becomes, standing or lying down.

Ptah-hotep then proceeds to petition the king to be released of his duties, so that his son may succeed him. He desires to address to the young man the words of wisdom uttered by sages of old who listened when the gods spake to them.

His Majesty at once gives his consent, and expresses the hope that Ptah-hotep's son will hearken with understanding and become an example to princes. "Speak to him", adds the king, "without making him feel weary."

The "Instruction" is fairly long—over 4000 words—so that it was necessary to have it copied out. We select a few of the most representative maxims.

Do not be vain although you are well educated; speak to an illiterate man as you would to a wise one. After all, there is a limit to cleverness; no worker is perfect. Courteous speech is more uncommon than the emeralds which girl slaves find among the stones.

If you speak with an argumentative man who really knows more than you do yourself, listen respectfully to him, and do not lose your temper if he differs from you.

If, however, an argumentative man knows less than you do, correct him and show him that you are the wiser of the two; others will approve of you and give you an excellent reputation.

If a man of low rank argues without knowledge, be silent. Do not speak angrily to him. It is not very creditable to put such an one to shame.

When you become a leader, be courteous and see that your conduct is exemplary. . . . Do not tyrannize over men. . . . It is he who gives to those who are in need that prospers; not the man who makes others afraid. . . . Listen graciously to one who appeals to you. Let him speak frankly, and be ever ready to put an end to a grievance. If a man is not inclined to tell everything he knows, it is because he to whom he speaks has the reputation of not dealing fairly. A mind that is well controlled is always ready to consider. . . . See that your employees are adequately rewarded, as is proper on the part of one to whom the god has given much. It is well known that it is no easy thing to satisfy employees. One says to-day: " He is generous; I may get much ", and to-morrow: " He is a mean, exacting man ". There is never peace in a town where workers are in miserable circumstances.

That man is never happy who is always engaged reckoning his accounts, but the man whose chief concern is to amuse himself does not provide for his household. . . . If you become rich after having been poor, do not bind your heart with your wealth; because you are the administrator of what the god has given you. Remember that you are not the last, and that others will become as great as you. . . . Enjoy your life, and do not occupy the entire day at your work. Wealth is no use to a worn-out man.

Love your wife; feed her and clothe her well; make her happy; do not deal sternly with her; kindness makes her more obedient than harshness; if she yearns for something which pleasures her eye, see that she gets it. . . . Do not be jealous, or despondent, or cross if you have no children. Remember that a father has his own sorrows, and that a mother has more troubles than a childless woman. . . . How beautiful is the obedience of a faithful son. The god loves obedience; he hates disobedience. A father rejoices in a son's obedience and honours him. A son who hearkens to counsel guards his tongue and conducts himself well. A disobedient son is foolish and never prospers. He blunders continually. . . . In the end he is avoided because he is a failure. . . . A father should teach wisdom to his sons and daughters, so that they may be of good repute. When others find them faithful and just, they will say: " That father has trained them well ". . . . A good son is a treasure given by the god.

Ptah-hotep reminds his son that when he goes to dine with a great man he should take what is given to him. A nobleman gives the daintiest portions to those he likes best. He must not keep staring at his host, or speak until he is spoken to; then he should answer readily. . . . When he is sent with a message from one nobleman to another he should take care not to say anything which will cause strife between them. He should not repeat what a nobleman said when in a temper

"Let your heart be more generous than your speech," advises Ptah-hotep as he draws his "Instruction" to a close. He hopes that his son will prosper as well as he himself has prospered, and that he will satisfy the king by his actions. "I have lived", he adds, "for a hundred and ten years, and have received more honours from His Majesty than did any of my ancestors, because I have been just and honourable all through life."

Such was the ethical, but there was also a superstitious element in Egyptian domestic life. The people believed that the world swarmed with spirits which were continually desiring to inflict injuries upon living beings, and were abroad by day as well as by night. An amulet on which was depicted a human hand was considered to be efficacious, and the Egyptian mother suspended it from a cord which was put round the baby's neck. She tied a knot in the morning and another in the evening until there were seven knots in all. On each occasion she repeated a formula over a knot, which was to the following effect: "Isis has twisted the cord; Nepthys has smoothed it; and it will guard you, my bonnie bairn, and you will become strong and prosper. The gods and the goddesses will be good to you, and the evil ones will be thwarted, the mouths of those who utter spells against you will be closed. . . . I know all their names, and may those, whose names I know not, suffer also, and that quickly."[1]

Erman, the German Egyptologist, has translated an interesting papyrus by an unknown scribe, which contains the formulæ used to protect children. Some children were more liable to be attacked by evil spirits than

---

[1] The knotted cord was in general use throughout Europe. It is not yet uncommon in the Highlands of Scotland, where red neck cords protect children against the evil eye, while sprains, &c., are cured by knotted cords, a charm being repeated as each knot is tied.

others. In Europe pretty children require special protection against the evil eye. Red-haired youngsters were
disliked because the wicked god Set was red-haired, and
was likely to carry them away. Their mothers, therefore, had to exercise special care with them, and there was
a particular charm for their use. In Russia red-haired
people are believed to have more knowledge of magic
than others, and are disliked on that account.

The Egyptian ghosts, the enemies of the living, like
the archaic deities, were of repulsive aspect. They came
from tombs in mummy bandages with cheeks of decaying
flesh, flat noses, and eyes of horror, and entered a room
with averted faces,[1] which were suddenly turned on children, who at once died of fright. They killed sleeping
babes by sucking their breath[2] when they kissed, or
rather smelled, them, and if children were found crying
they rocked them to sleep—the sleep of death.

When an infant was being hushed to sleep the
Egyptian mother sang a ditty to scare away the ghosts
of dead men, and then made a protecting charm with
lettuce, garlic, tow, bones, and honey. The following
is a rendering of one of the old " sleepy songs ":—

> Oh, avaunt! ye ghosts of night,
>   Nor do my baby harm;
> Ye may come with steps so light,
>   But I 'll thwart you with my charm.

> For my babe you must not kiss,
>   Nor rock if she should cry—
> Oh! if you did aught amiss,
>   My own, my dear, would die.

---

[1] Like Turnface in the boat of the dead.

[2] Cats are credited in Europe with taking away life by sucking children's breath as
they lie asleep.

O ye dead men, come not near—
　Now I have made the charm—
There's lettuce to prick you here,
　Garlic with smell to harm;

There's tow to bind like a spell,
　The magic bones are spread;
There's honey the living love well—
　'T is poison to the dead.

According to tradition, the Sixth-Dynasty kings were not descendants of Mena. Teta, the first king, may have come to the throne as a result of a harem conspiracy. He was a Ra worshipper, and probably a powerful nobleman, supported by a well-organized military force, which held the balance of power. The kingdom was in a state of political unrest. In every nome the hereditary chieftains clamoured for concessions from the royal house, and occasionally their requests were couched in the form of demands. Pepi I, the third king of the line, who was a strong monarch, appears to have secured the stability of the throne by promoting a policy of military aggression which kept the ambitious nobles fully engaged on the northern and southern frontiers. Nubia was invaded with success, and expeditions visited the land of Punt.

The Egyptians had imagined that the edge of the world was somewhere a little beyond the first cataract, and that the intervening space was peopled by demigods, called "Manes". Now the horizon was considerably widened. The heavenly Nile was believed to descend in a cascade much farther south than had hitherto been supposed, and the region of mystery was located beyond the area occupied by the too-human and ever-aggressive Nubians.

Pepi selected capable officials of proved loyalty to hold

the noblemen in check and secure the equitable distribu
tion of water throughout the kingdom.   These were
liberally rewarded, and were privileged to erect elaborate
tombs, like the nome governors, and in these they had
their biographies inscribed.

On an Abydos tomb wall we have recorded the achievements of Uni, who rose from humble official rank to be
Pharaoh's intimate confidant and counsellor. He was, he
says, Pepi's "guardian of heart", and he "knew everything that happened and every secret affair".   Although
he was only "superintendent of irrigated lands", he
exercised more influence over the kingdom than any
other dignitary.   Royal journeys were arranged by him,
and at Court ceremonies he marshalled the nobles, which
was, no doubt, a delicate task.   The perils which continually beset the throne are indicated in his reference to
a harem conspiracy.   "When one visited the palace to
give secret information against the great royal wife Ametsi,
His Majesty selected me to enter the harem to listen to
business.   No scribe was called, nor any other except me
alone.   I was selected because of my probity and discretion.   I recorded everything."

He was only, he repeats, "superintendent of irrigated
lands".   It was the first occasion on which a man of his
rank had listened to harem secrets.   Uni tells us no
more.   We do not even know what fate befell the plotting queen.

When military campaigns were carried out, Uni was
placed in command of the army. He tells that there were
generals in it, mamelouks from Lower Egypt, friends of
the king, and princes from the north and south, besides
a host of officials of high rank.   But they had all to obey
the man who was only the superintendent of irrigated
lands.   Evidently the commissariat arrangements were of

a simple character. Each man carried his own supply of bread. The inhabitants of the towns they passed through had to supply the soldiers with beer and "small animals".

Several campaigns were successfully conducted by Uni, and on each occasion large numbers of the enemy were slain, while "fig trees were cut down and houses burned". So firmly was peace established in the south that Merenra, the next monarch, was able to visit the first cataract, where he received the homage of the nobles.

After Uni's death, the chief of a warlike tribe at Elephantine, who was a veritable Rob Roy, came into royal favour. He made several raids into Nubia, and brought back ivory and ebony and gold. On one occasion he returned with a pygmy or "Deng". It was a great triumph, for "Dengs" belonged to the land of the "Manes" (demigods), and were able to charm even the sulky ferryman who transported the dead over the river of Hades. King Merenra had just died, and his successor, Pepi II, a young man, was greatly excited over the coming of the "Deng". Orders were sent to guard the pygmy carefully; and those who slept beside him in the boat were changed ten times each night. The little fellow was welcomed like royalty at Memphis, and he delighted the Pharaoh with his strange antics, boisterous manners, and war dances. It was the desire of everyone who watched him to be transformed into a "Deng" after death, so that the ferryman of Hades might come to the bank at once to transport the waiting soul to the other side.

These military expeditions taught the Nubians to respect the power of Egypt, and they subsequently became subjects of the Pharaohs.

The Sixth Dynasty, however, was doomed. Conspiring nobles regarded one another with suspicion, and cast ambitious eyes upon the throne. Local religious cults also gathered strength, and the political influence exercised by the priests of Heliopolis suffered decline. For about three centuries Ra had remained supreme; now his power was being suppressed. Serious revolts occurred. Merenra II—the successor of Pepi II, who is credited with a reign of over ninety years—was deposed twelve months after he ascended the throne. According to Herodotus, who is supported in this connection by Manetho, his queen immediately seized the reins of power. The Egyptian priests informed the Greek historian that Merenra was murdered, and that the queen Nitocris avenged his death in the following manner. She caused a large subterranean hall to be made for the purpose of celebrating festivals, as she pretended, and invited a number of noblemen to visit it. As the conspirators sat feasting, the waters of the Nile flooded the artificial cave through a secretly constructed canal, and the guests were all drowned. Great indignation was aroused throughout the kingdom, and the queen committed suicide by suffocation in an apartment filled with the fumes of burning wood. The story appears to be more mythical than historical.

At the close of the Sixth Dynasty the kingdom was plunged in anarchy. The nobles attempted to establish a government in which they were to hold power in rotation. It was impossible for such an arrangement to succeed, because the interests of each feudal lord were centred in his own particular nome. The Seventh Dynasty was brief. According to tradition there were " seventy kings in seventy days ". Egypt was then divided into a number of small separated states, which were adminis-

trated by the hereditary owners of the soil, and we find
one of them declaring, significantly enough, in his tomb
inscription that he had "freed his city in a time of war
from the oppression of the king".

Thus came to an end the Old Kingdom, which had
existed for about 1700 years from the time of Mena.
A great civilization had evolved during that period. It
had grown rich in art and architecture. Indeed, the
artistic achievements of the Old Kingdom were never
afterwards surpassed either in technique or naturalism;
the grandeur of its architectural triumphs is emphasized
by the enduring Pyramids, and especially Khufu's great
tomb with its finely wrought stonework, which remains
unequalled to the present day.

The people, too, had prospered and made great progress. Refined and cultured faces appear in the surviving
statuary; indeed many of the men and women look much
like those of the present day. Agriculture flourished,
the industries developed, and commerce made the people
prosperous. Education appears to have been thorough
within its limits, and had gradually become more widespread.

Although the power of the monarchy declined, the
people as a whole did not lapse back into a state of semi-
savagery. The nomes were well governed by the nobles,
but a system of detached local administration was fore-
doomed to failure on account of the physical conditions
of the country. Egypt required then, as now, a strong
central government to promote the welfare of the entire
country. A noble might continue to cut canals, but there
was no guarantee that he would receive an equitable and
regular supply of water. In an irrigated country water
laws must be strictly observed, otherwise the many will
suffer because of the heedlessness or selfishness of the

few. When the power of the Pharaoh was shattered, the natural resources of Egypt declined, and a great proportion of the people were threatened with periodic famines.

The demands of the Court when at the height of its power may have seemed oppressive to the feudal lords. Pharaoh required a proportion of their crops and of their live stock, much free labour, and many fighting men, because he gave them water and protected them against the inroads of invaders. He had also private ambitions, and desired to erect a great tomb for himself. Yet he governed Egypt for the good of the greater number, and the conflicts between the Court and the feudal lords were really conflicts between national and local interests. The country as a whole suffered from the effects of extreme governmental decentralization—a policy inaugurated by priestly Pharaohs, who were, perhaps, too greatly concerned about promoting a national religion based upon sun worship.

The ascendancy of the nobles was impossible so long as the Pharaohs were, in a practical sense, the chief priests of each particular cult. Diplomatic rulers honoured local gods and attended to the erection and endowment of temples. They wedged themselves in between the hereditary chieftains and the priests who exercised so powerful an influence over the people. When, however, the nobles became the sole patrons of their nome cults, they were able to openly defy the Court.

So, when the throne tottered, a plague of anarchy fell upon Egypt, and the forces of reaction were let loose. Nome warred against nome, and the strong prevailed over the weak. Temples were ruthlessly pillaged, and tombs were raided by robber bands; the mummies of hated kings were torn from the Pyramids; statuary was shattered and inscriptions were destroyed.   Only in those provinces where good government was maintained did the old order of things remain.   But Egypt was so thoroughly disorganized as a whole that several centuries had to elapse before the central government could be once again firmly established in the interests of progress and the welfare of the great mass of the people.

Occasionally a strong Pharaoh arose to compel the rival lords to make truce one with another, but such successes were only temporary.   The feudal system was deeply rooted, and all a king could do was to organize a group of nobles to deal with those who threatened to grow too powerful.   He could not raise or maintain a standing army, for each lord commanded all the fighting men in his own nome, and they owed allegiance to him alone; nor could the Pharaoh employ mercenaries, because the resources of the royal treasury were strictly limited.

CHAPTER XIV

Father Gods and Mother Goddesses

An Obscure Period—Popularity of Osiris Worship—A Mythical Region
—The Lake of Fire—Her-shef, who resembles Ptah—Links with Khnûmû—A
Wind God and Earth God—Giants and Elves—The God of Mendes—The
Ram a Corn Spirit—Deities fused with Osiris—Feline Goddesses—Flying
Serpents—The Mother of Mendes—Abydos, the Egyptian Mecca—Foreign
Invaders—A Buffer State—North and South in Revolt.

WE have entered upon an obscure and disturbed period
which extends over an interval of about three hundred
years. The petty states of Egypt continued to wage spo-
radic wars of conquest one against another, and a prolonged struggle was in progress for supreme power. In
time the political units grew less numerous, and several
federated tribes were ruled over by powerful feudal lords.
The chief centres of government in Upper Egypt were
established at Thebes, Siut, and Heracleopolis. Memphis was for a time the capital of a group of allied nomes
in Middle Egypt, and at Sais in the north there was a
reigning family of whom we know nothing except from
casual references in later times. The eastern Delta lay
open to the invader, and it is believed that foreign settlements were effected there. Ultimately Egypt was divided
into two great states. The southern group of allies was
governed by the Theban power, and the northern by the
Heracleopolitan. Then history repeated itself, and the
kingdom was once again united by a conqueror who
pressed northward from Upper Egypt.

The Eighth-Dynasty kings claimed to be descended from those of the Sixth. But, although they reigned at Memphis, their control of the disordered kingdom was so slight that they were unable to erect any monuments. No royal inscriptions survive at the quarries. After a quarter of a century of weak Memphite rule, the powerful nome governor of Heracleopolis Magna seized the throne and established the Ninth Dynasty. The kings of the Tenth Dynasty are believed to have been also his descendants.

Manetho calls the new king Akhthoes, and his name in the hieroglyphs is usually rendered as Kheti. He is also known as Ab-meri-ra. Like Khufu, he was reputed in the traditions of later times to have been a great tyrant, who in the end went mad, and was devoured by a crocodile. He seems to have held in check for a period the ambitious feudal nobles whose rivalries so seriously retarded the agricultural prosperity of the kingdom. No doubt famines were common.

Each nome promoted its own theological system, and that of Heracleopolis Magna now assumes special interest because of its association with the monarchy. The political influence of the priests of Heliopolis had passed away, but the impress of their culture remained. Osiris worship continued to be popular on account of its close association with agriculture. A Horus temple had existed at Heracleopolis from early Dynastic times, but the identity of the god does not appear to have survived the theological changes of the intervening period.

Heracleopolis Magna, which the Egyptians called Khenen-su, is of special mythological interest. It came to be recognized as the scene of the great creation myth of the sun worshippers. There Ra, at the beginning, rose from the primeval deep in the form of the sun egg, or the lotus flower—

> He that openeth and he that closeth the door;
> He who said: " I am but One ".
> Ra, who was produced by himself;
> Whose various names make up the group of gods;
> He who is Yesterday (Osiris) and the Morrow (Ra).

Khenen-su district was the scene of the " war of the gods ", who contended against one another at Ra's command—a myth which suggests the everlasting struggle between the forces of nature, which began at Creation's dawn, and is ever controlled by the sun.   Somewhere in the nome were situated the two mythical lakes, " the lake of natron " and " the lake of truth ", in which Ra cleansed himself, and there, too, at the height of their great struggle—symbolized as the struggle between good and evil—Set flung filth in the face of Horus, and Horus mutilated Set. The ultimate victory was due to Ra, who, in the form of the Great Cat that haunted the Persea tree at Heliopolis, fought with the Apep serpent and overcame it.   " On that day ", according to *The Book of the Dead*, " the enemies of the inviolable god (Osiris) were slain."

In the vicinity of Khenen-su was the fiery region. At its entrance crouched the demon who had human skin and the head of a greyhound.   He was concealed by the door, and pounced unexpectedly upon " the damned "; he tore out their hearts, which he devoured, and he swallowed their spirits.   So the faithful sun worshippers were wont to pray :

O Ra-tum give me deliverance from the demon who devoureth those who are condemned—he who waits at the door of the fiery place and is not seen. . . . Save me from him who clutcheth souls, and eateth all filth and rottenness by day and by night. Those who dread him are helpless.

At Khenen-su lived the Phoenix[1]—the "Great Bennu". It resembled an eagle, and had feathers of red and golden colour. Some authorities identify this mythical bird with the planet Venus, which, as the morning star, was "the guide of the sun god".

The religion of Heracleopolis Magna was, no doubt, strongly tinged by the theology of the sun worshippers. It seems also to have been influenced by Memphite beliefs. The chief god was Her-shef, who bears a stronger resemblance to Ptah Tanen than to Horus. He was a self-created Great Father, whose head was in the heavens while his feet rested upon the earth. His right eye was the sun and his left the moon, while his soul was the light that he shed over the world. He breathed from his nostrils the north wind, which gave life to every living being.

"Wind" and "breath" and "spirit" were believed by many primitive peoples to be identical.[2] Her-shef was therefore the source of universal life. As a "wind god" he resembles the southern deity Khnûmû, who was also called Knef (the Kneph of the Greeks). The Egyptian *knef* means "wind", "breath", and "spirit"—"the air of life". In Hebrew *nephesh ruach*, and in Arabic *ruh* and *nefs* have similar significance.

Ptah Tanen, Khnûmû, and Her-shef, therefore, combined not only the attributes of the earth giant Seb, but also those of Shu, the wind god, whose lightness is symbolized by the ostrich feather, but who had such great strength that he was the "uplifter" of the heavens.

---

[1] At a later date it was located in Arabia.

[2] "Spirit" is derived from *spiro*, "I breathe". The Aryan root "an" also signifies "wind" and "spirit", and survives in words like "animal", "animate", &c.

Both Seb and Shu are referred to as self-created deities.

It has been suggested that the elfin Khnûmû, of whom Ptah was the chief, had a tribal origin, and were imported into Egypt. In European lore, dwarfs and giants are closely associated, and are at times indistinguishable. The fusion of the dwarf Ptah with the giant Tanen is thus a familiar process, and in the conception we may trace the intellectual life of a mountain people whose giants, or genii, according to present-day Arabian folk belief, dwell in the chain of world-encircling hills named "Kaf".

In what we call "Teutonic" lore, which has pronounced Asiatic elements, the giant is the "Great Father", and in what we call "Celtic", in which the Mediterranean influence predominates, the giantess is the "Great Mother". The Delta Mediterranean people had "Great Mother" goddesses like Isis, Neith, the virgin deity of Buto, and Bast. At Mendes there was a "Great Father" deity who links with Ptah, Her-shef, and Khnû-mû. He is called Ba-neb-tettu, the ram god, and "lord of Tettu", and he became, in the all-embracing theology of Heliopolis, "the breath (life) of Ra". In the *Book of the Dead* there is a reference to Ra as "the Lord of Air who giveth life to all mortals".

The god of Mendes was reputed to have made "the wind of life" for all men, and was called "chief of the gods", "ruler of the sky", and "monarch of all deities". The earth was made fertile by his influence, and he was the origin of the passion of love; he caused the fertilizing Nile flood. Like Ptah Tanen, from whose mouth issued forth the waters, and like Ptah, Khnûmû, and Shu, he was the pillar (*dad*) of the sky. Osiris is also associated with the sky prop or props. All these deities appear to have had their origin in crude conceptions which survive in various stages of development in European lore.[1]

Like Ba-neb-tettu, the Mendes "Great Father", Her-shef of Heracleopolis was also a ram god, symbolizing the male principle; so was Khnûmû of the First Cataract district. In some representations of Ptah the ram's horns appear on his head. The ram was the primitive Min, who was worshipped throughout Egypt, and was absorbed by all the Great Father deities, including Ra. Min was honoured at harvest festivals, and was therefore a corn god, a character assumed by the deified King Osiris.

One of the figures of Her-shef of Heracleopolis is almost as complex as that of Sokar, the Memphite god of the dead. He is shown with four heads—a ram's head, a bull's head, and two heads of hawks. The bull was Mentu, who, like Min, represented the male principle, and was also a war god, the epitome of strength and bravery.

All the Great Fathers—Her-shef, Ptah, Khnûmû, and Ba-neb-tettu—were fused with Osiris. Ptah united with Osiris as ruler of the dead, Khnûmû became a form of Osiris at Heliopolis, Ba-neb-tettu of Mendes was also Ba-neb-ded, another name for Osiris, and Her-shef of Heracleopolis was "he on the sand", a form of Osiris, who is called "the god on the sand".

Her-shef is usually represented as a ram-headed man, wearing the white crown with plumes, surmounted by two

[1] In Scottish archaic lore the mountains are shaped by the wind hag, who is the mother of giants. The Irish Anu or Danu, associated with the "Paps of Anu", has the attributes of a wind goddess and is the mother of deities; the Irish hag Morrigu and her two sisters are storm hags and war hags. On Jochgrimm Mountain in Tyrol three hags brew the breezes. The Norse Angerboda is an east-wind hag, and she is the enemy of the gods of Asgard. The gods who are wind deities include Zeus and Odin, "the Wild Huntsman in the Raging Host". The Teutonic hags are evidently of pre-Teutonic origin; they are what the old Irish mythologists called in Gaelic "non gods".

disks (sun and moon) and two serpents with disks on their heads. Plutarch regarded him as the symbol of "strength and valour", a conception which accords with the military reputation of at least some of the kings of Heracleopolis who lived in stormy times.

The goddess associated with Her-shef was Atet, who was also call Mersekhnet, a "Great Mother" deity similar to Hathor, Isis, Neith, and others. She was a cat goddess, and in her cat form was called Maau, an appropriate name. She slew the Apep serpent—a myth which, as we have seen, was absorbed by Ra. Other feline deities are Bast of Bubastis, Sekhet, wife of Ptah, and Tefnut.[1]

At Heracleopolis there was a shrine to Neheb-Kau, who, like the virgin deity of Buto in the Delta, was a serpent goddess, symbolizing the female principle. She is represented as a flying serpent,[2] a reptile which Herodotus heard much about in Egypt but searched for in vain; she also appears as a serpent with human head, arms, and legs. She was worshipped at the Ploughing Festival before the seed was sown. Like the sycamore goddess, she was believed to take a special interest in the souls of the dead, whom she supplied with celestial food and drink.

Another Heracleopolitan deity was the vine god Heneb, who suggests an Egyptian Bacchus; he was probably a form of Osiris.

The female counterpart of the northern god, Baneb-tettu, was Heru-pa-Kaut, "Mother of Mendes", who was represented as a woman with a fish upon her head.

---

[1] The Norse Freyja, goddess of love, is also a cat goddess. In the Empire period Astarte was added to the Egyptian collection of feline deities.

[2] Isaiah refers to Egypt as "the land of trouble and anguish, from whence come the young lion and old lion, the viper and fiery flying serpent" (*Isaiah*, xxx, 6; see also *Isaiah*, xiv, 29).

She was in time displaced by Isis, as her son was by Horus. The ceremonies associated with all the " mother goddesses " were as elaborate as they were indecent.

Osiris worship flourished at Abydos, which became an Egyptian Mecca with its holy sepulchre. The tomb of King Zer, of the First Dynasty, was reputed to be that of the more ancient deified monarch Osiris, and it was visited by pious pilgrims and heaped with offerings. Elaborate religious pageants, performed by priests, illustrated the Osiris-Isis story. Set, the fearful red demon god, was execrated, and the good Osiris revered and glorified. Isis, mother of the god Horus, was a popular figure. " I who let fall my hair, which hangs loosely over my forehead, I am Isis when she is hidden in her long tresses."

Pious worshippers sought burial at Abydos, and its cemetery was crowded with the graves of all classes. Nome governors, however, were interred in their own stately tombs, like those at Beni Hassan and elsewhere, but their mummies were often carried first to Abydos, where " the Judgment of the Dead " was enacted. The Pharaohs appear to have clung to the belief in the Ra bark, which they entered, as of old, by uttering the powerful magic formulæ. The victory of the early faith was, however, complete among the masses of the people. With the exception of the Ra believers the worshippers of every other deity in Egypt reposed their faith in Osiris, the god of the dead.

Some Egyptologists regard the Heracleopolitans as foreign invaders. Their theology suggests that they were a mountain people of similar origin to the Memphite worshippers of Ptah. But no records survive to afford us definite information on this point. The new monarchs were evidently kept fully engaged by their military opera-

tions, and not until nearly the close of the Tenth Dynasty
do we obtain definite information regarding the conditions
which prevailed during the obscure period. There then
came into prominence a powerful nome family at Siut
which remained faithful to the royal house and kept at
bay the aggressive Thebans. In their cliff tombs we read
inscriptions which indicate that for a period, at least, the
Pharaohs were able to maintain peace and order in the
kingdom. One of these records that the royal officials
performed their duties effectively, and that war had
ceased. Children were no longer slain in their mother's
arms, nor were men cut down beside their wives. The
rebels were suppressed, and people could sleep out of
doors in perfect safety, because the king's soldiers were the
terror of all doers of evil. Further, we learn that canals
were constructed, and that there were excellent harvests
—a sure indication that a degree of order had been restored. A standing army was in existence, and could be
dispatched at short notice to a disturbed area. The Siut
nobles appear to have been Pharaoh's generals. They
enjoyed intimate relations with the ruling house. One,
who was named Kheti, was educated with the Pharaoh's
family, and learned to swim with them, and his widowed
mother governed the nome during his minority. He
married a princess. His son, Tefaba, reduced the south
by military force, and won a great naval battle on the
Nile. The younger Kheti, Tefaba's son, was also a
vigorous governor, and stamped out another southern
rebellion, and made a great display with his fleet, which
stretched for miles. But although southern Egypt was
temporarily pacified, a rebellion broke out in the north,
and the Pharaoh Meri-ka-ra was suddenly driven from
Heracleopolis. He took refuge with Kheti, who pressed
northward and won a decisive victory. Meri-ka-ra was

again placed on the throne.   But his reign was brief, and he was the last king of the Tenth Dynasty.

The Delta was now in a state of aggressive revolt, and the power of the Theban house was growing in Upper Egypt.   Ultimately the Siut house fell before the southern forces, and a new official god and a new royal family appeared in the kingdom.

CHAPTER XV

The Rise of Amon

The Theban Rulers—Need for Centralized Government—·Temple Building—The first Amon King—Various Forms of Amon—The Oracle—Mentu the War God—Mut, Queen of the Gods—The Egyptian Cupid—Story of the Possessed Princess—God casts out an Evil Spirit—A Prince's Dream—The God of Spring—Amenemhet's Achievements—Feudal Lords held in Check—The Kingdom United—A Palace Conspiracy—Selection of Senusert—The first Personality in History.

ANTEF, the feudal lord of the valley of Thebes, was the next Pharaoh of Egypt. With him begins the Eleventh Dynasty, which covers a period of over a century and a half. His power was confined chiefly to the south, but he exercised considerable influence over the whole land by gaining possession of sacred Abydos. The custodians of the "holy sepulchre" were assured of the allegiance of the great mass of the people at this period of transition and unrest.

The new royal line included several King Antefs and King Mentuhoteps, but little is known regarding the majority of them. Antef I, who was descended from a superintendent of the frontier, had probably royal blood in his veins, and a remote claim to the throne. He reigned for fifty years, and appears to have consolidated the power of his house. Mentuhotep II, the fifth king, was able to impose his will upon the various feudal lords, and secured their allegiance partly, no doubt, by force of arms, but mainly, it would appear, because the prosperity

of the country depended upon the establishment of a
strong central government, which would secure the distribution of water for agricultural purposes. Famine
may have accomplished what the sword was unable to
do. Besides, the road to sacred Abydos had to be kept
open. The political influence of the Osirian cult must
therefore have been pronounced for a considerable time.

Under Mentuhotep II the country was so well settled
that a military expedition was dispatched to quell the
Nubian warriors. Commerce had revived, and the arts
and industries had begun to flourish again. Temples
were built under this and the two succeeding monarchs
of the line. The last Mentuhotep was able to organize
a quarrying expedition of ten thousand men.

Meantime the power of the ruling house was being
securely established throughout the land. The Pharaoh's
vizier was Amenemhet, and he made vigorous attacks
upon the feudal lords who pursued a policy of aggression
against their neighbours. Some were deposed, and their
places were filled by loyal supporters of the Pharaoh.
After a long struggle between the petty "kings" of the
nomes and the royal house, Amenemhet I founded the
Twelfth Dynasty, under which Egypt became once again
a powerful and united kingdom. He was probably a
grandson of the vizier of the same name.

A new god—the chief god of Thebes—has now risen
into prominence. His name is Amon, or Amen. The
earliest reference to him appears in the Pyramid of the
famous King Unas of the Fifth Dynasty, where he and
his consort are included among the primeval gods associated with Nu—"the fathers and mothers" who were
in "the deep" at the beginning. We cannot, however,
attach much importance to the theorizing of the priests
of Unas's time, for they were busily engaged in absorbing

every religious myth in the land. Amon is evidently a strictly local god, who passed through so many stages of development that it is impossible to grasp the original tribal conception, which may, perhaps, have been crude and vague enough. His name is believed to signify " The Hidden One "—he concealed his " soul " and his " name ", like the giant who hid his soul in an egg.[1] Sokar of Memphis was also a " hidden " god, and was associated with the land of the dead. Amon may have been likewise a deity of Hades, for he links with Osiris as a lunar deity (Chapter XXII). In fact, as Amon Ra he displaced Osiris for a time as judge of the dead.

Amon is represented in various forms: (1) As an ape;[2] (2) as a lion resting with head erect, like the primitive earth lion Aker; (3) as a frog-headed man accompanied by Ament, his serpent-headed female counterpart; (4) as a serpent-headed man, while his consort is cat-headed;[3] (5) as a man god with the royal sceptre in one hand and the symbol of life (ankh) in the other; (6) as a ram-headed man.

In the Twelfth Dynasty a small temple was erected to Amon in the northern part of the city which was called Apet, after the mother goddess of that name who ultimately was fused with Hathor. " Thebes " is believed to have been derived from her name, the female article " T ", being placed before " Ape "; Tap or Tape was pronounced Thebai by the Greeks, who had a town of that name.[4] The sacred name of the city was Nu or Nu-Amon. " Art thou better than populous No ? " cried

---

[1] Osiris Sokar " dost hide his essence in the great shrine ot Amon ".—*The Burden of Isis*, p. 54.

[2] Osiris Sokar is addressed: " Hail, thou who growest like unto the ape of Tehuti " (Thoth). The Thoth-ape appears to be a dawn god.

[3] Seb is depicted with a serpent's head. The cat goddess is Bast, who links with other Great Mothers.   [4] Budge's *Gods of the Egyptians*.

the Hebrew prophet, denouncing Nineveh; "Ethiopia and Egypt were her strength and it was infinite."

Amon, the ram god, was the most famous oracle in Egypt. Other oracles included the Apis bull; Sebek, the crocodile; Uazit, the serpent goddess of Buto; and Bes, the grotesque god who comes into prominence later. Revelations were made by oracles in dreams, and when Thutmose IV slept in the shadow of the Sphinx it expressed its desire to him that the sand should be cleared from about its body. Worshippers in a state of religious ecstasy were also given power to prophesy.

The oracle of Amon achieved great renown. The god was consulted by warriors, who were duly promised victory and great spoils. Wrongdoers were identified by the god, and he was even consulted regarding the affairs of State. Ultimately his priests achieved great influence owing to their reputation as foretellers of future events, who made known the will of the god. A good deal of trickery was evidently indulged in, for we gather that the god signified his assent to an expressed wish by nodding his head, or selected a suitable leader of men by extending his arm.

Amon was fused with several deities as his various animal forms indicate. The ram's head comes, of course, from Min, and it is possible that the frog's head was from Hekt. His cult also appropriated the war god Mentu, who is depicted as a bull. Mentu, however, continued to have a separate existence, owing to his fusion with Horus. He appears in human form wearing a bull's tail with the head of a hawk, which is surmounted by a sun disk between Amon's double plumes; he is also depicted as a hawk-headed sphinx. As a bull-headed man he carries bow and arrows, a club, and a knife.

In his Horus form Mentu stands on the prow of

the sun bark on the nightly journey through Duat, and slays the demons with his lance. He was appropriated, of course, by the priests of Heliopolis, and became the "soul of Ra" and "Bull of Heaven". A temple was erected to him near Karnak, and in late times he overshadowed Amon as Mentu-ra.

Amon was linked with the great sun god in the Eleventh Dynasty, and as Amon-ra he ultimately rose to the supreme position of national god, while his cult became the most powerful in Egypt. In this form he will be dealt with in a later chapter.

Amon's wife was Mut, whose name signifies "the mother", and she may be identical with Apet. She was "queen of the gods" and "lady of the sky". Like Nut, Isis, Neith, and others, she was the "Great Mother" who gave birth to all that exists. She is represented as a vulture and also as a lioness. The vulture is Nekhebet, "the mother", and the lioness, like the cat, symbolizes maternity. Mut wears the double crown of Egypt, which indicates that she absorbed all the "Great Mother" goddesses in the land. Her name, in fact, is linked with Isis, with the female Tum, with Hathor, the Buto serpent, &c. In the *Book of the Dead* she is associated with a pair of dwarfs who have each the face of a hawk and the face of a man. It was to Mut that Amenhotep III, the father of Akenaton, erected the magnificent temple at Karnak with its great avenue of ram-headed sphinxes. Queen Tiy's lake in its vicinity was associated with the worship of this "Great Mother".

The moon god Khonsu was at Thebes regarded as the son of Amon and Mut. At Hermopolis and Edfu he was linked with Thoth. In the Unas hymn he is sent forth by Orion to drive in and slaughter the souls of gods and men—a myth which explains why stars vanish before the moon. His name means "the traveller".

As a lunar deity Khonsu caused the crops to spring up and ripen. He was also the Egyptian Cupid, who touched the hearts of lads and girls with love. The Oracle of Khonsu was consulted by those who prayed for offspring. Agriculturists lauded the deity for increasing their flocks and herds.

This popular god also gave "the air of life" to the newly born, and was thus a wind god like Her-shef and Khnûmû. As ward of the atmosphere he exercised control over the evil spirits which caused the various diseases and took possession of human beings, rendering them epileptic or insane. Patients were cured by Khonsu, "giver of oracles", whose fame extended beyond the bounds of Egypt.

An interesting papyrus of the Ramessid period relates the story of a wonderful cure effected by Khonsu. It happened that the Pharaoh, "the Horus, he who resembles Tum, the son of the sun, the mighty with scimitars, the smiter of the nine-bow barbarians", &c., was collecting the annual tribute from the subject kings of Syria. The Prince of Bakhten,[1] who brought many gifts, "placed in front of these his eldest daughter". She was very beautiful, and the Pharaoh immediately fell in love with her, and she became his "royal wife".

Some time afterwards the Prince of Bakhten appeared at Uas (Thebes) with an envoy. He brought presents to his daughter, and, having prostrated himself before the "Son of the Sun", announced:

"I have travelled hither to plead with Your Majesty for the sake of Bent-rash, the younger sister of your royal wife; she is stricken with a grievous malady which

[1] Identified with the King of the Hittites who became the ally of Ramesis II.

causes her limbs to twitch violently. I entreat Your Majesty to send a learned magician to see her, so that he may give her aid in her sore distress."

Pharaoh said: "Let a great magician who is learned in the mysteries be brought before me."

As he desired, so was it done. A scribe of the House of Life appeared before him, and His Majesty said: "It is my will that you should travel to Bakhten to see the younger daughter of the royal wife."

The magician travelled with the envoy, and when he arrived at his journey's end he saw the Princess Bent-rash, whom he found to be possessed of a hostile demon of great power. But he was unable to draw it forth.

Then the Prince of Bakhten appeared at Uas a second time, and addressing the Pharaoh said: "O King, my lord, let a god be sent to cure my daughter's malady!"

His Majesty was compassionate, and he went to the temple of Khonsu and said to the god: "Once again I have come on account of the little daughter of the Prince of Bakhten. Let your image be sent to cure her."

Khonsu, "giver of oracles" and "expeller of evil spirits", nodded his head, assenting to the prayer of the king, and caused his fourfold divine nature to be imparted to the image.

So it happened that the statue of Khonsu was placed in an ark, which was carried on poles by twelve priests while two chanted prayers. When it was borne from the temple, Pharaoh offered up burning incense, and five boats set forth with the ark and the priests, accompanied by soldiers, a chariot, and two horses.

The Prince of Bakhten came forth from his city to meet the god, accompanied by many soldiers, and prostrated himself.

"So you have indeed come," he cried. "You are not hostile to us; the goodwill of the Pharaoh has caused you to come hither."

Khonsu was then carried into the presence of the Princess Bent-rash, who was immediately cured of her malady. The evil demon was cast out, and it stood before the god and said: "Peace be with you, O mighty god. The land of Bakhten is your possession, and its people are your slaves. I am your slave also. As you desire, I will return again to the place whence I came. But first let the Prince of Bakhten hold a great feast that I may partake thereof."

Khonsu then instructed a priest, saying: "Command the Prince of Bakhten to offer up a great sacrifice to the evil spirit whom I have expelled from his daughter."

Great dread fell upon the prince and the army and all the people when the sacrifice was offered up to the demon by the soldiers. Then amidst great rejoicings that spirit of evil took its departure and went to the place whence it came, according to the desire of Khonsu, "the giver of oracles".

Then the Prince of Bakhten was joyful of heart, and he desired that Khonsu should remain in the land. As it happened, he kept the image of the god for over three years.

One day the prince lay asleep upon his couch, and a vision came to him in a dream. He saw the god rising high in the air like a hawk of gold and taking flight towards the land of Egypt. He awoke suddenly, trembling with great fear, and he said: "Surely the god is angry with us. Let him be placed in the ark and carried back to Uas."

The prince caused many rich presents to be laid in the temple of the god when his image was returned.

One of Khonsu's popular names was "The Beautiful One at Rest". He was depicted, like the Celtic love god Angus, "the ever-young", as a handsome youth. The upper part of a particularly striking statue of this comely deity was found in the ruins of his temple at Karnak.

As a nature god Khonsu was a hawk-headed man, crowned with a crescent moon and the solar disk; he was a sun god in spring. Like Thoth, he was also an architect, "a deviser of plans", and a "measurer", for he measured the months. Both the lunar deities are evidently of great antiquity. The mother-goddess-and-son conception is associated with the early belief in the female origin of the world and of life. The "Great Mother" was self-begotten as the "Great Father" was self-begotten, and the strange Egyptian idea that a god became "husband of his mother" arose from the fusion of the conflicting ideas regarding creation.

Amenemhet I, the first great ruler who promoted the worship of Amon, was also assiduous in doing honour to the other influential deities. From Tanis in the Delta, southward into the heart of Nubia, he has left traces of his religious fervour, which had, of course, a diplomatic motive. He erected a red granite altar to Osiris at sacred Abydos, a temple to Ptah at Memphis; he honoured the goddess Bast with monuments at Bubastis, and duly adored Amon, of course, at Thebes. His Ka statues were distributed throughout the land, for he was the "son of Ra", and had therefore to be worshipped as "the god"—the human incarnation of the solar deity.

Amenemhet was an active military ruler. Not only did he smite the Syrians and the Nubians, but also punished the rebellious feudal lords who did not bend to his will. New and far-reaching changes were introduced into the system of local, as well as central, government. The powers of nome governors were restricted. When one was forcibly deposed an official took his place, and the appointment of town rulers and headmen of villages became once again vested in the Crown. This policy was followed by Amenemhet's successors, until ultimately the feudal system, which for centuries had been a constant menace to the stability of the throne, was finally extinguished. The priestly allies of the provincial nobles were won to the Crown by formal recognition and generous gifts, and all the chief gods, with the exception of Ptah, were included in the "family" of Amon-ra.

Amenemhet gathered about him the most capable men in the kingdom. Once again it was possible for humble officials to rise to the highest rank. The industries of the country were fostered, and agriculture received special attention, so that harvests became plentiful again and there was abundance of food in Egypt.

When the king was growing old he selected his son Senusert to succeed him. Apparently the choice was not pleasing to some of the influential members of the royal house. In the "Instruction of Amenemhet", a metrical version of which is given at the end of the next chapter, we learn that a harem conspiracy was organized to promote the claims of a rival to the throne. A band of conspirators gained access to the palace through a tunnel which had been constructed secretly, and burst upon the old monarch as he lay resting after he had partaken of his evening meal. He "showed fight", although unarmed, and in the parley which ensued was evidently successful. It appears to have been accepted that the succession of Senusert was inevitable.

How the conspirators were dealt with we have no

means of knowing. It is possible that the majority of
them were pardoned. So long as Amenemhet remained
alive they were safe; but they must have feared the
vengeance of Senusert, who was a vigorous and warlike
prince, and eminently worthy to succeed his father. The
papyrus story of "The Flight of Senuhet" is evidently
no mere folktale, but a genuine fragment of history.
It is possible that Senuhet was one of the sons of
Amenemhet; at any rate he appears to have been com-
promised in the abortive palace conspiracy. When the
old king died at Memphis, where he appears to have
resided oftenest, a messenger was hurriedly dispatched
to Senusert, who was engaged leading an army against
the troublesome Libyans. None of the other princes
was informed, and Senuhet, who overheard the messenger informing the new king of his father's death,
immediately fled towards Syria. He found that other
Egyptians had taken refuge there.

After many years had elapsed his whereabouts were
revealed to King Senusert, who was evidently convinced
of his innocence. Senuhet was invited to return to
Egypt, and was welcomed at the palace by his royal
kinsman.

The narrative is of homely and graceful character,
and affords us more intimate knowledge of the life of
the period than can be obtained from tomb inscriptions
and royal monuments. Senuhet is one of the earliest
personalities in history. We catch but fleeting glimpses
of the man Amenemhet in his half-cynical "Instruction"
with its vague references to a palace revolt. In the
simple and direct narrative of the fugitive prince, however, we are confronted by a human being whose emo-
tions we share, and with whom we are able to enter
into close sympathy. The latter part of the story has

some of the happiest touches.   Our old friend rejoices because he is privileged once again to sleep in a comfortable bed after lying for long years in the desert sand; he throws away his foul rustic clothing and attires himself in perfumed linen, and feels young when his beard is shaved off and his baldness is covered by a wig.   He is provided with a mansion which is decorated anew, but what pleases him most is the presence of the children who come to visit him.   He was fond of children. . . . Our interest abides with a man who was buried, as he desired to be, after long years of wandering, in the land of his birth, some forty centuries ago!

CHAPTER XVI

Tale of the Fugitive Prince

A Libyan Campaign—Death of King Amenemhet—The Prince's Flight—Among the Bedouins—An Inquisitive Chief—The Prince is honoured—A Rival Hero—Challenge to Single Combat—Senuhet victorious—Egyptian Love of Country—Appeal to Pharaoh—Prince returns Home—Welcome at the Court—A Golden Friend—An Old Man made Happy.

SENUHET, "son of the sycamore", was a hereditary prince of Egypt. When war was waged against the Libyans he accompanied the royal army, which was commanded by Senusert, the chosen heir of the great Amenemhet. As it fell, the old king died suddenly on the seventh day of the second month of Shait. Like the Horus hawk he flew towards the sun. Then there was great mourning in the palace; the gates were shut and sealed and noblemen prostrated themselves outside; silence fell upon the city.

The campaign was being conducted with much success. Many prisoners were taken and large herds of cattle were captured. The enemy were scattered in flight.

Now the nobles who were in possession of the palace took counsel together, and they dispatched a trusted messenger to Prince Senusert, so that he might be secretly informed of the death of his royal father. All the king's sons were with the army, but none of them were called when the messenger arrived. The messenger spoke unto no man of what had befallen save Senusert alone.

Now it chanced that Senuhet was concealed nigh to

the new king when the secret tidings were brought to him. He heard the words which the messenger spoke, and immediately he was stricken with fear; his heart shook and his limbs trembled. But he retained his presence of mind. His first thought was for his own safety; so he crept softly away until he found a safe hiding place. He waited until the new king and the messenger walked on together, and they passed very close to him as he lay concealed in a thicket.[1]

No sooner had they gone out of hearing than Senuhet hastened to escape from the land of Egypt. He made his way southward, wondering greatly as he went if civil war had broken out. When night was far spent he lay down in an open field and slept there. In the morning he hastened along the highway and overtook a man who showed signs of fear. The day passed, and at eventide he crossed the river on a raft to a place where there were quarries. He was then in the region of the goddess Hirit of the Red Mountains, and he turned northward. On reaching a frontier fortress, which had been built to repel the raiding Bedouin archers, he concealed himself lest he should be observed by the sentinels.

As soon as it grew dark he continued his journey. He travelled all night long, and when dawn broke he reached the Qumor valley. . . . His strength was well-nigh spent. He was tortured by thirst; his tongue was parched and his throat was swollen. Greatly he suffered, and he moaned to himself: "Now I begin to taste of death". Yet he struggled on in his despair, and suddenly his heart was cheered by the sound of a man's voice and the sweet lowing of cows.

He had arrived among the Bedouins. One of them spoke to him kindly, and first gave him water to drink

[1] No reason is given in the story for Senuhet's sudden alarm.

and then some boiled milk.   The man was a chief, and
he perceived that Senuhet was an Egyptian of high rank.
He showed him much kindness, and when the fugitive
was able to resume his journey the Bedouin gave him safe
conduct to the next camp.   So from camp to camp
Senuhet made his way until he reached the land of the
Edomites, and then he felt safe there.

About a year went past, and then Amuanishi, chief
of Upper Tonu, sent a messenger to Senuhet, saying:
"Come and reside with me and hear the language of
Egypt spoken."

There were other Egyptians in the land of Edom,
and they had praised the prince highly, so that the chief
desired greatly to see him.

Amuanishi spoke to Senuhet, saying: "Now tell me
frankly why you have fled to these parts.   Is it because
someone has died in the royal palace?   Something appears to have happened of which I am not aware."

Senuhet made evasive answer: "I certainly fled
hither from the country of the Libyans, but not because
I did anything wrong.   I never spoke or acted treason-
ably, nor have I listened to treason.   No magistrate has
received information regarding me.   I really can give no
explanation why I came here.   It seems as if I obeyed
the will of King Amenemhet, whom I served faithfully
and well."

The Bedouin chief praised the great king of Egypt,
and said that his name was dreaded as greatly as that of
Sekhet, the lioness goddess, in the time of famine.

Senuhet again spoke, saying: "Know now that the
son of Amenemhet sits on the throne.   He is a just
and tactful prince, an excellent swordsman, and a brave
warrior who has never yet met his equal.   He sweeps
the barbarians from his path; he hurls himself upon

robbers; he crushes heads and strikes down those who oppose him, for he is indeed a valiant hero without fear. He is also a swift runner when pursuing his foes, and he smites them with the claws of a lion, for they cannot escape him. Senusert rejoices in the midst of the fray, and none can withstand him. To his friends he is the essence of courtesy, and he is much loved throughout the land; all his subjects obey him gladly. Although he extends his southern frontier he has no desire to invade the land of the Bedouins. If it happens, however, that he should come hither, tell him that I dwell amongst ye."

The chief heard, and then said: "My desire is that Egypt may flourish and have peace. As for yourself, you will receive my hospitality so long as you please to reside here."

Then Senuhet was given for wife the eldest daughter of the chief of Upper Tonu. He was also allowed to select for himself a portion of land in that excellent country which is called Aia. There was abundance of grapes and figs; wine was more plentiful than water; the land flowed with milk and honey; olives were numerous and there were large supplies of corn and wheat, and many cattle of every kind.

The chief honoured Senuhet greatly and made him a prince in the land so that he was a ruler of a tribe. Each day the Egyptian fared sumptuously on cooked flesh and roasted fowl and on the game he caught, or which was brought to him, or was captured by his dogs, and he ever had bread and wine. His servants made butter and gave him boiled milk of every kind as he desired.

Many years went past. Children were born to him and they grew strong, and, in time, each ruled over a tribe. When travellers were going past, they turned aside to visit Senuhet, because he showed great hospitality; he gave refreshment to those who were weary; and if it chanced that a stranger was plundered, he chastised the wrongdoers; he restored the stolen goods and gave the man safe conduct.

Senuhet commanded the Bedouins who fought against invaders, for the chief of Upper Tonu had made him general of the army. Many and great were the successes he achieved. He captured prisoners and cattle and returned with large numbers of slaves. In battle he fought with much courage with his sword and his bow; he displayed great cunning on the march and in the manner in which he arranged the plan of battle. The chief of Tonu loved him dearly when he perceived how powerful he had become, and elevated Senuhet to still higher rank.

There was a mighty hero in Tonu who had achieved much renown, and he was jealous of the Egyptian. The man had no other rival in the land; he had slain all who dared to stand up against him. He was brave and he was bold, and he said: "I must needs combat with Senuhet. He has not yet met me."

The warrior desired to slay the Egyptian and win for himself the land and cattle which he possessed.

When the challenge was received, the chief of Tonu was much concerned, and spoke to Senuhet, who said:

"I know not this fellow. He is not of my rank and I do not associate with his kind. Nor have I ever done him any wrong. If he is a thief who desires to obtain my goods, he had better be careful of how he behaves himself. Does he think I am a steer and that he is the bull of war? If he desires to fight with me, let him have the opportunity. As it is his will, so let it be. Will the god forget me? Whatever happens will happen as the god desires."

Having spoken thus, Senuhet retired to his tent and rested himself. Then he prepared his bow and made ready his arrows, and he saw that his arms were polished.

When dawn came, the people assembled round the place of combat. They were there in large numbers; many had travelled from remote parts to watch the duel. All the subjects of the chief of Tonu desired greatly that Senuhet should be the victor. But they feared for him. Women cried "Ah!" when they saw the challenging hero, and the men said one to another: "Can any man prevail over this warrior? See, he carries a shield and a lance and a battleaxe, and he has many javelins."

Senuhet came forth. He pretended to attack, and his adversary first threw the javelins; but the Egyptian turned them aside with his shield, and they fell harmlessly to the ground. The warrior then swung his battleaxe; but Senuhet drew his bow and shot a swift arrow. His aim was sure, for it pierced his opponent's neck so that he gave forth a loud cry and fell forward upon his face. Senuhet seized the lance, and, having thrust it through the warrior's body, he raised the shout of victory.

Then all the people rejoiced together, and Senuhet gave thanks to Mentu, the war god of Thebes, as did also the followers of the slain hero, for he had oppressed them greatly. The Chief Ruler of Tonu embraced the victorious prince with glad heart.

Senuhet took possession of all the goods and cattle which the boastful warrior had owned, and destroyed his house. So he grew richer as time went on. But old age was coming over him. In his heart he desired greatly to return to Egypt again and to be buried there. His thoughts dwelt on this matter and he resolved to make appeal unto King Senusert.   Then he drew up a petition and dispatched it in the care of a trusted messenger to the royal palace.   Addressing His Majesty, "the servant of Horus" and "Son of the Sun", Senuhet wrote :—

I have reposed my faith in the god, and lo! he has not failed me. . . . Although I fled away from Egypt my name is still of good repute in the palace.   I was hungry when I fled and now I supply food unto others; I was naked when I fled and now I am clad in fine linen; I was a wanderer and now I have many followers; I had no riches when I fled and now possess land and a dwelling. . . . I entreat of Your Majesty to permit me to sojourn once again in the place of my birth which I love dearly so that when I die my body may be embalmed and laid in a tomb in my native land.   I, who am a fugitive, entreat you now to permit me to return home. . . . Unto the god I have given offerings so that my desire may be fulfilled, for my heart is full of regret—I who took flight to a foreign country.

May Your Majesty grant my request to visit once again my native land so that I may be your favoured subject.   I humbly salute the queen.   It is my desire to see her once again and also the children so that life may be renewed in my blood.   Alas! I am growing old, my strength is diminishing; mine eyes are dim; I totter when I walk and my heart is feeble.   Well, I know that death is at hand.   The day of my burial is not far off. . . . Ere I die, may I gaze upon the queen and hear her talk about her children so that my heart may be made happy until the end.

King Senusert read the petition which Senuhet had sent unto him and was graciously pleased to grant his request.   He sent presents to his fugitive subject, and messages from the princes, his royal sons, accompanied His Majesty's letter, which declared:

These are the words of the King. . . . What did you do,

or what has been done against you, that you fled away to a foreign country? What went wrong? I know that you never calumniated me, but although your words may have been misrepresented, you did not speak next time in the gathering of the lords even when called upon. . . . Do not let this matter be remembered any longer. See, too, that you do not change your mind again. . . . As for the queen, she is well and receives everything she desires. She is in the midst of her children. . . .

Leave all your possessions, and when you return here you may reside in the palace. You will be my closest friend. Do not forget that you are growing older each day now; that the strength of your body is diminishing and that your thoughts dwell upon the tomb. You will be given seemly burial; you will be embalmed; mourners will wail at your funeral; you will be given a gilded mummy case which will be covered with a cypress canopy and drawn by oxen; the funeral hymn will be sung and the funeral dance will be danced; mourners will kneel at your tomb crying with a loud voice so that offerings may be given unto you. Lo! all shall be as I promise. Sacrifices will be made at the door of your tomb; a pyramid will be erected and you will lie among princes. . . . You must not die in a foreign country. You are not to be buried by Bedouins in a sheepskin. The mourners of your own country will smite the ground and mourn for you when you are laid in your pyramid.

When Senuhet received this gracious message he was overcome with joy and wept; he threw himself upon the sand and lay there. Then he leapt up and cried out: "Is it possible that such good fortune has befallen an unfaithful subject who fled from his native land unto a hostile country? Great mercy is shown unto me this day. I am delivered from the fear of death."

Senuhet sent an answer unto the king saying:

Thou mighty god, what am I that you should favour me thus? . . . If Your Majesty will summon two princes who know what occurred they will relate all that came to pass. . . . It was not my desire to flee from Egypt. I fled as in a dream. . . . I was not followed. I had not heard of any rebellious movement, nor did any magistrate receive my name. . . . I fled as if I had been ordered to flee by His Majesty. . . . As you have commanded, I will leave my riches behind me, and those who are my heirs here will inherit them. . . . May Your Majesty have eternal life.

When he had written this to His Majesty, Senuhet gave a great feast and he divided his wealth among his children. His eldest son became the leader of the tribe, and he received the land and the corn fields, the cattle and the fruit trees, in that pleasant place. Then Senuhet turned his face towards the land of Egypt. He was met on the frontier by the officer who commanded the fort, who sent tidings to the palace of Senuhet's approach. A boat laden with presents went to meet him, and the fugitive spoke to all the men who were in it as if he were of their own rank, for his heart was glad.

A night went past, and when the land grew bright again he drew nigh to the palace. Four men came forth to conduct him, and the children waited his coming in the courtyard as did also the nobles who led him before the king.

His Majesty sat upon his high throne in the great hall which is adorned with silver and gold. Senuhet prostrated himself. The king did not at first recognize him, yet he spoke kindly words; but the poor fugitive was unable to make answer; he grew faint; his eyes were blinded and his limbs were without strength; it seemed as if he were about to die.

The king said: "Help him to rise up so that we may converse one with another."

The courtiers lifted Senuhet, and His Majesty said: "So you have returned again. I perceive that in skulking about in foreign lands and playing the fugitive in the desert you have worn yourself out. You have grown old, Senuhet. . . . But why do you not speak? Have you become deceitful like the Bedouin. Declare your name. What causes you to feel afraid?"

Senuhet found his tongue and said: "I am unnerved, Your Majesty. I have naught to answer for. I have not done that which deserves the punishment of the god. . . . I am faint, and my heart has grown weak, as when I fled. . . . Once again I stand before Your Majesty; my life is in your hands; do with me according to your will."

As he spoke, the royal children entered the great hall, and His Majesty said to the queen:

"This is Senuhet. Look at him. He has come like a desert dweller in the attire of a Bedouin."

The queen uttered a cry of astonishment, and the children laughed, saying: "Surely it is not him, Your Majesty?"

The king said: "Yes, it is Senuhet."

Then the royal children decked themselves with jewels and sang before the king, each tinkling a sweet sistrum. They praised His Majesty and called upon the gods to give him health and strength and prosperity, and they pleaded for Senuhet, so that royal favours might be conferred upon him.

> Mighty thy words and swift thy will!
> Then bless thy servant in thy sight—
> With air of life his nostrils fill,
> Who from his native land took flight.
> Thy presence fills the land with fear;
> Then marvel not he fled away—
> All cheeks grow pale when thou art near;
> All eyes are stricken with dismay.

The king said: "Senuhet must not tremble in my presence, for he will be a golden friend and chief among the courtiers. Take him hence that he may be attired as befits his rank."

Then Senuhet was conducted to the inner chamber, and the children shook hands with him. He was given apartments in the house of a prince, the son of the king, in which he obtained dainties to eat. There he could sit in a cool chamber; there he could eat refreshing fruit; there he could attire himself in royal garments and anoint his body with perfumes; and there courtiers waited to converse with him and servants to obey his will.

He grew young again. His beard was shaved off, and his baldness was covered with a wig. The smell of the desert left him when his rustic garments were thrown away, and he was dressed in linen garments and anointed with perfumed oil. Once again he lay upon a bed—he who had left the sandy desert to those accustomed to it.

In time Senuhet was provided with a house in which a courtier had dwelt, when it had been repaired and decorated. He was happy there, and his heart was made glad by the children who visited him. The royal children were continually about his house.

King Senusert caused a pyramid to be erected for Senuhet; his statue was also carved at His Majesty's command, and it was decorated with gold.

"It was for no ordinary man," adds the scribe, who tells us that he copied the story faithfully, "that the king did all these things. Senuhet was honoured greatly by His Majesty until the day of his death."

The Instruction of Amenemhet

Be thou in splendour like the god, my son . . .
Hearken and hear my words, if thou wouldst reign
In Egypt and be ruler of the world,
Excelling in thy greatness. . . . Live apart
In stern seclusion, for the people heed
The man who makes them tremble; mingle not
Alone among them; have no bosom friend,
Nor intimate, nor favourite in thy train—
These serve no goodly purpose.

                       Ere to sleep
Thou liest down, prepare to guard thy life—
A man is friendless in the hour of trial. . . .
I to the needy gave, the orphan nourished,
Esteemed alike the lowly and the great;
But he who ate my bread made insurrection,
And those my hands raised up, occasion seized
Rebellion to create. . . . They went about
All uniformed in garments that I gave
And deemed me but a shadow. . . . Those who shared
My perfumes for anointment, rose betimes
And broke into my harem.

                    Through the land
Beholden are my statues, and men laud
The deeds I have accomplished . . . yet I made
A tale heroic that hath ne'er been told,
And triumphed in a conflict no man saw. . . .

Surely these yearned for bondage when they smote
The king who set them free. . . . Methinks, my son,
Of no avail is liberty to men
Grown blind to their good fortune.

                      I had dined
At eve and darkness fell. I sought to rest

For I was weary. On my bed I lay
And gave my thoughts release, and so I slept . . .
The rebels 'gan to whisper and take arms
With treacherous intent . . . I woke and heard
And like the desert serpent waited there
All motionless but watchful.

                     Then I sprang
To fight and I alone. . . . A warrior fell,
And lo! he was the captain of my guard.
Ah! had I but his weapons in that hour
I should have scattered all the rebel band—
Mighty my blows and swift! . . . but he, alas!
Was like a coward there. . . . Nor in the dark,
And unprepared, could I achieve renown.

Hateful their purpose! . . . I was put to shame.
Thou wert not nigh to save. . . . Announced I then
That thou didst reign, and I had left the throne.
And gave commands according to thy will. . . .
Ah! as they feared me not, 't was well to speak
With courtesy before them. . . . Would I could
Forget the weakness of my underlings!

My son, Senusert, say—Are women wont
To plot against their lords? Lo! mine have reared
A brood of traitors, and assembled round
A rebel band forsworn. They did deceive
My servants with command to pierce the ground
For speedy entry.

                Yet to me from birth
Misfortune hath a stranger been. I ne'er
Have met mine equal among valiant men. . .
Lo! I have set in order all the land.
From Elephantinè adown the Nile
I swept in triumph: so my feet have trod
The outposts of my kingdom. . . . Mighty deeds
Must now be measured by the deeds I've done.

I loved the corn god. . . . I have grown the grain
In every golden valley where the Nile
Entreated me; none hungered in my day,
None thirsted, and all men were well content—
They praised me, saying: "Wise are his commands".

I fought the lion and the crocodile,
I smote the dusky Nubians, and put
The Asian dogs to flight.

                         Mine house I built.
Gold-decked with azure ceilings, and its walls
Have deep foundations; doors of copper are,
The bolts of bronze. . . . It shall endure all time.
Eternity regards it with dismay!
I know each measurement, O Lord of All!

Men came to see its beauties, and I heard
In silence while they praised it. No man knew
The treasure that it lacked. . . . I wanted thee,
My son, Senusert. . . . Health and strength be thine!
I lean upon thee, O my heart's delight;
For thee I look on all things. . . . Spirits sang
In that glad hour when thou wert born to me.

All things I've done, now know, were done for thee;
For thee must I complete what I began
Until the end draws nigh. . . . O be my heart
The isle of thy desire. . . . The white crown now
Is given thee, O wise son of the god—
I'll hymn thy praises in the bark of Ra. . . .
Thy kingdom at Creation was. 'T is thine
As it was mine—how mighty were my deeds!
Rear thou thy statues and adorn thy tomb. . . .
I struck thy rival down. . . . 'T would not be wise
To leave him nigh thee. . . . Health and strength be thine!

CHAPTER XVII

Egypt's Golden Age

A Leader of Men—Gloomy Prophecy—Agriculture flourishing—The Chief Treasurer and his Auditors—Great Irrigation Scheme—Lake Mœris formed—Military Expeditions—A Murdered King—Disturbing Race Movements—First Mention of Hittites—Abraham in Egypt—Syria invaded—The Labyrinth—Like Mazy Cretan Palaces—Fall of Knossos—Bronze in Egypt—Copper and Iron—Trade in Tin—The British Mines—Spiral Ornament in Egypt and Europe.

THE Twelfth Dynasty, which embraces about two centuries, was a period of industrial and intellectual activity, and is appropriately called "The Golden Age of Egypt". It was ushered in, as we have seen, by Amenemhet I, whose name signifies "Amon leads". The king was, in a true sense, a leader of men; he displayed great military and administrative genius, and proved to be a saviour of the people. He rose to power at a time when a great crisis was approaching. The kingdom had grown weak as a result of prolonged internal dissensions, and its very existence as a separate power was being threatened by invaders on the northern and southern frontiers. The hour had come, and with it the man.

Amenemhet subdued the Nubians, who were as warlike and aggressive as the modern Sudanese; he cleared the eastern Delta of hordes of Asiatics, attracted thither by the prospects of plunder and the acquisition of desirable territory, and he reduced by shattering blows the growing power of the Libyans. His administrative reforms were beneficial to the great mass of the people, for the establishment of a strong central government protected them from brigandage and periodic visitations of devastating famines. Agriculture was promoted, and the revival of trade ensured a more equitable distribution of wealth. As the influence of the feudal lords declined, it became possible for capable men of humble rank to attain high official positions.

In a striking literary production of the age, a prophetic scribe, named Apura, stands before his king, uttering grave warnings of approaching national disaster. He pictures Egypt in the throes of revolution; brothers contend against brothers; men cease to till the soil. The prophet exclaims:

In vain will the Nile rise in flood, for the land will lie barren. Men who were wont to plough will say: "What is the good of it? We know what is coming." No children will be born in Egypt. Poor people will seize upon treasure. A man hitherto unable to purchase sandals will obtain possession of much grain. Diseases will decimate all classes; a terrible plague will smite the land; there will be war and much shedding of blood. Rich men will sorrow and poor men will laugh. All the cities will desire to throw off the yoke of their rulers. . . . Slaves will plunder their masters, and their wives will be decked with fine jewellery. Royal ladies will be driven from their homes; they will sit in the dust, wailing: "Oh! that we had bread to eat."

Thus, he declared, Egypt would suffer from the Conquest of Evil. But a more terrible conquest would immediately follow. Suddenly foreigners would enter the land to set up barbarous rule. Then all classes of Egyptians would endure great afflictions.

Having drawn this dark and terrible picture, the prophet foretells that a great deliverer is to arise. He will "cool the fire of oppression" and will be called "The Shepherd of his People". He will gather together his wandering flocks; he will smite the wrong-doer; he will stir up enthusiasm in the hearts of the men of Egypt and become their leader. "May he indeed be their deliverer!" exclaims the scribe. "Where is he to be found? Is he already here, waiting among the people?"

It is possible that at this period contemporary historical events were narrated in the prophetic manner, and that the scribe was eulogizing the reigning Pharaoh and justifying his reforms. In the "Instruction of Amenemhet" the old king reflects with astonishment that those he set free should rise up against him. A more literal rendering of his remark is: "He struggles for an ox that is bound who hath no memory of yester-day". Amenemhet had set the people free, and those who had received benefits showed that they failed to appreciate them by espousing the cause of their old oppressors. Was it their desire to become serfs again?

The condition of the past is reflected in the tomb inscription of one of the nome lords whose family owed its rise to its loyalty to the monarch. He boasts that every available piece of land under his jurisdiction was thoroughly cultivated. He protected the lives of the people. None starved, for he saw that all received food. A widow was treated in the same manner as a woman whose husband was alive, and when relief was given the poor received the same treatment as the powerful. Lord Kitchener has recently commented upon the financial embarrassments of the present-day fellahin of Egypt. Apparently the problem is one of long standing, for this governor — Ameni of the Gazelle nome — states that when the river rose high, and there was an abundance of produce, he "did not oppress the peasant because of his arrears".

It was the duty of the Chief Treasurer to see that the various nomes were administered in such a manner that they yielded adequate surpluses. A " sinking fund" was instituted for bad years, and relief was given in those localities where harvests were insufficient. The problem of irrigation received constant attention, and it became customary to measure the rise of the Nile on the rocks of the second cataract. The statistics thus obtained made possible the calculation of the probable yield of grain, so that the assessments might be fixed in the early part of each year. The royal auditors were constantly engaged throughout the land "taking stock" and checking the transactions of those who collected taxes "in kind", and references are made to their operations in tomb inscriptions. Their returns were lodged in the office of the Chief Treasurer at Memphis, who was ever in a position to advise the Pharaoh regarding the development of a particular district, and, in times of distress, to know where to find supplies to relieve the needy.

During the reign of Amenemhet III, the sixth monarch of the Dynasty, a great water storage and irrigation scheme was successfully carried out. The possibilities of the swampy Fayum had been recognized by certain rulers. King Den, of the First Dynasty, began the work of reclamation there, and some of his successors continued to deal with the problem. Amenemhet's operations were conducted on a grand scale. The famous Lake Mœris was formed by the erection of a reclaiming wall which extended for nearly thirty miles. It was connected with the Nile by a broad canal, and its largest circumference was 150 miles, while its area was about 750 square miles. It served the same purpose as the Assouan dam of the present day, but of course benefited only the province of the Fayum and the district

below it.   Strabo, writing long centuries after it was constructed, said: "The Lake Mœris, by magnitude and
depth, is able to sustain the superabundance of water
which flows into it when the river rises, without overflow-
ing the inhabited and cultivated parts of the country.
When the river falls the lake distributes the excess of
water through its canal, and both the lake and the canal
retain a remainder which is used for irrigation. . . .
There are locks on both mouths of the canal, and the
engineers use these to store up and distribute the
water."

When the scheme was completed the area of land
reclaimed embraced, according to Major R. H. Brown,
R.E., about 27,000 acres.   He has calculated that a
sufficient quantity of water was conserved to double the
flow of the Nile during the period between April and
July, when it is very low.   The extension of the culti-
vatable area increased greatly the drawings of the Chief
Treasurer.   Pharaoh, in a generous moment, being, no
doubt, well pleased with the success of the scheme,
made over the revenue from the fishing rights of the
lake to his queen, so that she might provide luxurious
attire and jewellery for herself and her train.

Senusert I, the friend of Senuhet, was an able and
vigorous ruler.   During his reign of about forty years
he appears to have engaged himself mainly in carrying
out the policy inaugurated by his father.   The results
were eminently satisfactory.   Peace was maintained with
a firm hand on the northern frontier, and the Libyans
were kept at bay.   He found it necessary, however, to
lead in person a strong army into Nubia.   There does
not appear to have been much fighting, for in the tomb
of his general, the favoured Ameni, it is recorded that
the losses were insignificant.   Apparently the most not-

able event of the campaign was the capture of an elephant.   Other expeditions followed, the last being in the year before the king's death.   The Nubians never ceased to give trouble.

Senusert restricted at every opportunity the powers of the feudal lords, and pursued the diplomatic policy of conciliating the various religious cults.   He erected a great temple at Heliopolis, and its site is marked to-day by a stately obelisk which bears his name.   He also repaired or extended temples at Coptos, Abydos, Hierakonpolis, and Karnak, and his monuments were judiciously distributed throughout the land.

Two years before his death Senusert appointed as regent his son, who became the second Amenemhet. After reigning for thirty years, Amenemhet II lost his life, according to Manetho, in a palace revolution. Senusert II, who followed, appears to have resided chiefly at Illahun, a town which is of special interest to us, because a plan of it was discovered by Petrie in the royal tomb.   We are not impressed by the accommodation provided for the great mass of the inhabitants.   The workers resided in narrow slums.   Many of the living rooms in the blocks run one into another, so that there could not have been either great comfort or much privacy.

A new type of face begins to appear in the royal house, as is shown by the smaller sculpture work of the time.   This matter will be dealt with in the next chapter. Nomadic tribes were also settling in Egypt.   In the well-known Beni-hassan tomb of the loyal nome governor Khnûmûhotep ("the god Khnûmû is satisfied") appears an interesting and significant wall painting of a company of Semites, who are presenting gifts of perfumes to the Pharaoh.   They are accompanied by their wives and families, as if they desired to become faithful subjects in the land of prosperity and good government.

Syria at this period was in a state of constant unrest. Great race movements were in progress over a considerable area in Asia and Europe. These were caused by one of those periodic waves of migration from Arabia, the southward and westward pressure of hill tribes in middle Asia, and by the aggressive tendencies of the Hittites. The earliest mention of the latter is made in the reign of Amenemhet I. Their seat of power was at Boghaz-Koi in Asia Minor, and they were raiding Mesopotamia and gradually pressing down through northern Syria. The smaller tribes were displaced by the larger, and migrations by propulsion were, in consequence, frequent and general. Many privations were endured by the scattered people, and of course agricultural operations must have been completely suspended in some districts.

About this time Abraham sojourned in Egypt, because "the famine was grievous in the land" (Canaan). After he returned he purchased from Ephron, the Hittite, the cave of Machpelah, in which to bury his dead. This landowner was evidently a pioneer settler from Asia Minor. He was friendly to the patriarch, whom he addressed as "a mighty prince among us". The Hittites may have penetrated Canaan as far south as Jerusalem.

Owing to the unrest on his northern frontier Senusert III found it necessary to invade Syria. A stela of his has been found at Gezer. It is recorded at Abydos that a battle was fought in which the Asiatics were defeated, and Sebek-khu, an Egyptian dignitary, to whom we are indebted for this scrap of interesting history, boasts of the gifts he received from the Pharaoh for his bravery on the field.   Nubia was also giving trouble again during this reign.   A vigorous campaign against the restless warriors resulted in the extension of the Egyptian frontier to the third cataract.   Two great forts were afterwards erected and garrisoned.   It was also decreed that no negroes with cattle or merchandise should pass northward by land or water beyond a certain point.   Traders were followed by colonists, and then fighting men desired to take forcible possession of territory.   A second campaign was conducted against the dusky tribes eight years after the first, and three years later there was another.   The flesh pots of Egypt were attracting all sorts and conditions of peoples.

The interests of the next king, Amenemhet III, were centred chiefly in the Fayum, where he saw completed the great Lake Mœris scheme.   His reign, which lasted for nearly half a century, was peaceful and prosperous. He was one of the great Pharaohs of Egypt.   Under his jurisdiction the country developed rapidly, commerce increased, and the industries were fostered.   Instead of sending periodic expeditions to Sinai for copper and turquoise, as had been the custom hitherto, he established a colony there.   A reservoir was constructed and a temple built to the goddess Hathor.   The colonists suffered greatly from the heat during the summer months.   A nobleman recorded on a stela the hardships endured by a pioneer expedition which visited the mines at an earlier date than usual, before permanent settlement was effected in that tropical land.   "The mountains are hot," he says, "and the rocks brand the body."   He endured his hardships with exemplary fortitude, and expressed the hope that others would similarly show their readiness to obey royal commands.

It was a building age, and Amenemhet honoured the

gods and at the same time humoured the growing communities of priests by erecting and enlarging temples. He gave special recognition to Osiris at sacred Abydos, where many Egyptians of all ranks continued to seek sepulture; to Amon, the family deity at Karnak; and to Her-shef at Heracleopolis. Ptah, the god of the artisans, appears to have been neglected, which seems to indicate that he had absorbed, or was absorbed by, Her-shef, whom he so closely resembles.

This Amenemhet is credited with having erected the great Labyrinth in the vicinity of Lake Mœris. The mosque-building Arabs must have used it as a quarry, for no trace of it remains. It appears to have been an immense temple, with apartments for each of the Egyptian gods. "All the works of Greece", declared Herodotus, "are inferior to it, both in regard to workmanship and cost." The Greek historian was of opinion that it surpassed even the Pyramids. There were twelve covered courts with entrances opposite to each other—six to the north and six to the south, and the whole was enclosed by a wall. Of the three thousand apartments half were underground. "The numerous winding passages through the various courts", Herodotus wrote, "aroused my warmest admiration. I passed from small apartments to spacious halls, and from these to magnificent courts, almost without end. Walls and ceilings were of marble, the former being sculptured and painted, and pillars of polished marble surrounded the courts. At the end of the labyrinth stood Pharaoh's Pyramid, with figures of animals carved upon its casement. "No stranger", Strabo informs us, "could find his way in or out of this building without a guide." The brick pyramids of the Twelfth Dynasty were also constructed with winding passages to baffle the tomb robbers; but they were "jerry built ", compared with those of the Khufu type, and survive to us in various stages of decay.

The idea of a labyrinth may have come from Crete. The palaces of the island kingdom were of mazy character, and the earliest at Knossos and Phaestos were erected in the First Middle Minoan period, which is parallel with the Eleventh Egyptian Dynasty. Their fame must have reached the Nile valley, for the influence of the island kingdom's architecture is traceable in the construction of Mentuhotep's complicated temple at Der el Bahari. A people who appear to have been "broadheaded" mountaineers invaded Crete at the close of its Second Middle Minoan period, which is parallel with the Twelfth Egyptian Dynasty. Their success culminated in the destruction of the earlier palace of Knossos. At a later age, when a similar invasion occurred, large numbers of Cretans fled to Asia Minor, and it is possible that in the time of Amenemhet III many of the island refugees settled in the Nile valley. If these included architects and skilled artisans, they must have received most hospitable welcome.

Egypt, we know, was at this period in close touch with Crete. The numerous relics of the Twelfth Dynasty which have been found in the palace ruins of the island show how free and continuous was the sea trade between the two kingdoms. No doubt it was greatly stimulated by the Egyptian demand for tin. We find that bronze came into more general use during the Twelfth Dynasty than had previously been the case. In Old-Kingdom times tools were made chiefly of copper, and occasionally of iron. The latter was called "The Metal of Heaven", and is referred to in the Pyramid texts of King Unas. If it was obtained originally from meteorites, as has been suggested, we can understand why, in Egypt as elsewhere, it was supposed to possess magical qualities. It does not seem to have been excavated in great quantities by the early Egyptians; the difficulty of smelting it must have been great, owing to the scarcity of timber.

Copper was used in the late pre-Dynastic period, when expeditions from the southern kingdom began to visit the mines of the Sinaitic peninsula. The Delta people may have also obtained it from Cyprus, where the earliest weapons and pottery resemble Egyptian forms. At the close of the Third Dynasty bronze was introduced or manufactured; the bronze "rod of Medum" was found deeply embedded in the fillings of a mastaba associated with the pyramid of King Sneferu. A bronze socketed hoe of the Sixth Dynasty bears resemblances to examples from Cyprus and South Russia preserved in the British Museum. Trade with the copper island did not assume any dimensions, however, until the Eighteenth Dynasty, and the Cypriote weapons which were imported into the Nile valley before that period may have come along the trade route through Syria, if they were not captured in frontier conflicts with Asiatic invaders.

Egypt manufactured its own bronze, and the suggestion of W. M. Muller, that certain figures on a Sixth-Dynasty relief are "Ægeans bringing tin into Egypt" is therefore of special interest. If such a trade existed, it must have been hampered greatly, if not entirely cut off, during the disturbed period prior to the rise of Amenemhet I.

Whence were the liberal supplies of bronze obtained by the Egyptians in the Twelfth Dynasty? The unrest in Asia must have interrupted trade along the great caravan routes to the ancient tin mines of Khorassan in Persia, from which Babylonia received supplies. The Phœnician mariners had scarcely yet begun to appear in

the Mediterranean. Tin must have come mainly through
Crete therefore; indeed the island traders could not have
had anything more valuable to offer in exchange for the
corn of Egypt.

Crete had long been familiar with bronze. The First
Early Minoan period, which marks the transition from
stone, began in Egypt's Third Dynasty, or slightly earlier.
Was its tin obtained from Central Europe or Brittany?
Dr. Duncan Mackenzie, the distinguished archæologist,
says in this connection: "By the beginning of the Bronze
Age (in Crete) the valley of the Rhone must have played
a dominant rôle of communication between the great
world of the Mediterranean and the north; by that time
it was probably the high continental trade route towards
the tin mines of Britain". If so, the tin-mining industry
of Cornwall and the Scilly islands must have been increased greatly by the demand created by the tin-
importing and temple-building Pharaohs of the Twelfth
Dynasty, who flourished long before Joseph appeared in
the land of Egypt.

Another link between ancient Britain and the Nile
valley is the spiral ornament, which appears in "degene-
rate form" on the so-called "spectacle stones" of Scotland.
The spiral is common on Egyptian scarabs of the Twelfth
Dynasty. We find that it passed to Crete, and then along
the Danube trade route to Denmark, where the ornaments on which it appeared were possibly given in
exchange for the much-sought-for Baltic amber. It spread
in time through Scandinavia. The spiral must also have
followed the Rhone-valley route, for it was passed on
from France to the British Isles, through which it was
widely diffused in the Bronze Age. In Ireland it was
carved on the stones of the famous New Grange barrow,
County Meath.

The brilliant Twelfth Dynasty came to an end soon after the death of the great Amenemhet III. His closing years were shadowed by domestic grief, for his favourite son, Ewib-ra, predeceased him. A wooden statue of the prince is preserved in the Cairo museum, and is that of a handsome and dignified youth. The next king, Amenemhet IV, ruled for about nine years. He left no son, and was succeeded by Queen Sebeknefru-ra, a daughter of Amenemhet III, and the last of her "line", who sat on the throne for four years. With her passed away the glory and grandeur of the "Golden Age", the latter half of which had special features of much interest. These are dealt with in the next chapter.

CHAPTER XVIII

Myths and Lays of the Middle Kingdom

Foreign Brides—Succession by Male and Female Lines—New Religious Belief—Sebek the Crocodile God—Identified with Set and Sutekh—The Crocodile of the Sun—The Friend and Foe of the Dead—Sebek Kings—The Tame Crocodile—Usert, the Earth Goddess—Resemblance to Isis and Neith —Sutekh and Baal—Significance of Dashur Jewellery—The Great Sphinx— Literary Activity—Egyptian Folksongs—Dialogue of a Man with his Soul —"To be or not to be"—Sun Cult Doctrines—"The Lay of the Harper".

DURING the Twelfth Dynasty Babylon fell and Crete was invaded. Egypt alone among the older kingdoms successfully withstood the waves of aggression which were passing over the civilized world. It was not immune, however, to foreign influence. A controlling power in Syria had evidently to be reckoned with, for raiding bands were constantly hovering on the frontier. It has been suggested that agreements were concluded, but no records of any survive. There are indications, however, that diplomatic marriages took place, and these may have been arranged for purposes of conciliation. At any rate foreign brides were entering the royal harem, and the exclusive traditions of Egypt were being set at defiance.

Senusert II had a favourite wife called Nefert, "the beautiful", who appears to have been a Hittite. Her son, Senusert III, and her grandson, Amenemhet III, have been referred to as "new types".[1] Their faces, as is shown plainly in the statuary, have distinct non-Egyptian and non-Semitic characteristics; they are long

Newberry and Garstang, and Petrie.

and angular—the third Senusert's seems quite Mongoloid —with narrow eyes and high cheek bones. There can be no doubt about the foreign strain.

It is apparent that Senusert III ascended the throne as the son of his father. This fact is of special interest, because, during the Twelfth Dynasty, succession by the female line was generally recognized in Egypt. Evidently Senusert II elevated to the rank of Crown Prince the son of his foreign wife. Amenemhet III appears to have been similarly an arbitrary selection. No doubt the queens and dowager queens were making their presence felt, and were responsible for innovations of far-reaching character, which must have aroused considerable opposition. It may be that a legitimist party had become a disturbing element. The high rate of mortality in the royal house during the latter years of the Dynasty suggests the existence of a plot to remove undesirable heirs by methods not unfamiliar in Oriental Courts.

Along with the new royal faces new religious beliefs also came into prominence. The rise of Sebek, the crocodile god, may have been due to the tendency shown by certain of the Pharaohs to reside in the Fayum. The town of Crocodilopolis was the chief centre of the hitherto obscure Sebek cult. It is noteworthy, however, that the reptile deity was associated with the worship of Set—not the familiar Egyptian Set, but rather his prototype, Sutekh of the Hittites. Apparently an old tribal religion was revived in new and developed form.

In the texts of Unas, Sebek is referred to as the son of Neith, the Libyan "Earth Mother", who personified the female principle, and was believed to be self-sustaining, as she had been self-produced. She was "the unknown one" and "the hidden one", whose veil had never been uplifted. Like other virgin goddesses, she had a father-

less son, the "husband of his mother", who may have
been identified with Sebek as a result of early tribal
fusion.

It is suggested that in his crocodile form Sebek was
worshipped as the snake was worshipped, on account
of the dread he inspired.   But, according to Diodorus,
crocodiles were also regarded as protectors of Egypt,
because, although they devoured the natives occasionally,
they prevented robbers from swimming over the Nile.
Opinions, however, differed as to the influence exercised
by the crocodile on the destinies of Egypt.   Some Indian
tribes of the present day worship snakes, and do everything they can to protect even the most deadly specimens.
In Egypt the crocodile was similarly protected in particular localities, while in others it was hunted down by
sportsmen.[1]   We also find that in religious literature the
reptile is now referred to as the friend and now as the
enemy of the good Osiris.   He brings ashore the dead
body of the god to Isis in one legend,[2] and in another he
is identified with his murderers.   In the "Winged Disk"
story the followers of Set are crocodiles and hippopotami,
and are slain by Horus because they are "the enemies of
Ra".   Yet Sebek was in the revolutionary Sixth Dynasty
identified with the sun god, and in the *Book of the Dead*
there is a symbolic reference to his dwelling on Sunrise
Hill, where he was associated with Hathor and Horus—
the Great Mother and son.

Sebek-Tum-Ra ultimately became the crocodile of the
sun, as Mentu became "bull of the sun", and he symbolized the power and heat of the orb of day.   In this

---

[1] Herodotus says: "Those who live near Thebes, and the Lake Mœris, hold the
crocodile in religious veneration. . . . Those who live in or near Elephantine make
the beasts an article of food."

[2] This is of special interest, because Hittite gods appear upon the backs of animals.

form he was the "radiant green disk"—"the creator", who rose from Nu "in many shapes and in many colours".

At Ombos, Sebek was a form of Seb, the earth giant, the son of Nut, and "husband of his mother". He was called the "father of the gods" and "chief of the Nine Bow Barbarians".

In his Set form, Sebek was regarded in some parts as an enemy and devourer of the dead. But his worshippers believed that he would lead souls by "short cuts" and byways to the Egyptian paradise. In the Pyramid Texts he has the attributes of the elfin Khnûmû, whose dwarfish images were placed in tombs to prevent decay, for he renews the eyes of the dead, touches their tongues so that they can speak, and restores the power of motion to their heads.

The recognition which Sebek received at Thebes may have been due to the influence of the late kings of the Twelfth Dynasty, and those of the Thirteenth who had Sebek names. The god is depicted as a man with a crocodile's head, and he sometimes wears Amon plumes with the sun disk; he is also shown simply as a crocodile. He was familiar to the Greeks as Sukhos. Strabo, who visited Egypt in the Roman period, relates that he saw a sacred crocodile in an artificial lake at Crocodilopolis in the Fayum. It was quite tame[1] and was decorated with gold ear-rings, set with crystal, and wore bracelets on its fore paws. The priests opened its jaws and fed it with cakes, flesh, and honey wine. When the animal leapt into the water and came up at the other side, the priests followed it and gave it a fresh offering. Herodotus tells that the fore feet of the sacred crocodile which he saw were secured by a chain. It was fed not only with

[1] The god was not feared. It had been propitiated and became the friend of man.

choice food, but with "the flesh of sacred victims". When the reptile died its body was embalmed, and, having been deposited in a sacred chest, was laid in one of the lower chambers of the Labyrinth. These subterranean cells were reputed to be of great sanctity, and Herodotus was not permitted to enter them.

The deity Usert, whose name is associated with the kings Senusert (also rendered Usertesen), was an earth goddess. She is identified with Isis, and closely resembles Neith—the Great Mother with a son whose human incarnation is the Pharaoh. Usert worship may have been closely associated, therefore, with Sebek worship, because Sebek was the son of an earth goddess. He rose from Nu, the primordial deep, as the crocodile rose from Lake Mœris, the waters of which nourished the "earth mother", and caused green verdure to spring up where formerly there was but sandy desert.[1] Sebek was thus in a new sense a form of Ra, and a "radiant green sun disk". His association with Set was probably due to Asiatic influence, and the foreign strain in the royal house may have come from a district where Set was worshipped as Sutekh. The Egyptian Set developed from an early conception of a tribal Sutekh as a result of Asiatic settlement in the eastern Delta in pre-Dynastic times. The Hittite Sutekh was a sun god and a weather god. But there were many Sutekhs as there were many Baals. Baal signifies "lord" or "chief god", and in Egypt was identified with Set and with Mentu, the bull of war. At Tanis he was "lord of the heaven". Sutekh, also a "baal" or "lord", appears to have been similarly adaptable in tendency. If it was due to his influence that the crocodile god of the Fayum became a solar deity, the

---

[1] When the Nile rises it runs, for a period, green and foul, after running red with clay. The crocodile may have been associated with the green water also.

foreign ladies in the Pharaoh's harem must have been Hittites, whose religious beliefs influenced those of their royal sons.

Exquisite jewellery has been found at Dashur, where Amenemhet II and his grandson Senusert III resided and erected their pyramids—two diadems of princesses of the royal house, the daughters of the second Senusert's foreign wife, at Dashur. One is a mass of little gold flowers connected by gold wires, which recall the reference, in *Exodus*, xxxix, 3, to the artisans who "did beat the gold into thin plates, and cut it into wires". The design is strengthened by large "Maltese crosses" set with gems.[1] Other pieces of Twelfth-Dynasty jewellery are similarly "innovations", and of the character which, long centuries afterwards, became known as Etruscan. But they could not have come from Europe at this period. They resemble the work for which the Hittites were famous.

The great sphinx may have also owed its origin to the influence exercised by the Hittites, whose emblem of power was a lion. Certain Egyptologists[2] are quite convinced that it was sculptured during the reign of Amenemhet III, whose face they consider it resembles. Nilotic gods had animal heads with human bodies. The sphinx, therefore, could not have been a god of Egypt. Scarab beetle seals were also introduced during the Twelfth Dynasty. The Dynastic civilization of Egypt began with the use of the Babylonian seal cylinder.

The "Golden Age" is distinguished not only for its material progress, but also for its literary activity. In this respect it may be referred to as the "Elizabethan Age" of Ancient Egypt. The compositions appear to

---

[1] The Maltese cross is believed to be of Elamite origin. It is first met with in Babylon on seals of the Kassite period. It appears on the neolithic pottery of Susa.
[2] Newberry and Garstang.

have been numerous, and many were of high quality. During the great Dynasty the kingdom was "a nest of singing birds", and the home of storytellers. There are snatches of song even in the tomb inscriptions, and rolls of papyri have been found in mummy coffins containing love ditties, philosophic poems, and wonder tales, which were provided for the entertainment of the dead in the next world.

It is exceedingly difficult for us to enter into the spirit of some of these compositions. We meet with baffling allusions to unfamiliar beliefs and customs, while our ignorance of the correct pronunciation of the language make some ditties seem absolutely nonsensical, although they may have been regarded as gems of wit; such quaint turns of phrase, puns, and odd mannerisms as are recognizable are entirely lost when attempts are made to translate them. The Egyptian poets liked to play upon words. In a Fifth-Dynasty tomb inscription this tendency is apparent. A shepherd drives his flock over the wet land to tramp down the seed, and he sings a humorous ditty to the sheep. We gather that he considers himself to be in a grotesque situation, for he "salutes the pike", and is like a shepherd among the dead, who converses with strange beings as he converses with fish. "Salutes" and "pike" are represented by the same word, and it is as if we said in English that a fisherman "flounders like flounders" or that joiners "box the box".

A translation is therefore exceedingly bald.

> The shepherd is in the water with the fish;
> He converses with the sheath fish;
> He salutes the pike;
> From the West—the shepherd is a shepherd from the West.

"The West" is, of course, the land of the dead.

Some of the Twelfth-Dynasty "minor poems" are, however, of universal interest because their meaning is as clear as their appeal is direct. The two which follow are close renderings of the originals.

THE WOODCARVER

The carver grows more weary
    Than he who hoes all day,
As up and down his field of wood
    His chisel ploughs away.
No rest takes he at even,
    Because he lights a light;
He toils until his arms drop down
    Exhausted, in the night.

THE SMITH

A smith is no ambassador—
    His style is to abuse;
I never met a goldsmith yet
    Able to give one news.
Oh, I have seen a smith at work,
    Before his fire aglow—
His "claws" are like a crocodile;
    He smells like fish's roe.

The Egyptian peasants were great talkers. Life was not worth living if there was nothing to gossip about. A man became exceedingly dejected when he had to work in solitude; he might even die from sheer ennui. So we can understand the ditty which tells that a brickmaker is puddling all alone in the clay at the time of inundation; he has to talk to the fish. "He is now a brickmaker in the West." In other words, the lonely task has been the death of him.

This horror of isolation from sympathetic companionship pervades the wonderful composition which has been called "The Dialogue of a Man with his Soul". The opening part of the papyrus is lost, and it is uncertain whether the lonely Egyptian was about to commit suicide or was contemplating with feelings of horror the melancholy fate which awaited him when he would be laid in the tomb. He appears to have suffered some great wrong; his brothers have deserted him, his friends have proved untrue, and—terrible fate!—he has nobody to speak to. Life is, therefore, not worth living, but he dreads to die because of the darkness and solitude of the tomb which awaits him. The fragment opens at the conclusion of a speech made by the soul. Apparently it has refused to accompany the man, so that he is faced with the prospect of not having even his soul to converse with.

"In the day of my sorrow", the man declares, "you should be my companion and my sympathetic friend. Why scold me because I am weary of life? Do not compel me to die, because I take no delight in the prospect of death; do not tell me that there is joy in the 'after-time'. It is a sorrowful thing that this life cannot be lived over again, for in the next world the gods will consider with great severity the deeds we have done here."

He calls himself a "kindly and sympathetic man", but the soul thinks otherwise and is impatient with him. "You poor fool," it says, "you dread to die as if you were one of these rich men."

But the Egyptian continues to lament his fate; he has no belief in joy after death. The soul warns him, therefore, that if he broods over the future in such a spirit of despondency he will be punished by being left forever in his dark solitary tomb. The inference appears to be that those who lack faith will never enter Paradise.

" The thought of death ", says the soul, " is sorrow in itself, it makes men weep; it makes them leave their homes and throw themselves in the dust."

Men who display their unbelief, never enjoy, after death, the light of the sun. Statues of granite may be carved for them, their friends may erect pyramids which display great skill of workmanship, but their fate is like that of " the miserable men who died of hunger at the riverside, or the peasant ruined by drought or by the flood—a poor beggar who has lost everything and has none to talk to except the fishes ".

The soul counsels the man to enjoy life and to banish care and despondency. He is a foolish fellow who contemplates death with sorrow because he has grown weary of living; the one who has cause to grieve is he whose life is suddenly cut short by disaster. Such appears to be the conclusion which should be drawn from the soul's references to some everyday happenings of which the following is an example:—

" A peasant has gathered in his harvest; the sheaves are in his boat; he sails on the Nile, and his heart is filled with the prospect of making merry. Suddenly a storm comes on. He is compelled to remain beside his boat, guarding his harvest. But his wife and his children suffer a melancholy fate. They were coming to meet him, but they lost their way in the storm, and the crocodiles devoured them. The poor peasant has good cause to lament aloud. He cries out, saying:

" ' I do not sorrow for my beloved wife, who has gone hence and will never return, so much as for the little children who, in the dawn of life, met the crocodile and perished.' "

The man is evidently much impressed by the soul's reasoning. He changes his mind, and praises the tomb as a safe retreat and resting place for one who, like himself, cannot any longer enjoy life. Why he feels so utterly dejected we cannot tell; the reason may have been given in the lost portion of the old papyrus. There is evidently no prospect of enjoyment before him. His name has become hateful among men; he has been wronged; the world is full of evil as he is full of sorrow.

At this point the composition becomes metrical in construction:

> Hateful my name! . . . more hateful is it now
> Than the rank smell of ravens in the heat;
> Than rotting peaches, or the meadows high
> Where geese are wont to feed; than fishermen
> Who wade from stinking marshes with their fish,
> Or the foul odour of the crocodile;
> More hateful than a husband deems his spouse
> When she is slandered, or his gallant son
> Falsely accused; more hateful than a town
> Which harbours rebels who are sought in vain.
>
> Whom can I speak to? . . . Brothers turn away;
> I have no friend to love me as of yore;
> Hearts have turned cold and cruel; might is right;
> The strong are spoilers, and the weakly fall,
> Stricken and plundered. . . . Whom can I speak to?
>
> The faithful man gets sorrow for reward—
> His brother turns his foe—the good he does,
> How swiftly 'tis undone, for thankless hearts
> Have no remembrance of the day gone past.
> Whom can I speak to? I am full of grief—
> There is not left alive one faithful man;
> The world is full of evil without end.

Death is before me like a draught prepared
To banish sickness; or as fresh, cool air
To one who, after fever, walks abroad.
Death is before me sweet as scented myrrh;
Like soft repose below a shelt'ring sail
In raging tempest. . . . Death before me is
Like perfumed lotus; like a restful couch
Spread in the Land of Plenty; or like home
For which the captive yearns, and warriors greet
When they return. . . . Ah! death before me is
Like to a fair blue heaven after storm—
A channel for a stream—an unknown land
The huntsman long has sought and finds at last.

He who goes Yonder rises like a god
That spurns the sinner; lo! his seat is sure
Within the sun bark, who hath offered up
Choice victims in the temples of the gods;
He who goes Yonder is a learnèd man,
Whom no one hinders when he calls to Ra.

The soul is now satisfied, because the man has professed his faith in the sun god. It promises, therefore, not to desert him. "Your body will lie in the earth," it says, "but I will keep you company when you are given rest. Let us remain beside one another."

It is possible that this composition was intended to make converts for the sun cult. The man appears to dread the judgment before Osiris, the King of the Dead, who reckons up the sins committed by men in this world. His soul approves of his faith in Ra, of giving offerings in the temples, and of becoming a "learned man"—one who has acquired knowledge of the magic formulæ which enables him to enter the sun bark. This soul appears to be the man's Conscience. It is difficult to grasp the Egyptian ideas regarding the soul which enters Paradise, the soul which hovers over the mummy, and the conscious

life of the body in the tomb.   These were as vague as
they appear to have been varied.

One of the most popular Egyptian poems is called
"The Lay of the Harper".   It was chanted at the
banquets given by wealthy men.   "Ere the company
rises," wrote Herodotus, "a small coffin which contains
a perfect model of the human body is carried round, and
is shown to each guest in rotation.   He who bears it
exclaims: 'Look at this figure. . . . After death you
will be like it.   Drink, therefore, and be merry.'"   The
"lay" in its earliest form was of great antiquity.   Probably a real mummy was originally hauled through the
banquet hall.

LAY OF THE HARPER

'Tis well with this good prince; his day is done,
His happy fate fulfilled. . . . So one goes forth
While others, as in days of old, remain.
The old kings slumber in their pyramids,
Likewise the noble and the learned, but some
Who builded tombs have now no place of rest,
Although their deeds were great. . . . Lo! I have heard
The words Imhotep and Hordadaf spake—
Their maxims men repeat. . . . Where are their tombs?—
Long fallen . . . e'en their places are unknown,
And they are now as though they ne'er had been.

No soul comes back to tell us how he fares—
To soothe and comfort us ere we depart
Whither he went betimes. . . . But let our minds
Forget of this and dwell on better things. . . .
Revel in pleasure while your life endures
And deck your head with myrrh.   Be richly clad
In white and perfumed linen; like the gods
Anointed be; and never weary grow
In eager quest of what your heart desires—
Do as it prompts you . . . until that sad day

Of lamentation comes, when hearts at rest
Hear not the cry of mourners at the tomb,
Which have no meaning to the silent dead. . .
Then celebrate this festal time, nor pause—
For no man takes his riches to the grave;
Yea, none returns again when he goes hence.

CHAPTER XIX

The Island of Enchantment

A Sailor's Story—Shipwrecked—The Sole Survivor—A Lonely Island—
A Voice like Thunder—The Giant Serpent God—A Threat—Sailor given
Protection—Sacrifice of Asses--Rescued by a Ship—The Parting—A Man of
Wisdom.

ONCE upon a time a ship set forth on a voyage to the
mines of Sinai, and it was swamped in a storm.   All
the sailors were drowned save one, who swam to the Isle
of Enchantment, which was inhabited by the "manes"—
serpent gods who have heads and arms like to human
beings and are able to hold converse in speech.

When this man returned to Egypt he related his
wonderful story unto his lord, saying: "Now, be well
satisfied that I have come back although alone.   Your
ship on which I have returned is safe, and no men are
missing.   I was rescued by it, and I had no other means
of escape.   When you have cleansed your limbs, I pray
you to inform the Pharaoh of the things which have
befallen me."

The master said: "So you persist in repeating this
tale of yours.   But speak on.   I will hear you to the
end, and, perchance, your words will betray the truth.
But lower your voice and say what you have to say without excitement."

The sailor said: "I will begin at the beginning, and
relate what happened to myself.   I voyaged towards the
mines in your great ship, in which were 150 of the finest

sailors in Egypt. They were all stout-hearted men. Now, some said that the wind would be unfavourable, and others said that there would be no wind at all. As it chanced, a great storm arose, and the ship was tossed about in the midst of high billows so that it was swamped. When I found myself in the angry waters, I clung to a floating spar. All the others were drowned. In time I was cast ashore, and I found myself on a lonely island, where I lay helplessly for three days and three nights. Then I began to revive. I was faint with hunger and thirst, and went to search for food, and I found fruit and birds and fishes, and ate thereof. I gave thanks to the god because that I was alive, and offered up a sacrifice.

"No sooner had I given thanks in this manner than I heard a loud noise like to thunder, and the earth trembled beneath me and the trees were stricken as with tempest. I hid my face with terror, and after I had lain a time on the ground I looked up and beheld a giant serpent god with human face and arms. He wore a long beard, and his body was golden and blue.

"I prostrated myself before him, and he spake, saying: 'Speak and tell, little fellow, speak and tell why you have come hither. If you do not speak without delay, I will cause your life to end. If you do not tell me what I have not heard and what I do not know,[1] I will cause you to pass out of existence like a flame which has been extinguished.'

"Ere I answered him he carried me inland and set me down without injury, whereupon I said that I had come from the land of Egypt in a great ship which perished in the storm, and that I had clung to a spar and was washed ashore.

---

[1] The Norse giant Vafthrudner similarly puts to death those who cannot tell him something he does not know.

"The serpent god heard, and said: 'Do not be terrified, little fellow, do not be terrified, and be cheerful of countenance, for it is the god who sent you hither to me. Here you may dwell until four moons wax and wane; then a ship will come, and you will depart in it and return once again to the land of Egypt. . . . It is pleasant to hold converse. Know, then, that I dwell here with my kind, and I have children, and there is also a girl who perished by accident in a fire. I will take you to my home, and you will return to yours again in time.'

"When the giant serpent god had spoken thus I prostrated myself before him, and I said: 'To the King of Egypt I will relate the things I have seen. I will laud your name, and offerings of oil and perfumes will be made to you. Asses[1] and birds will I sacrifice to you, and the king will send you rich offerings because you are a benefactor of mankind.'

"'I need not your perfumes,' answered the serpent god. 'I am a ruler of Punt, and these I possess in abundance, but I have no oil of Egypt here. But know that when you go away this island will never again be seen by any man; it will vanish in the midst of the sea.'

"When four moons had waxed and waned, a ship appeared as the serpent god had foretold. I knelt down and bade farewell to the inhabitants of the island of enchantment, and the great god gave me gifts of perfumes and ivory and much treasure, and he gave me also rare woods and baboons. I took my leave with grateful heart, and I thanked the god because of my deliverance. Then I went to the shore and hailed the ship, and was taken aboard it.

---

[1] The reference is unique. Set is associated with the wild ass, but except in this tale there is no indication that asses were sacrificed in Egypt. The Aryans sacrificed the horse.

"These are the things which happened unto me, my lord and master. Now conduct me, I pray you, before His Majesty that I may present him with the gifts of the serpent god. . . . Look upon me, for I have returned to tell of the wonders I did behold with mine eyes. . . . In my youth I was instructed to acquire wisdom so that I might be highly esteemed. Now I have become a wise man indeed."

Apparently "the master" was convinced by this wonderful story, which was duly recorded by a scribe of the temple of Amon.

CHAPTER XX

The Hyksos and their Strange God

The Sebek-Ra Rulers—A Great Pharaoh—The Shadow of Anarchy—Coming of the "Shepherd Kings"—Carnival of Destruction—A Military Occupation—Causes of World-wide Unrest—Dry Cycles—Invasions of Pastoral Peoples—History in Mythology—Tribal Father and Mother Deities—Sutekh, Thor, Hercules—Mountain Deities and Cave Demons—Hyksos Civilization—Trade with Europe and Asia—The Horse—Hittite Influence in Palestine—Raid on Babylon—Kassites and Aryans—Aryan Gods in Syria—Mitanni Kingdom.

AFTER the close of the Golden Age the materials for Egyptian history become somewhat scanty. The Thirteenth Dynasty opened peacefully, and the Sebek-Ra names of its kings indicate that the cults of the crocodile and the sun held the balance of power. The influence exercised by the Pharaohs, however, appears to have been strictly circumscribed. Some of them may have reigned in Crocodilopolis or its vicinity, but Thebes ultimately became the capital, which indicates that the Delta region, with its growing foreign element, was considered insecure for the royal house. The great kings of the Twelfth Dynasty had established their power in the north, where they found it necessary to keep watchful eyes on the Libyan and Syrian frontiers.

Succession to the throne appears to have been regulated by descent in the female line. Evidently the Legitimists were resolved that alien influence should not predominate at Court, and in this regard they must have received the support of the great mass of the Egyptian

252

people, of whom Herodotus said: "They contentedly adhere to the customs of their ancestors, and are averse from foreign manners". It is significant to find that the father of one of the Sebekhotep kings was a priest who achieved greatness because he married a princess. This Sebekhotep was followed by his son, who had a Hathor name, but he was dethroned after a brief reign. The next Pharaoh was the paternal uncle of the fallen monarch. His royal name was Neferkhara-Sebekhotep, and he proved to be the greatest ruler of this obscure period. He controlled the entire kingdom, from the shores of the Mediterranean to the second cataract, where records were made of the rise of the Nile. On the island of Argo, near the third cataract, he erected two granite statues over 20 feet in height, which stood in front of a large temple. Nubian aggression must have been held firmly in check by a considerable garrison. But not for long. After two weak kings had reigned, the throne was seized by Neshi, "the negro", a worshipper of Ra and Set. His colossal statue of black granite testifies to the supremacy achieved by the Nubian raiders. In the north another usurper of whom we have trace is Mermenfatiu, "Commander of the Soldiers".

The shadow of anarchy had again fallen upon Egypt. Once more, too, the feudal lords asserted themselves, and the kingdom was broken up into a number of petty states. A long list of monarchs is given by Manetho, and these may include many of the hereditary nome governors who became Pharaohs in their own domains and waged war against their neighbours. Thebes remained the centre of the largest area of control, which may have enjoyed a meed of prosperity, but the rest of Egypt must have suffered greatly on account of the lack of supervision over the needful distribution of

water. Peasants may well have neglected to till the soil
in districts ever open to the raids of plunderers, exclaim-
ing, in the words of the Twelfth-Dynasty prophet:
"What is the good of it? We know what is coming."

Egypt was thoroughly disorganized and unable to
resist its enemies. These were ever watchful for an opportunity to strike. The Nubians had already achieved
some success, although they were ultimately expelled by
the Thebans; the Libyans must have been active in the
north, while the Asiatics were pouring over the Delta
frontier and possessing themselves of great tracts of
territory. Then came the Hyksos invaders, regarding
whose identity much controversy has been waged. They
were evidently no disorganized rabble, and there are
indications that under their sway Egypt became, for an
uncertain period, a part of a great empire of which we,
as yet, know very little.

Josephus, the patriotic Jewish historian, who believed
that the Hyksos were "the children of Israel", quoted
Manetho as saying that "they were a people of ignoble
race who had confidence to invade our country, which
they subdued easily without having to fight a battle.
They set our towns on fire; they destroyed the temples
of the gods, and caused the people to suffer every kind
of barbarity. During the entire period of their dynasty
they waged war against the people of Egypt, desiring to
exterminate the whole race. . . . The foreigners were
called Hyksos, which signifies 'Shepherd Kings'."

Manetho's reference to a carnival of destruction is
confirmed by the inscription of Queen Hatshepsut of
the Eighteenth Dynasty, who declared with characteristic
piety:

> I have restored what was cast down,
> I have built up what was uncompleted,

Since the Asiatics were in Avaris of the north land,
And the barbarians were among them, destroying buildings,
While they governed, not knowing Ra.

But if the hated Hyksos were wreckers of buildings, so were the Egyptians, who were ever prone to obliterate all records of unpopular rulers. Khufu's enduring pyramid defied them, but they destroyed his mummy and perpetuated his memory in a spirit of undeniable bitterness, although he was one of their greatest men. He was an enemy of their gods, which means that he laid too firm a hand upon the ambitious and acquisitive priests. Thutmose III and Akenaton also undertook in their day the vengeful work of erasing inscriptions, while Rameses II and others freely appropriated the monuments of their predecessors. It is not surprising, therefore, to find that few traces of the Hyksos rulers survive, and that, in a folktale, they are referred to as "the impure". They ruled "not knowing Ra", and were therefore delivered to oblivion. Manetho, who compiled his history about a thousand years after they were driven from the country, was unable to ascertain much about them. Only a few of the kings to whom he makes reference can be identified, and these belong to the Fifteenth Dynasty. Of the Sixteenth Dynasty he knew little or nothing, but in dealing with the Seventeenth he was on surer ground, because Upper Egypt had then regained its freedom, and was gradually reconquering lost territory in the north.

The Hyksos overwhelmed the land at the close of the Fourteenth Dynasty. Then they chose for a king "one of their own people". According to Manetho his name was Salatis, and with him begins the Fifteenth Dynasty. He selected Memphis as his capital, and there "he made Upper and Lower Egypt pay tribute", while he left garrisons at places which were "considered to be proper for them". Did the Hyksos, therefore, effect merely a military occupation of Egypt and compel the payment of tribute to a controlling power in Asia? On this point we obtain no clear idea from Manetho, who proceeds to state that the foreigners erected a strongly fortified town called Avaris—afterwards destroyed by the Egyptians—and there they kept a garrison of 240,000 men, so as to secure the frontier from the attacks of the Assyrians, "who, they foresaw, would invade Egypt". Salatis held military reviews to overawe all foreigners.

Whatever enemy the Hyksos feared, or prepared to meet, it was certainly not the Assyrians, who were at the time fully occupied with their own affairs; they had not yet attained to that military strength which subsequently caused the name of their god Ashur to be dreaded even in the Nile valley.

The reference, however, may be to Babylonia, where, as we shall see, an aggressive people had made their appearance.

In absence of reliable records regarding the Hyksos people, or perhaps we should say peoples, for it is possible that there was more than one invasion, we must cross the frontier of Egypt to obtain some idea of the conditions prevailing in Asia during this obscure but fascinating period.

Great changes were passing over the civilized world. Old kingdoms were being broken up, and new kingdoms were in process of formation. The immediate cause was the outpourings of pastoral peoples from steppes and plateaus in quest of "fresh woods and pastures new", because herbage had grown scanty during a prolonged "dry cycle" in countries like Arabia, Turkestan, and the Iranian plateau. Once these migrations by propulsion began, they were followed by migrations caused by expulsion. The movements were in some districts accompanied by constant fighting, and a people who displayed the best warlike qualities ultimately became conquerors on a gradually increasing scale. Another cause of migration was the growth of population. When an ancestral district became crowded, the surplus stock broke away in "waves". But movements of this kind invariably followed the line of least resistance, and did not necessarily involve marked changes in habits of life, for pastoral peoples moved from upland to upland, as did agriculturists from river valley to river valley and seafarers from coast to coast. When, however, peaceful settlements were effected by nomads in highly civilized areas an increased impetus must have been given to migration from their native country, where their kindred, hearing of their prosperity, began to dream dreams of the land of plenty. Nomads who entered Babylon or Egypt became "the outposts" of those sudden and violent migrations of wholesale character which occurred during prolonged periods of drought. The Hyksos conquest of Egypt is associated with one of these "dry cycles".

In an earlier chapter[1] we have referred to the gradual expansion from North Africa of the early Mediterranean "long heads", who spread themselves over the unoccupied or sparsely populated valleys and shores of Palestine, Asia Minor, and Europe. Simultaneously, or not much later, Asiatic "broad heads" moved in successive "waves" along the mountain ranges; these are the Alpine people of the ethnologists, and they are traced from the Himalayas to Brittany and the British Isles. The beliefs and

[1] Chapter III.

tribal customs of the Mediterraneans appear to have been
mainly of Matriarchal character, while those of the Alpine
folk were mainly Patriarchal.

The mixture of these peoples caused the development
of a great civilization in Asia Minor, and so, it is believed, had origin the Hittite kingdom.   Other races
were embraced, however, in the Hittite confederacy.
Mongols from Turkestan moved southward during a
dry period apparently, and became a strong element in
the Hittite area of control, while Semites from Arabia,
who appeared at very early times in Syria, became allies
of the rising people, with whom they fused in some districts.   The eagle-nosed, bearded Alpine Hittites are
believed to be represented by the present-day Armenians
and the Mongolian Hittites by the Kurds.   Some ethnologists are of opinion that the characteristic Jewish nose
indicates an early fusion of Hittites and Syrians.   There
was also an Alpine blend in Assyria, where the Semites
had facial characteristics which distinguished them from
the ancestral stock in Arabia.

Hittite theology is of special interest to us because
its influence can be traced in Egypt immediately before
and especially during the Hyksos period.   Some of the
tribes of Asia Minor worshipped the Great Mother deity
Ma or Ammas, who, like the Libyan Neith and other
virgin goddesses of the Delta, was self-created and had
a fatherless son.   She was essentially an earth goddess,
and of similar character to Astarte, Aphrodite, the Cretan
serpent goddess, "Our Lady of Doves" in Cyprus, the
Celtic Anu or Danu in Ireland, and the Scottish Cailleach
Bheur who shaped the hills, let loose the rivers, and
waved her hammer over the growing grass.

In Cilicia the male deities predominated, and in
southern Cappadocia, where primitive tribal beliefs appear

to have fused early, we find a great rock sculpture, depicting, it is believed, the marriage of the Great Father and Great Mother deities of the Alpine and Mediterranean peoples.

The Great Father god of the Hittites is Pappas or Attis ("father"), who was best known to the Egyptians as Sutekh. He is identified with Baal, "the lord," a deity no longer regarded as Semitic in origin. It was the moon god Sin, for instance, who gave his name to Sinai, and the Arabian sun deity was female.

Sutekh is depicted on a cliff near Smyrna as a bearded god with curly hair and a high, curving nose. He looks a typical mountaineer, clad in a tunic which is tightened round the waist by the "hunger belt" so familiar in Scottish hill lore, and wearing boots with turned-up toes, specially suited for high snow-covered altitudes.

Sutekh was a sky and atmosphere deity who caused the storms and sent thunder. He was a god of war, and wore goat's horns to symbolize fertility and the male principle. As Tark or Tarku he is depicted carrying in one hand a hammer and in the other three wriggling flashes of lightning, suggesting the Teutonic Thor. He is also shown grasping a mace and trident or a double battleaxe. As Ramman,[1] with double horns, and bearing his axe and three thunderbolts, he received adoption in Babylonia after the Hittite conquest.

When the Great Mother was wedded to the Great Father, her son may have been regarded as the son of Tarku also. It was probably the younger deity who was identified by the Greeks with Hercules, son of Zeus. But we need not expect a continuity of well-defined ideas regarding deities of common origin who have developed

---

[1] "When I bow down myself in the house of Rimmon, the Lord pardon thy servant in this thing."—2 *Kings*, v, 18.

separately. These two gods, the Great Father and the son of the Great Mother, are sometimes indistinguishable. They not only varied in different districts, but also at different periods. In the latest phase of Hittite religion the Great Father, the conquering war god of the Alpine people, predominated, and he absorbed the attributes of other deities in localities where Hittite influence became supreme.

The Hittite deities were associated with mountains and mysterious caves, which indicates that in their earliest stages they were giants and hags of the type familiar among the Tyrol mountains, in the Scottish highlands, and in Scandinavia. They had also their animal affinities and were depicted standing on the backs of lions and lionesses. The double-headed eagle and the three-legged symbol had also religious significance.

In addition to the deities there were fearsome demons. The Hittite Typhoon, like the Egyptian Set and Apep serpent, warred against the gods. He was half-human and half-reptile—the upper part of his body was that of a man and the lower that of a serpent. He lived in a cave which was connected by an underground passage with the cave of the gods. Tempests issued from his jaws and lightning flashed from his terrible flaming eyes. He was slain by Tarku, as the Hydra was slain by Hercules, and the various dragons of European story were slain by heroes of popular romance.

Egypt also had its somewhat colourless dragon legend, which was probably imported. In one of the Horus stories, Set became a " roaring serpent ", and in this form he concealed himself in a hole (a cave) which, by command of the ubiquitous Ra, he was not permitted to leave. He thus became identified with the Apep serpent. Sutekh, the later Set, who was regarded in the Delta as the true sun god, displaced Ra and Horus and figured as the "dragon slayer". The earlier Set was not originally a demon. He was, it would appear, the god of a foreign people who entered Egypt in pre-Dynastic times and were ultimately associated with all that was evil and impure, like the later Hyksos who worshipped Sutekh.

In Syria and Mitanni, prior to the Hyksos period, the Great Father deity of the Hittites became the supreme god. The most reasonable inference is that he was the divine representative of the conquering people in Asia Minor. He bore several territorial names: he was Hadad or Dad in Syria and Teshub (or Teshup) in Mitanni; he was Tarku farther north. But that he was identical with Sutekh there can be little doubt, for when Rameses II entered into a treaty with the Hittites, Sutekh and Amon Ra were referred to as the chief representative gods of the two great empires.

Now it is a significant fact that the Hittite war god was the chief deity of the Hyksos. Like Ra-Tum of Heliopolis and Horus of Edfu his appearance in Egypt points to a definite foreign influence. He was the deity of a people who exercised control over subject states— a strange god who was adopted by compulsion because he represented the ruling Power. The Hyksos kings endeavoured to compel the Egyptians to recognize Sutekh, their official non-Arabian god—an indication that their organization had a religious basis.

From Manetho's references to this obscure period we gather that the invaders of Egypt were well organized indeed. Their raid was not followed by those intertribal feuds which usually accompanied forcible settlement in a country by Semitic hordes from Arabia. They did not break up into warring factions, like the early invaders of Palestine. Before reaching Egypt they must have come under the influence of a well-organized State. They had attained, at any rate, that stage of civilization when a people recognize the necessity for establishing a strong central government.

The Hyksos must be credited with military and administrative experience, seeing that they garrisoned strategic points, and maintained a standing army like the greatest of the Pharaohs. The collection of tribute is also significant. In like manner did the later Egyptian emperors extract revenue from the petty kings of subject states in Syria. What Power received the tribute gathered by the Hyksos? All the indications point to the Hittites. If the Hyksos people were not wholly from Asia Minor, it is highly probable that the army of occupation was under Hittite control.

It may be that the invading forces included Semites from Arabia, plundering Bedouins, Amorites, and even Phœnicians who had migrated from the north of the Persian Gulf to the Palestine coast, and that assistance was given by the Libyans, reinforced by mercenaries from Crete or the Ægean Peninsula. But it is inconceivable that a hungry horde of desert dwellers, or an uncontrolled and homogeneous rabble from Arabia, could have maintained firm control of Egypt for a prolonged period. The nomads, however, who accompanied the Hyksos forces, may have been " the barbarians in the midst of them " who are referred to in the inscription of Queen Hatshepsut. No doubt the invaders were welcomed and assisted by those troublesome alien peoples, who, during the Twelfth Dynasty, had settled in Egypt and absorbed its civilization. But the army of occupation was ever regarded as a foreign element, and in all probability it was reinforced mainly from without. The country must have been well governed. Queen Hatshepsut admits as much, for she condemns the Hyksos chiefly on religious grounds; they destroyed the temples—perhaps some were simply allowed to fall into disrepair—and they ruled " not knowing Ra ". Had the foreign kings followed the example of some of the most popular Pharaohs, they might have purchased the allegiance of the priests of the various cults; but their desire was to establish the worship of the Hittite Sutekh as a result, it may be inferred, of political influence exercised by the foreign power which received the tribute. One or two of the Hyksos kings affected a preference for Egyptian gods.

We must take at a discount the prejudiced Egyptian reference to the hated alien rulers. During the greater part of the Hyksos period peaceful conditions prevailed not only in Egypt but over a considerable area in Asia. The great trade routes were reopened, and commerce appears to have been in a flourishing condition. Agriculture, therefore, must have been fostered; a surplus yield of corn was required not only to pay tribute but also to offer in exchange for the commodities of other countries. We meet, in Manetho's King Ianias, a ruler who was evidently progressive and enterprising. He is identified with Ian, or Khian, whose name appears on Hyksos relics which have been found at Knossos, Crete, and Bagdad in Persia. His non-Egyptian title " ank adebu ", which signifies " Embracer of Countries ", suggests that he was a representative of a great power which controlled more than one conquered kingdom. Breasted, the American Egyptologist, translates Hyksos as " rulers of countries ", which means practically the same thing, although other authorities show a preference for Manetho's rendering, " Shepherd Kings ", or its equivalent " Princes of Desert Dwellers ". It may be, of course, that "Hyksos" was a term of contempt for a people whom the proud Egyptians made scornful reference to as "the polluted" or "the impure". To this day Europeans are regarded in China as "foreign devils".

We regard the Hyksos period as "a dark age" mainly because of the absence of those records which the Egyptians were at pains to destroy. Perhaps we are also prone to be influenced by their denunciations of the foreigners. We have no justification for assuming, however, that progress was arrested for a prolonged period extending over about two centuries. The arts did not suffer decline, nor did the builders lose their skill. So thoroughly was the kingdom reorganized that the power of the feudal lords was completely shattered. Even the Twelfth-Dynasty kings were unable to accomplish as much. The Hyksos also introduced the domesticated horse into Egypt, but at what period we are unable to ascertain. Manetho makes no reference to it in his brief account of the invasion. If, however, there were charioteers in the foreign army when it swept over the land, they could not have come from Arabia, and Bedouins were not likely to be able to manufacture or repair chariots. Only a rich country could have obtained horses at this early period. They had newly arrived in western Asia and must have been scarce and difficult to obtain.

Whence, then, came the horse which shattered and built up the great empires? It was first tamed by the Aryans, and its place of origin is signified by its Assyrian name "the ass of the East". How it reached Western Asia and subsequently made its appearance in the Nile valley, is a matter of special interest to us in dealing with the Hyksos problems.

We must first glance, however, at the conditions

which prevailed in the immediate neighbourhood of Egypt prior to the invasion. During the "Golden Age" the Pharaohs were much concerned about maintaining a strongly defended north-eastern frontier. No Egyptian records survive to throw light on the relations between Egypt and Syria, but the large number of Twelfth-Dynasty ornaments, scarabs, and amulets, bearing hieroglyphic inscriptions, which have been excavated at Gezer and elsewhere, indicate that trade was brisk and continuous. A great change had meantime passed over Palestine. "Sometime about 2000 to 1800 B.C.", says Professor Macalister, the well-known Palestinian explorer, "we find a rather sudden advance in civilization to have taken place. This, like all the other forward steps of which recent excavation in the country has revealed traces, was due to foreign interference. The Semitic nations, Amorite, Hebrew, or Arab, never invented anything; they assimilated all the elements of their civilization from without."

During the Twelfth Dynasty, therefore, Palestine came under the sway of a people who had attained a high degree of culture. But they could not have been either Assyrian or Babylonian, and Egypt exercised no control beyond its frontier. The great extending Power at the time was the Hittite in the north. Little is known regarding the early movements of its conquering peoples, who formed small subject states which were controlled by the central government in Asia Minor. That they penetrated into southern Palestine as traders, and effected, at least, a social conquest, is certain, because they were known to Amenemhet I, although he never crossed the Delta frontier. The northern war god was established at an early period in Syria and in Mitanni, and Biblical references indicate that the Hittites were prominent land owners. They were probably the people who traded with Egypt at Gezer, and with whom the Twelfth-Dynasty Pharaohs arrived at some understanding. It is unlikely that the influential foreign princesses who were worthy to be introduced into the royal harem were the daughters of rough desert dwellers. The Dashur jewellery suggests that the ladies were of refined tastes and accustomed to luxurious living.

We have no means of ascertaining why Senusert III, the son of one of the alien wives, invaded Syria and fought a battle at Gezer. It may be that the Hittites had grown restless and aggressive, and it is also possible that he co-operated with them to expel a common enemy—perhaps Semites from Arabia.

Some time prior to the Hyksos invasion the Hittites raided Babylon and overthrew the Hammurabi Dynasty. But they were unable to enjoy for long the fruits of conquest. An army of Kassites pressed down from the mountains of Elam and occupied northern Babylonia, apparently driving the Hittites before them. The Kassites are a people of uncertain origin, but associated with them were bands of Aryans on horseback and in chariots. This is the first appearance in history of the Indo-European people.

A westward pressure of tribes followed. The Kassites and Aryans probably waged war against the Hittites for a period, and the Hyksos invasion of Egypt may have been an indirect result of the migrations from the Iranian plateau and the conquest of Babylonia. At any rate it is certain that the Aryans continued to advance, for, prior to the close of the Hyksos period, they had penetrated Asia Minor and reached the Syrian coastland. Whether or not they entered Egypt we have no means of knowing. All foreigners were Hyksos to the

Egyptians at this time, as all northern barbarians were Celts to the Greeks at a later period. Some change occurred, however, for there was a second Hyksos Dynasty. What we know for certain is that a military aristocracy appeared in Mitanni, where Tushratta, who had an Aryan name, subsequently paid tribute to Egypt in the time of Amenhotep III and his son Akhenaton. He is believed to have been educated in the land of the Pharaohs, and his ancestors must have been the expellers from Mesopotamia of the Hittite rulers; the Mitanni rulers were for a period overlords of Assyria. In addition to the Hittite Sutekh-Teshub, the Mitanni Pantheon then included Indra, Mithra, and Varuna, the well-known Iranian gods. These had been introduced into the Punjab by an earlier Aryan "wave" which swept towards India about the beginning of the Twelfth Egyptian Dynasty.

It may also be noted here that when the Egyptians expelled the weakened Hyksos army of occupation they possessed horses and chariots. They afterwards pressed into Syria, but the danger of subsequent invasion was not secured until Thutmose III overcame the Mitanni Power, which apparently was not unconnected with the later "Hyksos" overlordship of Egypt.

During the Hyksos period the children of Israel appear to have settled in Egypt.

CHAPTER XXI

Joseph and the Exodus

Biblical References to Hyksos Period—Joseph as Grand Vizier—His Sagacity—Reorganizing the Kingdom—Israelites in Goshen—A Jacob King—Period of the Exodus—Egyptian References to Hebrews—A Striking Folk-tale—Cause of Theban Revolt—A National Hero—A Famous Queen Mother—A Warrior King—"Battles Long Ago"—Expulsion of Foreigners—Unrest in Syria—New Methods of Warfare.

IN the familiar Bible story of Joseph, the young Hebrew slave who became grand vizier in the land of the Nile, there is a significant reference to the nationality of his master Potiphar. Although that dignitary was "an officer of Pharaoh, captain of the guard", he was not of alien origin; we are pointedly informed that he was "an Egyptian". We also gather that Hyksos jurisdiction extended beyond the Delta region. During the dry cycle, when the great famine prevailed, Joseph "gathered up all the money that was found in the land of Egypt and in the land of Canaan" for the corn which the people purchased. Then he proceeded to acquire for the Crown all the privately owned estates in the Nile Valley and Delta region, with purpose, it would appear, to abolish the feudal system. An exception was made, however, of the lands attached to the temples. Apparently Pharaoh desired to conciliate the priests, whose political influence was very great, because we find that he allowed them free supplies of corn; indeed he had previously selected for Joseph's wife, " Asenath, the daughter of Potiphera, priest of On"; an indication that he specially favoured the influential sun cult of Heliopolis. Queen Hatshepsut's assertion that the foreign kings ruled in ignorance of Ra was manifestly neither strictly accurate nor unbiased.

The inference drawn from the Biblical narrative that the Hyksos Pharaohs adopted a policy of conciliation is confirmed by the evidence gleaned amidst the scanty records of the period. We find that some of these rulers assumed Ra titles, although they were also "beloved of Set" (Sutekh), and that one of them actually restored the tomb of Queen Apuit of the Sixth Dynasty. The Egyptians apparently indulged in pious exaggerations. That the Hyksos influence was not averse to culture is evidenced by the fact that the name of King Apepa Ra-aa-user is associated with a mathematical treatise which is preserved in the British Museum.

If learning was fostered, the arts and industries could not have been neglected. The Egyptian iconoclasts systematically destroyed practically all the monuments of the period, so that we have no direct evidence to support the assumption that it was characterized by a spirit of decadence due to the influence of uncultured desert dwellers. The skill displayed at the beginning of the Eighteenth Dynasty was too great to be of sudden growth, and certainly does not suggest that for about two centuries there had existed no appreciation of, or demand for, works of art. Although sculpture had grown mechanical, there had been, apparently, progressive development in other directions. We find, for instance, a marked and increased appreciation of colour, suggesting influence from a district where Nature presents more variety and distinguishing beauty than the somewhat monotonous valley of the Nile; ware was

being highly glazed and tinted with taste and skill un
known in the Twelfth Dynasty, and painting had become
more popular.

But, perhaps, it was in the work of administration
that the Egyptians learned most from their Hyksos
rulers. Joseph, who was undoubtedly a great statesman, must have impressed them greatly with his sound
doctrines of political economy. That sagacious young
vizier displayed an acute and far-sighted appreciation of
the real needs of Egypt, a country which cannot be made
prosperous under divided rule. No doubt he was guided
by the experienced councillors at Court, but had he not
been gifted with singular intelligence and strong force
of character, he could never have performed his onerous
duties with so much distinction and success. He fostered
the agricultural industry during the years of plenty, and
"gathered corn as the sand of the sea, very much, until
he left numbering; for it was without number".

Then came the seven years of famine. "And when
all the land of Egypt was famished, the people cried to
Pharaoh for bread. . . . And Joseph opened all the
storehouses and sold unto the Egyptians." Much wealth
poured into the Imperial Exchequer. "All countries
came into Egypt to Joseph for to buy corn." The dry
cycle prevailed apparently over a considerable area, and
it must have propelled the migrations of pastoral peoples
which subsequently effected so great a change in the
political conditions of Asia.

It is interesting to note that at this period the horse
was known in Egypt. On the occasion of Joseph's ele-
vation to the post of grand vizier, Pharaoh "made him
to ride in the second chariot which he had". Then
when the Egyptians, who found it necessary to continue
purchasing corn, cried out "the money faileth", the

young Hebrew "gave them bread in exchange for horses", &c.

The wholesale purchase of estates followed. "Buy us and our land for bread," said the Egyptians, "and we and our land will be servants unto Pharaoh. . . . So the land became Pharaoh's. . . . And as for the people, he (Joseph) removed them to cities from one end of the borders of Egypt even to the other end thereof."

The work of reorganization proceeded apace. Joseph in due season distributed seed, and made it conditional that a fifth part of the produce of all farms should be paid in taxation. A strong central government was thus established upon a sound economic basis, and it may have flourished until some change occurred of which we have no knowledge. Perhaps the decline of the Hyksos power was not wholly due to a revolt in the south; it may have been contributed to as well by interference from without.

Meanwhile the children of Israel "dwelt in the land of Egypt, in the country of Goshen; and they had possessions therein and multiplied exceedingly". Josephus's statement that they were identical with the Hyksos hardly accords with the evidence of the Bible. It is possible, however, that other Semites besides Joseph attained high positions during the period of foreign control. In fact, one of the Pharaohs was named Jacob-her, or possibly, as Breasted suggests, "Jacob-El". Such a choice of ruler would not be inconsistent with the policy of the Hittites, who allowed subject peoples to control their own affairs so long as they adhered to the treaty of alliance and recognized the suzerainty of the supreme Power.

It is impossible to fix with any certainty the time at which the Israelites settled in Egypt. They came, not as conquerors, but after the Hyksos had seized the crown. Apparently, too, they had no intention of effecting permanent settlement, because the bodies of Jacob and Joseph, having been embalmed, were carried to the family cave tomb "in the land of Canaan", which Abraham had purchased from "Ephron the Hittite".

No inscription regarding Joseph or the great famine has survived. But the Egyptians were not likely to preserve any record of a grand vizier who starved them into submission. A tablet which makes reference to a seven years' famine during the Third Dynasty has been proved to be a pious fraud of the Roman period. It was based, in all probability, on the Joseph story. The alleged record sets forth that King Zoser, who was greatly distressed regarding the condition of the country, sent a message to the Governor of Nubia, asking for information regarding the rise of the Nile. Statistics were duly supplied according to his desire. Then Pharaoh "dreamed a dream", and saw the god Khnûmû, who informed him that Egypt was being afflicted because no temples had been erected to the gods. As soon as he woke up, His Majesty made gifts of land to the priests of Khnûmû, and arranged that they should receive a certain proportion of all the fish and game caught in the vicinity of the first cataract.

There is no agreement as to when the Exodus of the Israelites took place. Some authorities are of opinion that it coincided with the expulsion of the Hyksos. Such a view, however, conflicts with the Biblical reference to a period of bondage. The Pharaoh of the Oppression was a "new king" and he "knew not Joseph". He enslaved and oppressed the Israelites, who had been so singularly favoured by the foreign rulers. According to tradition, he was Rameses II, during whose reign Moses acquired "all the wisdom of the Egyptians" and became "mighty in words and deeds". The next king was Mene-ptah, but he cannot be regarded as the Pharaoh of the Exodus. He reigned little over ten years, and one of his inscriptions makes reference to the Israelites as a people resident in Canaan, where they were attacked by the Egyptian army during a Syrian campaign. It is probable that the Hebrews were the Khabri mentioned in the Tell el Amarna letters, two centuries before Mene-ptah's time. They were then waging war against Canaan-itish allies of Egypt, and the Prince of Gezer sent an urgent but ineffectual appeal to the Pharaoh Akenaton for assistance. The Exodus must have taken place in the early part of the Eighteenth Dynasty, and possibly during the reign of Thothmes I—about a generation after Ahmes expelled the Asiatics from Avaris.

During the latter part of the Hyksos period the Theban princes, whom Manetho gives as the kings of the Seventeenth Dynasty, were tributary rulers over a goodly part of Upper Egypt. Reinforced from Nubia, and aided by the princes of certain of the nomes, they suddenly rose against their oppressors, and began to wage the War of Independence, which lasted for about a quarter of a century.

An interesting papyrus, preserved in the British Museum, contains a fragmentary folktale, which indicates that the immediate cause of the rising was an attempt on the part of the Hyksos overlord to compel the Egyptians to worship the god Sutekh.

"It came to pass", we read, "that Egypt was possessed by the Impure, and there was no lord and king."

This may mean that either the Hyksos rule had limited power in Upper Egypt or was subject to a higher authority in Asia. The folktale proceeds:

"Now King Sekenenra was lord of the south. . . . Impure Asiatics were in the cities (? as garrisons), and Apepa was lord in Avaris. They worked their will in the land, and enjoyed all the good things of Egypt. The god Sutekh was Apepa's master, for he worshipped Sutekh alone, and erected for him an enduring temple. . . . He sacrificed and gave offerings every day unto Sutekh. . . ."

The tale then goes on to relate that Apepa sent a messenger to Sekenenra, the lord of Thebes, "the city of the south", with an important document which had been prepared after lengthy consultation with a number of learned scribes.

Sekenenra appears to have received the messenger with undisguised alarm. He asked: "What order do you bring? Why have you made this journey?"

The document was read, and, so far as can be gathered from the blurred and mutilated papyrus, it was something to the following effect:—

The King Ra Apepa sends to you to say: Let the hippopotami, be put out of the pool in the city of Thebes. I cannot get sleep, either by day or by night, because their roaring is in my ear.

No wonder that "the lord of the south" was astounded. The sacred animals at Thebes could not possibly be disturbing the slumbers of a monarch residing on the Delta frontier. Apepa was evidently anxious to pick a quarrel with the Thebans, for his hypocritical complaint was, in effect, an express order to accomplish the suppression of a popular form of worship. Well he knew that he could not adopt more direct means to stir up a spirit of rebellion among his Egyptian subjects. Possibly the growing power of the Theban ruler may have caused him to feel somewhat alarmed, and he desired to shatter it before it became too strong for him.

Sekenenra was unable for a time to decide what reply he should make.   At length, having entertained the messenger, he bade him to convey the following brief but pointed answer to Apepa: "I intend to do as is your wish ".

Apparently he desired to gain time, for there could remain no doubt that a serious crisis was approaching. No sooner did the messenger take his departure than the Theban ruler summoned before him all the great lords in the district, and to them he related " what had come to pass ".   These men were likewise "astounded "; they heard what Sekenenra had to tell them " with feelings of sorrow, but were silent, for none knew what to say ".

The fragmentary tale then ends abruptly with the words: "The King Ra Apepa sent to——"

We can infer, however, that his second message roused a storm of opposition, and that whatever demand it contained was met with a blank refusal.   King Ra Apepa must have then sent southward a strong army to enforce his decree and subdue the subject princes who dared to have minds of their own.

If we identify Sekenenra with the Theban king of that name, whose mummy was found at Der el Bahari, and is now in the Cairo museum, we can conclude that the ancient folktale contained a popular account of the brief but glorious career and tragic death of a national hero, who, like the Scottish Sir William Wallace, inspired his countrymen with the desire for freedom and independence.

Sekenenra died on the battlefield.   We can see him pressing forward at the head of the Egyptian army, fighting with indomitable courage and accomplishing mighty deeds.   Accompanied by his most valiant followers, he hews his way through the Hyksos force.   But "one by one they fall around him ". . . . Now he is alone. He is surrounded. . . . The warriors in front of him are mowed down, for none can withstand his blows. But an Asiatic creeps up on his left side, swings his battleaxe, and smites a glancing blow. Sekenenra totters; his cheek bone and teeth have been laid bare. Another Asiatic on his right leaps up and stabs him on the forehead. Ere he falls, his first successful assailant strikes again, and the battleaxe crashes through the left side of the hero's skull. The Hyksos shout triumphantly, but the Egyptians are not dismayed; clamouring in battle fury, they rush on to avenge the death of Sekenenra. . . . That hero has not died in vain.

The mummy of the great prince bears the evidence of the terrible wounds he received. In his agony he had bitten his tongue between his teeth. But it is apparent that before he fell he turned the tide of battle, and that the Hyksos were compelled to retreat, for his body was recovered and carried back to Thebes, where it was embalmed after putrefaction had set in.

Sekenenra appears to have been a handsome and dashing soldier. He was tall, slim, and active, with a strong, refined face of dark Mediterranean type. Probably he was a descendant of one of the ancient families which had taken refuge in the south after the Hyksos invaders had accomplished the fall of the native monarchy.

His queen, Ah-hotep, who was a hereditary princess in her own right, lived until she was a hundred years old. Her three sons reigned in succession, and continued the war against the Hyksos. The youngest of these was Ahmes I, and he was the first Pharaoh of the Eighteenth Dynasty. Ah-hotep must have followed his career with pride, for he drove the Asiatics across the frontier. She survived him, and then lived through the reign of

Amenhotep I also, for she did not pass away until Thotmes I ruled in splendour over united Egypt, and caused its name to be dreaded in western Asia.

Ahmes I, like the heroic Sekenenra, received the support of the El Kab family, which was descended from one of the old feudal lords. His successes are recorded in the tomb of his namesake, the son of Ebana, a princess, and of Baba, the lord of El Kab, who had served under Sekenenra. This El Kab Ahmes was quite a youth—he tells us that he was "too young to have a wife"—when he fought on foot behind the chariot of the Pharaoh. He was afterwards promoted to the rank of admiral, and won a naval victory on a canal. So greatly did the young nobleman distinguish himself that he received a decoration —a golden collar, the equivalent of our "Victoria Cross". Indeed he was similarly honoured for performing feats of valour on four subsequent occasions, and he also received gifts of land and of male and female slaves who had been taken captive.

The progress northward of Ahmes I, with army and river fleet, was accompanied by much hard fighting. But at length he compelled the Hyksos force, which had suffered heavily, to take refuge in the fortified town of Avaris. After a prolonged siege the enemy took flight, and he pursued them across the frontier.

We have followed, so far, the narrative of Ahmes, son of Ebana. According to Manetho's account of the expulsion, as quoted by Josephus, who, perhaps, tampered with it, King Ahmes was unable to do more than shut up the Asiatics in Avaris. Then Thummosis (Thothmes), successor of Ahmes, endeavoured to carry the town by assault, but failed in the attempt. Just when he was beginning to despair of accomplishing his purpose, the enemy offered to capitulate if they would be allowed to depart in peace. This condition was accepted, whereupon 240,000 men, women, and children evacuated Avaris and crossed the frontier into Syria. Manetho adds that they migrated to the district afterwards known as Judea, and built Jerusalem, because "they were in dread of the Assyrians". But, as we have seen, the Assyrians were not at this period the predominating power in the East. Manetho (or Josephus) was plainly wrong. A new and hostile enemy, however, had appeared at Mitanni—the dreaded Aryans, who worshipped the strange gods Indra, Mithra, and Varuna.

After clearing the Delta of Asiatic soldiers, Ahmes I turned his attention to Nubia. He did not meet with much opposition, and succeeded in extending the southern frontier to the second cataract, thus recovering the area which had been controlled by the great Pharaohs of the Twelfth Dynasty. He had afterwards to suppress two abortive risings in the heart of the kingdom, which may have been engineered by Hyksos sympathizers. Then he devoted himself to the work of restoring the monuments of his ancestors and the temples of the gods. After a strenuous reign of over twenty years he died in the prime of life, lamented, no doubt, by the people whom he had set free, and especially by the queen mother, Ahhotep, that wife of a mighty leader and nurse of valiant heroes—one of the first great women in history.

The military successes of the Egyptians were largely contributed to by their use of the horse, which the Aryans had introduced into the West.

New methods of fighting had also been adopted by the Egyptians. When the Eighteenth-Dynasty soldiers were depicted on the monuments and in the tombs the artists had for their models highly disciplined and well-organized bodies of men who had undergone a rigorous training. The infantry were marshalled in regular lines, and on battlefields made vigorous and orderly charges. Charioteers gathered into action with the dash and combination of modern-day cavalry. Had this new military system evolved in Upper Egypt as a result of the example shown by the Hyksos? Or had the trade in horses brought into the Nile valley Aryan warriors who became the drill sergeants and adjutants of the army which drove the Hyksos from the land of the Pharaohs?

CHAPTER XXII

Amon, the God of Empire

Lunar Worship—The Great Mother of Darkness.—Amon as a Moon God—Fusion with Ra—Ptah a Form of the Theban Deity—"Fenkhu" and "Fenish" Artisans—Osiris and Amon—Veneration of Religious Pharaohs—Amon's Wife and Concubine—Conquests of Thothmes I—Rival Claimants to the Throne—Queen Hatshepsut—Her Famous Expedition—Rise of Thothmes III—A Great Strategist—His Conquests—The Egyptian Empire—Amon's Poetic Praise—The Emperor's Buildings and Obelisks.

THE moon god Ah comes into prominence during the Egyptian War of Independence. This ancient deity must have been closely associated with the Theban religious cult which Ra Apepa, the Hyksos king, singled out for attack, because the name of the queen mother, Ah-hotep, signifies "Ah is satisfied", and that of her victorious son Ah-mes, "born of Ah".

It is highly probable that Ah was the son of the great Mother deity Apet, who was identified with the female hippopotamus Taurt, "the mighty one", goddess of maternity, and "mother of the gods". At Thebes and Ombos, Osiris was regarded as the son of the sacred hippopotamus. As we have seen in the Introduction, he was, like Ah, identified with the moon spirit, which symbolized the male principle. The Apet hippopotamus was the animal incarnation of the Great Mother; as a water goddess, therefore, Apet links with Nut, who rose from the primordial deep and was "the waters above the firmament".

At the beginning there was naught save darkness and water. The spirit of the night was the Great Mother, and her first-born was the moon child. Life came from death and light from darkness. Such appears to have been the conception of the worshippers of the sky-and-water goddess and the lunar god.

On the other hand, the worshippers of the male earth spirit believed that the firmament was made of metal which was beaten out by the Great Father, Ptah, at the beginning. Ere metal came into use it may have been conceived that the sky was made of stone. Hathor, the sky goddess, was significantly enough "the lady of turquoise", and Ra, the sun god, was in the Fifth Dynasty symbolized by an obelisk.

Osiris, the human incarnation of primitive Nilotic deities, absorbed the attributes of the moon spirit and the male earth spirit. Isis, on the other hand, apparently absorbed those of Nut, the sky-and-water goddess, and of Neith, the earth goddess, who symbolized growth.

As moon worship was of greater antiquity in Egypt than sun worship, and was associated with agricultural rites, the Theban cult must have made popular appeal, and helped to rally the mass of the people to throw off the yoke of the Hyksos Ra and Sutekh worshippers. The political significance of Apepa's order to slay the hippopotami is therefore apparent.

When the influence of the southern conquerors extended to Hermopolis, Ah was merged with Thoth, who was originally a lunar deity. In fact, as we have shown in our Introduction, he was another form of Khonsu. With Mut, "the mother", who is indistinguishable from Apet, Khonsu and Thoth formed a Theban triad. In Nubia, where archaic Mediterranean beliefs appear to have been persistent, Thoth was the son of Tefnut, the lioness-headed goddess, who was given arbitrary association with Shu, the atmosphere god, by the theorists of Heliopolis. Mut was also depicted at Thebes with the head of a lioness.

As we have already suggested, it is possible that Amon was originally the son of Mut-Apet. He may have developed as a symbolized attribute of Ah. Fragments of old hymns make reference to him as a lunar deity, and as a "traverser" of space like Khonsu-Thoth. Indeed, even in his hawk-headed form, he retains his early association with the moon, for he wears the solar disk with the lunar crescent.[1]

Amon, like the sons of all the Great Mother deities, represented in his animal forms the "male principle" and the "fighting principle". He became "the husband of his mother" when the Great Father and Great Mother conceptions were fused. This process is illustrated in the triad formed by Ptah, the father, Mut, the mother, and Thoth, the son. Ptah's wife Sekhet, with the head of a lioness, is indistinguishable from Mut, Tefnut, and Bast.

As a Great Father deity, Amon, "husband of his mother" became "king of the gods",[2] and lost his original lunar character. His fusion with the sun god of Heliopolis, which was accomplished for political purposes, made the change complete, for he became Amon-Ra, the great representative deity of Egypt, who combines the attributes of all other gods.

Amon-Ra was depicted as a great bearded man, clad in a sleeveless tunic suspended from his shoulders, with the tail of an animal hanging behind. His headdress of

---

[1] In an Amon-Ra hymn the deity is called "maker of men, former of the flocks, lord of corn" (*Religion of the Ancient Egyptians*, Wiedemann, p. 116).

[2] "The gods gather as dogs round his feet."—*Hymn to Amon-ra.*

high double plumes, with lunar and solar symbols, was coloured in sections red and blue, and red and green, as if to signify an association with the river flowing between its banks and the growth of verdure.   Sometimes he is shown with Min's ram's horns curving downwards round his ears, and sometimes with those of Khnûmû spreading outward.[1]   He wore a collar and armlets and bracelets.

As a god of war he rose into great prominence during the Eighteenth Dynasty.   The victorious kings, who became owners of all the land in Egypt, and returned with great spoils from many battlefields, were lavish in their gifts to his temple, and his priests became exceedingly wealthy and powerful.   There never was in Egypt a more influential cult than that of Amon-Ra.

His solar attributes, however, were not so prominent in the Eighteenth as in the Nineteenth and Twentieth Dynasties.   The influence of the moon cult remained for a considerable period.   As much is suggested by the names of the kings.   Ah-mes I, "born of Ah", was followed by four rulers called Amen-hotep, "Amon is satisfied", and four called Thoth-mes, "born of Thoth".

The influence of the Ra cult at Heliopolis was tempered by that of the Amon cult at Thebes, with the result that the old Egyptian lunar gods came into prominence. Nor were Ptah and other kindred deities excluded from the group of official gods as in the Fifth Dynasty.   At Memphis Amon-Ra was worshipped as Ptah.   In a hymn addressed to the great Theban deity it was declared—

> Memphis receives thee in the form of Ptah—
> He who is the first-born of all gods;
> He who was at the beginning.

It would appear that the Memphites had combined

---

[1] "Amon of the two horns."

with the Thebans to drive the Hyksos out of Egypt. When Ahmes began the work of reconstructing the temples, the first gods he honoured were Amon and Ptah. In the limestone quarries near Cairo two tablets record that stone was excavated for the great temples at Memphis and Thebes. No reference is made to Heliopolis. It is of special interest to find that the workmen who were employed were of the Fenkhu, a Syrian tribe. There can be no doubt these quarriers were foreigners. In an Assouan inscription of Thothmes II it is stated that the boundary of the Egyptian empire on the north extended to the Syrian lakes, and that the Pharaoh's arms were " not repulsed from the land of the Fenkhu ". A stele erected by Thothmes III at Wady Halfa records a victory during a Syrian campaign over " the Fenkhu ". Ahmes must have obtained these skilled quarriers from the Fenkhu for the purpose of hastening on the work of restoring the temples in return for some favour conferred, for he did not wage war against the tribe, which remained powerful at the time of Thothmes III. It is impossible, however, to identify them with certainty. To this day the inhabitants of Palestine still credit all the surviving works of antiquity to the " Fenish ", and although the reference is evidently to the Philistines and Phœnicians, as well as to the hewers of the great artificial caves, it is possible that the latter, who are referred to in the Bible as the Rephaim or Anakim, were originally the " Fenish " and the Egyptian " Fenkhu ". Ahmes may have followed the example of his temple- and pyramid-building predecessors in drawing fresh supplies of skilled stoneworkers from southern Palestine.

Osiris worship was combined with that of Amon at Thebes, but, as we have seen, Osiris and Amon had much in common, for both gods had lunar attributes.

Osiris " hides his essence in the great shrine of Amon ".[1]
The Amon ram was an animal incarnation of the corn
spirit.   It is significant to find, in this connection, that
the priests of Amon for a long period sought sepulture
at sacred Abydos, which had become closely associated
with Osirian worship.   But there was a strange fusion of
beliefs regarding the other world.   Men died believing
that they would enter the bark of Ra and also reach
the Osirian Paradise.   Ultimately the Heliopolitan belief in the efficacy of magical formulæ impaired the
ethical character of the Ptah-Osirian creed.

Although Ahmes I was the liberator of Egypt, his
memory was not revered so greatly as that of his son
and successor Amenhotep I (Amenophis).   The great
Pharaohs of the records were the religious Pharaohs ;
if a monarch was assiduous in venerating the gods, and
especially in erecting and endowing temples, his fame
was assured; the grateful priests " kept his memory
green ".   Amenhotep I and his wife Aahmes-Nefertari
were, after their death, revered as deities; references are
made to them as protectors and punishers of men in
the Nineteenth Dynasty.

Nefertari was during her life " Amon's wife ".   She
slept in the temple, and her children were reputed to be
the sons and daughters of the god.   The high priest's
wife was " the concubine of Amon ".   It was Amenhotep I who founded the endowments of the Amon cult
at Thebes which ultimately became so wealthy and powerful.   He also began the erection of the magnificent buildings at Karnak, which were added to by his successors.
His reign, which lasted for only about ten years, was

---

[1] That is, the soul of Osiris is in Amon, as the soul of the giant is in the egg, the
ram, &c., "doubly hidden".   Amon-Ra is addressed in a temple chant: "Hidden is thy
abode, lord of the gods ".

occupied chiefly in reorganizing the kingdom and in establishing the new national religion. Assisted by the veteran military nobles of El Kab, he waged war against the Libyans on the north and the Nubians on the south. He appears also to have penetrated Syria, but no records of the campaign survive. His successors, however, ere he invaded Asia, claimed to hold sway as far north as the Euphrates.

The next king, Thothmes I, came to the throne as the husband of a princess of the royal line. He found it necessary to invade Nubia. Ahmes of Ebana, who accompanied him, records in his tomb that a battle was fought between the second and third cataract. The Pharaoh slew the Nubian leader who opposed him, and, on his return, had the body suspended head downwards at the bow of the royal ship. Thothmes penetrated Nubia beyond the third cataract, and reached the island of Arko, where Sebekhotep had undertaken the erection of his great statues. A fortress was erected and garrisoned on the island of Tombos at the third cataract. Nubia thus became once again an Egyptian province.

A campaign of conquest was next waged in Syria, where Egyptian dominance was continually challenged by the rival powers in Asia Minor and Mesopotamia. "It was probably", write King and Hall, "with the Iranian kingdom of Mitanni, between Euphrates and Tigris, that the Dynasty carried on its struggle for Syria." No royal records of the campaign of Thothmes I survive, but we gather from the tomb inscriptions of Ahmes of Ebana and Ahmes of El Kab, that a great victory was won in Naharina, "the land of the rivers", which secured Egyptian supremacy. The king was afterwards able to boast that the northern boundary of the Empire extended "as far as the circuit of the sun"—

it was believed that the world's edge was at the source of
the Euphrates on the north and of that of the Nile on the
south, and that both rivers flowed from the ocean, "the
great Circle" surrounding the earth, in which lay the
great serpent.

Thothmes I made an addition to the Karnak temple,
and erected two great pylons on the thirtieth anniversary
of his reign, when, at the Sed festival, he appears to have
selected his successor.   On one of the pylons he recorded
that he had established peace in Egypt, ended lawlessness,
and stamped out impiety, and that he had subdued the
rebels in the Delta region.   He also implored Amon to
give the throne to his daughter Hatshepsut.

The closing period of the king's reign is obscure, and
there is no agreement as to the events which occurred in
connection with the family feud which ensued.   Thothmes
III dated his reign from the year preceding the death
of Thothmes I, but in the interval Thothmes II and
Hatshepsut sat on the throne.

The children of the royal princess who was the wife
of Thothmes I included two sons and two daughters, but
they all died young with the exception of the Princess
Hatshepsut.   Another wife was the mother of Thothmes
II, while a concubine gave birth to Thothmes III.

Such is Breasted's reading of the problem, which is
made difficult on account of the mutilation of inscriptions
by the rival claimants.   Other Egyptologists suggest that
Thothmes III was the son of Thothmes II.

Thothmes III was a priest in the temple of Amon.
He secured his succession by marrying either Hatshepsut
or her daughter.   According to Breasted, he superseded
Thothmes I at a festival at which the Oracle of Amon
proclaimed him as the Pharaoh.   Thothmes III then
began his reign, and the old king lived in retirement.

After a time the usurping prince had to recognize the co-regency of Hatshepsut. But, ere long, he was thrust aside, and the queen reigned alone as "the female Horus". Thothmes II then seized the throne on his own and his father's behalf, and when Thothmes I died, Thothmes II allied himself with Thothmes III. When they had reigned about two years Thothmes II died, but Thothmes III was not able to retain his high position. Once again Hatshepsut, who had evidently won over a section of the priesthood, seized the reins of government, and Thothmes III was once again "relegated to the background ".[1] At the festivals he appeared as a priest.

Hatshepsut must have been a woman of great ability and force of character to have displaced such a man as Thothmes III. For about fourteen years she ruled alone, and engaged herself chiefly in restoring the religious buildings which had either been demolished or had fallen into disrepair during the Hyksos period. She completed the great mortuary temple at Der-el-Bahari, which had been begun under Thothmes II. It was modelled on the smaller temple of Mentuhotep, and is still magnificent in ruin. Situated against the western cliffs at Thebes, it was constructed in three terraces with sublime colonnades finely proportioned and exquisitely wrought. An inner chamber was excavated from the rock. On the temple walls the mythical scenes in connection with the birth of the queen were sculptured in low relief, and to get over the difficulty of being recognized as a "son of the sun ", Hatshepsut was depicted in company of her male "double ". On state occasions she wore a false beard.

The queen's most famous undertaking was to send an

---

[1] *A History of Egypt*, James Henry Breasted, London, 1906.

expedition of eight ships to the land of Punt to obtain myrrh trees, incense, rare woods, and sacred animals for the temple. It was her pious wish that Amon should have a garden to walk in.

To celebrate her jubilee Hatshepsut had erected two magnificent obelisks, nearly a hundred feet high, in front of the Karnak temple in which Thothmes III was a priest. One of these still stands erect, and is greatly admired by visitors. The obelisks, like the temple, were designed by the much-favoured architect Senmut, an accomplished artist and scheming statesman, who was a prominent figure in the party which supported the queen.

But so deeply was Hatshepsut concerned in devoting the revenues of the State to religious purposes that the affairs of empire were neglected. The flame of revolt was spreading through Syria, where the tribal chiefs scorned to owe allegiance to a woman, especially as she neglected to enforce her will at the point of the sword. Apparently, too, the Mitanni power had recovered from the blows dealt by the military Pharaohs of a previous generation and had again become aggressive. Then Hatshepsut died. She may have fallen a victim of a palace revolt of which no record survives. Her mummy has never been discovered. When the deep tunnel which she had constructed for her tomb was entered, it was found to have been despoiled. It may be that her body was never deposited there. After her death no more is heard of her favourite Senmut, or her daughter, whom she had selected as her successor. Her name was ruthlessly erased from her monuments. All the indications point to a military revolt, supported by a section of the priesthood, at a time of national peril.

Thothmes III, who immediately came to the throne, lost no time in raising an army and pressing northward to subdue the Syrian rebellion. Although he has been referred to as "this little man with coarse features, as we know from his mummy", it would be a mistake to retain the impression that he was of repulsive aspect. He died when he was an old man; his jaw was not tied up before embalmment, which was not highly successful, for his nose was disfigured, and has partly crumbled away. The statues of the king present the striking face of a vigorous and self-contained man; in one he has a nose which rivals that of Wellington, and an air of dignity and refinement which accords with what we know of his character; for not only was he a great leader who, as his grand vizier has informed the ages, knew all that happened and never failed to carry out a matter he took in hand, he was also a man of artistic ability, accustomed, as Breasted informs us, to spend his leisure time "designing exquisite vases".

The hour had come and the man! With a well-organized army, in which he had placed the most capable men in command, he swept his victorious way through Syria and struck terror to the hearts of the rebels. His name—Manakhpirria (Men-kheper-ra) Thothmes—was dreaded long after his death, and may have originated the Semitic title "Pharaoh", which was never used by the native kings of Egypt.

The greatest triumph of the various Syrian campaigns conducted by Thothmes III was the capture of Megiddo, in the Hebrew tribal area of Issachar. That fortified stronghold, situated on the plain of Jezreel, was a point of great strategic importance—"the Key", indeed, of northern Palestine. It had to be approached over the ridge of Carmel, and was partly surrounded by the tributary known as "the brook Kina", which flows into the Kishon River. Two highways leading to Megiddo lay before the Egyptian army, like the legs of inward curving calipers, and between these a narrow mountain pass cut in an almost straight and direct line into the town.

The Egyptian generals intended to advance along the northern curving highway, but Thothmes III was, like Nelson, a great strategist who ever did the unexpected. He decided to push through the pass, although along the greater part of it his horsemen would have to advance in Indian file. To inspire his followers with his own great courage, the fearless monarch rode in front. His daring manœuvre was a complete success. Ere it was comprehended by the enemy, his army was pouring down upon the plain.

He completely upset the plans of the Asiatic allies, who had divided their forces to await the advance of the Egyptians by the north and the south, occupying the while, no doubt, strong positions.

The battle took place next day on the river bank. Thothmes led on a victorious charge, and scattered the enemy so that they retreated in confusion and took refuge in the city. Had the Egyptians not been too eager to secure the spoils of victory, they might have captured Megiddo, as Thothmes informed them afterwards. A long siege followed, but at length the town was starved into submission, and the princes came forth to swear allegiance to the Pharaoh. They also made payment of the tribute which they had withheld during the closing years of Hatshepsut's reign. Thothmes took the eldest sons of the various revolting princes as hostages, and deported them to Thebes. The spoils of victory included over 900 chariots and 200 coats of mail and much gold and silver. Ere he returned home he captured three towns in Lebanon, and reorganized the administration of northern Palestine.

Other campaigns followed. On one of these Thoth-mes made swift attack upon some revolting princes by crossing the sea and landing on the Phœnician coast. The Hittites gave trouble on the north, and he pushed on to Carchemish, their southern capital, and captured it. At Kadesh, on the Orontes, he also dealt a shattering blow against the Hittites and their allies from Mitanni. He had previously subdued the Libyans, and conducted a successful campaign into Nubia. Thus he built up a great empire, and made Egypt the foremost power in the world. Tribute poured into the royal exchequer from the various subject states, and peace offerings were made by the Hittites and even by the rulers of Cyprus and Crete. Both Assyria and Babylonia cultivated friendly relations with Thothmes III, who appears to have been as distinguished a diplomatist as he was a conqueror.

The priests of Amon composed a great hymn in his honour, which, they pretended, had been recited by their god.

I have come, I have given to thee to smite the land of the Syrians—
Under thy feet they lie through the length and breadth of the
    god's land;
I have made them see thy might like to a star revolving
When it sheds its burning beams and drops its dew on the
    meadows.

I have come, I have given to thee to vanquish the Western peoples.
Crete is stricken with fear, terror is reigning in Cyprus;
Like to a great young bull, I have made them behold thy power,
Fearless and quick to strike, none is so bold to resist thee.

I have come, I have given to thee to conquer the folk of the
    marshes,
The terror of thee has fallen over the lands of Mitanni;
Like to a crocodile fierce they have beheld thee in glory;
O monarch of fear at sea, none is so bold to approach thee.

The chief buildings of Thothmes III were erected to Amon at Thebes, but he did not fail to honour Ra at Heliopolis, Ptah at Memphis, and Hathor at Dendera. One of his jubilee obelisks, which he erected at Thebes, now stands in Constantinople; another is in Rome; the pair set up at Heliopolis have been given prominent sites on either side of the Atlantic Ocean—one in New York and the other on the Thames Embankment, London. His reign, which he dated from his first accession prior to the death of Thothmes I, extended over a period of fifty-four years.   He died on 17 March, 1447, B.C., and was buried in the lonely "Valley of Kings' Tombs".

CHAPTER XXIII

Tale of the Doomed Prince

Pharaoh's Heir—Decree of the Fates—Son must die a Sudden Death—
His Lonely Childhood—The Dog—Prince goes upon his Travels—The Lady
of the Tower—Won by the Disguised Prince—An Angry Father—Prince
returns Home—Perils of Darkness—The Giant and the Crocodile—The
Serpent slain—Mystery of the Prince's Fate—Resemblances to European
Stories—An Unsolved Problem.

Now hear the tale of the doomed prince. Once upon a
time there was a king in Egypt whose heart was heavy
because that he had no son. He called upon the gods,
and the gods heard, and they decreed that an heir should
be born to him. In time came the day of the child's
birth. The seven Hathors (Fates) greeted the prince
and pronounced his destiny; they said he would meet
with a sudden death, either by a crocodile, or a serpent,
or a dog.

The nurses informed the king what the Hathors had
said, and the heart of His Majesty was troubled. He
commanded that a house should be erected in a lonely
place, so that the child might be guarded well, and he
provided servants, and all kinds of luxuries, and gave
orders that the prince should not be taken outside his
safe retreat.

It came to pass that the boy grew strong and big.
One day he climbed to the flat roof of the house. Looking down, he saw a dog which followed a man, and
wondered greatly thereat.

Then he spoke to one of the servants, saying: "What is that which follows the man walking along the road?"

"That," answered the servant, "is a dog."

The boy said: "I should like to have one for myself. Bring a dog to me."

When he spoke thus, the servant informed the king. His Majesty said: "Let him have a young boar hunter, so that he may not fret."

So the prince was given a dog as he had desired.

The boy grew into young manhood, and his limbs were stout; he was indeed a prince of the land. He grew restless in the lonely house, and sent a message to his royal father, saying: "Hear me. Why am I kept a prisoner here? I am destined to die either by a crocodile, a serpent, or a dog; it is the will of the gods. Then let me go forth and follow my heart's desire while I live."

His Majesty considered the matter, and said he would grant the lad's wish. So he caused him to be provided with all kinds of weapons, and consented that the dog should follow him.

A servant of the king conducted the young prince to the eastern frontier,[1] and said: "Now you may go wherever you desire."

The lad called his dog, and set his face toward the north. He hunted on his way and fared well. In time he reached the country of Naharina (Mitanni), and went to the house of a chief.

Now the chief was without a son, and he had but one daughter and she was very fair. He had caused to be erected for her a stately tower with seventy windows, on the summit of a cliff 700 feet from the ground. The fame of the girl went abroad, and her father sent for all the sons of chiefs in the land and said to them:

[1] Apparently the prince was safe from attack so long as he was away from Egypt.

" My daughter will be given in marriage to the youth who can climb up to her window."

Day after day the lads endeavoured to scale the cliff, and one afternoon when they were so engaged the young prince arrived and saw them. He was given hearty welcome. They took him to their house, they cleansed him with water and gave him perfumes, and then they set food before him and gave fodder to his horse. They showed him great kindness, and brought sandals to him.

Then they said: " Whence come ye, young man ? "

The prince answered: " I am the son of one of the Pharaoh's charioteers. My mother died, and my father then took another wife, who hates me. I have run away from home."

He said no more. They kissed him as if he were a brother, and prevailed upon him to tarry with them a while.

" What can I do here ? " asked the prince.

The young men said: " Each day we try to scale the cliff and reach the window of the chief's daughter. She is very fair, and will be given in marriage to the fortunate one who can climb up to her."

On the next day they resumed their wonted task, and the prince stood apart, watching them. Then day followed day, and they endeavoured in vain to reach the window, while he looked on.

It came to pass at length that the prince said to the others: " If you consent, I will make endeavour also; I should like to climb among you."

They gave him leave to join them in the daily task. Now it chanced that the beautiful daughter of the chief in Naharina looked down from her window in the high tower, gazing upon the youths. The prince saw her, and he began to climb with the sons of the chiefs, and he went up and up until he reached the window of the great chief's daughter, the fair one.   She took him in her arms and she kissed him.

Then one who had looked on, sought to make glad the heart of the girl's father, and hastened to him and spoke, saying:

"At last one of the youths has reached the window of your daughter."

"The great chief asked: "Whose son is he?"

He was told: "The youth is the son of one of the Pharaoh's charioteers, who fled from Egypt because of his stepmother."

Then was the great chief very angry, and he said: "Am I to give my daughter in marriage to an Egyptian fugitive?   Order him to return at once to his own land."

Messengers were sent to the youth in the tower, and they said to him: "Begone!   You must return to the place whence you came."

But the fair maid clung to him.   She called upon the god, and swore an oath, saying: "By the name of Ra Harmachis, if he is not to be mine, I will neither eat nor drink again."

When she had spoken thus she grew faint, as if she were about to die.

A messenger hastened to her father and told him what the girl had vowed and how she thereupon sank fainting.

The great chief then sent men to put the stranger to death if he remained in the tower.

When they came nigh the girl, she cried: "By the god, if you slay my chosen one, I will die also.   I will not live a single hour if he is taken from me."

The girl's words were repeated to her father, and he,

the great chief, said: "Let the young man, this stranger, be brought into my presence."

Then was the prince taken before the great chief. He was stricken with fear, but the girl's father embraced him and kissed him, saying: "You are indeed a noble youth. Tell me who you are. I love you as if you were mine own son."

The prince made answer: "My father is a charioteer in the army of the Pharaoh. My mother died, and my father then took another wife, who hates me. I have run away from home."

The great chief gave his daughter to the prince for wife, and provided a goodly dwelling, with servants, a portion of land, and many cattle.

It came to pass some time after this that the prince spoke to his wife, saying:

"It is my destiny to die one of three deaths—either by a crocodile, or a serpent, or a dog."

"Let the dog be slain at once," urged the woman.

Said the prince: "I will not permit that my dog be slain. Besides, he would never do me harm."

His wife was much concerned for his safety. He would not let the dog go out unless he went with it.

It came to pass that the prince travelled with his wife to the land of Egypt, and visited the place in which he had formerly dwelt. A giant was with him there. The giant would not allow him to go out after dark, because a crocodile came up from the river each night. But the giant himself went forth, and the crocodile sought in vain to escape him. He bewitched it.

He continued to go out each night, and when dawn came the prince went abroad, and the giant lay down to sleep. This continued for the space of two months.

It came to pass on a certain day that the prince made

merry in his house.   There was a great feast.   When
darkness fell he lay down to rest, and he fell asleep.   His
wife busied herself cleansing and anointing her body.
Suddenly she beheld a serpent which crept out of a hole
to sting the prince.   She was sitting beside him, and she
called the servants to fill a bowl with milk and honeyed
wine for the serpent, and it drank thereof and was intoxicated.   Then it was rendered helpless, and rolled over.
The woman seized her dagger and slew the serpent, which
she flung into her bath.

When she had finished, she awoke the prince, who
marvelled greatly that he had escaped, and his wife said:
" Behold the god has given me the chance to remove one
of your dooms.   He will let me strike another blow."

The prince made offerings to the god, and prostrated
himself, and he continued so to do every day.

It came to pass many days afterwards that the prince
went out to walk some distance from his house.   He did
not go alone, for his dog followed him.   It chanced that
the dog seized an animal in flight, and the prince followed
the chase, running.   He reached a place near the bank
of the river and went down after the dog.   Now the dog
was beside the crocodile, who led the prince to the place
where the giant was.   The crocodile said: " I am your
doom and I follow you . . . (I cannot contend) with the
giant, but, remember, I will watch you. . . . You may
bewitch me (like) the giant, but if you see (me coming
once again you will certainly perish).

Now it came to pass, after the space of two months,
that the prince went . . .

Note.—Here the British Museum papyrus, which contains several doubtful sentences,
is mutilated and ends abruptly.   The conclusion of the story is left, therefore, to our
imaginations.

One cannot help being struck with certain resem-

blances in the ancient narrative to a familiar type of
Celtic story, which relates the adventures of a king's son
who goes forth disguised as "a poor lad" to seek his
fortunes and win a bride by performing some heroic
deed in a foreign country. The lady in the lofty tower
is familiar. In Irish mythology she is the daughter of
Balor, King of Night, who had her secluded thus because it was prophesied that her son would slay him.
But the Cyclopean smith, Mackinley, won her, and her
son Lugh, the dawn god, killed Balor with the "round
stone", which was the sun. The mother of the Greek
Hermes, who slew his grandson, Argus, with the "round
stone", was concealed in a secret underground chamber,
from which her lover rescued her.

Apparently the Egyptian prince was safe so long as
he resided in a foreign country, and that may be the
reason why his father had him conducted to the frontier.
It would appear also that he has nothing to fear during
the day. The crocodile is bewitched so long as the giant
lies in slumber. In certain European stories a man who
works a spell must similarly go to sleep. When Sigurd
(the Norse Siegfried) roasts the dragon's heart, Regin lies
down to sleep, and when Finn-mac-Coul (the Scottish
Finn) roasts the salmon, Black Arky, his father's
murderer, lies asleep also. (See *Teutonic Myth and
Legend.*) In a Sutherlandshire story a magician goes
to sleep while snakes are being boiled to obtain a curative
potion.

The Egyptian protecting giant (also translated
"mighty man") is likewise familiar in a certain class of
Scottish (? Mediterranean) folktales.

In our Northern legends which relate the wonderful
feats of the disguised son of a king he invariably lies
asleep with his head on the knees of the fair lady who

"combs his hair". She sees "the beast" (or dragon) coming against her and awakens him. In this Egyptian tale the woman, however, slays the serpent, which comes against the man instead.

Readers will naturally ask: "Was the prince killed by the crocodile or by the dog? . . . Or did he escape? Was his wife given the opportunity to strike a blow?"

In "Celtic" stories the "first blow" is allowed, and it is invariably successful. One relates that a woman saved a hero's life by striking, as was her privilege, the first blow, and, as she used a magic wand, she slew the sleeping giant who was to strike the next "trial blow".

Was the crocodile slain in the end, and did the dog kill his master by accident? This faithful animal is of familiar type. He is one of the dogs "which has its day". In Northern tales the dog is sometimes slain by its master after it has successfully overcome a monster of the night. The terrible combat renders it dangerous afterwards. Besides, "it had its day".

Did the Egyptian dog kill the crocodile? Or did the prince's wife slay the dog, thinking the crocodile was unable to injure her husband? And was the spell then broken, and the crocodile permitted to slay the prince?

The problem may be solved if, and when, another version of this ancient story is discovered.

CHAPTER XXIV

Changes in Social and Religious Life

Wealth and Luxury—Gaiety of Town Life—Social Functions—Ancient Temperance Lectures—The Judges—Mercenary Soldiers—Foreign Brides and their Influence—Important Deities worshipped—Sutekh and Baal—The Air God—The Phœnician Thor—Voluptuous Goddesses—Ashtoreth of the Bible—References to Saul and Solomon—The Strange God Bes—Magic and Ethics—New Ideas of the Judgment—Use and Significance of Amulets—Jacob's Example—New Burial Customs.

In less than a century after the expulsion of the Hyksos a great change passed over the social conditions of Egypt. The kingdom was thoroughly organized under the supreme control of the Court. Every inch of land which the Pharaohs reconquered was vested in the Crown; the estates of the old nobility who had disappeared under the regime of Joseph were administered by officials; all the peasants became serfs of the king and paid a proportion of their produce in rent and taxation. The law was firmly administered, and the natural resources of the country were developed to the utmost.

When the arms of the Pharaoh secured settled conditions in Syria, the trade routes were reopened and the merchant class increased and prospered. There was no lack of employment. Temple building nursed the various industries into prosperity, and careers were opened for capable men in the civil service and the army. When the wealth of Asia poured into Egypt not only through the ordinary channels of commerce, but also in tribute from the dependencies, the nation assumed that air of comfort and prosperity which we find reflected in the artistic productions of the time. The tomb scenes no longer reveal a plain-living, scantily attired people or dignified and barefooted noblemen and Pharaohs amidst scenes of rural simplicity. Egypt of the Eighteenth Dynasty has a setting of Oriental splendour. Its people are gaily attired and richly bejewelled, and the luxurious homes of the wealthy resound with music and song and the clatter of wine cups.

When the Egyptian nobles of the Old and Middle Kingdoms had carved in their tombs the scenes of every-day life which they desired to be repeated in Paradise, they were content to have ploughmen and builders and domestic servants to provide them with the simple necessaries of life: the leisured classes of the Empire sought more after amusements; they could not be happy without their society functions, their merry feasts and rich attire, their troops of singers and dancers, their luxurious villas with elaborate furnishings, and their horses and chariots and grooms.

Town life was full of gaiety under the Empire. Wealthy people had large and commodious houses and delighted to entertain their friends, who drove up in chariots, attended by servants, and clad in many-coloured and embroidered garments. As the guests gathered and gossiped in these ancient days the hired musicians played harps and lyres, guitars, flutes, and double pipes; the lords and ladies seated themselves on single and double chairs, and wine and fruits were brought in by slaves, who also provided garlands and bouquets of scented flowers, perfumes, and oil for anointment. The drinking cups were of artistic shape, and might be either of glass or porcelain, or of silver or gold, finely engraved, and perhaps studded with precious stones. Joseph's cup was of silver (*Genesis*, xliv, 2).

The dinner consisted of many courses. These Eighteenth-Dynasty guests ate the flesh of the ox, the wild goat, or the gazelle, and certain fish, but never the tabooed eel, and they partook of geese and ducks and other birds in season; pork and mutton were rigidly excluded.[1] A variety of vegetables, and fruit and pastries, were included in the menu. In fact all classes feasted well. It is not surprising to find that when the Israelites were starving in the deserts of Arabia they sighed for the food of Egypt, and said: "Who shall give us flesh to eat? We remember the fish which we did eat in Egypt freely; the cucumbers, and the melons, and the leeks, and the onions, and the garlick" (*Numbers*, xi, 4 and 5). They also longed for Egyptian bread (*Exodus*, xvi, 3).

The society guests of Egypt were served at little tables, or as they sat in rows according to rank, by the nude or scantily attired servants, who handed round the dishes and napkins. All the guests ate with their fingers; they used knives for cutting and spoons for liquids; they washed before and after meals.

Ere wine drinking was resumed, the model of a mummy, or perhaps a real mummy, was drawn round the feasting hall, while the musicians chanted "The Lay of the Harper". (Chapter XVIII.) Then came a round of amusements. Jugglers and acrobats performed feats, nude girls danced, and songs were sung; again and again the drinking cups were replenished with wine. Many drank heavily. It was no uncommon thing in ancient

---

[1] Sheep and pigs were "taboo" because they were sacred animals which were eaten sacrificially only. Shepherds appear to have been shunned like swineherds. Joseph informed his brethren that "every shepherd is an abomination unto the Egyptians" (*Genesis*, xlvi, 34). (See Chapter V.)

Egypt to see intoxicated people. Even in the Middle Kingdom tombs at Beni Hassan there are evidences that the priestly exhortations to live temperate lives were necessitated by the habits of the time; servants are depicted carrying home their masters in various stages of intoxication. Nor were the women guiltless in this respect. In the Empire tomb scenes at Thebes tipsy ladies are seen supported by servants or attended with bowls when they turn sick and their embroidered robes slip from their shoulders.[1]

A temperance advocate in ancient Egypt, who lamented the customs of his age, addressed his friends as follows: "Do not drink beer to excess. . . . When you are intoxicated you say things which you are unable to recall; you may trip and break your limbs, but no one goes to your assistance, and your friends who continue to drink despise you and call out: 'Put this fellow away; he is drunk!' If, perchance, someone desires to ask your advice when you are intoxicated, you are found lying in the dust like a senseless child."

A teacher once wrote to his pupil, saying: "I am told that you are neglecting your studies, and that you are giving yourself up to enjoyment. It is said that you wander about through the streets of an evening smelling of wine. The smell of wine will make men avoid you. Wine will destroy your soul; you will become like a broken oar which cannot steer on either side; like a temple in which there is no god, or like a house without bread. Wine is an abomination."

In sharp contrast to the merrymakers of the Empire period are the stern and just administrators of the law.

---

[1] Hebrew women were also addicted to drinking. "Now Hannah, she spake in her heart; only her lips moved, but her voice was not heard; therefore Eli thought she had been drunken." Eli said: "Put away thy wine from thee" (*1 Samuel*, i, 13–14).

Judges were expected to make no distinction between rich and poor, and exemplary punishments were meted out to those who, by showing favour or accepting bribes, were found to be unworthy stewards. Daily courts were held, at which the evidence was taken down by scribes; cases were debated, the forty law rolls were always referred to and consulted, and decisions were enforced by the officers of the court. The king boasted not only of the victories he achieved on foreign campaigns; he desired also to have his memory revered as "the establisher of law"; when ineffectual appeal was made to him as the supreme judge, he "spoke not; the law remained".

But although Egypt was being governed by men of high ideals, influences were at work which were sapping the vitality of the nation. The accumulation of wealth and the increasing love of luxury made men less prone to undertake severe and exacting duties. It was ultimately found impossible to recruit a large army in Egypt. The pleasure-loving gentlemen preferred the excitement of the chase to the perils of the battlefield, and the pleasures of cities to the monotony of the garrison life and the long and arduous marches on foreign campaigns. "Soldiers of fortune" were accordingly enlisted, so that a strong standing army might be maintained. The archers known as the "Nine-bow Barbarians" came from Nubia, and from Europe were obtained the fierce "Shardana", the Mycenæan people who gave their name to Sardinia. Ultimately Libyans, and even Asiatics, were recruited; one of the regiments which followed Rameses II in his Syrian campaign was named after the alien god Sutekh. The foreign section of the Egyptian army was acknowledged to be the best. Its loyalty, however, depended on the condition of the Imperial exchequer, and it ultimately became a menace instead of a support to the empire.

Foreign traders were also being attracted to Egypt, while the kings and the noblemen showed such a decided preference for handsome alien wives that a new type of face appeared in society, as may be seen in the pictures and statuary of the times. Instead of the severe and energetic faces of the Old and Middle Kingdoms, we find among the upper classes effeminate-looking noblemen with somewhat languid expressions, and refined ladies with delicately cut features, languorous eyes, and sensitive lips. Occasionally, however, a non-Egyptian face is at once cultured and vigorous.

The foreign elements in society exercised a marked influence on the religious beliefs of the age. Strange gods were imported, and the voluptuous worship of the goddesses of love and war became increasingly popular; the former included Baal, Sutekh, and Reshep, and the latter Astarte, Anath, and Kadesh. Ere we deal with the changes which were effected by foreign influence in the Egyptian religion, we will pass these deities briefly under review.

Baal signifies "the god", "the lord", or "the owner", and was a term applied to the chief or ruler of one of the primitive groups of nameless deities[1]; his spouse was called "Baalath", "the lady". The Baal of Tyre was Melkarth; the Baal of Harran was Sin, the moon god; the Baal of Tarsus was an atmospheric or wind god; the Baal of Heaven was the sun god.[2] There were as many Baals in Asia as there were Horuses in Egypt.

Sutekh and Baal were generic terms. As we have indicated, Sutekh was the prototype of the Egyptianized Set, the terminal "kh" signifying "majesty". Indeed

---

[1] Nameless deities are the oldest.　　　　[2] Philo of Byblus.

Set and Sutekh were identified in the Nineteenth Dynasty. The "roaring Set" was the atmospheric or storm god Sutekh, the "Baal" or "lord" of all other deities. Possibly the Egyptian "Neter" was similarly a term applied originally to the nameless chief god of primitive conception.

Baal and Sutekh were, like Ptah and Khnûmû, the Great Father deities of the tribes who conceived that life and the world were of male origin. Some people identified the Great Father with the earth or water, as others identified him with the sun or the moon. The Baal and Sutekh worshippers, on the other hand, believed that the "air god" was the originator of life; he was the "soul" of the world. Like the Egyptian Shu, he was "the uplifter". According to Wiedemann, the root "shu" signifies "to uplift oneself". As the "Uplifter" of himself and the heavens, Shu was "the Baal". Primitive peoples all over the world have identified "air" and "breath" with "spirit". As we have shown (Chapter XIV), Khnûmû's name "Kneph" signifies "wind" and "spirit"—the "air of life". The Aryan root "an", "to blow" or "breathe", is found in the Latin "anima", "air" and "breath"; the Gaelic "anal"; the Greek "anemos"; and in English words like "animate", &c. The significance of Baal and Sutekh as atmospheric or wind gods is thus quite apparent; they were the sources of "the air of life".

As "the creator god" was the originator of both good and evil, he was worshipped as the giver of food, the nourisher of crops, and the generative principle in nature, and also propitiated as a destroying and blighting and avenging influence. His wrath was made manifest in the storm; he was then "the roaring Set", or the thunder god, like the Norse Thor. In the Bible the

God of Israel is contrasted with "the Baal" when Elijah, after exposing and slaying Baal's false prophets (*1 Kings*, xviii), took refuge in a cave.

> Behold, the Lord passed by, and a great and strong wind rent the mountains and brake in pieces the rocks before the Lord; but the Lord was not in the wind; and after the wind an earthquake; but the Lord was not in the earthquake; and after the earthquake a fire; but the Lord was not in the fire; and after the fire a still small voice (*1 Kings*, xix, 11-12).

Baal was thus "the lord" of wind, earthquake, and fire. "In Egypt", says Wiedemann,[1] "Baal was regarded as a god of the sky—a conception which fairly corresponds to his original nature—and as a great but essentially a destructive deity." He was "a personification", says Budge,[2] "of the burning and destroying sun heat and the blazing desert wind". Similarly Shu, "the uplifter", was identified with the hot desert winds, while his consort Tefnut symbolized the blazing sunlight, and was the bringer of the pestilence; she was also "the spitter" who sent the rain.

Baal was worshipped in Egypt at Tanis (Zoan); a temple was also erected to him at Memphis. Rameses II boasted that he was a warrior lord like Baal, and showed much respect for the imported deity.

Sutekh, "lord of heaven", was the "Sutekh of Kheta" (the Hittites), the god of the North Syrian allies of the Hittites, the god of the Hyksos, and the god of the early invaders who attacked the Osirian people of pre-Dynastic Egypt. As we have seen (Chapter XVIII), Sutekh came into prominence as a great god during the Twelfth Dynasty, in connection with the worship of the crocodile. Seti I, father of

---

[1] *Religion of the Ancient Egyptians.*   [2] *Gods of the Egyptians.*

Rameses II, was named after Sutekh, and a temple was erected for his worship by Rameses III at Thebes.

Sutekh is shown on a scarab with wings and a horned cap, standing upon the back of a lion. He was respected by the Egyptians because he represented the Hittite power; he was the giver of victory and territory.[1] As Set he was despised in Egypt during the period that he represented a repulsed and powerless enemy.

Another Asiatic deity who was honoured in Egypt was Reshep (or Reshpu), the Resef of the Phœnicians. He was another form of Baal, a "heaven lord", "lord of eternity", "governor of the gods", &c. His name signifies "lightning", or "he who shoots out fire". As the thunder god he was the god of battle. The Egyptians depicted him as a bearded man with Semitic profile, carrying a club and spear, or a spear and the symbol of life (ankh). From his helmet projects the head and neck of a gazelle, one of the holy animals associated with Astarte. A triad was formed in Egypt of Min, Reshep, and Kadesh.

Astarte was the most popular of the imported deities. Her worship became widespread during the later dynasties. At Memphis she was adored with the moon god Ah, and when Herodotus visited the city he found a small temple dedicated to "the strange Aphrodite" (Venus). She was the goddess of the eastern part of Tanis (Zoan). Astarte is the goddess of ill repute referred to in the Bible as Ashtaroth and Ashtoreth "of the Zidonians". Solomon "went after Ashtoreth" (*1 Kings*, xi, 5). The Israelites were condemned when "they forsook the Lord and served Baal and Ashtaroth"

---

[1] This belief is emphasized in *Judges*, xi, 24: "Wilt not thou possess that which Chemosh thy god giveth thee to possess?" Chemosh was the god of the Moabites.

(*Judges*, ii, 13). Samuel commanded: "Put away the strange gods and Ashtaroth from among ye". This goddess was worshipped both by the Phœnicians and the Philistines, and when the latter slew Saul they hung his armour in her temple (*1 Samuel*, xxxi, 10). Temples were erected to her in Cyprus and at Carthage. As Aphrodite she was the spouse of Adonis, and at Apacha in Syria she was identified with the planet Venus as the morning and evening star; she fell as a meteor from Mount Lebanon into the River Adonis. As a goddess of love and maternity she links with Isis, Hathor, Ishtar, "Mother Ida", Mylitta, and Baalath. Among the mountains this Mother Goddess had herds of deer and other animals like the Scottish hag "Cailleach Bheur".

Astarte was worshipped in Egypt early in the Eighteenth Dynasty, and was a lunar deity and goddess of war. She appears to have been introduced into the Nile valley with the horse. Like Tefnut, and other Egyptian feline goddesses, she was depicted with the head of a lioness. As the "Lady of Horses" she stands in a chariot driving four horses over a fallen foe.

There were many local types of this Great Mother deity in Asia. Another who was honoured in Egypt was Anthat (Anta), who was associated in ancient Arabia with the moon god Sin, and in Cappadocia, Asia Minor, with Ashir (Ashur). Several towns in northern and southern Syria bear her name. Thothmes III erected a shrine to her at Thebes, and in a treaty between Rameses II and the Hittites she and Astarte are coupled like Isis and Nepthys. Anthat is also the spouse of Sutekh. She is depicted on the Egyptian monuments as a goddess of battle, holding a spear in one hand and swinging a battle-axe in the other, seated on a throne or armed with shield and club riding on a horse in her Aasith form, favoured by Seti I. Rameses III named a favourite daughter Banth-anth, "daughter of Anthat".

Kadesh (Quedesh) "the holy one", was another form of Astarte. As the "mistress of all the gods", and the patroness of the "unmoral" women connected with her temples, she emphasized the licentious phase of the character of Ashtoreth which was so warmly denounced by the Hebrew prophets. The Egyptians depicted her as a moon goddess, standing nude on the back of a lioness, which indicated that she was imported from the Hittites; in one hand she carries lotus flowers and what appears to be a mirror, and in the other two serpents. As "the eye of Ra" she links with Hathor and Sekhet.

The grotesque god Bes also came into prominence during the Eighteenth Dynasty; it is possible that he was introduced as early as the Twelfth. Although his worship spread into Syria he appears to have been of African origin and may have been imported from Somaliland. Like the Deng, he was a dwarf with long arms and crooked legs; his nose was broad and flat, his ears projected like those of a cat, he had bushy hair and eyebrows and a beard, his lips were thick and gross. Over his back he wore the skin of a wild animal, the tail trailing behind. He was always drawn full face, like Kadesh and unlike typical Egyptian deities. He was a war god, a god of music playing a harp, and a love god. The oldest surviving representation of Bes is found in the Der el Bahari temple of Amon, where he attends at the birth of Hatshepsut. As late as Roman times he was known by his oracle at Abydos. Absorbed by the sun worshippers, he became the nurse of Harpokrates (Horus) whom he nourished and amused. He also guarded the child god against the attacks of serpents, which he tore to pieces between his teeth. As Sepd he was given a handsome body and a leonine face.

The luxury-loving and voluptuous worshippers of the Empire period found the ethical principles of the Ptah-Osirian creed little to their taste. They appear to have argued that if men and women were to be judged by the King of the Dead, according to the deeds they committed upon earth, there was little hope of the rich ever entering Paradise. Apparently belief in the heaven of the sun worshippers had faded away; it was incomprehensible, especially to the foreign element, that generations of Ra believers could be accommodated in the sun bark, to which entry was obtained by uttering magic "passwords".

The priests of Amon-Ra, who combined the worship and conceptions of the sun and moon cults, solved the problem of securing admission to the happy fields of Osiris, in Nether Egypt, by the use of charms and formulæ. It was unnecessary for worshippers who believed the priests either to live moral lives or to commit to memory the "confession of faith" which they must repeat before Osiris; the necessary formulæ were inscribed on the rolls of papyri which form the *Book of the Dead*, and when one of these was purchased, to be laid beside the mummy, the name of the dead was written in the spaces left blank for that purpose. But another difficulty had to be surmounted. When the heart was weighed before Osiris it made confession, according to the conception of the Old Kingdom, of the sins of which it was guilty. The priests effectually silenced the heart by using as a charm the scarabæus, the symbol of resurrection, on which was inscribed: "Oh, my heart, confess not against me as a witness!" These words were believed to have magical potency, and the scarabæus and other amulets became increasingly popular during the Empire period. The "tet" amulet was a symbol of the blood of Isis and protected the dead against the demons; the "dad" amulet, a fourfold altar, symbolized the backbone of Osiris and gave strength to the body and secured entrance to Paradise; the "ankh", a symbol of life, renewed vitality; the oval shaped "cartouche", which gave magical protection to the names of monarchs on their monuments, was also used as an amulet—evidently to prevent the demons from devouring the name of the dead.

Among the numerous charms were the "Horus eyes",[1] which were ever vigilant to detect evil influences. The right eye was the sun and the left the moon, so that protection was secured by day and by night.

Charms were in use from the earliest times, but the elaborate use of them in connection with burials begins with the Eighteenth Dynasty. They are, of course, relics of stone worship. Young and old in primitive times wore "luck stones" to protect themselves against the "evil eye", to prevent and cure diseases, and to secure good fortune. Indeed all personal ornaments appear to have had origin as charms. That they were recognized by the Hebrews as having idolatrous significance is clearly indicated in the Bible. After Jacob had met Esau, and slain the Hivites who desired to marry his daughters and female followers, he commanded his household to "put away the strange gods that are among you"; then we read: "And they gave unto Jacob all the strange gods which were in their hand, and all their ear-rings which were in their ears; and Jacob hid them under the oak which was by Shechem" (*Genesis*, xxxv, 3, 4). Evidently the ear-rings were connected with pagan worship and were as unworthy of Israel as the idols.

[1] These are still on sale in the East.

The changes which passed over the religious beliefs of the Egyptians during the Empire period were accompanied by new burial customs. Instead of constructing pyramids and mastabas, the Pharaohs and his lords had tomb chambers excavated among the hills. The cliffs opposite Thebes are honeycombed with the graves of the nobility; behind them lies the lonely "Valley of the Kings' Tombs". Some of the royal tombs are of elaborate structure, with many chambers and long narrow passages, but none surpass the greatest of the mysterious artificial caves of southern Palestine, on which they may have been modelled.

The splendour and wealth of this age is reflected in the elaborate furnishing of the tombs and the expensive adornment of mummies. Even among the middle and lower classes comparatively large sums were expended in performing the last material services to the departed.

CHAPTER XXV

Amenhotep the Magnificent and Queen Tiy

Prejudice against Thothmes III—Religion of Amenhotep II—Human
Sacrifices in his Tomb—Thothmes IV and the Sphinx—Amenhotep III half
a Foreigner—Queen Tiy's Father and Mother—A Royal Love Match—
Recreations of the King—Tiy's Influence upon Art—A Stately Palace—The
Queen's Pleasure Lake—Royalty no longer exclusive—The "Vocal Memnon"—King stricken with a Malady—Tiy's Powerful Influence—Relations
with the Priests of Amon—Akhenaton's Boyhood.

FOR some unexplained reason the memory of Thothmes
III was not revered by the priests, although he had once
been a priest himself, and never failed, on returning
from his victorious campaigns, to make generous gifts
to Amon's temple at Karnak. No folktales about his
tyranny and impiety survive, as in the case of the great
Khufu, the Pyramid builder. He has suffered more
from a conspiracy of silence. The prejudice against him
remained even until Roman times, when an elderly priest
translated to Germanicus the annals of Egypt's greatest
emperor and coolly ascribed them to Rameses II. This
intentional confusion of historical events may have given
origin to the legends recorded by Greek writers regarding the mythical Pharaoh Sesostris, to whom was credited,
with exaggerations, not only the achievements of Thothmes III and Rameses II, but also those of Senusert III
the first Pharaoh who invaded Syria. Herodotus believed that one of the sculptured representations of the

Hittite Great Father deity in Lydia was a memorial of Sesostris.

It may be that Thothmes III and Hatshepsut were supported by rival sects of the Theban priesthood, and that the disposal of Senmut and his friends, who were probably executed, was never forgiven. The obliteration of the great queen's name from the monuments, as we have suggested, may have been associated with a revolt which was afterwards regarded as heretical. We know little regarding the religious beliefs of Thothmes, but those of his son, Amenhotep II, were certainly peculiar, if not reactionary. He adored, besides Amon, Khnûmû, Ptah, and Osiris, the crocodile god Sebek, and the voluptuous goddess Astarte (Ashtoreth), Bast and Sekhet the feline deities, and Uazit the virgin serpent, and two of the Hathors. In his tomb there are evidences that he revived human sacrifice, which was associated with sun worship in the Fifth Dynasty; the body of a man with a cleft in his skull was found bound to a boat, and the mummies of a woman and child in an inner chamber suggest that he desired the company in the Osirian Paradise of his favourites in the royal household. Although he reigned for twenty years we know little regarding him. Possibly some of his greater monuments were either destroyed or appropriated by his successors. He conducted a campaign in Syria soon after he ascended the throne, and returned in triumph with the bodies of seven revolting princes suspended, heads downward, at the prow of the royal barge; six of these were afterwards exposed on the walls of Thebes, and one was sent to Napata in Nubia. He also conducted a military expedition as far south as Khartoum.

Another mysterious revolt, which may mark the return to power of the anti-Thothmes party, brought to

the throne the next king, the juvenile Thothmes IV, who
was not, apparently, the prince selected as heir by Amenhotep II. The names of the half-dozen brothers of the
new Pharaoh were erased in the tomb of the royal tutor,
and they themselves disappear from history. According
to a folktale, Thothmes IV was the chosen of the sun
god—a clear indication of priestly intervention—who was
identified for the first time, as Ra Harmachis, with the
great Sphinx at Gizeh. Thothmes had been out hunting,
and lay to rest at noonday in the shadow of the Sphinx.
He dreamt that the sun god appeared before him and
desired that the sand should be cleared away from about
his body. This was done, and a temple erected between
the paws, which was soon afterwards covered over by the
sand drift.

Thothmes IV was evidently favoured by the priests.
His distinctly foreign face indicates that his mother was
an Asiatic beauty; it is handsome but somewhat effemi-
nate. He died when he was about thirty, after a reign
of from eight to ten years. His royal wife was a daughter
of Artatama I, the Aryan king of Mitanni; she was the
mother of Amenhotep III, and grandmother of Akhenaton.

The third Amenhotep had a distinctly non-Egyptian
face, but of somewhat different type to that of his father;
the cheeks are long, the nose curves upwards, and he has
the pointed chin and slim neck which distinguished his
favourite wife Queen Tiy and their son Akenaton.

Much controversy has been waged over the racial
origin of Queen Tiy, who was one of Egypt's most
notable women. While some authorities regard her as
an Asiatic—either Semite, Hittite, or Aryan—others
believe her to be either an Egyptian or Libyan. It is
impossible to confirm either of the conflicting views that
she was a fair-haired, rosy-cheeked beauty with blue eyes,

or that she was dark, with lustrous eyes and a creamy complexion; but there can be no doubt that she was a lady of great personal charm and intellectual power. One of her portraits, sculptured in low relief, is a delicately cut profile. Her expression combines sweetness with strength of will, and there is a disdainful pout in her refined and sensitive mouth; her upper lip is short, and her chin is shapely and protruding. Whether she was born in Egypt or not, there can be little doubt that she had alien blood in her veins. Her father, Yuaa, appears to have been one of those Asiatic noblemen who was educated in Egypt and settled there. He held the honorary, but probably lucrative, position of superintendent of Amon's sacred cattle. His mummy shows him to have been a handsome, lofty-browed man with a Tennysonian nose of Armenoid rather than Semitic type; he had also the short upper lip and chin of his daughter. Tiy's mother appears to have been an Egyptian lady. The marriage of the King Amenhotep III to Tiy had no political significance; the boy and girl—they could not have been much more than sixteen—had evidently fallen in love with one another. The union proved to be a happy one; their mutual devotion continued all through life. Tiy was no mere harem favourite; although not of royal birth she was exalted to the position of queen consort, and her name was coupled with that of her husband on official documents.

Amenhotep's reign of thirty-six years (1411 to 1375 B.C.) was peaceful and brilliant, and he earned his title "The Magnificent" rather by his wealth and love of splendour than by his qualities as a statesman. The Asiatic dependencies gave no trouble; the grandsons of the martial princes whom Thothmes III subdued by force of arms had been educated at Thebes and thoroughly Egyptianized. Amenhotep would have, no doubt, distinguished himself as a warrior had occasion offered, for on the single campaign of his reign, which he conducted into Nubia, he displayed the soldierly qualities of his ancestors. He was a lover of outdoor life and a keen sportsman. During the first ten years of his life he slew 102 lions, as he has recorded, and large numbers of wild cattle.

Queen Tiy, on the other hand, was a lady of intellectual attainments and artistic temperament. No doubt she was strongly influenced by her father. When we gaze on Yuaa's profound and cultured face we cannot help concluding that he was "the power behind the throne". The palace favourites included not only highborn nobles and ladies, but the scholars and speculative thinkers to whom the crude beliefs and superstitious conventionalities associated with the worship of Amon and the practices of the worldly minded priests had become distasteful and obsolete; architects and artists and musicians also basked in royal favour. The influence of Queen Tiy on the art of the age was as pronounced as it was beneficial; she encouraged the artists to shake off the stiff mannerisms of the schools, to study nature and appreciate its beauties of form and colour, to draw "with their eyes on the object". And so Egypt had not only its "revolution of artistic methods", but its "renascence of wonder". No doubt the movement was stimulated by the wonderful art which had reached so high a degree of perfection in Crete. Egypt at the time was the most powerful state in the civilized world, and was pulsating with foreign influences; the old giant, shackled by ancient customs and traditions, was aspiring to achieve intellectual freedom.

The new movement was accompanied by a growing love of luxury and display of Oriental splendour which

appealed to the young king. To please his winsome
bride he caused to be erected a stately palace on the
western bank of the Nile at Thebes. It was constructed
of brick and rare woods; the stucco-covered walls and
ceilings of its commodious apartments were decorated
with paintings, which included nature studies, scenes of
Egyptian life, and glimpses of Paradise, exquisitely drawn
and vividly coloured; here and there were suspended those
beautiful woven tapestries which were not surpassed by
the finest European productions of later times, and there
was a wealth of beautiful vases in coloured glass, porcelain,
and silver and gold. The throne room, in which Queen
Tiy held her brilliant Courts, was 130 feet long and
40 feet wide. Papyri and lotus-bud pillars of haunting
design supported the roof and blossomed against a sky-
blue ceiling, with its flocks of pigeons and golden ravens
in flight. The floor was richly carpeted and painted
with marsh and river scenes, snarers capturing the " birds
of Araby ", huntsmen slaying wild animals, and fish
gaping wide-eyed in clear waters. Amidst the carved
and inlaid furniture in this scene of beauty the eye was
taken by the raised golden thrones of the king and queen,
over which the great gleaming pinions of the royal vulture
were displayed in noble proportions.

A shady balcony protruded from the outer decorated
walls; it was radiant with greenery and brilliant flowers
from Asia, covered with coloured rugs, and provided
with cushioned seats. When the invigorating wind from
the north blew cool and dry over the desert, Queen Tiy
and her artistic friends, lingering on the balcony, must
have found much inspiration in the prospect unfolded
before them. The grounds within the palace walls, bask-
ing in the warm sunlight, were agleam with Asian and
Egyptian trees, shrubs, and many-coloured flowers. On

the west rose in light and shadow the wonderful Theban
hills of every changing hue; eastward between the blue,
palm-fringed Nile, with its green banks and background
of purple hills, lay a great mile-long artificial lake, spark-
ling in sunshine and surrounded by clumps of trees and
mounds ablaze with strange and splendid blossoms.   On
this cool stretch of restful water the king and queen were
wont to be rowed in their gorgeous barge of purple
and gold named *Beauties of Aton*, while girl voices rose
bird-like in song, and sweet music came from many--
stringed harps and lyres, and from guitars, and lutes, and
warbling double pipes.   On nights of festival, religious
mysteries were enacted on the illuminated waters, which
reflected the radiance of many-coloured lights, the brilliant
stars, and the silver crescent of the moon.

In the vicinity of the palace were the luxurious villas
and beautiful gardens, with bathing pools and summer
houses, of the brilliant lords and ladies who attended the
state banquets and entertainments organized by Queen
Tiy.

Egypt's king and queen no longer held themselves
aloof from the people with the Chinese-like exclusiveness
of the Old and Middle Kingdoms. They were the leaders
of social life; their everyday doings were familiar to the
gossipers. No air of mystery and idolatrous superstition
pervaded the Court; domestic life in its finest aspects was
held up as an ideal to the people. Public functions were
invested with great splendour, royalty drove out in chariots
of silver and gold, brilliantly costumed, and attended by
richly attired lords and ladies and royal attendants and
guards. The king was invariably accompanied by the
queen.

Amenhotep vied with his predecessors in erecting
magnificent temples. His favourite architect was Amen-

hotep, son of Hapi, a remarkable man whose memory was long venerated; by the common people he was regarded as a great magician. It must have been he who appealed to the vanity of the king by designing the two colossal royal statues which were erected on the western plain of Thebes; they were afterwards known as the "vocal Memnon", because they were reputed to utter sounds at sunrise, caused, no doubt, by some ingenious device. These representations of Amenhotep III rose to a height of seventy feet, and still dominate the landscape in mutilated condition; they guarded the entrance of the royal mortuary temple which was demolished in the following Dynasty. Amenhotep was worshipped in his temple at Memphis, while Queen Tiy was similarly honoured in Nubia.

Great wealth accumulated in Egypt during this period. Tushratta, the subject king of Mitanni, writing to Amenhotep, declared, when he asked for gold "in great quantity" that "in the land of my brother gold is as plentiful as dust". The Pharaoh had added to his harem a sister of Tushratta's, his Asian cousin, named Gilu-khipa,[1] and she arrived with over three hundred ladies and attendants, but she did not displace Queen Tiy.

Much light has been thrown on the relations between Egypt and other countries by the Tell-el-Amarna letters—a number of clay tablets inscribed in Babylonian script which were discovered a few years ago. Babylonian was at the time the language of diplomacy. In these we find rulers writing in affectionate terms to one another and playing the game of politics with astuteness and Oriental duplicity.

---

[1] Her father was King Sutarna, whose sister was the wife of Thothmes IV. Sutarna's father was Artatama I, a contemporary of Thothmes III.

In the beautiful Theban palace was born to Queen Tiy, in the twentieth year of her husband's reign, the distinguished Akhenaton, who was to become the most remarkable Pharaoh who ever sat on the throne of Egypt. He was the only son; several princesses had preceded him. The young heir of the favourite wife was called Amenhotep, and when his father died he ascended the throne as Amenhotep IV. He was then about fourteen years of age, but had already married Nerfertiti, an Asiatic princess, apparently a daughter of Tushratta.

The last half-dozen years of the life of Amenhotep III were clouded in gloom. He was laid aside by some disease—either paralysis or insanity—which Tushratta of Mitanni sought to cure by sending on two occasions images of the goddess Ishtar.[1]   Queen Tiy appears to have governed the kingdom in the interval, and it is possible that she inaugurated the religious revolt, which became so closely associated with the name of her son, to counteract not only the retrogressive tendencies of the priests of Amon, but also, perhaps, to curb their political power; for, no doubt, they did their utmost to exercise a direct influence on the affairs of state. The existence of strained relations between the Amon temple and the royal palace during the boyhood of the future Pharaoh may well have infused his mind with that bitterness against the great religious cult of Thebes which he afterwards did his utmost to give practical expression to by doctrinal teachings and open persecution.

[1] The goddess of Nineveh. Tushratta must therefore have held sway over part of Assyria. The Mitanni King Saushatar, great-grandfather of Tushratta, captured and plundered Ashur.

CHAPTER XXVI

The Religious Revolt of the Poet King

The Shelley of Egypt—King as a Prophet—The Need of the Empire—Disturbing Race Movements—Fall of Cretan Kingdom—Hittites press Southward—Khabri advance on Palestine—Akhenaton's War on Amon—The New Capital—A Poet's Dream—Empire going to Ruin—Aton the "First Cause"—A Grand Theology—Origin of the New Deity—Shu in the Sun—The Soul in the Egg—The Air of Life—A Jealous God—The Future Life—Paradise or Transmigration of Souls — Death of Akhenaton — Close of a Brilliant Dynasty.

HERODOTUS was informed by the sages of Egypt that the souls of the dead passed through "every species of terrestrial, aquatic, and winged creatures", and, after a lapse of about three thousand years, "entered a second time into human bodies". If that belief were as prevalent at present in these islands as it was in early Celtic times, we might be at pains to convince the world that Shelley was a reincarnation of Akhenaton. The English poet was born about 3150 years after the death of Egypt's "heretic King", and both men had much in common; they were idealists and reformers at war with the world, and "beautiful but ineffectual angels". With equal force these lines by William Watson may be applied to the one as to the other:—

> Impatient of the world's fixed way,
> He ne'er could suffer God's delay,
> But all the future in a day
> Would build divine. . . .

Shelley's reference to himself in "Adonais" is admirably suited for Akhenaton.

> Mid others of less note, came one frail form,
> A phantom among men; companionless
> As the last cloud of an expiring storm,
> Whose thunder is its knell; he, as I guess,
> Had gazed on Nature's naked loveliness,
> Actæon-like, and now he fled astray
> With feeble steps o'er the world's wilderness. . . .
>
> A pard-like spirit beautiful and swift—
> A Love in desolation masked;—a Power
> Girt round with weakness; it can scarce uplift
> The weight of the superincumbent hour;
> It is a dying lamp, a falling shower,
> A breaking billow;—even whilst we speak
> Is it not broken? . . .

Like Shelley, too, Akhenaton appears to have resolved, while yet a boy, to fight against "the selfish and the strong", whom he identified particularly with the priests of Amon, for these were prone indeed to "tyrannize without reproach and check". The Egyptian prince, like the young English gentleman, began to "heap knowledge from forbidden mines of lore", and "from that secret store wrought linked armour for his soul"; he embraced and developed the theological beliefs of the obscure Aton cult, and set forth to convince an unheeding world that—

> The One remains, the many change and pass,
> Heaven's light forever shines, Earth's shadows fly. . . .

From the point of view of the Egyptian Imperialists the reign of Akhenaton, like that of Queen Hatshepsut, was a distinct misfortune. As it happened, the dreamer king ascended the throne with the noble desire to make all men "wise, and just, and free, and mild", just when

CHAPTER XXVI

The Religious Revolt of the Poet King

HERODOTUS was informed by the sages of Egypt that the souls of the dead passed through "every species of terrestrial, aquatic, and winged creatures", and, after a lapse of about three thousand years, "entered a second time into human bodies". If that belief were as prevalent at present in these islands as it was in early Celtic times, we might be at pains to convince the world that Shelley was a reincarnation of Akhenaton. The English poet was born about 3150 years after the death of Egypt's "heretic King", and both men had much in common; they were idealists and reformers at war with the world, and "beautiful but ineffectual angels". With equal force these lines by William Watson may be applied to the one as to the other:—

> Impatient of the world's fixed way,
> He ne'er could suffer God's delay,
> But all the future in a day
> Would build divine. . . .

Shelley's reference to himself in "Adonais" is admirably suited for Akhenaton.

> Mid others of less note, came one frail form,
> A phantom among men; companionless
> As the last cloud of an expiring storm,
> Whose thunder is its knell; he, as I guess,
> Had gazed on Nature's naked loveliness,
> Actæon-like, and now he fled astray
> With feeble steps o'er the world's wilderness. . . .
>
> A pard-like spirit beautiful and swift—
> A Love in desolation masked;—a Power
> Girt round with weakness; it can scarce uplift
> The weight of the superincumbent hour;
> It is a dying lamp, a falling shower,
> A breaking billow;—even whilst we speak
> Is it not broken? . . .

Like Shelley, too, Akhenaton appears to have resolved, while yet a boy, to fight against "the selfish and the strong", whom he identified particularly with the priests of Amon, for these were prone indeed to "tyrannize without reproach and check". The Egyptian prince, like the young English gentleman, began to "heap knowledge from forbidden mines of lore", and "from that secret store wrought linked armour for his soul"; he embraced and developed the theological beliefs of the obscure Aton cult, and set forth to convince an unheeding world that—

> The One remains, the many change and pass,
> Heaven's light forever shines, Earth's shadows fly. . . .

From the point of view of the Egyptian Imperialists the reign of Akhenaton, like that of Queen Hatshepsut, was a distinct misfortune. As it happened, the dreamer king ascended the throne with the noble desire to make all men "wise, and just, and free, and mild", just when

the Empire was in need of another ruler like Thothmes III to conduct strenuous military campaigns against
hordes of invaders and accomplish the subjection of the
rebellious Syrian princes. Once again, as in the Twelfth
Dynasty, the civilized world was being disturbed by the
outpourings from mountainous districts of pastoral
peoples in quest of "fresh woods and pastures new".
Crete had been invaded during the reign of Amenhotep
III; the "sack of Knossos" was already a thing of the
past; the great civilization of the island kingdom had
received its extinguishing blow, and thousands of the
"Kheftiu" were seeking permanent homes in the Ægean,
Asia Minor, Phœnicia, and Egypt. Ere Akhenaton's
father had died, Thebes received ominous intelligence
of the southward pressure of the Hittites and also of the
advance on Palestine of the Khabri (? Hebrews)—the
first "wave" of the third great Semitic migration from
eastern Arabia, known as the "Aramæan". The days
of the half-Iranian, half-Egyptian Tushratta were num-
bered; the civilization of Mitanni was doomed to vanish
like that of Crete.

Akhenaton began to reign as Amenhotep IV. With
purpose, apparently, to effect the immediate conversion
of Thebes, he began the erection of a temple to Aton
(or Aten) in close proximity to that of Amon. Ere long
an open rupture between the priesthood and the Pharaoh
became the chief topic of political interest. Amon's high
priests had been wont to occupy high and influential
positions at Court; under Amenhotep III one had been
chief treasurer and another grand vizier. Akhenaton
was threatening the cult with complete political extinction.
Then something was done, or attempted to be done, by
the priestly party, which roused the ire of the strong-
minded young king, for he suddenly commenced to wage

a war of bitter persecution against Amon. Everywhere the god's name was chipped from the monuments; the tombs were entered, and the young Pharaoh did not spare even the name of his father. It was at this time that he himself became known officially as Akhen-aton, "the spirit of Aton"[1]—the human incarnation of the strange god. Then he decided to desert Thebes, and at Tell-el-Amarna, about 300 miles farther south, he caused to be laid out a "garden city", in which were built a gorgeous palace which surpassed that of his father, and a great temple dedicated to "the one and only god". Aton temples were also erected in Nubia, near the third cataract, and in Syria at a point which has not been located.

When he entered his new capital, which was called "Horizon of Aton", the young king resolved never to leave it again. There, dwelling apart from the unconverted world, and associating with believers only, he dedicated his life to the service of Aton, and the propagation of those beliefs which, he was convinced, would make the world a Paradise if, and when, mankind accepted them.

Meanwhile more and more alarming news poured in from Syria. "Let not the king overlook the killing of a deputy", wrote one subject prince. . . . "If help does not come, Bikhura will be unable to hold Kumidi." . . . In a later communication the same prince "begs for troops"; but he begged in vain. "If the king does not send troops," he next informed Akhenaton, "all the king's lands, as far as Egypt, will fall into the hands of the Khabri." Another faithful ally wrote: "Let troops be sent, for the king has no longer any territory; the Khabri have wasted all". To this communication was

[1] Or, "Aton is satisfied" (Sethe).

added a footnote addressed to the royal scribe, which reads: "Bring *aloud* before my lord, the king, the words, '*The whole territory of my lord, the king, is going to ruin*'."[1]

In the stately temple at Tell-el-Amarna, made beautiful by sculptor and painter, and strewn daily with bright and perfumed flowers, the dreamer king, oblivious to approaching disaster, continued to adore Aton with all the abandon and sustaining faith of a cloistered medieval monk.

"*Thou hast made me wise in thy designs and by thy might*", he prayed to the god. . . . "*The world is in thy hand.*"

Akhenaton accounted it sinful to shed blood or to take away the life which Aton gave. No sacrifices were offered up in his temple; the fruits of the earth alone were laid on the altars. He had already beaten the sword into a ploughshare. When his allies and his garrison commanders in Syria appealed for troops, he had little else to send them but a religious poem or a prayer addressed to Aton.

Hard things are often said about Akhenaton. One writer dismisses him as an "æsthetic trifler", others regard him as "a half-mad king"; but we must recognize that he was a profoundly serious man with a great mission, a high-souled prophet if an impractical Pharaoh. He preached the gospel of culture and universal brotherhood, and his message to mankind is the only vital thing which survives to us in Egypt amidst the relics of the past.

> 'T is naught
> That ages, empires, and religions there
> Lie buried in the ravage they have wrought;
> For such as he can lend,—they borrow not

---

[1] "Tell-el-Amarna Letters" in Professor Flinders Petrie's *History of Egypt*, Vol. II.

> Glory from those who made the world their prey;
> And he is gathered to the kings of thought
> Who waged contention with their time's decay,
> And of the past are all that cannot pass away.

He remains to us as one of "the inheritors of unfulfilled renown",

> Whose names on earth are dark
> But whose transmitted effluence cannot die
> So long as fire outlives the parent spark. . . .

He believed in the "one and only god", Aton, whose power was manifested in the beneficent sun; the great deity was Father of all mankind, and provided for their needs and fixed the length of their days. Aton was revealed in beauty, and his worshippers were required to live beautiful lives—the cultured mind abhorred all that was evil, and sought after "the things which are most excellent"; it shrank from the shedding of blood; it promoted the idea of universal brotherhood, and conceived of a beautiful world pervaded by universal peace.

No statues of Aton were ever made; Akhenaton forbade idolatrous customs. Although Aton was a sun god, he was not the material sun; he was the First Cause manifested by the sun, "from which all things came, and from which ever issued forth the life-giving and life-sustaining influence symbolized by rays ending in hands that support and nourish human beings". "No such grand theology had ever appeared in the world before, so far as we know," says Professor Flinders Petrie, "and it is the forerunner of the later monotheist religions, while it is even more abstract and impersonal, and may well rank as scientific theism."[1] The same writer says: "If this were a new religion, invented to satisfy our modern

[1] *The Religion of Egypt*, London, 1908.

scientific conceptions, we could not find a flaw in the correctness of its view of the energy of the solar system. How much Akhenaton understood we cannot say, but he had certainly bounded forward in his views and symbolism to a position which we cannot logically improve upon at the present day. No rag of superstition or of falsity can be found clinging to this new worship evolved out of the old Aton of Heliopolis, the sole lord or Adon of the Universe".[1]

The chief source of our knowledge of Akhenaton's religion is his great hymn, one of the finest surviving versions of which has been found in the tomb of a royal official at Tell-el-Amarna. It was first published by Bouriant, and has since been edited by Breasted, whose version is the recognized standard for all translations.[2]

The development of Aton religion may have been advanced by Yuaa, Queen Tiy's father, during the reign of Amenhotep III, when it appears to have been introduced in Court circles, but it reached its ultimate splendour as a result of the philosophical teachings of the young genius Akhenaton. It has its crude beginnings in the mythological beliefs of those nature worshippers of Egypt and other countries who conceived that life and the universe were of male origin. We can trace it back even to the tribal conception that the soul of the world-shaping giant was in the chaos egg. In the Theban Recension of the *Book of the Dead* Ra is addressed:

O thou art in thine Egg, who shinest from thy Aton. . . .

---

[1] *A History of Egypt*, Vol. II, London.

[2] The most important of these appear in the following publications: Breasted's *A History of Egypt*, Petrie's *A History of Egypt* (version by Griffiths), Budge's *Gods of the Egyptians*, and Wiedemann's *Religion of the Ancient Egyptians*. In Naville's *The Old Egyptian Faith* (English translation by Rev. C. Campbell) the view is urged that Akhenaton's religious revolt was political in origin.

O thou beautiful being, thou dost renew thyself, and make
thyself young again under the form of Aton. . . .

Hail Aton, thou lord of beams of light; thou shinest and all
faces (i.e. everybody) live.[1]

There was an Aton cult at Heliopolis which taught that
the creator Ra was "Shu in his Aton". Aton is the
solar disk and Shu is the air god, the source of "the air
of life", the Great Father who is the soul of the universe.
Like "the Baal", Shu is also associated with the sun;
the atmospheric god is manifested by lightning and fire
as well as by tempest. Shu is thus not only "air which
is in the sun", but also, according to Akhenaton's religion, "heat which is in Aton". In the Tell-el-Amarna
poem, Aton, who creates all things, "makest the son to
live in the body of his mother". Then follows a reference to "the egg":

When the chick is in the egg and is making a sound within the
shell,
Thou givest it *air* inside it so that it may keep alive.
                                                    Budge's trans

The small bird in the egg, sounding within the shell,
Thou givest to it *breath* within the egg
To give life to that which thou makest.
                                                    Griffith's trans.

When the chicklet crieth in the egg-shell,
Thou givest him *breath* therein, to preserve him alive.[2]
                                                    —*Breasted's trans.*

When Akhenaton and his queen were depicted worshipping Aton, the rays which stretched out from the
sun and ended in hands not only supported their bodies

---

[1] Budge's *Gods of the Egyptians* and *Book of the Dead.*
[2] Amon-ra also "giveth breath to that which is in the egg" (*Religion of the Ancient Egyptians*, Wiedemann, p. 115).

but pressed towards their nostrils and lips the "ankh", the "symbol of life". The air of life was the sun-heated air; life was warmth and breath.[1] Why the "ankh" touched the lips is clearly indicated in the great hymn. When the child is born, Aton—

> Openest his mouth that he may speak.

Aton was thus, like certain other Egyptian gods, "the opener",[2] who gave power of speech and life to a child at birth or to the mummy of the dead. In this connection Wiedemann says that Ptah "bore a name which is probably derived from the root *pth*, "to open", especially as used in the ritual term "opening of the mouth". Porphyrius,[3] "who was well informed in Egyptian matters", tells us that the god (Ptah) came forth from an egg which had issued from the mouth of Kneph (a word signifying "air", "breath", and "spirit"). Kneph is Khnûmû in his character as an atmosphere god.

Some authorities identify Aton with the old Syrian god Adon. The root "ad" or "dad" signifies "father". As "ad" becomes "at" in "Attis", it may be that, as a result of habitual phonetic conditions, Adon became Aton. But Akhenaton's Aton was a greater conception than Adon.

The marked difference between the various Egyptian and Asiatic "Great Fathers" and the god of Akhenaton consists in this—Aton was not the chief of a Pantheon: he was the one and only god. "The Aton", says Professor Petrie, "was the only instance of a 'jealous god' in

---

[1] A ray of light from the moon gave origin to the Apis bull. See Chapter V.

[2] Osiris Sokar is "the opener of the mouth of the four great gods who are in the underworld" (*The Burden of Isis*, p. 54).

[3] Eusebius, *Præparatio Evangelica*, III, 11; Wiedemann, *Religion of the Ancient Egyptians*.

Egypt, and this worship was exclusive of all others, and claims universality."[1]   Had Akhenaton's religion been the same as that of the Aton cult at Heliopolis we might expect to find him receiving direct support from that quarter.   To the priests of Ra he was as great a "heretic" as he was to the priests of Amon, or Amon-Ra, at Thebes.

Akhenaton's conception of the material universe did not differ from that which generally obtained in his day in Egypt.   There was a Nile in heaven and a Nile in the underworld.   In rainless Upper Egypt he believed that—

The Nile in heaven is for the strange people. . . .
Thou (Aton) placest a Nile in heaven that it may rain upon them.
Griffiths.

The Nile of the underworld was "for the land of Egypt".

When thou hast made the Nile beneath the earth
Thou bringest it according to thy will to make the people live. . . .
That it may nourish every field.
Griffiths.

Aton also made the firmament in which to rise:

Rising in thy forms as the living Aton,
Shining afar off and returning . . .
All eyes see thee before them.
Griffiths.

We do not obtain from the hymn any clear idea of Akhenaton's conception of evil.   There is no reference to the devil serpent, or to the war waged against the sun god in Heliopolitan myth.   But it appears that as light was associated with life, goodness, and beauty, darkness was similarly filled with death and evil.   At night men lie down to sleep and "their nostrils are stopped", or

[1] *The Religion of Ancient Egypt*, p. 54.

"their breath is shut up". Then creatures of evil are abroad; "every lion cometh from his den and serpents of every kind bite" (Budge). Nor is there any reference to the after life. "When thou (Aton) settest in the western horizon the earth is in darkness, and is like a being that is dead" (Budge) or "like the dead" (Breasted and Griffiths). Akhenaton appears to have believed in the immortality of the soul—the bodies of Queen Tiy, his mother, and of his daughter and himself were embalmed —but it is not certain whether he thought that souls passed to Paradise, to which there is no reference in the poem, or passed from egg, or flower, to trees, animals, &c., until they once again entered human bodies, as in the Anpu-Bata story and others resembling it which survive in the folktales of various ages and various countries.

Akhenaton's hymn to Aton is believed to have been his own composition. Its beauty is indicated in the following extracts from Prof. Breasted's poetic translation:—

When thou risest in the eastern horizon of heaven,
Thou fillest every land with thy beauty.

When thou settest in the western horizon of heaven,
The world is in darkness like the dead.

Bright is the earth when thou risest in the horizon,
When thou shinest as Aton by day.
The darkness is banished, when thou sendest forth thy rays.

How manifold are all thy works,
They are hidden from before us,
O thou sole god, whose powers no other possesseth,
Thou didst create the earth according to thy desire
While thou wast alone.

The world is in thy hand,
Even as thou hast made them.
When thou hast risen, they live.
When thou settest, they die.
For thou art duration, beyond thy mere limbs.
By thee man liveth,
And their eyes look upon thy beauty
Until thou settest.

Thou makest the beauty of form. . . .
Thou art in my heart.

The revolution in art which was inaugurated under Amenhotep III is a marked feature of Akhenaton's reign. When sculptors and painters depicted the king he posed naturally, leaning on his staff with crossed legs, or accompanied by his queen and children. Some of the decorative work at Tell-el-Amarna will stand comparison with the finest productions of to-day.

The records which survive to us of the Akhenaton period are very scanty, for when the priests of the old faith again came to power they were at pains to obliterate them. Queen Tiy does not appear to have taken a prominent part in the new movement, which had developed beyond her expectations; and although she occasionally visited the city of Aton, her preference for Thebes, the scene of her social triumphs, remained to the end. Akhenaton's wife was a queen consort, as Tiy had been, and the royal couple delighted to appear among the people accompanied by their children.

The fall of the Amon party was complete. For several years the eight temples of Amon at Thebes lay empty and silent; their endowments had been confiscated for Aton, to whom new temples were erected in the Fayum and at Memphis, Heliopolis, Hermonthis, and Hermopolis.

An endeavour was made to enforce the worship of Aton by royal decree all over Egypt, with the result that the great mass of the people, who appear to have shown little concern regarding the fall of the tyrannical Amon party, were aroused to oppose with feelings of resentment an uncalled-for interference with the immemorial folk customs and beliefs which were so closely associated with their habits of life. But still the power of the "heretic king" remained supreme. The army remained loyal, although it had shrunk to an insignificant force, and when Akhenaton placed in command Horemheb it appears to have effectively controlled the disturbed areas.

Akhenaton died while still a young man, and left no son to succeed him. Semenkh-ka-ra, who had married a princess, became the next Pharaoh, but he appears to have been deposed by another son-in-law of the "heretic", named Tutenk-aton, who returned to Thebes, allied himself with the priests, and called himself Tutenk-amon, "Image of Amon". He was followed in turn by Ai (Eye), who called himself "Divine Father", and then a military revolt, instigated by the priests, brought to the throne, after a brief period of anarchy, Horemheb, who secured his position by marrying a princess of the royal line. He popularized himself with the worshippers of the ancient cults by ruthlessly persecuting the adherents of the religion of Akhenaton, erasing the name of Aton everywhere. He appears to have re-established the power of Egypt over a part of Palestine, and he restored order in the kingdom. So the Eighteenth Dynasty came to an end about two and a half centuries after the expulsion of the Hyksos.

CHAPTER XXVII

The Empire of Rameses and the Homeric Age

Sectarian Rivalries—Struggles for Political Ascendancy—New Theology —The Dragon Slayer—Links between Sutekh, Horus, Sigurd, Siegfried, Finn-mac-Coul, Dietrich, and Hercules—Rameses I and the Hittites—Break-up of Mitanni Empire—Seti's Conquests—Wars of Rameses II—Treaty with the Hittites—Pharaoh's Sublime Vanity—Sea Raids by Europeans on Egypt— The Last Strong Pharaoh—The Great Trojan War.

THE Nineteenth Dynasty opens with Rameses I, but no record survives to throw light on his origin, or the political movement which brought him to the throne. He was an elderly man, and does not appear to have been related to Horemheb. When he had reigned for about two years his son Seti was appointed co-regent.

But although history is silent regarding the intrigues of this period, its silence is eloquent. As the king's throne name indicates, he was attached to the cult of Ra, and it is of significance to note that among his other names there is no recognition of Amon.

The history of Egypt is the history of its religion. Its destinies were controlled by its religious cults and by the sects within the cults. Although Ra was fused with Amon, there are indications that rivalries existed not only between Heliopolis and Thebes, but also between the sects in Thebes, where several temples were dedicated to the national god. The theological system which evolved from the beliefs associated with Amon, the old lunar deity, must have presented many points of difference to those which emanated from Heliopolis, the home of scholars and speculative thinkers. During the Eighteenth Dynasty the priesthood was divided into two great parties: one supported the claims of Queen Hatshepsut, while the other espoused the cause of Thothmes III. It may be that the queen was favoured by the Ra section of the Amon-ra cult, and that her rival was the chosen of the Amon section. The Thothmes III party retained its political ascendancy until Thothmes IV, who worshipped Ra Harmachis, was placed upon the throne, although not the crown prince. It is possible that the situation created by the feuds which appear to have been waged between the rival sects in the priesthood facilitated the religious revolt of Akhenaton, which, it may be inferred, could have been stamped out if the rival sects had presented a united front and made common cause against him.

With the accession of Rameses I we appear to be confronted with the political ascendancy of the Ra section. It is evident that the priests effected the change in the succession to the throne, for the erection was at once undertaken of the great colonnaded hall at Karnak, which was completed by Rameses II. The old Amon party must have been broken up, for the solar attributes of Amon-ra became more and more pronounced as time went on, while lunar worship was associated mainly with Khonsu and the imported moon goddesses of the type of Astarte and the "strange Aphrodite". To this political and religious revolution may be attributed the traditional prejudice against Thothmes III.

The new political party, as its "new theology" suggests, derived its support not only from Heliopolis, but also from half-foreign Tanis in the Delta. Influences from without were evidently at work. Once again, as in the latter half of the Twelfth Dynasty and in Hyksos times, the god Set or Sutekh came into prominence in Egypt. The son of Rameses I, Seti, was a worshipper of Set—not the old Egyptianized devil Set, but the Set who slew the Apep serpent, and was identified with Horus.

The Set of Rameses II, son of Seti I,[1] wore a conical hat like a typical Hittite deity, and from it was suspended a long rope or pigtail; he was also winged like the Horus sun disk. On a small plaque of glazed steatite this " wonderful deity " is depicted " piercing a serpent with a large spear ". The serpent is evidently the storm demon of one of the Corycian caves in Asia Minor—the Typhon of the Greeks, which was slain by the deity identified now with Zeus and now with Hercules. The Greek writers who have dealt with Egyptian religion referred to " the roaring Set " as Typhon also. The god Sutekh of Tanis combined the attributes of the Hittite dragon slayer with those of Horus and Ra.

It is possible that to the fusion of Horus with the dragon slayer of Asia Minor may be traced the origin of Horus as Harpocrates (Her-pe-khred), the child god who touches his lips with an extended finger. The Greeks called him " the god of silence "; Egyptian literature throws no light on his original character. From what we know of Horus of the Osirian legends there is no reason why he should have considered it necessary to preserve eternal silence.

In a particular type of the dragon-slaying stories of Europe,[2] which may have gone north from Asia Minor

---

[1] Griffiths in *Proceedings of the Society of Biblical Archæology*, Volume XVI, pp. 88–9.

[2] One must distinguish between the various kinds of mythical monsters slumped as " dragons ". The " fiery flying serpent " may resemble the " fire drake ", but both

with the worshippers of Tarku (Thor or Thunor), the hero—a humanized deity—places his finger in his mouth for a significant reason. After Siegfried killed the dragon he roasted its heart, and when he tasted it he immediately understood the language of birds. Sigurd, the Norse dragon slayer, is depicted with his thumb in his mouth after slaying Fafner.[1] The Highland Finn, the slayer of Black Arky, discovered that he had a tooth of knowledge when he roasted a salmon, and similarly thrust his burnt finger into his mouth.[2] In the Nineteenth-Dynasty fragmentary Egyptian folktale, "Setna and the Magic Book", which has been partially reconstructed by Professor Petrie,[3] Ahura relates: "He gave the book into my hands; and when I read a page of the spells in it, I also enchanted heaven and earth, the mountains and the sea; I also knew what the birds of the sky, the fishes of the deep, and the beasts of the hill all said". The prototype of Ahura in this "wonder tale" may have been Horus as Harpocrates. Ahura, like Sigurd and Siegfried, slays a "dragon" ere he becomes acquainted with the language of birds; it is called "a deathless snake". "He went to the deathless snake, and fought with him, and killed him; but he came to life again, and took a new form. He then fought again

---

differ from the "cave dragon" which does not spout fire and the "beast" of Celtic story associated with rivers, lakes, and the sea. The latter is found in Japan and China, as well as in Scotland and Ireland. In "Beowulf", Grendel and his mother belong to the water "beast" order; the dragon which causes the hero's death is a "fire drake". Egypt has also its flood and fire monsters. Thor slew the Midgard serpent at the battle of the "Dusk of the Gods".

[1] *Teutonic Myth and Legend.*

[2] *Finn and His Warrior Band.* The salmon is associated with the water "dragon"; the "essence", or soul, of the demon was in the fish, as the "essence" of Osiris was in Amon. It would appear that the various forms of the monster had to be slain to complete its destruction. This conception is allied to the belief in transmigration of souls.

[3] *Egyptian Tales* (second series), London, 1895.

with him a second time; but he came to life again, and took a third form.   He then cut him in two parts, and put sand between the parts, that he should not appear again" (Petrie).   Dietrich von Bern experienced a similar difficulty in slaying Hilde, the giantess, so as to rescue Hildebrand from her clutches,[1] and Hercules was unable to put an end to the Hydra until Iolaus came to his assistance with a torch to prevent the growth of heads after decapitation.[2]   Hercules buried the last head in the ground, thus imitating Ahura, who "put sand between the parts" of the "deathless snake".   All these versions of a well-developed tale appear to be offshoots of the great Cilician legend of "The War of the Gods".   Attached to an insignificant hill cave at Cromarty, in the Scottish Highlands, is the story of the wonders of Typhon's cavern in Sheitandere (Devil's Glen), Western Cilicia.   Whether it was imported from Greece, or taken north by the Alpine people, is a problem which does not concern us here.

At the close of the Eighteenth Dynasty the Hittites were pressing southward through Palestine and were even threatening the Egyptian frontier.   Indeed, large numbers of their colonists appear to have effected settlement at Tanis, where Sutekh and Astarte had become prominent deities.   Rameses I arranged a peace treaty[3] with their king, Sapalul (Shubiluliuma), although he never fought a battle, which suggests that the two men were on friendly terms.   The mother of Seti may have been a Hittite or Mitanni princess, the daughter or grandchild

[1] *Teutonic Myth and Legend*.   In Swedish and Gaelic stories similar incidents occur.
[2] *Classic Myth and Legend*.   The colourless character of the Egyptian legend suggests that it was imported, like Sutekh; its significance evidently faded in the new geographical setting.
[3] It is referred to in the subsequent treaty between Rameses II and the Hittite king.

of one of the several Egyptian princesses who were given as brides to foreign rulers during the Eighteenth Dynasty. That the kings of the Nineteenth Dynasty were supported by the foreign element in Egypt is suggested by their close association with Tanis, which had become a city of great political importance and the chief residence of the Pharaohs. Thebes tended to become more and more an ecclesiastical capital only.

Seti I was a tall, handsome man of slim build with sharp features and a vigorous and intelligent face. His ostentatious piety had, no doubt, a political motive; all over Egypt his name appears on shrines, and he restored many monuments which suffered during Akhenaton's reign. At Abydos he built a great sanctuary to Osiris, which shows that the god Set whom he worshipped was not the enemy of the ancient deified king, and he had temples erected at Memphis and Heliopolis, while he carried on the work at the great Theban colonnaded hall. He called himself "the sun of Egypt and the moon of all other lands", an indication of the supremacy achieved by the sun cult.

Seti was a dashing and successful soldier. He conducted campaigns against the Libyans on the north and the Nubians in the south, but his notable military successes were achieved in Syria.

A new Hittite king had arisen who either knew not the Pharaoh or regarded him as too powerful a rival; at any rate, the peace was broken. The Hittite overlord was fomenting disturbances in North Syria, and probably also in Palestine, where the rival Semitic tribes were engaged in constant and exhausting conflicts. He had allied himself with the Aramæans, who were in possession of great tracts of Mesopotamia, and with invaders from Europe of Aryan speech in the north-west of Asia Minor.

The Hittite Empire had been broken up. In the height of its glory its kings had been overlords of Assyria. Tushratta's great-grandfather had sacked Ashur, and although Tushratta owed allegiance to Egypt he was able to send to Amenhotep III the Nineveh image of Ishtar, a sure indication of his supremacy over that famous city. When the Mitanni power was shattered, the Assyrians, Hittites, and Aramæans divided between them the lands held by Tushratta and his Aryan ancestors.

Shubululiuma was king of the Hittites when Seti scattered hordes of desert robbers who threatened his frontier. He then pressed through war-vexed Palestine with all the vigour and success of Thothmes III. In the Orontes valley he met and defeated an army of Hittites, made a demonstration before Kadesh, and returned in triumph to Egypt. Seti died in 1292, having reigned for over twenty years.

His son Rameses II, called " The Great " (by his own command), found it necessary to devote the first fifteen of the sixty-seven years of his reign to conducting strenuous military operations chiefly against the Hittites and their allies. A new situation had arisen in Syria, which was being colonized by the surplus population of Asia Minor. The Hittite army followed the Hittite settlers, so that it was no longer possible for the Egyptians to effect a military occupation of the North Syrian territory, held by Thothmes III and his successors, without waging constant warfare against their powerful northern rival. Rameses II appears, however, to have considered himself strong enough to reconquer the lost sphere of influence for Egypt. As soon as his ambition was realized by Mutallu, the Hittite king, a great army of allies, including Aramæans and European raiders, was collected to await the ambitious Pharaoh.

Rameses had operated on the coast in his fourth year, and early in his fifth he advanced through Palestine to the valley of the Orontes.   The Hittites and their allies were massed at Kadesh, but the Pharaoh, who trusted the story of two natives whom he captured, believed that they had retreated northward beyond Tunip.   This seemed highly probable, because the Egyptian scouts were unable to get into touch with the enemy.   But the over-confident Pharaoh was being led into a trap.

The Egyptian army was in four divisions, named Amon, Ra, Ptah, and Sutekh.   Rameses was in haste to invest Kadesh, and pressed on with the Amon regiment, followed closely by the Ra regiment.   The other two were, when he reached the city, at least a day's march in the rear.

Mutallu, the Hittite king, allowed Rameses to move round Kadesh on the western side with the Amon regiment and take up a position on the north.   Meanwhile he sent round the eastern side of the city a force of 2500 charioteers, which fell upon the Ra regiment and cut through it, driving the greater part of it into the camp of Amon.   Ere long Rameses found himself surrounded, with only a fragment of his army remaining, for the greater part of the Amon regiment had broken into flight with that of Ra and were scattered towards the north.

It was a desperate situation.   But although Rameses was not a great general, he was a brave man, and fortune favoured him.   Instead of pressing the attack from the west, the Hittites began to plunder the Egyptian camp. Their eastern wing was weak and was divided by the river from the infantry.   Rameses led a strong force of charioteers, and drove this part of the Hittite army into the river.   Meanwhile some reinforcements came up and fell upon the Asiatics in the Egyptian camp, slaying them almost to a man. Rameses was then able to collect some of his scattered forces, and he fought desperately against the western wing of the Hittite army until the Ptah regiment came up and drove the enemies of Egypt into the city.

Rameses had achieved a victory, but at a terrible cost. He returned to Egypt without accomplishing the capture of Kadesh, and created for himself a great military reputation by recording his feats of personal valour on temple walls and monuments. A poet who sang his praises declared that when the Pharaoh found himself surrounded, and, of course, "alone", he called upon Ra, whereupon the sun god appeared before him and said: "Alone thou art not, for I, thy father, am beside thee, and my hand is more to thee than hundreds of thousands. I who love the brave am the giver of victory." In one of his inscriptions the Pharaoh compared himself to Baal, god of battle.

Rameses delayed but he did not prevent the ultimate advance of the Hittites. In his subsequent campaigns he was less impetuous, but although he occasionally penetrated far northward, he secured no permanent hold over the territory which Thothmes III and Amenhotep II had won for Egypt. In the end he had to content himself with the overlordship of Palestine and part of Phœnicia. Mutalla, the Hittite king, had to deal with a revolt among his allies, especially the Aramæans, and was killed, and his brother Khattusil II,[1] who succeeded him, entered into an offensive and defensive alliance with Rameses, probably against Assyria, which had grown powerful and aggressive. The treaty, which was drawn up in 1271 B.C., made reference to previous agreements, but these, un-

---

[1] Known to the Egyptians as Khetasar.

fortunately, have perished; it was signed by the two
monarchs, and witnessed by a thousand Egyptian gods
and a thousand Hittite gods.

Several years afterwards Khattusil visited Egypt to
attend the celebration of the marriage of his daughter
to Rameses. He was accompanied by a strong force
and brought many gifts. By the great mass of the
Egyptians he was regarded as a vassal of the Pharaoh;
he is believed to be the prince referred to in the folktale which relates that the image of the god Khonsu
was sent from Egypt to cure his afflicted daughter (see
Chapter XV).

Rameses was a man of inordinate ambition and sublime vanity. He desired to be known to posterity as
the greatest Pharaoh who ever sat upon the throne of
Egypt. So he covered the land with his monuments
and boastful inscriptions, appropriated the works of his
predecessors, and even demolished temples to obtain
building material. In Nubia, which had become thoroughly Egyptianized, he erected temples to Amon, Ra,
and Ptah. The greatest of these is the sublime rock
temple at Abu Simbel, which he dedicated to Amon and
himself. Beside it is a small temple to Hathor and his
queen Nefertari, "whom he loves", as an inscription sets
forth. Fronting the Amon temple four gigantic colossi
were erected. One of Rameses remains complete; he
sits, hands upon knees, gazing contentedly over the
desert sands; that of his wife has suffered from falling
debris, but survives in a wonderful state of preservation.

At Thebes the Pharaoh erected a large and beautiful
temple of victory to Amon-ra, which is known as the
Ramesseum, and he completed the great colonnaded hall
at Karnak, the vastest structure of its kind the world
has ever seen. On the walls of the Ramesseum is the

well-known Kadesh battle scene, sculptured in low relief. Rameses is depicted like a giant bending his bow as he drives in his chariot, scattering before him into the River Orontes hordes of Lilliputian Hittites.

But although the name of Rameses II dominates the Nile from Wady Halfa down to the Delta, we know now that there were greater Pharaohs than he, and, in fact, that he was a man of average ability. His mummy lies in the Cairo museum; he has a haughty aristocratic face and a high curved nose which suggests that he was partly of Hittite descent. He lived until he was nearly a century old. A worshipper of voluptuous Asiatic goddesses, he kept a crowded harem and boasted that he had a hundred sons and a large although uncertain number of daughters.

His successor was Seti Mene-ptah. Apparently Ptah, as well as Set, had risen into prominence, for Rameses had made his favourite son, who predeceased him, the high priest of Memphis. The new king was well up in years when he came to the throne in 1243 B.C. and hastened to establish his fame by despoiling existing temples as his father had done before him. During his reign of ten years Egypt was threatened by a new peril. Europe was in a state of unrest, and hordes of men from "the isles" were pouring into the Delta and allying themselves with the Libyans with purpose to effect conquests and permanent settlement in the land of the Pharaohs. About the same time the Phrygian occupation of the north-western part of Asia Minor was in progress. The Hittite Empire was doomed; it was soon to be broken up into petty states.

The Egyptian raiders appear to have been a confederacy of the old Cretan mariners, who had turned pirates, and the kinsfolk of the peoples who had overrun the island kingdom. Included among them were the Shardana[1] and Danauna (? the " Danaoi" of Homer) who were represented among the mercenaries of Pharaoh's army, the Akhaivasha, the Shakalsha, and the Tursha. It is believed that the Akhaivasha were the Achæans, the big, blonde, grey-eyed warriors identified with the "Keltoi" of the ancients, who according to the ethnologists were partly of Alpine and partly of Northern descent. It is possible that the Shakalsha were the people who gave their name to Sicily, and that they and the Tursha were kinsmen of the Lycians.

Pharaoh Mene-ptah was thoroughly alarmed, for the invaders penetrated as far as Heliopolis. But the god Ptah appeared to him in a dream and promised victory. Supported by his Shardana and Danauna mercenaries, who had no scruples about attacking their kinsmen, he routed the army of allies, slaying about 9000 men and taking as many prisoners.

A stele at Thebes makes reference to a campaign waged by Mene-ptah in Palestine, where the peoples subdued included the children of Israel.

Although the son of the great Rameses II boasted that he had "united and pacified all lands", Egypt was plunged in anarchy after his death, which occurred in 1215 B.C. Three claimants to the throne followed in succession in ten years, and then a Syrian usurper became the Pharaoh. Once again the feudal lords asserted themselves, and Egypt suffered from famine and constant disorders.

The second king of the Twentieth Dynasty, Rameses III, was the last great Pharaoh of Egypt. In the eighth

---

[1] The old Cretans, the "Keftiu", are not referred to by the Egyptians after the reign of Amenhotep III. These newcomers were evidently the destroyers of the great palace at Knossos.

year of his reign a second strong sea raid occurred; it is dated between 1200 and 1190 B.C. On this occasion the invading allies were reinforced by tribes from Asia Minor and North Syria, which included the Tikkarai, the Muski (? Moschoi of the Greeks), and the Pulishta or Pilesti who were known among Solomon's guards as the Peleshtem. The Pulishta are identified as the Philistines from Crete who gave their name to Palestine, which they occupied along the seaboard from Carmel to Ashdod and as far inland as Beth-shan below the plain of Jezreel.

It is evident that the great raid was well organized and under the supreme command of an experienced leader. A land force moved down the coast of Palestine to co-operate with the fleet, and with it came the raiders' wives and children and their goods and chattels conveyed in wheel carts.[1] Rameses III was prepared for the invasion. A land force guarded his Delta frontier and his fleet awaited the coming of the sea raiders. The first naval battle in history was fought within sight of the Egyptian coast, and the Pharaoh had the stirring spectacle sculptured in low relief on the north wall of his Amon-ra temple at Medinet Habu, on the western plain of Thebes. The Egyptian vessels were crowded with archers who poured deadly fusillades into the enemies' ships. An overwhelming victory was achieved by the Pharaoh; the sea power of the raiders was completely shattered.

Rameses then marched his army northwards through Palestine to meet the land raiders, whom he defeated somewhere in southern Phœnicia.

The great Trojan war began shortly after this great

---

[1] When the Philistines were advised by their priests to return the ark to the Israelites it was commanded: "Now, therefore make a new cart and take two milch kine and tie the kine to the cart".—(*1 Samuel*, vi, 7).

attack upon Egypt. According to the Greeks it was waged between 1194 and 1184 B.C. Homer's Troy, the sixth city of the archæologists, had been built by the Phrygians. Priam was their king, and he had two sons, Hector, the crown prince, and Paris. Menelaus had secured the throne of Sparta by marrying Helen, the royal heiress. When, as it chanced, he went from home —perhaps to command the sea raid upon Egypt—Paris carried off his queen and thus became, apparently, the claimant of the Spartan throne. On his return home Menelaus assembled an army of allies, set sail in a fleet of sixty ships, and besieged the city of Troy. This war of succession became the subject of Homer's great epic, the *Iliad*, which deals with a civilization of the "Chalkosideric" period—the interval between the Bronze and Iron Ages.[1]

Meanwhile Egypt had rest from its enemies. Rameses reigned for over thirty years. He had curbed the Libyans and the Nubians as well as the sea and land raiders, and held sway over a part of Palestine. But the great days of Egypt had come to an end. It was weakened by internal dissension, which was only held in check and not stamped out by an army of foreign mercenaries, including Libyans as well as Europeans. The national spirit flickered low among the half-foreign Egyptians of the ruling class. When Rameses III was laid in his tomb the decline of the power of the Pharaohs, which he had arrested for a time, proceeded apace. The destinies of Egypt were then shaped from without rather than from within.

---

[1] The Cuchullin saga of Ireland belongs to the same archæological period; bronze and iron weapons were used. Cuchullin is the Celtic Achilles; to both heroes were attached the attributes of some old tribal god. The spot on the heel of Achilles is shared by the more primitive Diarmid of the Ossianic saga.

CHAPTER XXVIII

Egypt and the Hebrew Monarchy

"THE burden of Egypt.   Behold, the Lord rideth upon
a swift cloud, and shall come into Egypt: and the idols
of Egypt shall be moved at his presence, and the heart
of Egypt shall melt in the midst of it.   And I will set
the Egyptians against the Egyptians: and they shall
fight every one against his brother, and every one against
his neighbour; city against city, and kingdom against
kingdom.   And the spirit of Egypt shall fail in the
midst thereof. . . . The brooks of defence shall be
emptied and dried up; the reeds and flags shall wither.
The paper reeds[1] by the brooks, by the mouth of the
brooks, and everything sown by the brooks, shall wither,
be driven away, and be no more.   The fishers also shall
mourn, and all they that cast angle into the brooks shall
lament, and they that spread nets upon the waters shall
languish.   Moreover, they that work in fine flax, and
they, that weave networks, shall be confounded.   And
they shall be broken in the purposes thereof, all that
make sluices and ponds for fish" (*Isaiah*, xix).

From the death of Rameses III to the period of

---

[1] Papyri.

Isaiah, the great Hebrew prophet and politician, we must pass in review about five centuries of turbulence and change. The last great Pharaoh of the Nineteenth Dynasty was followed by nine weak rulers bearing the name of Rameses. Little is known, or is worth knowing, regarding them. They were but puppets in the hands of the powerful priests of Amon-ra, who had become the commanders of the army, the chief treasurers, grand viziers, and high judges of Egypt. The Oracle of Amon-ra confirmed all their doings. In the end the great Theban god became the rival of Osiris as Judge of the Dead, and the high priest, Herihor, thrust aside Rameses XII and seized the crown. Another priest king reigned at Tanis (Zoan) in the Delta.

Egypt was thrown into confusion under ecclesiastical rule, and land fell rapidly in value. Robbery on the highways and especially in tombs became a recognized profession, and corrupt officials shared in the spoils; the mummies of great Pharaohs, including Seti I and Rameses II, had to be taken by pious worshippers from the sepulchral chambers and concealed from the plunderers. No buildings were erected, and many great temples, including the Ramesseum, fell into disrepair.

After the passing of an obscure and inglorious century we find that the mingled tribes of Libyans and their western neighbours and conquerors, the Meshwesh, had poured into the Delta in increasing numbers, and penetrated as far south as Heracleopolis. Egypt was powerless in Palestine. The Philistines had moved southward, and for a period were overlords of the Hebrews. They had introduced iron, and restricted its use among their neighbours, as is made evident in the Bible.

Now there was no smith found throughout all the land of Israel: for the Philistines said, Lest the Hebrews make them

swords or spears; but all the Israelites went down to the Philistines, to sharpen every man his share, and his coulter, and his axe,
and his mattock. Yet they had a file for the mattocks, and for
the coulters, and for the forks, and for the axes, and to sharpen the
goads. So it came to pass in the day of battle, that there was
neither sword nor spear found in the hand of any of the people that
were with Saul and Jonathan; but with Saul and with Jonathan
his son was there found (*1 Samuel*, xiii, 19–22).

Thus the Hebrews at the very beginning of their
history as a nation had experience of a commercial
"corner", which developed their business instincts, no
doubt. Their teachers were Europeans who represented
one of the world's oldest civilizations.[1] The oppression
which they endured welded together the various tribes,
and under Saul the Hebrews made common cause against
the Philistines. When handsome, red-cheeked David,[2]
who had probably a foreign strain in his blood, had consolidated Judah and Israel, the dominance of the Cretan
settlers came to an end; they were restricted to the sea
coast, and they ceased to have a monopoly of iron.
Solomon, the chosen of the priests, was supported by
a strong army, which included mercenaries, and became
a great and powerful monarch, who emulated the splendour of the Pharaohs of the Eighteenth Dynasty. His
supremacy in southern Syria was secured by an alliance
with Egypt.

And Solomon made affinity with Pharaoh king of Egypt, and
took Pharaoh's daughter, and brought her into the city of David,
until he had made an end of building his own house, and the
house of the Lord, and the wall of Jerusalem round about
(*1 Kings*, iii, 1).

The Pharaoh with whom Solomon had come to an

---

[1] "The remnant of the country of Caphtor" (Crete).—*Jeremiah*, xlvii, 4.
[2] "A youth and ruddy and of a fair countenance" (*1 Samuel*, xvii, 42).

understanding was Sheshonk (Shishak), a vigorous ruler and successful military leader, who established peace in his kingdom. He secured his Delta frontier from attack by laying a firm hand on the territory between Egypt and the "buffer state" of the Hebrews. In time we read that he had "taken Gezer" (an independent city state) "and burnt it with fire, and slain the Canaanites that dwelt in the city, and given it for a present unto his daughter, Solomon's wife" (*1 Kings*, ix, 16).

Sheshonk was the first king of the Libyan (Twenty-Second) Dynasty, which lasted for about two centuries. He was the descendant of a Meshwesh-Libyan mercenary who had become high priest of Her-shef at Heracleopolis and the commander of the local troops. Under this foreign nobleman and his descendants the nome flourished and became so powerful that Sheshonk was able to control the Delta region, where he allied himself with other Libyan military lords. In the end he married the daughter of the last weak priest king of Tanis, and was proclaimed Pharaoh of Egypt. He made Bubastis his capital, and the local goddess, the cat-headed Bast, became the official deity of the kingdom. Amon was still recognized, but at the expense of other Delta deities who shared in the ascendancy of "the kindly Bast". Sheshonk held nominal sway over Thebes, and appointed his son high priest of Amon-ra, and he was able to extract tribute from Nubia.

Sheshonk's chief need was money, for he had to maintain a strong standing army of mercenaries. He must have cast envious eyes on the wealth which had accumulated in Solomon's kingdom, and, as it proved, was not slow to interfere in its internal affairs when opportunity offered. He extended his hospitality to Jeroboam, the leader of the Israelites who desired to be relieved of the heavy taxes imposed by Solomon. "Solomon

sought therefore to kill Jeroboam" (*1 Kings*, xi, 40).
When Rehoboam came to the throne, Jeroboam pleaded
on behalf of the oppressed ten tribes of the north, but
the new king was advised to say: "My little finger shall
be thicker than my father's loins". A revolt ensued,
and Jeroboam became king of the north, supported, evidently, by Shishak. The golden calf was then worshipped
by Jeroboam's subjects; it was probably the symbol of
the Hathor-like "Lady of Heaven", whose worship was
revived even in Jerusalem, when Jeremiah said: "The
children gather wood, and the fathers kindle the fire, and
the women knead their dough, to make cakes to the
queen of heaven, and to pour out drink offerings unto
other gods" (*Jeremiah*, vii, 18). The religious organization, based upon the worship of the God of Israel, which
had been promoted by David, was thus broken up; "there
was war between Rehoboam and Jeroboam all their days"
(*1 Kings*, xiv, 30).

The opportunity afforded for invasion was quickly
seized by Sheshonk. According to his own annals, he
swept through Palestine, securing great spoils; indeed
he claims that his mercenaries penetrated as far north as
the River Orontes. It is stated in the Bible that he
plundered Jerusalem, and "took away the treasures of
the house of the Lord, and the treasures of the king's
house; he even took away all; and he took away all
the shields of gold which Solomon had made" (*1 Kings*,
xiv, 25–6).

About a century after the death of Sheshonk the
power of the royal house is found to have declined; the
various hereditary Libyan lords showed but nominal allegiance to the Crown. A rival kingdom had also arisen
in the south. When the priest kings were driven from
Thebes they founded a theocracy in the Nubian colony,

which became known as Ethiopia, and there the Oracle of Amon controlled the affairs of State.

In time the Ethiopian kingdom became strong enough to control a large part of Upper Egypt, and Thebes was occupied. Then Piankhy, the most capable of all the Ethiopian rulers, extended his conquests until he forced the princes of the north to acknowledge his supremacy.

Piankhy's most serious rival was Tefnekht, prince of Sais, who assembled an army of allies and fought his way southward as far as Thebes. He was driven back by Piankhy, who ultimately swept in triumph to Sais and compelled the submission of Tefnekht and his allies. He did not, however, effect the permanent occupation of Lower Egypt.

Shabaka, the first Pharaoh of the Ethiopian (Twenty-Fifth) Dynasty, ruled over all Egypt, having secured by force of arms the allegiance of the princes, or petty kings, of the north. He is believed to be the Biblical "So, King of Egypt" (*2 Kings*, xvii, 4). Syria and Palestine had become dependencies of the great Empire of Assyria, which included Babylonia and Mesopotamia and extended into Asia Minor. Shabaka had either dreams of acquiring territory in southern Syria, or desired to have buffer states to protect Egypt against Assyrian invasion, for he entered into an alliance with some of the petty kings. These included King Hoshea of Israel, who, trusting to Egypt's support, "brought no present (tribute) to the King of Assyria as he had done year by year" (*2 Kings*, xvii, 4). Sargon II of Assyria anticipated the rising, and speedily stamped it out. He had Ilu-bi'-di of Hamath flayed alive, he defeated a weak Egyptian force; and took Hanno, Prince of Gaza, and King Hoshea prisoners. Then he distributed, as he has re-recorded, 27,290 Israelites — "the ten lost tribes" —

between Mesopotamia and the Median highlands.[1] Large numbers of troublesome peoples were drafted from Babylonia into Samaria, where they mingled with the remnants of the tribes which remained. Thus came to an end the kingdom of the northern Hebrews; that of Judah—the kingdom of the Jews—remained in existence for another century and a half.

Taharka, the third and last Ethiopian Pharaoh, whose mother was a negress, is referred to in the Bible as Tirhakah (*Isaiah*, xxxvii, 9). Like Shabaka, he took an active part in Asian politics, and allied himself with, among others, Luli, King of Tyre, and Hezekiah, King of Judah. Sargon "the later", as he called himself, had been assassinated, and his son, Sennacherib, had to deal with several revolts during the early years of his reign. Ionians had invaded Cilicia, and had to be subdued; many of the prisoners were afterwards sent to Nineveh. Trouble was constantly brewing in Babylonia, where the supremacy of Assyria was being threatened by a confederacy of Chaldeans, Elamites, and Aramæans; a pretender even arose in Babylon, and Sennacherib's brother, the governor, was murdered, and the city had to be besieged and captured. This "pretender", Merodach-Baladan,[2] had been concerned in the Egypto-Syrian alliance, and Sennacherib found it necessary to push westward, as soon as he had overrun Chaldea, to deal with the great revolt. He conquered Phœnicia, with the

---

[1] These tribes were worshippers of the "golden calf". There is no proof that they were not absorbed by the peoples among whom they settled. A good story is told of a well-known archæologist. He was approached by a lady who supports the view that the British are descended from the "ten lost tribes". "I am not an Anglo-Israelite," he said; "I am afraid I am an Anglo-Philistine".

[2] He "sent letters and a present to Hezekiah" (*Isaiah*, xxxix, 1). The shadow of the sundial of Ahaz had gone "ten degrees backward". According to an astronomical calculation there was a partial eclipse of the sun—of the upper part—which was visible at Jerusalem on 11 January, 689, B.C., about 11.30 a.m. (See also *2 Chronicles*, xxxii.)

exception of Tyre, but King Luli had taken refuge in Cyprus. Hastening southward he scattered an army of allies, which included Pharaoh Taharka's troops, and, having captured a number of cities in Judah, he laid siege to Jerusalem. Hezekiah held out, but, according to the Assyrian account, made terms of peace with the emperor, and afterwards sent great gifts to Nineveh. A later expedition appears to have been regarded as necessary, however, and, according to the Biblical account, it ended disastrously, for Sennacherib's army was destroyed by a pestilence. Isaiah, who was in Jerusalem at the time, said: " Thus saith the Lord . . . Behold I will send a blast upon him, and he shall hear a rumour and shall return to his own land, and I will cause him to fall by the sword in his own land " (*2 Kings*, xix, 7).

And it came to pass that night, that the angel of the Lord went out, and smote in the camp of the Assyrians an hundred and four score and five thousand. . . . So Sennacherib, King of Assyria, departed (*2 Kings*, xix, 35, 36).

The Assyrian came down like the wolf on the fold,
And his cohorts were gleaming in purple and gold;
And the sheen of their spears was like stars on the sea,
When the blue wave rolls nightly on deep Galilee.

Like the leaves of the forest when summer is green,
That host with their banners at sunset was seen:
Like the leaves of the forest when autumn hath blown,
That host on the morrow lay withered and strown.

For the angel of death spread his wings on the blast,
And breathed in the face of the foe as he passed;
And the eyes of the sleepers waxed deadly and chill,
And their hearts but once heaved—and for ever grew still!

And there lay the steed with his nostril all wide,
But through it there rolled not the breath of his pride;

And the foam of his gasping lay white on the turf,
And cold as the spray of the rock-beating surf.

And there lay the rider distorted and pale,
With the dew on his brow, and the rust on his mail:
And the tents were all silent—the banners alone—
The lances unlifted—the trumpet unblown.

And the widows of Ashur are loud in their wail,
And the idols are broke in the temple of Baal;
And the might of the Gentle, unsmote by the sword,
Hath melted like snow in the glance of the Lord.

Byron.

Isaiah, statesman and scholar, had been no party to the alliance between Egypt and Judah and the other Powers who trusted in the Babylonian Pretender; in fact, he had denounced it at the very outset. He entertained great contempt for the Egyptians. "Lo, thou trustest in the staff of this broken reed, on Egypt; whereon if a man lean, it will go into his hand and pierce it" (*Isaiah*, xxxvi, 6). . . . "The princes of Zoan" (Tanis), he said, "are become fools, and the princes of Noph (Memphis[1]) are deceived" (*Isaiah*, xix, 13). He foretold the fall of Tyre and the subjection of Egypt, and admonished the pro-Egyptians of Judah, saying: "Woe to the rebellious children . . . that walk into Egypt . . . to strengthen themselves in the strength of Pharaoh, and to trust in the shadow of Egypt" (*Isaiah*, xxx, 1, 2). "For the Egyptians", he warned Hezekiah, "shall help in vain and to no purpose . . . their strength is to sit still . . . write it before them in a tablet", he added, "and note it in a book" (*Isaiah*, xxx, 7, 8). He had summed up the situation with characteristic sagacity.

Sennacherib's campaigns paralysed the kingdom of

---

[1] Or Napata, in Ethiopia.

the Jews. Thousands of prisoners were deported, and when peace again prevailed Hezekiah had left only "the remnant that is escaped of the house of Judah" (*2 Kings*, xix, 30).

After Sennacherib was murdered, as the result of a revolt which disturbed Babylon, his son, Assar-haddon,[1] had to deal with another western rising fomented by that scheming Ethiopian Pharaoh Taharka, who was riding speedily on the road to ruin.

About 674 B.C. the young Assyrian emperor conducted a vigorous campaign in Syria, and struck at the root of his imperial troubles by invading Egypt, which he conquered, and divided up between some twenty princes, the chief of whom was the half-Libyan Necho of Sais. Taharka endeavoured to reconquer his kingdom, and Assar-haddon set out with a strong army to deal with him, but died on the march.

A few years later Ashur-banipal, the new Assyrian emperor, defeated Taharka at Memphis. Necho of Sais, who had been intriguing with the Ethiopian king, was pardoned, and appointed chief agent of the emperor in Egypt, which had become an Assyrian province.

Taharka gave no further trouble. When he died, however, his successor, Tanut-amon, King of Ethiopia, endeavoured to wrest Upper and Lower Egypt from the Assyrians. Necho marched southward with a force of Assyrian troops, but was defeated and slain at Memphis. But the triumph of Tanut-amon was shortlived. Ashur-banipal once again entered Egypt and stamped out the last spark of Ethiopian power in that unhappy country. Thebes was captured and plundered, the images of the great gods were carried away to Nineveh, and the temples were despoiled of all their treasure. Half a century later,

[1] Or Esarhaddon

when Nahum, the Hebrew prophet, foretold the fall of Nineveh, "the bloody city . . . full of lies and robbery . . . the noise of the whip, and the noise of the rattling of the wheels, and of the prancing horses, and of the jumping chariots " . . . he referred in his own graphic manner to the disaster which fell upon Thebes at the hands of the vengeful Assyrians.

"Art thou better than populous No (Thebes) that was situate among the rivers", cried the prophet, "that had the waters round about it . . . Ethiopia and Egypt were her strength and it was infinite. . . . Yet was she carried away, she went into captivity: her young children also were dashed in pieces at the top of all the streets; and they cast lots for her honourable men, and all her great men were bound in chains" (*Nahum*, iii, 8–10).

So the glory departed from Thebes, never again to return. Amon was cast down from his high place, the priesthood was broken up, and the political schemers who escaped the Assyrians found refuge in Ethiopia, where the kings submitted to their rule and became "as clay in the hands of the potter ", with the result that the civilization of the Nubian power gradually faded away. Psamtek, who, according to Herodotus, had fled to Syria on the death of his father Necho, became Assyrian governor (Shaknu) in Egypt, and the country was left to settle down in its shame to produce the wherewithal demanded in tribute year by year by the mighty Emperor Ashurbanipal of Assyria.

CHAPTER XXIX

The Restoration and the End

The God of the People—Egypt yearns for the Past—Rise of Saite Kings
—Osiris as Great Father—Christianized Horus Legend—Scythians and Cimmerians—End of Assyrian Empire—Jeremiah and Pharaoh Necho—Surrender
of Jerusalem—Early Explorers—Zedekiah and Pharaoh Hophra—Jerusalem
sacked—Babylonian Captivity—Amasis and the Greeks—Coming of King
Cyrus—Fall of Babylon—Persian Conquest of Egypt—Life in the Latter Days
—Homely Letters—Cry of a Lost Soul.

THE civilization of ancient Egypt began with Osiris and
ended with Osiris. Although the deified king had been
thrust into the background for long centuries by the
noble and great, he remained the god of the common
people. "The dull crowd", as Plutarch called them,
associated the ideas about their gods, "with changes of
atmosphere according to the seasons, or with the generation of corn and sowings and ploughings, and in saying
that Osiris is buried when the sown corn is hidden by
the earth, and comes to life and shows himself again
when it begins to sprout. . . . They love to hear these
things, and believe them, drawing conviction from things
immediately at hand and customary." The peasant lived
and died believing in Osiris. "As Osiris lives, so shall
he also live; as Osiris died not, so shall he also not die;
as Osiris perished not, so shall he also not perish."[1]
Egypt was made prosperous by Osiris: he gave it the
corn which brought all its wealth and power. The

[1] Erman, *Handbuch.*
363

greatest Pharaohs were those who, reverencing Osiris, cut new irrigating canals, and boasted like Amenemhet I:

> I loved the corn god . . . I have grown the grain
> In every golden valley where the Nile
> Entreated me. . . .

Egypt's Bata-like peasants constituted the strongest army commanded by the Pharaohs; they won golden spoils from Nature, which were of more account than the spoils from Syrian battlefields and the tribute of subject kings. Those constant toilers, who were innately conservative in their methods and customs and beliefs, bulk largely in the background of ancient Egyptian history; they were little affected by the changes which passed over the country century after century; once a political storm died down, they settled back into their own habits of life; they were "the nails that held the world (of Egypt) together".

We have seen the Pharaohs and their nobles going after strange gods, marrying alien wives, and adopting new manners and customs, forgetting those traditions which are the inspiration of national life and the essence of true patriotism. When Egypt fell and was ground under the heel of the Assyrian it was from the steadfast, although unlettered, peasants that the strength of the restoration was derived; they remembered the days that were, and they remembered Osiris. "Those Egyptians who live in the cultivated parts of the country", wrote Herodotus, "are of all I have seen the most ingenious, being attentive to the improvement of memory beyond the rest of mankind."

The Assyrian conquest stirred Egypt to its depths. When Thebes was sacked, and Amon-ra cast down from his high place, the worshippers of Osiris were reviving the beliefs and customs of the Old Kingdom, for they had never gone wholeheartedly after Ra and Amon or Sutekh and Astarte. When Ashur-banipal shattered the power of the Asiatic nobles of Egypt and drove out the Ethiopians, he also rescued the Egyptian people from their oppressors and strengthened the restoration movement which had begun under the Ethiopian kings.

Ashur-banipal was unable to retain for long his hold upon the land of the Pharaohs. Persistent revolts occupied his attention at the very heart of his empire. His brother, the subject king of Babylon, had secured the co-operation of the Elamites, the Aramæans, the Chaldeans, and the Arabians, and a fierce struggle ensued, until in the end Babylon was besieged and captured and Elam was devastated. Meanwhile Cimmerians were invading Asia Minor and the Aryan Medes were pressing into Elam. When peace was at length restored Assyria, although triumphant, was weakened as a result of its terrible struggles, and the empire began to go to pieces.

Assyria's misfortunes gave Psamtek his opportunity. About two years after his rival, Tanut-amon, was driven out of Thebes, he had come to an understanding with King Gyges of Lydia, who, having driven off the first attack of Cimmerians, was able to send him Ionian and Carian mercenaries. Psamtek then ceased to pay tribute to Ashur-banipal, and was proclaimed Pharaoh of United Egypt. As he had married a daughter of Taharka, the Ethiopian, his succession to the throne was legalized according to the "unwritten law" of Egypt. The Assyrian officials and soldiers were driven across the Delta frontier.

Herodotus relates an interesting folktale regarding the rise of Psamtek. He was informed that the Egyp-

tians chose twelve kings to reign over them, and these
"connected themselves with intermarriages, and engaged
to promote the common interest", chiefly because an
oracle had declared that the one among them who offered
a libation to Ptah in a brazen vessel should become the
Pharaoh. One day in the labyrinth eleven of the kings
made offerings in golden cups, but the priest had brought
out no cup for Psamtek, who used his brazen helmet.
The future Pharaoh was promptly exiled to a limited area
in the Delta. He visited the oracle of the serpent goddess at Buto, and was informed that his cause would
prosper when the sea produced brazen figures of men.
Soon afterwards he heard that a body of Ionians and
Carians, clad in brazen armour, had come oversea and
were plundering on the Egyptian coast. He immediately
entered into an alliance with them, promising rich re-
wards, vanquished his rivals in battle, and thus became
sole sovereign of Egypt.

Sais was then the capital, and its presiding deity, the
goddess Neith, assumed great importance; but by the
mass of the people she was regarded as a form of Isis.
The great city of Memphis, however, was the real centre
of the social and religious life of the new Egypt which
was the old. Thebes had ceased to have any political
significance. No attempt was made to restore its dilapi-
dated temples, from which many of the gods had been
deported to Assyria, where they remained until the Persian
age. Amon had fallen from his high estate, and his cult
was presided over by a high priestess, a sister of Psamtek's
queen, the "wife" of the god. With this lady was afterwards associated one of Psamtek's daughters, so that the
remnant of the Amon endowments might come under
the control of the royal house. Ra of Heliopolis shrank
to the position of a local deity. The conservative Egyp-

tians, as a whole, had never been converted to sun worship.

Osiris was restored as the national god in his Old Kingdom association with Ptah, the Great Father, the world deity, who had his origin upon the earth; his right eye was the sun and his left eye was the moon. But although the sun was "the eye of Osiris", the ancient deity was no more a sun god than Ra was an earth god. As Osiris-ra he absorbed certain attributes of the solar deity, but as Ra had similarly absorbed almost every other god, the process was not one of change so much as adjustment.[1] Ra ceased to be recognized as the Great Father of the Egyptian Pantheon. "Behold, thou (Osiris) art upon the seat of Ra." Osiris was essentially a god of vegetation and the material world; he was the soul of Ra, but his own soul was the soul of Seb, the earth god, which was hidden now in a tree, now in an animal, now in an egg: the wind was the breath and spirit of Osiris, and his eyes gave light. He was not born from the sun egg like Ra. Seb, the earth giant, in his bird form was before the egg, and Osiris absorbed Seb. Osiris became "the Great Egg", which was "the only egg", for the Ra "egg" had been appropriated from the earth worshippers. He was both Seb and the "egg"—"thou egg who becometh as one renewed". The father of Ra was Nu (water); the father of Osiris was Tanen (earth).[2]

But although he fused with Ptah-Tanen and became the Great Father, Osiris was not divested of his ancient lunar attributes. He was worshipped as the Apis bull;

---

[1] The various gods became manifestations of Osiris. In the Osirian hymns, which were added to from time to time, Osiris is addressed: "Thou art Tum, the forerunner of Ra . . . the soul of Ra . . . the pupil of the eye that beholdest Tum . . . lord of fear, who causeth himself to come into being" (*The Burden of Isis*, Dennis).

[2] *The Burden of Isis*; the egg, pp. 39, 45, 55; the sun, pp. 23, 24, 41, 49, 53; Tatenen (Tanen), p. 49; Seb, pp. 32, 47.

his soul was in the bull, and it had come from the moon
as a ray of light.   Here then we have a fusion of myths
of divergent origin.   Osiris was still the old lunar god,
son of the Great Mother, but he had become "husband
of his mother" or mothers, and also his own father, because he was the moon which gave origin to the sacred
bull.   He was also the world giant whose soul was
hidden.   The Egyptian theologians of the restoration
clung to all the old myths of their mingled tribal ancestors
and attached them to Osiris.

So Osiris absorbed and outlived all the gods.   In
early Christian times the Serapeum, the earthly dwelling
place of Serapis (Osiris-Apis), was the haunt of society
Hadrian, writing to the consul Servian, said that the
Alexandrians "have one god, Serapis, who is worshipped
by Christians, Jews, and Gentiles".   The half-Christian-
ized Egyptians identified Christ with Horus, son of Osiris,
and spoke of the Saviour as the young avenger in the
"Legend of the Winged Disk", who swept down the
Nile valley driving the devil (Set) out of Egypt.   As
early Gaelic converts said: "Christ is my Druid", those
of the land of the Pharaohs appear to have declared
similarly: "Christ is my Horus".

Horus and his mother, Isis, came into prominence
with Osiris.   Set, as Sutekh, was banished from Egypt,
and was once again regarded as the devil.   The cult of
Isis ultimately spread into Europe.[1]

But not only were the beliefs of the Old Kingdom
revived; even its language was imitated in the literature
and inscriptions of the Saite period, and officials were
given the titles of their predecessors who served Zoser
and Khufu.   Art revived, drawing its inspiration from the
remote past, and once again the tomb scenes assumed a

[1] An image of Isis was found on the site of a Roman camp in Yorkshire.

rural character and all the mannerisms of those depicted in Old Kingdom times. Egypt yearned for the glories of other days, and became an imitator of itself. Everything that was old became sacred; antiquarian knowledge was regarded as the essence of wisdom. Hieroglyphic writing was gradually displaced by Demotic, and when the Greeks found that the learned priests alone were able to decipher the ancient inscriptions, they concluded that picture writing was a sacred art; hence the name " hieroglyphics ", derived from *hieros*, sacred, and *glypho*, I engrave.

The excess of zeal displayed by the revivalists is illustrated in their deification of Imhotep, the learned architect of King Zoser of the Third Dynasty (see Chapter VIII). His memory had long been revered by the scribes; now he was exalted to a position not inferior to that held by Thoth in the time of Empire. As the son of Ptah, he was depicted as a young man wearing a tight-fitting cap, sitting with an open scroll upon his knees. He was reputed to cure diseases by the power of spells, and was a patron of learning, and he was a guide or priest of the dead, whom he cared for until they reached the Osirian Paradise. In Greek times he was called Imûthes, and identified with Asklepios.

Animal worship was also carried to excess. Instead of regarding as sacred the representative of a particular species, the whole species was adored. Cats and rams, cows and birds, and fishes and reptiles were worshipped wholesale and mummified. The old animal deities were given new forms; Khnûmû, for instance, was depicted as a ram-headed hawk, Bast as a cat-headed hawk, and Anubis as a sparrow with the head of a jackal.

Psamtek reigned for over fifty-four years, and Egypt prospered. At Memphis he extended the temple of

Ptah and built the Serapeum, in which the sacred bull
was worshipped.   He waged a long war in Philistia and
captured Ashdod, and had to beat back from his frontier
hordes of Scythians and Cimmerians, peoples of Aryan
speech, who had overrun Asia Minor and were pressing
down through Syria like the ancient Hittites; during
their reign of terror King Gyges of Lydia was defeated
and slain.

The Greeks were encouraged to settle in Egypt, and
their folklays became current in the Delta region.   Herodotus related a version of the tale of Troy which was told
to him by the priests.   It was to the effect that Paris fled
to Egypt when Menelaus began military operations to
recover Helen, and that he was refused the hospitality
of the Pharaoh.   In the *Odyssey* Menelaus says to
Telemachus:

> Long on the Egyptian coast by calms confined,
> Heaven to my fleet refused a prosperous wind,
> No vows had we preferred, nor victim slain,
> For this the gods each favouring gale restrain.
>
> *Od.*, iv, 473.

When Psamtek's son, Necho, came to the throne the
Assyrian empire was going to pieces.   Nahum was warning Nineveh:

> Behold, I am against thee, saith the Lord of hosts. . . . I will
> shew the nations thy nakedness and the kingdoms thy shame. . . .
> The gates of thy land shall be set wide open unto thine enemies;
> the fire shall devour thy bars. . . . Thy shepherds slumber, O
> King of Assyria: thy nobles shall dwell in the dust: thy people is
> scattered upon the mountains, and no man gathereth them.   There
> is no healing of thy bruise; thy wound is grievous: all that hear
> the bruit of thee shall clap the hands over thee (*Nahum*, iii).

After Ashur-banipal had devastated Elam it was occupied by the Aryan Medes. About 607 B.C. Cyaxares, the Median king, who had allied himself with the revolting Babylonians, besieged Nineveh, which was captured and ruthlessly plundered. The last Assyrian king, Sin-shar-ishkun, the second son of Ashur-banipal, is identified with the Sardanapalus of legend who set fire to his palace and perished in its flames so that he might not fall into the hands of his enemies. Tradition attached to his memory the achievements of his father.

Pharaoh Necho took advantage of Assyria's downfall by seizing Palestine. King Josiah of Judah went against him at Megiddo and was defeated and slain. "And his servants carried him in a chariot dead from Megiddo and brought him to Jerusalem" (*2 Kings*, xxiii, 30). Jehoahaz was selected as Josiah's successor, but Necho deposed him and made him a prisoner, and, having fixed Judah's tribute at "an hundred talents of silver and a talent of gold", he "made Eliakim, the son of Josiah, king . . . and turned his name to Jehoiakim" (*2 Kings*, xxiii, 34). But although Necho had been strong enough to capture Kadesh, his triumph was shortlived. Less than four years later Nebuchadrezzar, King of Babylon, who claimed Syria, routed Necho's army at Carchemish, and the Egyptians were forced to hasten back to their own land. "This is the day of the Lord of hosts, a day of vengeance", cried Jeremiah. . . . "Come up ye horses; and rage ye chariots; and let the mighty men come forth: the Ethiopians and the Libyans, that handle the shield; and the Lydians (mercenaries) that handle and bend the bow. . . . The sword shall devour. . . . Let not the swift flee away, nor the mighty man escape. . . . The nations have heard of thy shame", cried the Hebrew prophet to the escaping Egyptians (*Jeremiah*, xlvi). "And the King of Egypt came not again any more out of his land: for the King of Babylon had taken from the river of Egypt unto the River Euphrates all that pertained to the King of Egypt (*2 Kings*, xxiv, 7).

Necho had come to an understanding with Nebuchadrezzar, and interfered no more in Palestine. A few years later Jehoiakim rebelled against the King of Babylon, expecting that Necho would support him, despite the warnings of Jeremiah, and Jerusalem was besieged and forced to surrender. Jehoiakim had died in the interval, and his son, Jehoiachin, and a large number of "the mighty of the land" were deported to Babylon (*2 Kings*, xxiv). Mattaniah, son of Josiah, was selected to rule over Jerusalem, his name being changed to Zedekiah.

Necho, according to Herodotus, had undertaken the construction of a canal between the Mediterranean and the Red Sea, but desisted after a time on account of a warning received from an oracle. He then devoted himself to building a large fleet. His father was reputed to have endeavoured to discover the source of the Nile, and it was probably with desire to have the problem solved that Necho sent an expedition of Phœnicians to circumnavigate Africa. When the vessels, which started from the Red Sea, returned three years later by the Straits of Morocco, the belief was confirmed that the world was surrounded by the "Great Circle"—the ocean.

Apries, the second king after Necho, is the Pharaoh Hophra of the Bible. He had dreams of conquest in Syria, and formed an alliance which included unfortunate Judah, so that "Zedekiah rebelled against the King of Babylon" (*Jeremiah*, lii, 3). Nebuchadrezzar took swift and terrible vengeance against Josiah's unstable son. Jerusalem was captured after a two years' siege and laid in ruins (about 586 B.C.). Zedekiah fled, but was captured, "And the King of Babylon slew the sons of

Zedekiah before his eyes. . . . Then he put out the eyes of Zedekiah; and the King of Babylon bound him in chains and carried him to Babylon, and put him in prison till the day of his death" (*Jeremiah*, lii, 10, 11). The majority of the Jews were deported; a number fled with Jeremiah to Egypt. So ended the kingdom of Judah.

> Oh! weep for those that wept by Babel's stream,
> Whose shrines are desolate, whose land a dream. . . .
> Tribes of the wandering foot and weary breast,
> How shall ye flee away and be at rest!
>
> *Byron.*

Jeremiah proclaimed the doom of Judah's tempter, crying: "Thus saith the Lord; Behold I will give Pharaoh-hophra, King of Egypt, into the hand of his enemies, and into the hand of them that seek his life; as I gave Zedekiah, King of Judah, into the hand of Nebuchadrezzar, King of Babylon, his enemy, and that sought his life" (*Jeremiah*, xliv, 30).

Apries fell about 568 B.C. According to Herodotus, the Egyptians revolted against him, apparently because of his partiality to the Greeks; his army of Ionian and Carian mercenaries was defeated by a native force under Amasis (Ahmes II), whose mother was a daughter of Psamtek II. A mutilated inscription at Babylon is believed to indicate that Nebuchadnezzar invaded Egypt about this time, but it is not confirmed by any surviving Nilotic record. Apries was kept a prisoner by the new king, but the Egyptians demanded his death, and he was strangled.

Amasis reigned for over forty years. He was well known to the Greeks. Herodotus says that he regulated his time in this manner: from dawn until the city square was crowded he gave audience to whoever required it; the rest of the day he spent making merry with friends of not very high morals.   Some of his nobles remonstrated with him because of his "excessive and unbecoming levities", and said he should conduct himself so as to increase the dignity of his name and the veneration of his subjects.   Amasis answered: "Those who have a bow bend it only when they require to; it is relaxed when not in use.   And if it were not, it would break and be of no service in time of need.   It is just the same with a man; if he continually engaged in serious pursuits, and allowed no time for diversion, he would suffer gradual loss of mental and physical vigour."

Amasis "was very partial to the Greeks, and favoured them at every opportunity", Herodotus says.   He encouraged them to settle at Naucratis,[1] where the temple called Hellenium was erected and Greek deities were worshipped.   Amasis erected a magnificent portico to Neith at Sais, had placed in front of Ptah's temple at Memphis a colossal recumbent figure 75 feet long, and two erect figures 20 feet high, and caused to be built in the same city a magnificent new temple to Isis.   To the Græco-Libyan city of Cyrene, with which he cultivated friendly relations, he gifted "a golden statue of Minerva".   He married a princess of the Cyrenians.   Herodotus relates that during the wedding celebrations Amasis "found himself afflicted with an imbecility which he experienced under no other circumstances"; probably he had been drinking heavily, as he was too prone to do.   His cure was attributed to Venus, who was honoured with a statue for reward.

Amasis was not over popular with the Egyptians. Not only did he favour the Greeks, but promulgated a

[1] "Mighty in ships."

law to compel every citizen to make known once a year the source of his earnings. It is not surprising to find that he had to send Greek soldiers to Memphis to over-awe the offended natives, who began to whisper treason-able sayings one to another.

His foreign policy was characterized by instability. Although he cultivated friendly relations for the purpose of mutual protection, he gave no assistance in opposing the Persian advance westward.

About the middle of the reign of Amasis a new power arose in the East which was destined to shatter the crumbling edifices of old-world civilization and usher in a new age. "Cyrus, the Achæmenian, King of Kings", who was really a Persian, overthrew King Astyages (B.C. 550) of the Medes and founded the great Aryan Medo-Persian empire and pressed westward to Asia Minor. Amasis formed alliances with the kings of Babylon, Sparta, and Lydia, and occupied Cyprus, which he evacuated when the Persians overthrew the Lydian power. Egypt had become "a shadow" indeed. Cyrus next turned his attention to Babylonia, besieging and capturing city after city. The regent, Belshazzar, ruled as king in Babylon, which, in 539 B.C., was completely invested. On the last night of his life, deeming himself secure, "Belshazzar the king made a great feast to a thousand of his lords, and drank wine before the thousand" (*Daniel*, v, 1).

> In that same hour and hall,
> The fingers of a hand
> Came forth against the wall,
> And wrote as if on sand:
> The fingers of a man;—
> A solitary hand
> Along the letters ran,
> And traced them like a wand.
>
> . . . . . .

"Belshazzar's grave is made,
    His kingdom passed away,
He, in the balance weighed,
    Is light and worthless clay;
The shroud his robe of state,
    His canopy the stone;
The Mede is at his gate!
    The Persian on his throne!"

                                        Byron.

So Babylon fell. Cyrus, who was proclaimed its king, allowed the Jews to return home, and the first lot saw the hills of Judah in 538 B.C., nearly half a century after Zedekiah was put to shame.

Cambyses, a man of ungovernable temper and subject to epileptic fits, succeeded Cyrus in 530 B.C. Nine months after the death of Amasis, the ineffectual intriguer (525 B.C.), he moved westward with a strong army and conquered Egypt. Psamtek III, after the defeat of his army of mercenaries at Pelusium, on the east of the Delta, retreated to Memphis. Soon afterwards a Persian herald sailed up the Nile to offer terms, but the Egyptians slew him and his attendants and destroyed the boat. Cambyses took speedy revenge. He invested Memphis, which ere long surrendered. According to Herodotus, he committed gross barbarities. Pharaoh's daughter and the daughters of noblemen were compelled to fetch water like slaves, nude and disgraced before the people, and Pharaoh's son and two thousand Egyptian youths, with ropes round their necks, were marched in procession to be cut to pieces as the herald of Cambyses had been, and even Pharaoh was executed. On his return from Nubia, where he conducted a fruitless campaign, Cambyses is said to have slain a newly found Apis bull, perhaps because Amasis had "loved Apis more than any other king ". At Sais the vengeful Persian, according to Egyptian tradition, had the mummy of Amasis torn to pieces and burned.

With the conquest by Persia the history of ancient Egypt may be brought to an end. Before the coming of Alexander the Great, in B.C. 332, the shortlived and weak Dynasties Twenty-eight to Thirty flickered like the last flames of smouldering embers. Then followed the Ptolemaic age, which continued until 30 B.C., when, with the death of the famous Cleopatra, Egypt became "the granary of Rome".

Under the Ptolemies there was another restoration. It was modelled on the civilization of the latter half of the Eighteenth Dynasty, and Amenhotep, son of Hapi, the architect and magician who had been honoured by Queen Tiy's royal husband, was elevated to the rank of a god. A large proportion of the foreign population embraced Egyptian religion, and the dead were given gorgeous mummy cases with finely carved or painted portraits.

Vivid glimpses of life in Egypt from the second to the fourth century A.D., are afforded by the papyri discovered at Oxyrhynchus, chiefly by Messrs. Grenfell and Hunt. Wealthy and populous Alexandria had its brilliant and luxury-loving social groups. Invitations to dinner were sent out in much the same form as at the present day. The following is dated second century A.D.:

Chæremon requests your company at dinner at the table of the lord of Serapis in the Serapeum to-morrow, the 15th, at 9 o'clock.

The worship of Apis was fashionable. A lady wrote to a friend about the beginning of the fourth century:

Greeting, my dear Serenia, from Petosiris. Be sure, dear, to come up on the 20th for the birthday festival of the god, and let me know whether you are coming by boat or by donkey in order that we may send for you accordingly. Take care not to forget. I pray for your continued health.

There were spoiled and petted boys even in the third century. One wrote to his indulgent father:

Theon to father Theon, greeting. It was a fine thing of you not to take me with you to the city. If you won't take me with you to Alexandria I won't write you a letter, or speak to you, or say goodbye to you, and if you go to Alexandria I won't take your hand or ever greet you again. This is what will happen if you won't take me. Mother said to Archelaus: "It quite upsets me to be left behind". It was good of you to send me presents. . . . Send me a lyre I implore you. If you don't, I won't eat, I won't drink—there now!

Alexandria was always a hotbed of sedition. A youthful citizen in good circumstances wrote to his brother:

I learned from some fishermen that Secundus's house has been searched and my house has been searched. I shall therefore be obliged if you will write me an answer on this matter so that I may myself present a petition to the Prefect. . . . Let me hear about our bald friend, how his hair is growing again on the top; be sure and do.

Marriage engagements were dissolved when prospective sons-in-law were found to be concerned in lawless actions; prisoners were bailed out; improvident people begged for loans from friends to take valuables and clothing out of pawn; country folk complained that merchants sent large cheeses when they ordered small ones. Young men were expected to write home regularly. The following is a father's letter:—

I have been much surprised, my son, at not receiving hitherto a letter from you to tell me how you are. Nevertheless, sir, answer me with all speed, for I am quite distressed at having heard nothing from you.

So the social life of an interesting age is made articulate for us, and we find that human nature has not changed much through the centuries.[1]

In the Ptolemaic age a papyrus was made eloquent with the lamentation of a girl wife in her tomb. At fourteen she was married to the high priest of Ptah, and after giving birth to three daughters in succession she prayed for a son, and a son was born. Four brief years went past and then she died. Her husband heard her crying from the tomb, entreating him to eat and drink and be merry, because the land of the dead was a land of slumber and blackness and great weariness. . . . "The dead are without power to move . . . sire and mother they know not, nor do they long for their children, husbands, or wives. . . . Ah, woe is me! would I could drink of stream water, would I could feel the cool north wind on the river bank, so that my mind might have sweetness and its sorrow an end."

It is as if the soul of ancient Egypt, disillusioned in the grave, were crying to us in the darkness "down the corridors of time".

---

[1] The translations are from *Oxyrhynchus Papyri* (Egyptian Fund) Parts 2 and 3.

INDEX